Altered States
of
Consciousness
and
Mental Health

Altered States
of
Consciousness
and
Mental Health

A Cross-Cultural Perspective

edited by COLLEEN A. WARD

CROSS-CULTURAL RESEARCH AND METHODOLOGY SERIES
VOLUME 12

SAGE PUBLICATIONS
The Publishers of Professional Social Science
Newbury Park   London   New Delhi

Copyright 1989 by Sage Publications, Inc.

All rights reserved. No part of this book may be reproduced or utilized in any form or by any means, electronic or mechanical, including photocopying, recording, or by any information storage and retrieval system, without permission in writing from the publisher.

For information address:

 SAGE Publications, Inc.
2111 West Hillcrest Drive
Newbury Park, California 91320

SAGE Publications Ltd.
28 Banner Street
London EC1Y 8QE
England

SAGE Publications India Pvt. Ltd.
M-32 Market
Greater Kailash I
New Delhi 110 048 India

Printed in the United States of America

Library of Congress Cataloging-in-Publication Data

Main entry under title:

Altered states of consciousness and mental health : a cross cultural
  perspective / Colleen A. Ward, editor.
       p. cm. — (Cross-cultural research and methodology series)
       Bibliography: p.
       Includes index.
       ISBN 0-8039-3277-4
       1. Mental health. 2. Psychical research 3. Consciousness.
    4. Ethnopsychology. 5. Psychiatry, Transcultural.   I. Ward,
    Colleen A.   II. Series.
    RA790.5.A44   1989
    616.89 — dc20   89-5872
                                                                 CIP

FIRST PRINTING, 1989

CONTENTS

ABOUT THE SERIES

The Sage Series on Cross-Cultural Research and Methodology was created to present comparative studies on cross-cultural topics and interdisciplinary research. Inaugurated in 1975, the series is designed to satisfy a growing need to integrate research method and theory and to dissect issues from a comparative perspective; a truly international approach to the study of behavioral, social, and cultural variables can be done only within such a methodological framework.

Each volume in the series presents substantive cross-cultural studies and considerations of the strengths, interrelationships, and weaknesses of its various methodologies, drawing upon work done in anthropology, political science, psychology, and sociology. Both individual researchers knowledgeable in more than one discipline and teams of specialists with differing disciplinary backgrounds have contributed to the series. While each individual volume may represent the integration of only a few disciplines, the cumulative totality of the series reflects an effort to bridge gaps of methodology and conceptualization across the various disciplines and many cultures.

This volume extends the series' concern with mental health across cultures to a realm that is not usually even acknowledged by Western societies as a natural psychological phenomenon: altered states of consciousness. Earlier series volumes dealing with health issues were concerned with the culturally appropriate delivery of mental health services (P. B. Pedersen, N. Sartorius, and A. J. Marsella, 1984) and the applications of cross-cultural psychology to health promotion (P. R. Dasen, J. W. Berry, and N. Sartorius, 1988). While breaking new ground, these two earlier volumes essentially extended a Western psychology to other cultures. In contrast, the present volume starts with a psychological phenomenon that is rooted in the cultural life of a wide variety of peoples and that has only recently come to the attention of Western researchers. The case is made in this volume that a knowledge of altered states of consciousness, while of interest in its own right, is also fundamental to our understanding of mental health. We welcome this examination of this new domain to our series.

—Walter J. Lonner
John W. Berry

7

INTRODUCTION
COLLEEN A. WARD

> It will ere long be seen, I trust, that . . . we gain much more by a broad
> than a narrow conception of our subject. At a certain stage in the de-
> velopment of every science a degree of vagueness is what best consists
> with fertility. James, 1890/1950.

Although originally applied to the development of the discipline
of psychology, William James's words are particularly apt in the description of the study of altered states of consciousness (ASC's) and
mental health in a cross-cultural milieu. The highly interesting, relatively young, but rapidly evolving field has attracted the attention of
psychologists, psychiatrists, and anthropologists. Scholars from
each specialty have made modest contributions to the field, but
progress has been hampered by controversies and limitations within
each of the disciplines and by criticisms from without. This book attempts to assist the development of scholarship in the field by presenting various perspectives on ASC's and mental health and by
placing them within the boundaries of cross-cultural psychology.
This seems particularly appropriate as cross-cultural psychologists
acknowledge that their goal is to "bring the total range, the broad
variability and all possible differences exhibited in human behavior
within the scope of psychological science" (Berry, 1980, p. 5) and to
incorporate a wide range of methodological approaches in this pursuit (Triandis & Berry, 1980).

From the psychological perspective, the study of altered states of
consciousness has long been fraught with difficulties. A strong
behavioristic approach in the discipline has resulted in the reluc-
tance to examine internal, intangible, inaccessible mental states that
are not readily amenable to experimental investigation. As a result,
the bulk of such research as was undertaken in the 1960s and 1970s
tended to be limited by three major constraints: a unidimensional,
experimental approach to research, the confinement of that research to predominantly artificially induced ASC's produced in laboratory settings (e.g. drugs, hypnosis), and an ethnocentric definition of normal and pathological states. While recent research has
become more imaginative with the rise of cognitive psychology and
the acknowledgment of rich and varied naturally occurring ASC's in
the context of religious and cultural traditions, a number of scholars

argue that the study of altered states of consciousness should be more comprehensive in the incorporation of physiological, psychological, and sociocultural dimensions and of experiential as well as experimental methods (Ornstein, 1973; Tart, 1975; Ward, 1985).

While psychologists have been criticized for their approach to the study of consciousness, psychiatrists have concomitantly come under heavy fire in their area of expertise. A major objection concerns the reliance on a medical model of psychopathology and its implications for understanding and analyzing altered states of consciousness. The medical or disease model of psychopathology assumes that mental disorders are predominantly biologically based illnesses that occur universally in response to specific etiological factors. Although this perspective has been undermined by psychologists who advocate a more psychosocial approach and by anthropologists who are concerned with the influence of sociocultural factors, it retains prominence in contemporary psychiatry. The model is apparently problematic in that it implics "objective" diagnostic criteria that are independent of both cultural appraisals and individuals' experiential interpretations. This is particularly important in that the diagnosis of certain mental "illnesses" is predicated on alterations or disturbances of consciousness as defined by Western, organic medical practices. As these ASC's are typically conceptualized as explicitly difficult, frightening, or unpleasant and debilitating, there is little acknowledgment of their multifaceted meanings and potential adaptive value (Fadiman & Kewman, 1979).

In contrast to the psychologists and psychiatrists, anthropologists emerge relatively unscathed by criticisms of ethnocentrism; they have been considered, after all, the undisputed experts on culture and have undoubtedly been exposed to a wide variety of rich and "exotic" altered states of consciousness on a cross-cultural basis. However, while it has been readily accepted that anthropologists effectively pursue studies of culture and society, there has been some skepticism about their expertise in specifically psychological domains. Many anthropologists themselves (e.g., Leighton & Hughes, 1976) acknowledge that "culture and personality," or psychological anthropology, is a subfield of anthropology that invites collaboration from psychiatrists. Moreover, a number of behavioral scientists are ill at ease with the limitations of anthropological field methods, which are often viewed as less powerful than experimental techniques.

In consideration of the limitations of each discipline's independent approach, the convergence of psychology, psychiatry, and anthropology is exceptionally useful in the study of ASC's and mental health on a cross-cultural basis, and the broad representation of scholars in this volume provides a multifaceted perspective that accurately reflects the current state of the field. Yet the book should be of special interest to cross-cultural psychologists in its presentation of various in-depth emic analyses and the speculative and theoretical working through toward universal etics.

The volume is divided into four parts. The first considers important theoretical and methodological issues in the study of altered states of consciousness; the second and third link altered states of consciousness and mental health by focusing on both therapeutic and pathological aspects of ASC's. The final section concentrates on models and methods, highlighting a variety of paradigms for the study of ASC's and diverse methodological approaches. The division of papers into these four sections is somewhat arbitrary in that the works more often reflect a difference of emphasis rather than a division of subject matter. In the end it is hoped that this book may provide a substantive basis for a broad, multifaceted framework for the study of altered states of consciousness and mental health and with that framework a promising future for the developing field.

REFERENCES

Berry, J. W. (1980). Introduction to methodology. In H. C. Triandis & J. W. Berry (Eds.), *Handbook of cross-cultural psychology* (Vol. 2). Boston: Allyn & Bacon.

Fadiman, J., & Kewman, D. (1979). *Exploring madness: Experience, theory and research*. Monterey, CA: Brooks/Cole.

James, W. (1890/1950). *The principles of psychology*. New York: Dover.

Leighton, A. H., & Hughes, J. H. (1976). Cultures as causative of mental disorder. In W. Katkovsky & L. Gorlow (Eds.), *The psychology of adjustment*. New York: McGraw-Hill.

Ornstein, R. (Ed.). (1973). *The nature of human consciousness*. San Francisco: Freeman.

Tart, C. (1975). *States of consciousness*. New York: Dutton.

Triandis, H. C., & Berry, J. W. (1980). *Handbook of cross-cultural psychology* (Vol. 2). Boston: Allyn & Bacon.

Ward, C. (1985). Scientific methodology and experiential approaches to the study of mental imagery. *Journal of Mental Imagery, 9*(2), 113-126.

PART I

Altered States of Consciousness and Mental Health: Theoretical and Methodological Issues

> When we turn to the prospects for the scientific observer of consciousness, we are immediately faced with a host of perplexing issues, entangling confusions [and] definitional obscurities. (Globus & Franklin, 1980, p. 465)

The scientific study of consciousness has traditionally been fraught with complications, due largely to the rather elusive nature of the subject matter. Controversies have long raged regarding the definition and classification of these phenomena and the most effective methods for their investigation. The already substantial problems inherent in undertaking mainstream research on states of consciousness, however, rise dramatically with the extension of scientific inquiry to the cross-cultural domain. Ward and Lambek, in this section, address a number of comparative theoretical and methodological topics, with particular emphasis on such issues as the distinction of normal and altered states, the construction of frameworks for relating shifts of consciousness to mental health, the diminution of ethnocentrism in cross-cultural research, the selection of appropriate methods for assessment of subjective experiences, the critical evaluation of explanatory paradigms, and the synthesis of multidisciplinary perspectives.

Although Lambek develops arguments from the perspective of a cultural anthropologist and Ward from the viewpoint of a cross-cultural psychologist, they share a core of common concerns. Both disparage the all-too-common reductionist approach in the study of complex altered states of consciousness (ASC's), particularly the tendency to interpret these phenomena predominantly in terms of physiological parameters. Lambek makes the point explicit: "We cannot peel back culture to reveal a purely biological level." Both authors also argue for a more holistic approach to the study of consciousness. This may reflect not only the recognition of the interweaving of biological, psychological, and sociocultural facets of ASC's, but also the acknowledgment of the value of bimodal approaches to their investigation, including objective-subjective, quantitative-qualitative, and experimental-experiential dimensions. Ward, particularly, posits that experiential perspectives are demanded to interpret, understand, and make sense of quantitative data on consciousness and that "although ASC's are also characterized by observable, psychological, and behavioral correlates, their definition is ultimately based upon subjective interpretation."

The two authors also share a respect for the social constructionist perspective and the significance of indigenous explanations for such phenomena as trance and possession, as well as cultural perceptions of ordinary and nonordinary states of consciousness and sociocultural models and interpretations of health and illness. Ward advances the position that ordinary states of consciousness are specialized constructs and are in many ways quite arbitrary and culturally relative. Similarly, Lambek argues that possession is a social phenomenon—institutionalized, socially legitimated, and rule bound—and that the trance experience is not equivalent in all societies. He further highlights the difficulty in relating various states of consciousness to "illness," an experience that is also, in part, culturally constructed.

Despite the commonality of themes, Lambek and Ward diverge on a range of issues. Most significantly, their contributions reflect the fundamental tension between the universalist and cultural relativist perspectives in cross-cultural research. While both acknowledge cross-cultural similarities and differences in altered states of consciousness and their relation to mental health, as well as the problems of equivalence in the comparative investigation of such phenomena, Ward still implicitly aspires to the search for universals. Lambek, on the other hand, argues that "in cultural matters the lowest common denominator cannot tell us very much." Perhaps this divergence is to be expected, as to a large extent it mirrors core differences in the values underlying anthropological and psychological approaches; however, it is also likely that these differences are a matter of degree and emphasis and that the positions are not really dichotomous or mutually incompatible.

In addition to broad cross-cultural concerns, Ward and Lambek take up issues that are particularly germane to their respective disciplines of psychology and anthropology. Ward concentrates on theoretical and methodological deficiencies in the field—the largely unsynthesized body of research on ASC's, the limitations of types and sources of data and methods of data collection, the ethnocentric biases in data interpretation, and, most importantly, the problematic issues of equivalence in the search for universals. Lambek, on the other hand, is able to offer a significant contribution by providing not only a critique of the field—particularly the "naturalizing paradigms" in use—but also a viable alternative for interpreting ASC's in terms of text and discourse. Taken together, Ward and Lambek provide a useful theoretical and methodological introduction to the chapters to follow on altered states of consciousness and mental health in the cross-cultural context

REFERENCE

Globus, G., & Franklin, S. (1980). Prospects for the scientific observer of perceptual consciousness. In J. M. Davidson & R. J. Davidson (Eds.), *The psychobiology of consciousness* (pp. 465-482). New York: Plenum.

1

THE CROSS-CULTURAL STUDY OF ALTERED STATES OF CONSCIOUSNESS AND MENTAL HEALTH

COLLEEN A. WARD

It is a curious but undeniable fact that consciousness, the essence of knowing, does not know itself very well. (Rossi, 1986, p. 97)

Although consciousness in general and altered states of consciousness (ASC's) more specifically have become relatively respectable in mainstream psychology in the last two decades, the analysis of these phenomena has suffered from a number of serious deficiencies. Tart (1980), one of the forerunners in the field, has criticized the study of altered states of consciousness primarily on theoretical grounds, pointing out that although we have "thousands of miscellaneous bits" of scientific data, most pieces have remained unsynthesized and contributed only in a limited fashion to a holistic perspective on consciousness (p. 243). Tart himself has countered this shortcoming by moving from the role of experimentalist into the role of theoretician and has proposed a systems approach to altered states of consciousness as a psychological framework for analysis. This approach allows for the incorporation of experiential and behavioral elements and biological and cultural components in ASC analysis and assists in the exploration of discrete but shifting states of consciousness and underlying patterns of organization (Tart, 1975). While Tart has remedied some theoretical deficits in the area, offered a useful framework for cross-cultural extension of ASC research, and developed a potential avenue for methodological innovations, the study of altered states of consciousness, by and large, continues to warrant criticisms on methodological grounds. These criticisms center on limitations relating to data types, data sources, and data collections, as well as on ethnocentric approaches to data interpretation.

ASC RESEARCH: PITFALLS AND PROSPECTS

As psychology regards itself as the scientific study of human behavior and experience, it bears a major responsibility for the exploration of human consciousness. Modeling itself on the natural sciences, the discipline has relied heavily on a nomothetic research approach with preference for experimental methods and causal explanations. The consequences of this for the study of ASC's is that the majority of investigations are limited to "objective" or readily quantifiable indices of consciousness and are undertaken in highly controlled but patently artificial laboratory conditions. This type of research is undoubtedly useful and has proved extremely valuable; however, as the sole psychological perspective on consciousness (or at least the only commendable viewpoint when dealing with such "fuzzy" subject matter) it is severely constrained. Cross-cultural approaches to the study of ASC's, by contrast, have been more diverse and varied and are able to offer some interesting prospects in the expansion of conventional boundaries of contemporary psychological research on consciousness.

Types of Data: "Objective" and "Subjective" Domains

Psychologists and philosophers of science have long been aware of the complementarity in objective and subjective routes to knowledge (Ward, 1985). Blackburn (1971) has referred to these pursuits as intellectual and sensuous complementarity in science, while Ornstein (1975) has contrasted argument (verbal, rational, propositional, analytical, and causal) with experience (intuitive, oppositional, and acausal). These dualistic approaches have also been acknowledged cross-culturally in Eastern philosophical and psychological systems concerned with human behavior and development (Akhilananda, 1951; Govinda, 1973; Tulku, 1975); however, the relative value placed on the two modes varies.

Argument, of course, represents the highly acclaimed and allegedly objective approach to knowledge preferred in scientific exploration, although we are well aware of the influence of experience in theory building and "pre-scientific" inquiry (Govinda, 1973; Kuhn, 1962). Goleman and Davidson (1979) summarize the position of contemporary Western psychology regarding the supremacy of objective data:

When researchers investigate states of consciousness they look for the most rigorous criteria to define the boundaries of various states. People have always known that the dream state is radically different from waking, but only with the discovery in the 1950's of rapid eye movement during dreaming have researchers been able to find the hard index of dreaming that lets them comfortably speak of it as a distinct state. (p. 86)

This can be contrasted with what Shah (1973) cites as essentially a Sufi position:

There are two modes of knowledge, through argument and experience. Argument brings conclusions and compels us to concede them, but it does not cause certainty nor remove doubt in order that the mind may remain at rest in truth, unless this is provided in experience. (p. 277)[1]

Despite the interesting accounts of altered states of awareness that are available (e.g., Castaneda, 1976; Huxley, 1954), psychological studies of ASC's have been geared toward, and in many cases limited to, objective, quantitative data. The effective investigation of ASC's, particularly in a cross-cultural context, however, demands the incorporation of subjective experiential data with the more objective indices. First, on the most basic level it would be nonsensical to approach the study of ASC's without the inclusion of the experiential domain, particularly as the defining characteristics of these states rest on qualitative alterations in the overall pattern of mental functioning that are recognized by the experiencer as being distinctly different from the ordinary operation of consciousness (Ludwig, 1966; Tart, 1969). Although ASC's are also characterized by observable pyschological, physiological, and behavioral correlates, their definition is ultimately based upon subjective interpretation.

Second, experiential elements are typically required to interpret, understand, or "make sense" of quantitative data. Take, for example, the abundant research on various forms of meditation, which most frequently demonstrates reduced arousal as evidenced by enhanced alpha waves and decreased pulse rate, respiration, and blood pressure (Kasamatsu & Hirai, 1969; Wallace, 1970). This is consistent with observable behavioral data, as subjects generally appear at rest, being seated comfortably in a quiet environment with eyes closed. Early studies of Kriya Yoga, however, have revealed the output of high-level beta waves, indicating an increase in mental activity and arousal despite the apparent psychological withdrawal and observable rested postures (Das & Gastaut, 1955). This is only interpretable if it is known that phenomenologically meditative states are distinct and that in Yogic terms the Kriya technique is dependent upon extensive visual imagery to control the flow of vital energy from the base of the spine to the brain—resulting in a highly aroused, ecstatic-like, imagery-laden altered state. Peper and Ancoli (1977) and Brown (1977) have since proposed that there are two distinct meditational styles characterized by different physiological and phenomenological indices; however, Schuman (1980) argues that meditative ASC's can *best* be understood in terms of the passive awareness of the ongoing experience rather than in terms of physiological conditions (p. 336).

Finally, from a different perspective and theoretical rationale, the limitations of objective data and need for the subjective complement have been highlighted by a minority of cross-cultural psychologists (e.g., Ward, 1985, 1987). These researchers have pointed out that despite the cross-cultural claim to be engaged in an enterprise dedicated to a universal psychology in content, theory, and methods (Berry, 1983), the nature of psychological inquiry has been noticeably restricted. Mitroff (1974) has argued that there are specific styles of inquiry in scientific endeavors and that these styles are likely to vary across cultures. Extending that premise, we find that experiential approaches have played a significant role in the formulation of theories of human nature in a number of traditional cultures that have not historically differentiated science, philosophy, psychology, and medicine (Akhilananda, 1951). Experiential inquiry has been particularly prominent in the study of consciousness, psychological well-being, and indigenous therapies (Fadiman & Frager, 1976; Ikemi & Ishikawa, 1979). Despite the preference for quantitative data in cross-cultural inquiry, it has been argued that the acceptance of the qualitative is also required; without this, cross-cultural researchers inadvertently generate methodolocial paradoxes in their quest for a universal psychology (Azuma, 1984).

This volume attempts to redress some of the imbalances generated by primary reliance on the "objective" approach by incorporating more substantial experiental data into the study of ASC's. This has been done in providing rich accounts of subjective experiences of various altered states of awareness. For example, Valla and Prince offer case reports of religious experiences, including shifts into altered states of consciousness, and discuss therapeutic aspects of these responses in terms of biopsychological factors. Zusne provides a vivid account of self-induced altered states of awareness as described by early-twentieth-century scientist and talented imager Ludwig Staudenmaier, and analyzes these states in a psychological framework, comparing controlled and autonomous imagery. The authors, then, are able to proceed from subjective, introspectionist reports of ASC experiences and to cast these experiences into theoretical frameworks derived from mainstream psychology. Valla and Prince adopt a stress and coping framework for analysis of therapeutic religious experiences, while Zusne employs signal detection theory in the analysis of imagery. The three authors adeptly demonstrate the utility of qualitative data in scientific inquiry.

Collection of Data: Experimental and Nonexperimental Methods

Linked to the understandable preference for "objective" data is the primary reliance on experimental methods. Psychologists employ a variety of quantitative approaches in scientific investigations: experimental, quasi-experimental, and descriptive, including correlational analyses, naturalistic observations, and surveys as well as single case studies. Nevertheless, an overwhelming preference for experimental methods has been retained, although only a portion of psychological studies meet these criteria. Reflecting trends in the mainstream discipline, the study of ASC's has been heavily weighted toward experimental and quasi-experimental investigations. In the context of mental imagery research, for example, Ashton (1982) has bemoaned observations conducted without the manipulation of experimental variables, describing research of this type as lacking in critical acumen and arguing that it may have serious, detrimental consequences for the study of mental imagery.

Although cross-cultural approaches to the analysis of psychological phenomena have been inspired by experimental and quasi-experimental techniques, the interdisciplinary nature of the research has demanded a wider variety of scientific methods. The more structured and intrusive methods of data collection and the experimental and quasi-experimental research preferred by psychologists are complemented by the anthropological emphasis on naturalism and observational techniques (Berry, 1980; Edgerton, 1974). The case study approach commonly utilized by psychiatrists adds to diversity in the cross-cultural enterprise. As Harré (1979) has argued that the experiment itself may be a cultural artifact, and prominent cross-cultural psychologists (e.g., Triandis, 1980) have maintained that multimethod approaches are the most powerful research techniques, ethnographic and systematic observational field techniques, survey methods, archival research, and holocultural approaches are valuable additions to the more conventional experimental and quasi-experimental designs.

This volume attempts to redress the imbalance in research work on ASC's by including a variety of research approaches. Some cross-cultural data on ASC's are extracted from larger ethnographic field studies; this is true for Stoller's study of spirit possession in the Songhay of Africa as well as for Lambek's analysis of trance in Mayotte. Lee's study of altered states of consciousness in Malaysian spirit seances employs similar naturalistic observation techniques, but derives from a more specifically defined area of interest. In addition to ethnographic techniques, case studies are employed, as demonstrated by Krippner's study of ASC's in Brazilian mediums and Chandra shekar's report of ASC's and spirit possession in rural India. Survey techniques are utilized by Valla and Prince in their study of the prevalence and experience of altered states of awareness in religious contexts, while Kemp and Dobkin de Rios rely on archival data for their respective analyses of demonology and mental illness in medieval Europe and hallucinogenic states of consciousness in ancient Moche healing practices. These approaches may be contrasted with the experimental work presented by Spanos on hypnosis and multiple personality.

Sources of Data: Laboratory and Real World

In addition to the preference for objective data obtained by experimental methods, and related to this preference, mainstream research has generally limited the context of ASC investigations to artificially induced states observed in laboratory settings. Most commonly, research has concentrated on experimentally controlled drug-induced, sensory deprivation, or hypnotic states and biofeedback techniques, although auto-induced conditions such as sleep, dreaming, and, more recently, meditation have been examined. From the subject's point of view, then, ASC research most frequently offers an unusual sensory experience in an isolated experimental session; the experiment is detached from rather than related to the individual's life more generally, and the ASC is likely to lack purpose or meaning. From the experimenter's perspective, the external validity of such ASC's must be seriously considered.

The concentration on experimenter-induced and decontextualized states of consciousness in ASC research is unnecessarily narrow, given that cross-cultural literature tells us that assorted varieties of ASC's have evolved naturally on a worldwide basis and that hallucination is a widely distributed mode of human psychological functioning. Bourguignon and Evascu (1977), for example, reported that in a worldwide sample of 488 societies, 90% (437) displayed naturally occurring trance (behavior traditionally linked to visions and hallucinations) and/or possession states (dissociation attributed to the intrusion of spirits). Krippner (1972) enumerated some 20 states of consciousness, and cross-cultural evidence suggests that certain types of ASC's in Krippner's taxonomy, such as trance, meditative states, and expanded consciousness, are readily apparent in non-Western cultures.[2] Deikman (1966) also argues that deautomatization, a perceptual and cognitive shift responsible for altered states of awareness, is more prevalent in "primitive" societies.

In addition to extending the range of variation in ASC's, cross-cultural research allows the states to be observed in their natural environments. A number of social scientists have argued that human behavior observed otherwise is meaningless, as it cannot be separated from context (Kluckhohn, 1959). Lambek, for example, in the following chapter, vigorously defends the necessity to appreciate the social construction and cultural reality of ASC's. Analysis of real world behaviors and appreciation of ASC's in terms of their cultural contexts and culture-specific explanations and interpretations add an important dimension to mainstream work on altered states of consciousness.

This volume attempts to redress the imbalance of laboratory versus real world investigations by presenting a variety of field studies that offer access to a wide range of ASC's. These altered states of awareness are not typically amenable to psychological investigation and include various forms of ceremonial trance, visions, religious ecstasy, and self-induced hallucinations. In addition, assorted exotic and mundane forms of psychopathology, such as culture-bound neuroses, psychoses, and multiple personality disorders, are examined. Ample opportunity is provided to observe and analyze these experiences in their natural contexts, from African rituals and Malaysian seances to Indian villages and Brazilian churches.

Interpretation of Data: Ethnocentric Perspectives

A final area of criticism of altered states of consciousness has been the historical tendency to naively equate ASC's with pathology—reflecting a misguided and often ethnocentric approach. Deikman (1971) has proposed a model of bimodal consciousness composed of active and receptive modes. The active mode is characterized by object-based logic, heightened boundary perception, and dominance of formal characteristics over sensory traits. The receptive mode, by contrast, is marked by diffuse attending, paralogical thought processes, decreased boundary perception, and dominance of sensory modalities. The two modes are also defined by discrete physiological processes, the active being associated with augmented sympathetic nervous system arousal and the receptive with parasympathetic activity. From a Western perspective it has been assumed that the active mode represents ordinary consciousness, a mental state of striving, organized to manipulate the environment and oriented toward achievement of personal goals. The receptive mode, in contrast, is seen as mysterious or even deviant, despite being the complement in a repertoire of cognitive states.

Tart (1980) discusses this in greater detail, referring to the implicit operating assumptions employed by laypeople and most scientists that tend to impede our understanding of ordinary consciousness and ASC's. Tart maintains that our most basic and implicit assumption is that our ordinary consciousness is in some way normal or natural and that altered states are odd or unusual. This assumption holds despite the fact that many routinely experienced phenomena are odd; because they are familiar, however, we do not attend to them. A second related assumption, according to Tart, is that ordinary consciousness is not only normal but also "best" or "optimal"; consequently, altered states of consciousness are perceived as in some way "inferior" or even "pathological." Tart (1980) succinctly summarizes: "Our ordinary state of consciousness is a construction, not a given, and a specialized construction that in many ways is quite arbitrary. Thus many of the values associated with it are quite arbitrary and culturally relative" (p. 245).

Tart also maintains that the human potentials for various states of consciousness are shaped by cultural conditioning. Through this process a finite number of a very wide range of potentials are fixed in a relatively stable way to produce a state of ordinary consciousness—"a characteristic and habitual patterning of mental functioning that adapts the individual, more or less successfully, to survive in his culture's consensus reality" (1980, p. 249). It becomes apparent, then, that cross-cultural differences in attitudes toward alterations of consciousness affect the prevalence and evaluation of alterations and may even, through conditioning, affect brain functioning, as hypothesized by Davidson (1980), who suggested differential readiness of certain limbic structures in activating and generating affective arousal.

This volume offers valuable cross-cultural data demonstrating that assorted ASC's not only are regarded as "normal" or commonplace but in many instances are encouraged and esteemed. Chandra shekar, for example, discusses certain forms of trance and ritual possession widely accessible to laypeople in India; the states frequently occur in ceremonial contexts and are viewed with awe and respect. Similarly, Jilek details therapeutic aspects of ASC's in Amerindian dance ceremonials that are increasing in popularity with the rise of nativist movements. Cross-cultural data also reveal that altered states of awareness occur in healing practices, as evidenced by Krippner's exposition of Brazilian mediumship, Lee's analysis of Malaysian spirit seances, and Katz's discussion of the !Kung "boiling energy" of *num!*

ALTERED STATES OF CONSCIOUSNESS AND MENTAL HEALTH

ASC's are multidimensional and complex phenomena, and considerable effort has been devoted to describing and classifying them—e.g., Krippner's (1972) 20 states of consciousness, Ludwig's (1966) ASC induction analysis, Tart's (1975) systems approach and experiential response criteria, and Fischer's (1986) cartography of nonordinary states. In addition, there has been substantial work devoted to the neurophysiology of altered states. Early studies by Neher, (1962) and Gellhorn and Kiely (1972), for example, have been expanded and synthesized by Lex (1979) in her work on the neurobiology of ritual trance. A main area of interest, however, has been and still is the relationship between ASC's and mental health.

While a portion of the inquiries concerning ASC's and mental health has been derived from psychological investigations of the phenomena, the historical development of this research has differed somewhat from the more experimental tradition of mainstream work on consciousness. In particular, greater contributions have sprung from psychiatrists and anthropologists, and there is a longer, though not necessarily more illustrious, history of cross-cultural research. In addition, in many instances "consciousness" per se has not been central to the researchers' interests. For psychiatrists the focal concern has been mental health and illness, with ASC's either contributing to or detracting from psychological well-being. For anthropologists a primary objective has been the collection of rich ethnographic data, of which ASC's may be a part; their relationship to mental health may be parenthetically contemplated. Despite the strong anthropological influence in this domain, however, the research has not been totally free of ethnocentric impositions; in particular, cultural biases have emerged in relation to a basic paradigm clash in the investigation of ASC's and mental health.

It is beyond the scope of this paper to detail the extensive literature on culture and psychopathology, the problems of definition of normal and abnormal, and the classification of psychiatric disorders; however, it should be acknowledged that the conflict between medical and psychosocial and sociocultural models of mental health and illness has had discernible consequences for the study of ASC's and psychological well-being. Medical models have maintained that abnormal behavior can be compared to or equated with disease. If this is the case, mental illnesses are expected to be universal, although the manifestation of the fundamental disturbances may be colored by culture. This position gives license to interpret exotic disorders involving ASC's in terms of standard psychiatric classification systems. *Pibloktoq*, for example, a disturbance of consciousness found in Eskimo populations and accompanied by erratic behaviors such as tearing off one's clothes and wandering around in a hostile climate, has been interpreted as a hysterical disorder (Gussow, 1985). Similarly, *hsieh-ping*, as observed in Taiwan and characterized by alterations in consciousness, disorientation, and visual and auditory hallucinations, has been described as a depressive condition (Hughes, 1985; Lin, Kleinman, & Lin, 1981). While this appears tenable, unusual behaviors, perhaps regarded as eccentric but not as disturbed or as warranting treatment in the indigenous cultural context, may be likewise diagnosed and classified.

As the definitional features of psychiatric taxonomies tend to imply that ASC's per se are pathological, there is a danger of overextending the diagnosis of pathology to most or all conditions involving altered states of awareness. This might be exemplified by the Group for the Advancement of Psychiatry's (1979) inability to distinguish mysticism and pathology. A more germane cross-cultural example is the case of *latah* often found in Malay women. A *latah* episode typically involves a temporary dissociative state of brief duration in which the individual exhibits a startle reaction with subsequent hypersuggestibility and mimicry, sometimes accompanied by obscene utterances. While the Malays tend to regard the behavior as harmless, eccentric, and often entertaining—Colson's (1971) ethnographic data reveal it is perceived as *lain dari biasa* (different from usual) but *betul* (correct)—it has been described in the psychiatric literature as a culture bound syndrome, sometimes as hysterical/ histrionic, and as a hyperstartle response (Simons, 1985). Perhaps a more dramatic example of ethnocentrism as a consequence of the assumptions implicitly underlying medical models is offered to us by Silverman's (1979) analysis of shamans, who are described as "instrumental medicine men who communicate directly with the spirits who exhibit the most blatant forms of psychotic-like behavior" (p. 120). Although Silverman notes the prestige accorded to shamans in their indigenous environments, he regards their ceremonial ASC's as hysterical and argues that the route to shamanism parallels that of acute schizophrenia.

Opposed to the medical model are various psychosocial and sociocultural theories of abnormal behavior that emphasize to varying degrees the cultural contribution to the creation, definition, explanation, manifestation, and treatment of psychological disorders. These may include social learning theories (Ullman & Krasner, 1975), stress and coping models (Lazarus, 1976), labeling and symbolic interactionist theories (Becker, 1963; Scheff, 1966), and a variety of existential theories (Laing, 1967). Some theorists extend these ideas to argue that psychopathology itself is a social construction cognitively imposed on certain types of behavior (Szasz, 1970). White and Marsella (1984) succinctly appraise the significance of sociocultural factors in the emergence of pathology: "A growing amount of cultural and psychiatric research is showing that illness experience is an interpretive enterprise which is constructed in social situations according to the premises of cultural theories about illness and social behavior generally" (p. 3). In short, the role of culture in the manifestation and interpretation of psychopathology can no longer be ignored.

With regard to ASC's and mental health, then, a key issue revolves around the indigenous cultural interpretation and explanation of, and reaction to, an altered state. Cross-cultural literature tells us that individuals in non-Western cultures are less prone to view ASC's as intrinsically pathological. This was elegantly demonstrated by Westermeyer and Wintrob's (1979) study of folk criteria in the diagnosis of mental illness in rural Laos. The researchers surveyed 27 villages, identified 35 people who were labeled *baa* (insane), and interviewed friends, families, and neighbors of those individuals to ascertain the defining characteristics of *baa*. In addition, a panel of four mental health professionals was provided clinical data summaries for the individuals and subsequently diagnosed 24 cases of functional psychoses, 9 instances of organic psychoses, and 2 borderline conditions. The categories of diagnostic criteria to emerge from the Laotian informants, however, were: (1) danger to self and others, (2) nonviolent but socially disruptive behaviors, (3) socially dysfunctional behavior, (4) problems with speech or communication, (5) impaired psychological functions (particularly delusions), (6) affective disturbances, and (7) somatic signs and symptoms. Westermeyer and Wintrob remark that notable by its absence was hallucination as a defining characteristic, despite the fact that it was found to be present in most of the 35 subjects. Similar findings were reported by Edgerton (1966) in his interviews with 500 East Africans; he uncovered only 5 reports of hallucination as defining criteria among 1,926 responses.

There has been a trend toward enhanced cultural sensitivity and the elimination of the uncritical supposition that unusual states are intrinsically pathological in current and recent research on ASC's and mental health. For example, Kane's (1974) analysis of ASC's in fire-walking and snake-handling Southern Appalachian religious sects rejects the pathological label sometimes attributed to those behaviors (Tseng & Hsu, 1980). Still other researchers have considered potentially therapeutic aspects of various ASC's. This has been explored in terms of neurophysiological explanations (Lex, 1979), including recent work on endorphins (Henry, 1982; Prince, 1982); in psychological terms, including both remedial (Prince, 1976) and preventative (Kiev, 1961) aspects; and in sociocultural terms, including social status, benefits, and supports (Walker, 1972; Ward, 1984).

The works presented in this volume, though differing in theoretical orientations, demonstrate an appreciation of indigenous interpretations of ASC's and reject the notion that ASC's are inherently pathological. The therapeutic features of ASC's discussed in Jilek's analysis of Amerindian dance ceremonials provide a good illustration. When pathological conditions involving ASC's are explored, as in Kemp's description of medieval madness or Ward's cross-cultural analysis of spirit possession, they are examined in a manner consistent with the indigenous evaluation of the states. The volume additionally offers alternative frameworks for examining ASC's: the political dimension discussed by Stoller in the analysis of Songhay possession, the dramaturgical dimensions of ritual trance in Malaysian healing practices described by Lee, and the analyses of hallucination and power explored by Dobkin de Rios.

PROBLEMS AND ISSUES IN CROSS-CULTURAL RESEARCH ON ASC's AND MENTAL HEALTH

The previous sections have been directed primarily toward mainstream researchers with interests in the exploration of consciousness and have attempted to demonstrate the value and necessity of a cross-cultural approach. This section shifts in emphasis and direction. It is concerned primarily with how such research is appraised from the perspective of cross-cultural psychology and emphasizes problems inherent in cross-cultural endeavors.

Cross-cultural psychology has been defined as the "systematic study of behavior and experience as it occurs in different cultures, is influenced by culture or results in changes in existing cultures" (Triandis, 1980, p. 1). An important objective has been the description of behavior in a given culture by the use of concepts/constructs found meaningful by people in that culture (Brislin, 1980), although primary emphasis has been placed on the testing of the generality of psychological laws and the construction of overarching psychological theory (Malpass, 1977). The cross-cultural perspective on ASC's and mental health has been recognized as a worthwhile addition to the field. It offers specific advantages in terms of variety of data sources, a multimethod approach to data collection, interdisciplinary collaboration, and cultural sensitivity in data interpretation. It provides advantages inherent in all cross-cultural enterprises by extending the range of variation of human behavior for psychological analyses and assessing a wider testing ground for psychological theories. But along with the advantages of a cross-cultural perspective, theoretical and methodological problems exist.

A fundamental dilemma in cross-cultural pursuits, and one demonstrated in the variety of papers presented here, is the tension between the universalist and cultural relativist positions. The former perspective emphasizes cross-cultural similarities. In its most extreme form, it overlooks specific differences or leaps to such high levels of abstraction to make comparisons that tautologies or mundane truisms result (Lonner, 1980). The latter position contends that culture should be understood in its own terms with an appreciation of context and arbitrariness (Shweder & Bourne, 1984). In its most extreme form, comparisons are not made and parallels not drawn due to the belief that either necessitates comparisons of incomparables. Although few scholars take the extremes of these positions, the differences in perspective are illustrated in this volume. Lambek, for example, elegantly argues that trance and possession cannot be separated from their sociocultural construction and reality, and therefore deserve to be analyzed in those terms. Ward, on the other hand, draws parallels between some cross-cultural forms of possession and neurosis, and between exorcism and psychotherapy.

Despite the fact that anthropologists—who have a longer and richer history of struggling with culture, the consequences of its definition, and the terms of its analysis—generally favor the relativist position (Rohner, 1984), cross-cultural psychologists, while hoping to maintain cultural sensitivity, have aspired to comparison in the search for universals. Berry (1969) has offered us a framework for these aspirations, though one that is not without its critics (e.g., Jahoda, 1983). Berry's proposition is simple and provides a compromise by combining a culture-specific or emic perspective with a comparative, etic, or culture-general approach in theory testing. While acknowledging that the origins of theory are always emically derived, Berry suggests we test it in the form of an imposed etic to see if it is appropriate, powerful, or predictive in a different cultural context. If so, a derived etic may emerge, although its recognition as a true etic, or universal, is only possible after multiple, often quasi-experimental comparisons. Of course, to undertake these comparisons the researcher must meet a number of stringent equivalence requirements (for detailed discussion, see Berry, 1980, or Poortinga, 1982).[3]

For those who maintain that this is the most appropriate framework for exploring ASC's cross-culturally, it must be acknowledged that research on ASC's and mental health lags behind more developed areas of cross-cultural psychology, such as social behavior (Bond, 1988) or cognitive development (Berry & Dasen, 1974). Derived etics are still in the making, as a substantial proportion of work has been undertaken by anthropologists, who often prefer emic or relativist approaches and/or psychologists and psychiatrists who have tended to implicitly utilize imposed etics in a cross-cultural context without the explicit or quasi-experimental comparison of two or more groups. Analysis of the requirements of equivalence may suggest why this has been the case.

The implicit etic imposition has been adapted by Ward (1982) and Ward and Beaubrun (1981) in the exploration of spirit possession in West Indian Pentecostals. The research poignantly demonstrates the problematic issues of equivalence in this type of cross-cultural enterprise. Ward's research began with field observations of Pentecostal services, which included the display of unusual behaviors termed possession and accompanying exorcistic healing rituals. The display of possession episodes typically involved dissociative states characterized by glazed eyes, psychomotor activity, change in facial expression and voice quality, and constricted attention. Case history materials indicated that the individuals who believed themselves to be subject to malevolent possession suffered a variety of complaints often associated with neurotic disorders—sleep disturbances, depressed mood, psychosomatic ailments, anxiety and panic attacks, and periods of dissociation. In addition, most commonly the individuals were undergoing significant life changes or crises that appeared to be temporally linked to their conditions of possession. In their own cultural context the individuals were regarded as troubled, and their symptomic possession behaviors required treatment; therefore, to further explore the possibility that the onset and duration of possession might be interpreted as stress-induced, neurotic coping responses, 10 possessed church members were matched with 10 controls in the congregation and were assessed by the neuroticism scales of the EPI and hysteria scale of the MMPI.[4] The data revealed that the possessed individuals demonstrated higher levels of neuroticism and hysteria than the controls.

On the positive side, the research utilizes multiple methods: field observations, case studies, and quasi-experimental psychometric assessment. It appears to be culturally sensitive in that possession is not interpreted as evidencing pathology on the basis of ASC display per se but rather on the basis of associated symptoms described as problematic by the individuals experiencing them. The indigenous evaluation of the condition is also considered. Yet despite the consistency between a Western notion of neurosis and the Trinidadian Pentecostal interpretation of possession, can the researchers really make a convincing case for conceptual equivalence?

Berry (1980) tells us that conceptual equivalence is a precondition for comparison and relies on a common meaning of concepts within the cognitive systems of people and groups being compared.

Despite the contention that in these instances possession and neuroses are likely to be functionally equivalent (or, more accurately, dysfunctionally equivalent), it is not highly plausible that either clinicians or laypeople in Trinidad or in other cultures would interchangeably use the concepts of "neuroses" and "possession." Furthermore, the term "possession" in Trinidad encompasses a wide range of behaviors and conditions, some esteemed and desirable (Ward, 1979-80), others pathological. A major difficulty arises as Lambek (this volume) notes, from the defining characteristics of the two concepts: possession in its various forms is *primarily* defined by the attribution of causality, whereas neurosis is *primarily* defined by its signs and symptoms.

Although a potential alternative is to commence with the study of ASC's that are deemed conceptually equivalent, this approach also confronts some thorny issues. Even such a basic and universal experience as dreaming has radically different functions across cultures, as evidenced by Stewart's (1969) work on the Temiar-Semoi of Malaysia and the proposition of dream therapy. As Dobkin de Rios (this volume) notes, there are vast differences in the purpose, function, and objectives of drug-induced hallucinogenic experiences on American university campuses and in Peruvian healing rituals. Evidence suggests that the same state of altered awareness may have radically different objectives across cultures and thus is ineligible for comparisons as the two experiences do not meet the criteria for functional equivalence.

Overall, while the cross-cultural perspective on ASC's and mental health has done much to enhance our understanding of consciousness, it has not met the goals set by cross-cultural psychologists in the search for universals. For the most part, research has been descriptive, and systematic cross-cultural comparisons that address the methodological issues of equivalence have not yet been achieved. Theory has not been truly decentered, and imposed etics still derive from Euro-American sources. In short, the objectives of cross-cultural research are ambitious, but the accomplishments have been modest.

CONCLUSION

This paper has argued that a cross-cultural approach to ASC's offers a substantial contribution to the field by extending the range of human variation in the search for universals. More specifically, cross-cultural endeavors have countered some of the pervasive limitations of traditional ASC research—constraints regarding data types, data sources, data collection, and ethnocentrism in data interpretation. Despite these preliminary contributions, it is acknowledged that the cross-cultural studies of ASC's and mental health are relatively young and predominantly descriptive. The challenges demanded by cross-cultural psychology in terms of more sophisticated and comparative research methodology in the pursuit of psychological universals remain to be met. It is hoped, nevertheless, that the cross-cultural perspective of this volume may assist in building a bridge to the next stage of more concentrated theory development and testing in ASC and mental health research.

NOTES

1. The quote is from Roger Bacon's *Opus Maius*, though Shah contends it is derived from Sufi authorities.
2. The 20 states are dreaming, sleeping, hypnagogic, hypnopompic, hyperalert, lethargic, rapture, hysteric, fragmentation, regressive, meditative, trance, reverie, daydreaming, internal scanning, stupor, coma, stored memory, expanded consciousness, and "normal."
3. This includes conceptual, functional, stimuli, linguistic, and metric equivalence.
4. These instruments were used for diagnostic purposes by clinical psychologists in Trinidad.

REFERENCES

Akhilananda, S. (1951). *Mental health and Hindu psychology.* Boston: Brandon Press.
Ashton, R. (1982). Mist: Comments on Marks and McKellar. *Journal of Mental Imagery, 6,* 31-32.
Azuma, H. (1984). Psychology in a non-Western country. *International Journal of Psychology, 19,* 45-55.
Becker, H. S. (1963). *Outsiders: Studies in the sociology of deviance.* New York: Free Press.
Berry, J. W. (1969). On cross-cultural comparability. *International Journal of Psychology, 4,* 119-128.
Berry, J. W. (1980). Introduction to methodology. In H. C. Triandis & J. W. Berry (Eds.), *Handbook of cross-cultural psychology* (Vol. 2, pp. 1-28). Boston: Allyn & Bacon.
Berry, J. W. (1983). The sociogenesis of social sciences: An analysis of the cultural rel-

ativity of social psychology. In B. Bain (Ed.), *The sociogenesis of language and human conduct* (pp. 449-458). New York: Plenum.

Berry, J. W., & Dasen, P. R. (Eds.). (1974). *Culture and cognition: Readings in cross-cultural psychology.* London: Methuen.

Blackburn, T. R. (1971). Sensuous-intellectual complementarity in science. *Science, 172,* 1003-1007.

Bond, M. (Ed.). (1988). *The cross-cultural challenge to social psychology.* Newbury Park, CA: Sage.

Bourguignon, E., & Evascu, T. (1977). Altered states of consciousness within a general evolutionary perspective: A holocultural analysis. *Behavior Science Research, 12,* 199-216.

Brislin, R. W. (1980). Introduction to social psychology. In H. C. Triandis & R. W. Brislin (Eds.), *Handbook of cross-cultural psychology* (Vol. 5, pp. 1-23). Boston: Allyn & Bacon.

Brown, D. P. (1977). Levels of concentrative meditation. *International Journal of Clinical and Experimental Hypnosis, 25*(4), 236-273.

Castaneda, C. (1976). *The teachings of Don Juan: A Yaqui way of knowledge.* Middlesex: Penguin.

Colson, A. C. (1971). Perceptions of abnormality in a Malay village. In N. N. Wagner & E. S. Tan (Eds.), *Psychological problems and treatments in Malaysia* (pp. 88-101). Kuala Lumpur: University of Malaya Press.

Das, N. N., & Gastaut, H. (1955). Variations de l'activité électrique du cerveau, du coeur, et de muscles squelliques au cours de la méditation et de l'extase yogique. *Electroencephalography and Clinical Neurophysiology, 6,* 211-219.

Davidson, R. J. (1980). Consciousness and information processing: A biocognitive perspective. In J. M. Davidson & R. J. Davidson (Eds.), *The psychobiology of consciousness* (pp. 11-46). New York: Plenum.

Deikman, A. J. (1966). Deautomatization and the mystic experience. *Psychiatry, 29,* 324-338.

Deikman, A. J. (1971). Bimodal consciousness. *Archives of General Psychiatry, 25,* 481-489.

Edgerton, R. B. (1966). Conceptions of psychosis in four East African societies. *American Anthropologist, 68,* 408-425.

Edgerton, R. B. (1974). Cross-cultural psychology and psychological anthropology: One paradigm or two? *Reviews in Anthropology, 1,* 52-65.

Fadiman, J., & Frager, R. (1976). *Personality and personal growth.* New York: Harper & Row.

Fischer, R. (1986). Toward a neuroscience of self-experience and states of self-awareness and interpreting interpretations. In B. B. Wolman & M. Ullman (Eds.), *Handbook of states of consciousness* (pp. 3-30). New York: Van Nostrand Reinhold.

Gellhorn, E., & Kiely, W. F. (1972). Mystical states of consciousness: Neurophysiological and clinical aspects. *Journal of Nervous and Mental Diseases, 154,* 399-405.

Goleman, D., & Davidson, R. J. (1979). The nature of altered states. In D. Goleman & R. J. Davidson (Eds.), *Consciousness: Brain, states of awareness and mysticism* (p. 86). New York: Harper & Row.

Govinda, L. (1973). The two types of psychology. In R. E. Ornstein (Ed.), *The nature of human consciousness* (pp. 234-236). San Francisco: Freeman.

Group for the Advancement of Psychiatry. (1979). What mysticism is. In D.

Goleman & R. Davidson (Eds.), *Consciousness: Brain, states of awareness and mysticism* (pp. 187-190). New York: Harper & Row.

Gussow, Z. (1985). *Pibloktoq* (hysteria) among the polar Eskimo: An ethnopsychiatric study. In R. C. Simons & C. C. Hughes (Eds.), *The culture bound syndromes* (pp. 271-288). Boston: Reidel.

Harré, R. (1979). *Social being.* Oxford: Basil Blackwell.

Henry, J. L. (1982). Possible involvement of endorphins in altered states of consciousness. *Ethos, 10,* 394-408.

Hughes, C. (1985). Glossary of "culture bound" or folk psychiatric syndromes. In R. C. Simons & C. C. Hughes (Eds.), *The culture bound syndromes* (pp. 469-505). Boston: Reidel.

Huxley, A. (1954). *The doors of perception.* New York: Harper & Row.

Ikemi, Y., & Ishikawa, H. (1979). The integration of occidental and oriental psychosomatic treatments. *Psychotherapy and Psychosomatics, 31,* 324-333.

Jahoda, G. (1983). The cross-cultural emperor's conceptual clothes: The emic-etic issue revisited. In J. B. Deregowski, S. Dziurawiec, & R. C. Annis (Eds.), *Expiscations in cross-cultural psychology* (pp. 19-38). Lisse: Swets & Zeitlinger.

Kane, S. M. (1974). Ritual possession in a South Appalachian religious sect. *Journal of American Folklore, 87,* 293-302.

Kasamatsu, A., & Hirai, T. (1969). An electroencephalographic study on Zen meditation. In C. Tart (Ed.), *Altered states of consciousness* (pp. 489-501). New York: John Wiley.

Kiev, A. (1961). Spirit possession in Haiti. *American Journal of Psychiatry, 118,* 133-138.

Kluckhohn, C. M. (1959). Common humanity and diverse cultures. In D. Lerner (Ed.), *The human meaning of the social sciences* (pp. 245-284). New York: Meridian Books.

Krippner, S. (1972). Altered states of consciousness. In J. White (Ed.), *The highest state of consciousness* (pp. 1-5). New York: Doubleday.

Kuhn, T. (1962). *The structure of scientific revolutions.* Chicago: University of Chicago Press.

Laing, R. D. (1967). *The politics of experience.* New York: Pantheon.

Lazarus, R. S. (1976). *Patterns of adjustment.* New York: McGraw-Hill.

Lex, B. W. (1979). The neurobiology of ritual trance. In E. G. d'Aquili, C. D. Laughlin, & J. McManus (Eds.), *The spectrum of ritual: A biogenetic structural analysis* (pp. 117-151). New York: Columbia University Press.

Lin, K. M., Kleinman, A., & Lin, T. Y. (1981). Overview of mental disorders in Chinese cultures: Review of epidemiological and clinical studies, In A. Kleinman & T. Y. Lin (Eds.), *Normal and abnormal behavior in Chinese culture* (pp. 237-272). Boston: Reidel.

Lonner, W. J. (1980). The search for psychological universals. In H. C. Triandis & W. W. Lambert (Eds.), *Handbook of cross-cultural psychology* (Vol.1, pp. 143-204). Boston: Allyn & Bacon.

Ludwig, A. M. (1966). Altered states of consciousness. *Archives of General Psychiatry, 15,* 225-234.

Malpass, R. (1977). Theory and method in cross-cultural psychology. *American Psychologist, 32,* 1069-1079.

Mitroff, J. J. (1974). *The subjective side of science.* New York: Elsevier.

Neher, A. (1962). A physiological explanation of unusual behavior in ceremonies involving drums. *Human Biology, 34,* 151-161.

Ornstein, R. (1975). *The psychology of consciousness.* San Francisco: Freeman.

Peper, E., & Ancoli, S. (1977). The two endpoints on an EEG continuum of meditation—alpha/theta and fast beta. *Biofeedback and Self Regulation, 2,* 289-290.

Poortinga, Y. (1982). Psychometric approaches of intergroup comparison: The problem of equivalence. In S. H. Irvine & J. W. Berry (Eds.), *Human assessment and cultural factors* (pp. 237-257). New York: Plenum.

Prince, R. H. (1976). Psychotherapy as the manipulation of endogenous healing mechanisms: A transcultural survey. *Transcultural Psychiatric Research Review, 13,* 115-133.

Prince, R. H. (1982). Shamans and endorphins: Hypothesis for a synthesis. *Ethos, 10,* 409-423.

Rohner, R. (1984). Toward a conception of culture for cross-cultural psychology. *Journal of Cross-cultural Psychology, 15,* 111-138.

Rossi, E. (1986). Altered states of consciousness in everyday life: Ultradian rhythms. In B. B. Wolman & M. Ullman (Eds.), *Handbook of states of consciousness* (pp. 97-132). New York: Van Nostrand Reinhold.

Scheff, T. J. (1966). *Being mentally ill: A sociological theory.* Chicago: Aldine.

Schuman, M. (1980). The psychophysiological model of meditation and altered states of consciousness: A critical review. In J. M. Davidson & R. J. Davidson (Eds.), *The psychobiology of consciousness* (pp. 333-378). New York: Plenum.

Shah, I. (1973). The Sufis. In R. Ornstein (Ed.), *The nature of human consciousness* (pp. 275-278). San Francisco: Freeman.

Shweder, R. A., & Bourne, E. J. (1984). Does the concept of the person vary cross-culturally? In A. J. Marsella & G. M. White (Eds.), *Cultural conceptions of mental health and therapy* (pp. 97-137). Boston: Reidel.

Silverman, J. (1979). Shamans and acute schizophrenia. In D. Goleman & R. J. Davidson (Eds.), *Consciousness: Brain, states of awareness and mysticism* (pp. 120-125). New York: Harper & Row.

Simons, R. C. (1985). The resolution of the *Latah* paradox. In R. C. Simons & C. C. Hughes (Eds.), *The culture bound syndromes* (pp. 43-62). Boston: Reidel.

Stewart, K. (1969). Dream theory in Malaya. In C. Tart (Ed.), *Altered states of consciousness* (pp. 159-167). New York: John Wiley.

Szasz, T. S. (1970). *The manufacture of madness.* New York: Harper & Row.

Tart, C. (1969). Introduction. In C. Tart (Ed.), *Altered states of consciousness* (pp. 1-6). New York: Wiley.

Tart, C. (1975). *States of consciousness.* New York: Dutton.

Tart, C. (1980). A systems approach to altered states of consciousness. In J. M. Davidson & R. J. Davidson (Eds.), *The psychobiology of consciousness* (pp. 243-269). New York: Plenum.

Triandis, H. C. (1980). Introduction. In H. C. Triandis & W. W. Lambert (Eds.), *Handbook of cross-cultural psychology* (Vol. 1, pp. 1-14). Boston: Allyn & Bacon.

Tseng, W. S., & Hsu, J. (1980). Minor psychological disturbances of everyday life. In H. C. Triandis & J. G. Draguns (Eds.), *Handbook of cross-cultural psychology* (Vol. 6, pp. 61-97). Boston: Allyn & Bacon.

Tulku, T. (Ed.). (1975). *Reflections of mind: Western psychology meets Tibetan Buddhism.* Emeryville, CA: Dharma Publishing.

Ullman, L. P., & Krasner, L. A. (1975). *A psychological approach to abnormal behavior.* Englewood Cliffs, NJ: Prentice-Hall.

Walker, S. (1972). *Ceremonial spirit possession in Africa and Afro-America.* Leiden: Brill.

Wallace, R. K. (1970). Physiological effects of transcendental meditation. *Science, 167,* 1751-1754.

Ward, C. (1979-80). Therapeutic aspects of ritual trance: The Shango cult in Trinidad. *Journal of Altered States of Consciousness, 5,* 19-29.

Ward, C. (1982). An examination of spirit possession in a West Indian Pentecostal community. In R. Rath, H. S. Asthana, D. Sinha, & J. B. H. Sinha (Eds.), *Diversity and unity in cross-cultural psychology* (pp. 352-359). Lisse: Swets & Zeitlinger.

Ward, C. (1984). Thaipusam in Malaysia: A psychoanthropological analysis of ritual trance, ceremonial possession and self-mortification practices. *Ethos, 12,* 307-334.

Ward, C. (1985). Scientific methodology and experiential approaches to the study of mental imagery. *Journal of Mental Imagery, 9,* 113-126.

Ward, C. (1987). Theory and method in cross-cultural psychology. In J. D. Greenwood (Ed.), *The idea of psychology: Conceptual and methodological issues* (pp. 13-40). Singapore: Singapore University Press.

Ward, C., & Beaubrun, M. (1981). Spirit possession and neuroticism in a West Indian Pentecostal community. *British Journal of Clinical Psychology, 20,* 295-296.

Westermeyer, J., & Wintrob, R. (1979). "Folk" criteria for the diagnosis of mental illness in rural Laos: On being insane in sane places. *American Journal of Psychiatry, 136,* 755-761.

White, G. M., & Marsella, A. J. (1984). Introduction: Cultural conceptions in mental health research and practice. In A. J. Marsella & G. M. White (Eds.), *Cultural conceptions of mental health and therapy* (pp. 3-38). Boston: Reidel.

2

FROM DISEASE TO DISCOURSE
Remarks on the Conceptualization of Trance and Spirit Possession

MICHAEL LAMBEK

A central concern of cultural anthropology is the inspection of categories that Western common sense and even science take for granted and assign existence in the world of nature. As Sahlins (1976) and others have pointed out, the naturalization of cultural practices, the projection of the variable, contigent, and fluctuating onto the fixed and autonomous categories of Nature, is an extremely powerful mechanism of legitimation in Western discourse. Following this critical tradition I shall argue that the cross-cultural literature on trance and spirit possession has suffered from a largely unexamined acceptance of the naturalist paradigm and that much is to be gained by recolonizing the terrain for culture. When spirit possession is seen as a human social and historical activity, constrained by cultural models, we can begin to understand what is valuable about any given case and to account for the diversity of trance phenomena, both between and within particular societies, synchronically or diachronically viewed. One of the main values of a cultural perspective is that it provides analytic room for a degree of freedom on the part of the human subject. The person who enters trance is not simply the victim of natural forces beyond his or her control (nor of cultural forces). Likewise, the collective model is itself mutable, a product of various historical and structural forces. Interpreting spirit possession in its cultural context also al-

AUTHOR'S NOTE: Fieldwork in Mayotte has been carried out in 1975-76, 1980, and, since the original draft of this paper was written, in 1985, together with Jacqueline Solway. The support of the National Science Foundation, the Social Sciences and Humanities Research Council of Canada, the University of Toronto, and the National Geographic Society, as well as the people of Mayotte, is gratefully acknowledged. A first version of the paper was presented at the joint meeting of the Canadian Association for Medical Anthropology and the Canadian Ethnology Society in Montreal, May 1984. I thank Ellen Corin for her comments on that occasion, Janice Boddy, Jackie Solway, and Colleen Ward for their comments on various drafts, and especially Paul Antze for his disquietingly sharp reading. None of them are responsible for what remains.

lows us to avoid the opposite fallacy (again, ultimately a naturalizing one) of seeing trance behavior as a purely instrumental strategy, a product of individual self-interest.

The arguments to be presented emerge primarily from my encounter with a single ethnographic case, selected aspects of which will be briefly summarized in the next section of the paper (cf. Lambek, 1981). Spirit possession, as it was found in the 1970s and 80s in Mayotte (Comoro Islands, Western Indian Ocean) is a complex, subtle, and supple phenomenon. However, the aim of this paper is not to investigate the subtleties of the case but rather to make a more general argument: that the subtleties are basic to what spirit possession in Mayotte, or anywhere else, is. While I attempt to clear up some misunderstandings that hinder the development of a comparative understanding of trance and spirit possession, I suggest that generalizations that attempt to smooth over the variability and complexity of the phenomena instead of giving them a central place are not particularly useful. In cultural matters, the lowest common denominator cannot tell us very much. Thus, the paper is concerned with alternative ways of conceptualizing trance phenomena.

After a largely critical consideration of a number of frameworks with strong naturalizing tendencies, I end by suggesting a few other approaches. However, I do not attempt to reach a unilateral conclusion; at this stage of our understanding, the very notion of a "general theory" of trance and possession would almost certainly entail the naturalizing assumptions I criticize. The chapter makes positive use of some recent anthropological work and is meant to complement the extremely insightful perspective on spirit possession put forward by Crapanzano (1977), with which it shares a concern with human cultural practice.[1] The reader who wishes to see a vivid account of diversity of trance phenomena within a given society as recorded by a master ethnographer (and one whose theory anticipated the current interest in practice) might turn to Firth (1967).

In order to speak comparatively, some sort of general language is necessary. I will be concerned primarily with what Bourguignon (1967) has labeled "possession trance," that is, the association of trance behavior with a cultural theory that attributes it to the possession of the self by an external agency.[2] However, it should be noted that Bourguignon's isolation of the categories "possession" and "trance" is heuristic and somewhat arbitrary, first, in the way it pries apart behavior and theory, and second, in the manner that these categories are imposed upon a range of otherwise diverse cultural phenomena. Such categories, if the distinction between them is considered to remain useful, might well be reconceptualized as polythetic (cf. Needham, 1971). Moreover, in any comparative work we need to keep in mind the point made by Dumont (1975) and others that we violate social wholes when we begin to fragment them so that the contents will fit the grid of our preconceived categories. The danger in applying monothetic, decontextualized categories is precisely that of reifying and naturalizing them, leading to such pseudo-problems as whether "shamanism" should be considered a form of "spirit possession" (or vice versa).

In an earlier draft of this paper I attempted to use "spirit possession" to refer to a whole social complex, of which states of "trance" form only a part. In this approach, essentially similar to Bourguignon's, "trance" refers to the temporary neurophysiological changes and largely unconscious psychological processes manifest in behavior that sometimes accompany assumptions about and activities interpreted as products of external agents, all of which (including the trance behavior) is called "spirit possession." While in some ways this seemed self-evident, I was unable, as several readers noted, to be consistent in my application of the terms. I think this is because although the distinction is easy enough to make in theory, at the level of the analyst's model, it simply does not fit the phenomena we observe. While trance, like sex, eating, or vocalization, is "natural" in the sense that, under the right stimuli, it is a condition or activity (or range of conditions or activities) of which the human species at large is capable, the form or manifestation of trance in any specific context is no more "natural" (necessary, unmediated, given) than the model that guides it. Trance may include certain universal features or attributes from which each culture selects points of emphasis (much as a language, viewed phenomically, selects from the range of possible human vocalizations). Yet the institutionalized appearance of trance—its form, meaning, incidence, etc.—is cultural. Except in rare or anomalous cases, the appearance of trance is not the direct effect of any particular set of physiological, psychological, or social forces. Rather, the appearance of trance is mediated by the cultural model, by its social reality; the collective representations of trance precede its incidence (Stirrat, 1977). And it is this social reality of trance in which most cross-cultural investigators, whether they recognize it or not, are interested.

It is the very distinction between "trance" and "possession" that lies at the heart of the naturalizing paradigm. Here trance is behavior and subject to "explanations" in straightforward causal terms, the product of certain psychological or social stimuli (which vary according to the theory being proposed). Possession is secondary, an indigenous hypothesis or theory put forward to account for the facts of trance and, in the more sophisticated models such as that of Lewis (1971), subtle enough to situate the behavior appropriately in its social context.

Lewis's work, which is both a major synthesis of previous accounts of "ecstatic religion" and the most original and explicit structural-functionalist perspective on the subject, has formed a point of departure for most subsequent anthropological thinking and hence, despite its evident value, must come in for a certain amount of criticism. An examination of some of his assumptions will direct us to the problematic relationship between trance and possession. In Lewis's model, spirits are amoral creatures in settings in which peripheral and subordinate members of the society (notably women) are possessed, whereas spirits uphold morality in societies where it is those in authority (notably men) who enter trance. In the situation of the peripheral cult, if the behavior of the women in trance expresses a rebellion against the dominant social order, the indigenous theory accommodates itself to the social facts and actually serves to legitimate and perpetuate those facts by objectifying the amoral quality of the spirits. Behavior and theory are quasi-independent of one another, though each is ultimately the product of the underlying social relations. Lewis's model is able to account for certain ethnographic facts (though in tending to reify the distinction between peripheral and main morality "cults" it polarizes them and ignores intermediate cases). The problem, however, is that Lewis may simply be replicating uncritically the naturalizing models that prevail in the societies under investigation instead of examining the construction of the models themselves. For both Lewis and the authoritative native view there is a certain inevitability in the relationships between the model and the behavior, for the natives because the model describes "natural" reality and for Lewis because especially the behavior, but also the model, are "natural" representations ("reflections") of social reality. However, I would suggest that whether the spirits are moral or amoral—and hence the manner in which they manifest themselves in human subjects, i.e., the very "nature" of trance—may itself be an area of contention. The ways in which models of possession incorporate instances of trance to legitimate certain kinds of social relations, and possibly even to construct new forms of social relations, must be investigated.

Ultimately, it is our conceptualization of the relationship between human thought and practice and human experience that must serve as a guide for how we view trance and possession. Yet such considerations are generally omitted from discussion or given second place to assumptions that grant the manifestations of trance a certain necessity. Trance is not prior to spirit possession in either a logical or causal sense, and possession cannot be viewed as a "model of" trance unless it is also well understood that it is equally a "model for" trance (cf. Geertz, 1973). Where it is meaningful, trance, like any other regular human activity, is shaped by culture. Hence, the "possession" and the "trance" in any given system of "possession trance" cannot be consistently isolated from each other in practice.

SPIRIT POSSESSION IN MAYOTTE

Spirit possession is a significant, if rather low-key, feature of life in Mayotte,[3] affecting the conduct of interpersonal relationships and the organization of the family, the construction of the self, and the conceptualization of the world and human experience in it. A large number of people, of whom all are adults—roughly five times as many women as men—are possessed by a spirit or spirits, manifested in intermittent states of trance, dreams, various illnesses, aches and pains, reactions to certain foods, and the like. I follow Mayotte usage in referring to the spirit as a distinct social person from the host. The spirit speaks and acts while the host is "absent" during trance, and there is consistency and continuity from one appearance of a given spirit to the next. Hosts by and large do not remember what occurred while they were in trance (since they were not present, how could they?), but they are often told by others what happened. (They are given, not descriptions of themselves in trance, but the gist of what was transacted with the spirit.)

At various stages of their lives hosts may be "patients" seeking "cures"; possession is often spoken of in a "medical" idiom, and a "cure" alleviates symptoms by adjusting the host's relationship with her spirit. A "cure" entails undergoing a sequence of rituals during which the presence of the spirit in the particular host is publicly legitimated and its identity and power established. The host and her immediate kin must also learn to come to terms with the spirit in their midst; in its external (objective) form this is primarily a matter of satisfying the spirit's (typical) requests and convincing the spirit to accede to certain human principles of social action. Thereafter, a host may enter trance intermittently, primarily for the spirit's amusement, but also in order to permit her spirit to pursue its social relationships (conceived and constructed independently of those of the host herself) with the host's kin or acquaintances. Finally, some hosts become curers, i.e., mediums.[4] Mediums treat illness related to sorcery, manage the spirit possession cures of others, and diagnose and consult over a wide variety of topics. A medium can maintain a public practice or else may operate primarily within the family context.

Exorcism is performed only rarely, when the host exhibits symptoms severe enough to indicate that an ongoing relationship with the spirit would not be possible. In contrast to ordinary possession, where the spirit is identified according to species, age grade, gender and eventually personal name, the spirit whose presence requires exorcism is defined much more vaguely as "just an evil spirit" (*lulu ratsy. tu*); social identity is not relevant here. A failed exorcism is often redefined as mental derangement (*ulu adala*). Spirits that are not exorcised but are individually identified are essentially amoral rather than evil; their relationships with the human host require attempts at socialization and negotiation. However, the spirits of curers often do become authority figures of a sort and articulate morality in certain contexts. Social relationships between a possessing spirit and the host or various members of the host's family are developed through material exchanges (which also help to differentiate host and spirit from one another), through expressions of mutual sentiment, accession to one another's requests, and the like. These relationships may become very solid (or, conversely, they may remain entirely undeveloped), but at the same time they are characterized by the superior power of spirits and by the uncertainty that is a feature of all things pertaining to the spirit world; and, like many intense human relationships, they have their ups and downs. Indeed, the ups and downs help to remind everyone that there *is* a social relationship.

The recognition of possession emerges in a variety of circumstances and is constructed from signs ranging from apparently psychotic breaks (sometimes during the postpartum period), to occasional dreams, a series of misfortunes, lingering or acute illness, or a sudden competent expression of trance behavior during the feast for spirits that accompanies someone else's curing ceremony. Typically, the affirmation of possession is made gradually, and it need not lead to full expression in trance at all. I have attended lengthy seances where a spirit in an inexperienced host was called up in vain. The gap between initial "diagnosis" and appropriate trance behavior

may take years. Some people with spirits have to observe various ta-
boos imposed upon them but never enter trance; others enter trance
frequently but never hold a full curing ceremony. Peoples' abilities
and circumstances vary, but the main point is that not every spirit
will make the same demands upon the host (although, when they are
made, the demands are quite conventional). In my view it is impossible to make universal, nontautological generalizations about the
conditions for possession (or trance) in Mayotte. Moreover, since
possession can change an individual host in varying directions and
to varying degrees, it is difficult to find a constant that explains all
stages of even a single particular case. These facts need surprise us
only if we are committed to a naturalist paradigm.

Trance behavior often strikes the inexperienced observer as wild,
uncoordinated, incoherent, and unpredictable, and, indeed, it is
meant to. However, close observation and discussion with various
mediums reveal an underlying "grammar" such that in a competent
trancer most behavior can be interpreted as an expression of the
identity or attitude of the spirit and the stage or immediate quality
of its relationship with the host or interlocutor. These socially relevant messages are not simply constructed ex post facto but may be
seen to generate much of the behavior, especially in a "cure" where
everything proceeds according to the ideal model. This model has
typical "difficulties," e.g., original intransigence of the spirit, built
into it. The obstacles that have to be overcome may have their
source partially in basic human problems of adjustment to an altered state of consciousness or to the creation of a secondary "self,"
but they are not determined by them. Rather, they are the conventional means by which possession can be and is established.

The source of particular messages or elements of behavior may lie
in the collective model or in the internal conflicts or interests of the
host, or in both, but the code, the chain of signifiers and the rules regarding their expression, is collective. To give but a single illustration, in 1976 a relatively new kind of spirit made its appearance, indicating its presence by causing the host to froth at the mouth at the
onset of trance during a public ceremony. Only individuals possessed by this kind of spirit frothed at the mouth, and they did so
only when actively manifesting that spirit (most of them had other
kinds of spirits as well). Moreover, the frothing stopped as soon as
certain substances were applied, such as a white sheet, said to be ap-
preciated by this kind of spirit.[5] People acknowledged the severity of
the entry into trance, and the spirit did not become popular. They
also acknowledged the similarity to epilepsy, but they pointed out

that the spirit only mimicked the latter. That epilepsy was only signifier but not signified, that it was not in fact present in these cases of possession, is indicated by the fact that the individuals concerned foamed at the mouth always and only at the culturally appropriate occasions and that they did not appear to have any other symptoms of the disease. The one acknowledged epileptic with whom I was familiar did not participate in this form of possession. Hence, even the most "natural" and apparently involuntary of signs appears only in highly restricted contexts and carries quite a particular meaning.

I have argued elsewhere (1980, 1981) that spirit possession in Mayotte can be viewed, in broad terms, as a system of communication. I will not discuss all the properties of this system here, but in any given appearance or manifestation of a spirit three sorts of messages are typically transmitted, distinguished according to whether the primary referent is the individual spirit, the nature of spirits in general, or specific human interlocutors. Admittedly, this is a rough-and-ready set of distinctions, and any given act of communication, viewed as performance, may contain several levels of message simultaneously (cf. Rappaport, 1979). In particular, the contrast between the body of the host and the voice (person) of the spirit encourages consideration of various metamessages concerning the host. However, I make the distinction here because it serves as a useful way to describe respectively the three major contexts, activities, or overlapping stages through which spirit possession is constituted in Mayotte as social practice. In each of these, the scope for inventiveness and innovation, for improvisation (Bourdieu, 1977), for "speaking the present" or "speaking the past" (Becker, 1979; Bloch, 1974) is rather different.

First, one must consider the period of the emergence of a spirit in a particular host, during which messages concerning its individual status and immediate and prospective social relationships predominate. The identity of the spirit emerges during the interpretations of signs and circumstances, the first appearances in the host, the planning of the curing ceremonies, the applications of medicine, and the performance of the ceremonies themselves. In the course of these events the identity of the spirit is established as separate from that of the human host and is given both psychological and social reality. The full identity of the spirit may be in some suspense until the enactment of the final ceremony; it is a product both of the host's deep motivation and the "fit" with the identities of the spirits of the host's consociates and predecessors.[6] In addition to discovering (or, from another point of view, constructing) this identity, the host has to learn to distinguish herself from the identity manifested in trance, and the latter has to take on the qualities of a self (though never a fully coherent or autonomous one) in a kind of Meadian dialog among the I, the Me, and the Generalized Other (cf. Boddy, 1988; Kapferer, 1979). For the host this is initially a matter of constructing a Not Me and defining herself in opposition to it. For society the emergence process is a matter of accepting and validating the difference between host and spirit and affirming the relationship between them and the identity and power of the latter.

Second, we can distinguish the play or performance activities that take place mostly among the spirits (i.e., the possessed hosts) themselves, but also between spirits and nonpossessed humans. These activities, which vary in their particulars according to the species and status of the spirit, are timeless in the sense that they enact and display the nature of Spiritness without reference to specific ends or problems. The behavior of spirits provides the substance of the public discourse on Otherness that is an essential interpretive function of possession (cf. Boddy, in press); the displays of Spiritness provide fertile ground for cultural reflection upon the taken-for-granted world, in particular upon power and morality. Although the behavior is conventional and highly constrained by the codes of performance, it is also symbolically rich and open-ended, both because it does not prescribe particular avenues of behavior to the onlookers and because of its playful quality, especially the use of music and dance and the comedic juxtapositions of phenomena that are usually kept apart. Spirit performances are both amusing and intellectually and aesthetically satisfying. Spirit behavior is endlessly fascinating to some people; the parties for spirits held at the final stage of a possession "cure" attract large audiences as well as hosts whose spirits would not rise otherwise, and the appearance of a spirit on any occasion produces general interest.

The spirits also refer to aspects of Mayotte history and social identity and hence may be politically resonant. Of the two main species of spirit found in Mayotte, the *patros* are creatures who live in underwater communities around the margins of the island and whose names derive from books of Islamic astrology and related lore. They form a "version" or transformation of spirits found throughout Muslim East Africa, but one that manifests the ties of people to their territory. The *trumba*, by contrast are deceased Malagasy; in particular, the leading *trumba* are former Sakalava sovereigns. The *trumba* ceremonies, which sit less easily alongside Islam,

reconstitute royal authority and enable the spirits to perform blessing rituals over the human populace.[7] The authority of spirits is a
key feature of their makeup and one that plays a central role in the
final sort of communication to be discussed.

Third, then, there are the substantive conversations held between
established spirits and their human consociates, including the "internal" conversations maintained by adepts, but also the conversations established between curers and clients, and within families, especially between the spirit and the host's spouse (Lambek, 1980) or
among the spirit and two generations of hosts (Lambek, 1988). Over
the course of time the Not Me (i.e., the host's spirit) may be assimilated into the enlarged and more mature self of the host. The host
develops a stronger, more complex self-identity, with greater confidence, awareness, and resources to deal with stress. Mature spirits
play an important role in advising and protecting their hosts and
their families (although their trickster qualities always remain a part
of their identities). Possession thus adds a critical dimension to the
construction and conduct of social relations and provides both an
idiom and a channel with which to speak about and to manage identity, personhood, conflict, and uncertainty.

In Mayotte spirits become social personas in the sense that
they maintain coherent identities and consistent relationships
with others, both ideally distinct from those of the host. Spirits
thus form part of Mayotte social organization, and indeed spirit
possession can be considered a "total social fact" in the sense proposed by Mauss (1954). Possession can enter into virtually all
areas of life: illness and therapy, interpersonal relations, private
experience, marriage, the articulation of family boundaries and
continuity between the generations, world view, divination, social
thought, morality, political process, conflict resolution, myth,
fantasy, and fun. It cannot be explained in simple terms. In fact,
its very penetration into so many areas of life, the diversity of its
functions and expressions, suggests turning away from causal, etiological explanations toward examining its structure, organization, reproduction, and meaning.[8]

ETIOLOGICAL FACTORS AND
NATURALIZING MODELS

Trance's somatic expression has led many observers to a focus on
physiological and psychological causes and functions. But posses-

sion is a social phenomenon, as social as marriage. In Mayotte, possession is an institutionalized, socially legitimated and rule-bound context for, among other things, trance, in somewhat the way that marriage forms a context for, among other things, sex. Anthropologists would not think of explaining the institution of marriage in terms of the motivations that underlie individual decisions to marry, nor explain individual marriages in terms of the physiological properties or psychological functions of sex. True, certain expressions of possession may indicate underlying social pathology, much as conflict-ridden marriages or high rates of serial monogamy can, but this is a matter of symptom, not structure. And trance itself, like human sex, occurring in several forms and many kinds of contexts, legitimate and illegitimate, clearly defined and vague, is never purely "natural," though we like to think it is or at least to imagine the limiting cases.[9] To put this in its bluntest terms, no theory of marriage is based on the physiological properties of orgasm. It is time students of spirit possession stopped apologizing for not doing EEG's in the field and accepted the social reality of what they observe.

To retrench a little, it is clear that one of the reasons that trance has proved difficult to understand is precisely that a large complex of factors, neurological and psychological as well as social, do play a role in its full articulation. It is difficult to model the relationships among these factors, especially in light of the fact that the balance among them may shift with the cultural context and with the individual. To deal only with the former here, the cultural models that serve to generate and constrain trance behavior, the movement between states of consciousness, and the interpretation of trance behavior affect the manner and degree to which factors such as physical illness, nutritional status, unconscious motivation, interpersonal or role conflict, and social contradiction or strain are likely to be expressed in one or another form of trance activity. However, to the degree that any of these factors does play a direct role, it is a secondary one. As we all know, the human potential for trance experience is not activated in equivalent circumstances in all societies.

Ultimately, it may be artificial to attempt to isolate neurobiological, psychological, social, and cultural factors from one another. There is a much-cited article by Geertz (1973) in which he criticizes the "layer cake" model of humanity: that we have a basic biological foundation surmounted by increasing superficial layers of psychology, society, and culture. Geertz argues that the evolution of the human species has included feedback processes among all these elements, each adapting to the emerging context provided by the others. Thus, we cannot peel back culture to reveal a purely "biological" layer. This should hold true for trance as well as for any other aspect of human behavior, but it is difficult, given our fundamental assumptions, to conceptualize. This is not to say that trance has no biological elements—obviously it does—but rather that they may not be any more basic than, or isolable from, the psychological and cultural ones. We may recognize similarities in overt behavior in two societies such that we want to label both "trance," but such recognition does not allow us to generalize from one case to the other. For example, there is nothing in the Mayotte material that allows us to predict the surprising—from the Mayotte point of view—fact that in the northern Sudanese *zar* the host retains a partial consciousness of her possession and "sees through the eyes of the spirit" (Boddy, 1988). Thus, while Mayotte possession is predicated on the sharp distinction between the social persons of host and spirit, the Sudanese case focuses critically upon the ambiguity. In sum, trance has no purely biological core. It must be understood as fully human (and therefore cultural), with all the complexity that that implies.

A reaction to the difficulty of handling the complexity of trance has been the attempt to define it as (or reduce it to) a behavioral manifestation of something *else*, i.e., something outside of itself. As an extreme illustration of this reaction, an ecologically oriented colleague once asked me if I could discover trace elements in the soil that might account for the strange behavior I was reporting! In this way trance is treated as "natural" in the sense that, while it is unusual, an oddity that cries out for explanation, it can, in fact, readily *be* explained (away) as the direct, unmediated outcome of a material process. Among other things, this ignores the widespread and great variability among trance phenomena, the fact that they can change in unexpected directions, and their complex elaboration in places like Mayotte. In this approach, secondary features are rendered primary and spirit possession is reduced to an expression, explanation, or rationalization of trance behavior.

Perhaps the most common set of variants of this approach is to assume that trance is a more or less direct manifestation of disease or illness. Spirit possession then becomes the social label or theory of the illness and/or the mode of therapy (e.g., see Jilek, this volume, Kennedy, 1967, and Messing, 1958, for psychiatric models; Kehoe and Giletti, 1981, for a nutritional one).[10] Writers who follow the psychiatric approach often are not able to distinguish clearly which elements of the "cult" are manifestations of illness and which are forms of therapy, but an underlying assumption, sometimes corresponding to the claims of the local people, is that illness is a necessary condition for participation in the activity. Possession is considered so "odd" that it cries out for explanation in functional, therapeutic terms. It is true that in many instances trance may be linked to illness and that it may be an idiom through which illness is expressed or resolved. Yet "illness" itself is a problematic category, since it too is, at least in part, culturally constructed (Kleinman, 1983; Ward, this volume). And the relationship between trance and illness is by no means either necessary or straightforward. Illness is not the only thing expressed in trance; nor do all people who enter trance regularly correspond to an independent condition that we would consider pathological. Nor do all equally or equivalently ill or disturbed people enter trance. Even within a single society, the etiologies of every case of possession are not going to be identical to one another. In sum, we might equally well ask upon observing the strange activities of joggers or poets whether their behavior must be ascribed to illness (or therapy).

In Mayotte some histories of possession begin during the course of an illness. On the other hand, I saw illness symptoms manufactured or used as signs of possession, and I have argued (1981) that in Mayotte illness is an idiom for possession rather than the reverse. Recently, Kapferer (1983) has taken a rather similar view regarding certain possession phenomena in Sri Lanka. Less controversially, it might be stated that illness and trance inform, rather than determine, each other. Perhaps there is a natural affinity for this sort of connection, since each works upon the body and the subject's consciousness of it. Moreover, the illness idiom lends to Mayotte possession a sense of the external and the inevitable; like many naturalizing ideologies, it performs a function of mystification. Viewed historically, the (indigenous) "medicalization" of possession in Mayotte may be understood as a defensive move in the context of Islam, colonialism, and the demise of an autonomous political structure that the *trumba* once helped to constitute (cf. Baré, 1977; Feeley-Harnik, 1984). Our own insistent "medicalization" of Mayotte possession and like phenomena can be related to the "triumph of the therapeutic" in Western discourse more generally.

Of course, in certain cultural contexts one could imagine the encouragement of an illness career for the individual who exhibits a primary manifestation of trance behavior. Likewise, given a primary manifestation of illness, a trance career could be encouraged. Here one could follow labeling theory and argue that the social reaction to primary deviance (a deviance that in the anthropological version of the model proposed by Wallace, 1972, is psychologically or biologically rooted) can lead to a career of secondary deviance as the victim begins a process of loss of self-esteem and progressive identification with her illness. But the likelihood of this happening, as Wallace asserts, depends precisely on how trance behavior is culturally viewed and on whether the society has particular models for interpreting and handling the behavior. These models certainly can *not* be explained in terms of illness. Moreover, contrary to Wallace, it seems likely that once coherent models exist, even the primary manifestation of trance will be an essentially cultural product, a sign of the subsequent career rather than a biological symptom (cf. Kehoe & Giletti, 1981). "Deviance" itself is an inappropriate concept here, especially since, if anything, the cultural models and labeling processes tend to be supportive rather than harmful.

An important factor in the possible development of an "illness" component is whether the cultural model and associated ritual process allow or encourage the trancer to construct a trance self or not. In the case of Sri Lankan demonic exorcisms, so effectively described by Kapferer (1979, 1983), where demonic possession *must* indicate psychic disruption and the aim of the cure is to permanently remove the spirit, the ritual breaks down the patient's disturbed self and rebuilds her original self. The trance state is associated with illness and loss of self and is embedded in a cultural process in which that occurs. In Mayotte, on the other hand, trance transcends the initial "illness." (In fact, this may be true of some Sri Lankan material not considered by Kapferer, such as the trance states of the exorcists themselves.) If we include Obeyesekere's (1981) discussion of Sri Lankans who are not exorcised, we notice an inversion of the Mayotte situation. In Mayotte exorcism is reserved for atypical cases, for people who are relatively seriously disturbed; in Sri Lanka, these appear to be the sorts of people who may reject exorcism (Figure 2.1).

Related to the illness models of trance are those formulations that would reduce trance to a manifestation of particular social relations, most frequently relations of unequal power. Here, psychological "stress" is replaced by social "strain," possession is treated as a symptom or index of social conflict that cannot be channeled in a more productive direction. Thus, for example, role conflict may be a significant factor in the trance "epidemics" among Malay factory girls (Ackerman & Lee, 1981; L. Suriyo, personal communication). In the well-known "relative deprivation" theory of I. M. Lewis

(1971) this conflict approach is joined to narrowly individualistic views of social life as competition and psychological motivation as self-interest, so that, in the "peripheral cults," "possession is concerned essentially with the enhancement of status" (p. 127). The "devious manoeuvre" (p. 33) of spirit possession is the means by which a woman "gets even" (my phrase) with her husband.

	relatively undisturbed, typical	relatively disturbed, atypical
Mayotte	ongoing possession	exorcism
Sri Lanka	exorcism	ongoing possession

Figure 2.1 Comparison of the Application of Dominant Trance Models in Mayotte and Sri Lanka

The arguments proposed to demonstrate the insufficiency of the illness paradigm hold here as well. While sociological factors may partially account for particular instances or for shifts in the incidence of trance behavior, including epidemics, and for changes in the content of the material expressed in trance (Janzen, 1983a, 1983b; Lambek, 1984), they cannot account for the structure of possession forms. Status competition does not explain particular ethnographic cases at all (Kapferer, 1983; Lambek, 1981; Stirrat, 1977). As Crapanzano (1977) rather generously concludes about this type of approach, we need to discover the context-specific rules for status manipulation and control instead of seeking tautological generalizations. Indeed, perhaps we should follow Burridge's (1969) lead in the study of millenarian movements, away from parallel arguments of utilitarian individualism and competitiveness and toward seeing these phenomena as contexts for and attempts toward moral and personal regeneration. This would imply a nondeterministic perspective on human action, a point of view for which, if it is true, the corporeal manifestation of trance hardly prepares us.

All this is not to suggest that power may not be central to possession. On the contrary, spirits are powerful creatures, and in their effects upon their human hosts and their demands upon others their power is vividly manifested. But this power is socially constructed, generated in the rituals and system of communication through which possession is constituted. Spirits act with a power and speak with an authority that transcends the mundane, and humans are not considered responsible for their actions or directives. In this way, depending on specific context and means, possession can provide a significant arena for expressing resistance, submitting acceptance, articulating consensus, negotiating or transcending contradictory values, raising unpalatable issues, and making or avoiding decisions, though it cannot be reduced to any of these. The field of power is much broader than individual status manipulation or getting even. In Foucault's (1980) terms the power is creative as well as repressive. At the end of his study Lewis (1971) appears to recognize this when he remarks that "possession . . . represents an assertion, in the most direct, dramatic, and conclusive form that the spirits are mastered by man" (p.204), even while he continues to seek the necessary socioeconomic conditions for "the possession response" (p.203). My concern is precisely whether it is appropriate to seek "necessary conditions" and whether possession should be reduced to a "response" at all.

Finally, a discussion of trance should not neglect the question of unconscious motivation. As Obeyesekere (1984) has pointed out, one should not confuse the notion of trance as illness (i.e., psychopathology) with the presence of deep motivational factors per se. However, it is by no means clear whether the deep motivations of trancers differ systematically or to any degree from those of nontrancers in a given social context. One must also ask what motivates some people to *refrain* from trance behavior (Lambek, 1985). It may be that Mayotte trancers are simply not as troubled as their Sri Lankan counterparts described by Obeyesekere (1981).[11] In general, however, psychoanalytic arguments must consider not only the fact of trance per se but the identity of the particular spirit and its psychological relevance for the host (Lambek, 1988).

To incorporate a psychoanalytic point of view is still to leave open numerous avenues of interpretation. Among the more promising directions is to view possession as an idiom through which individuals *may* articulate various problems (Boddy, in press; Crapanzano, 1977; Obeyesekere, 1970). For Mayotte I would emphasize less the symptomatic, symbolic expression of unconscious conflict than the role of possession in adepts' life trajectories or "projects" in terms of the growth of the self (cf. Zempleni, 1977). Possession provides an interesting idiom for reflexivity, and the separation between host and spirit can sometimes lead to a positive "working through" along something of the order of psychoanalytic process. The transference relationship is critical here. The parental authority figure is mediated by the curer and then internalized and transformed as the client's spirit. Over time the host comes increasingly to identify with the spirit, perhaps the very one who also possesses her parent or grandparent (Lambek, 1988)! The people who are able to become successful hosts of spirits in Mayotte may be equivalent personalities to those who make successful psychoanalytic patients in the West. More generally, the "rhetorical force of possession" (Crapanzano, 1977, p. 26) produces an autonomous internal as well as external discourse. The spirit may participate in the internalized, specialized, yet ultimately ambivalent object relationship that British analysts have seen as critical in the development of self experience (Masud Khan, 1974).

Another interesting link between Mayotte possession and psychoanalysis concerns the external form of therapy. The fact that a curer can enter trance and become temporarily someone else can have positive implications for her clients (whether or not the client's problems are viewed as possession-related). Paul Antze and I (Lambek & Antze, 1983) have likened possession to psychoanalysis in that both are examples of "privileged discourse," encounters in which the ordinary social implications of conversation are lifted and there is an uncoupling of the messages from the metamessages about the self (the persona, or "me") and its social relations with other participants in the conversation. This allows the exploration of new topics and the taking on of new perspectives. That the curer can become someone "other" may be of particular significance in a society characterized by multiplex social relations. It should be noted that this argument does not concern the quality of the trance experience or the content of any specific psychological processes, such as catharsis, but rather establishes the properties of spirit possession as a system of communication and their consequences, such as the manner in which transference is handled. In sum, psychoanalysis can help us to understand the *process* of having a spirit or speaking to spirits rather than simply to explain the occurrence of trance or possession.

TRANCE AS TEXT AND AS DISCOURSE

In many of its manifestations, possession violates our own cultural distinctions and deeply held assumptions concerning the "natural" differences between such pairs of opposites as self and other, seriousness and comedy, reality and illusion, and, perhaps most critically, art and life. Because possession transcends these oppositions, our models must, too. A feature of possession that may serve as a bridge toward a new sort of model is its essentially playful or paradoxical quality. This is an aspect of possession that is often explicitly elaborated and emphasized in its social context (e.g., Lambek, 1981), but omitted from the observer's analysis.

Possession contains the central paradox that an actor both is and is not who she claims to be, producing "a kind of incongruence between statement and intent" (Becker, 1979, p. 233). Following from this central ambiguity, spirit possession is often full of surprises, creativity, and comedy, and may carry an undermining of political authority, whether slyly or through open parody (e.g., Leacock & Leacock, 1975; Stoller, this volume). Possession tends to make fun of everything it comes into contact with. The trickster needs a straight man, and, of course, anthropologists are not exempt from mockery. Thus Janice Boddy (in press) has reported the anthropologist's *zar* spirit who appeared in a northern Sudanese village toward the end of her research there. The investigator is inevitably engaged in the discourse; without a sense of humor she is lost, doubly mystified and caught in a regress of parody. Hence, if the possessed never allow us to forget what Giddens (1982) has called the "dialogical quality of social science" (pp. 13-14), then equally, we should grasp the dialogical quality of spirit possession.

One strategy I have adopted in earlier work (Lambek, 1981) is to view possession as text. This clarifies both what is going on and the sorts of questions we can reasonably ask about it. The text model avoids categorizing or reducing trance to something else. It suggests looking for levels of constraints, grammars of production and interpretation, modes of representation, avenues of creativity. Possession occurs in the context of a tradition of possession. It is formed by specific genres, rhetorical devices, images, and metaphors, as well as by a confrontation with a specific historical and social experience. Like poetry, or the art of the diarist, possession is a means of symbolically articulating experience. Most of the time it makes use of an essentially public code. Like various forms of Western art, it can be self-reflective; it is superbly suited to handle paradox. Like much mythology, for example, the Native North American "trickster" tales, possession accepts ambiguity (cf. Diamond, 1972). As in the Winnebago trickster cycle, there is a creative tension in Mayotte possession between the syntagmatic dimension (the emergence of order from chaos) and the paradigmatic dimension (the opposition

between orderly human and chaotic spirit worlds). Frequently possession is a kind of serious parody of orthodox religion, social convention, or the accepted language of power relations. Possession
may even be self-parodic.

The text model aims neither to restrict comparison to fixed, autonomous, narrative, and realist works nor to place possession in a
peripheral domain. The critic René Wellek expresses the issue well:

> Art is "illusion," "fiction," the world changed into language, paint, or
> sound. It seems to me an oddity of our time that this simple insight
> into the aesthetic fact is construed as a denial of the relevance, the hu-
> manity and significance of art. The recognition of the difference be-
> tween life and art, of the "ontological gap" between a product of the
> mind, a linguistic structure, and the events in "real" life which it re-
> flects, does not and cannot mean that the work of art is a mere empty
> play of forms, cut off from reality. The relation of art to reality is not
> as simple as older naturalistic theories of copying or "imitation" or
> Marxist "mirroring" assume. "Realism" is not the only method of art.
> It excludes three-quarters of the world's literature. It minimizes the
> role of imagination ... (as quoted by Hutcheon, 1980, p. 17)

Viewing possession as art or text clarifies the limitations of attempting only to seek either literal or latent meanings and hence to
ground the work in something outside of itself, whether in the biography of the individual or in her historical situation (Frye, 1971).
Among the limitations of such "documentary and external approaches" to literature, Frye notes that "they do not account for the
literary form of what they are discussing ... [and] do not account for
the poetic and metaphorical language of the literary work, but assume its primary meaning to be a non-poetic meaning" (pp.19-20).
In other words, they leave out central questions—those things that
make literature "literary" (or possession, possession) and not merely
commonplace. Frye then emphasizes literary context: the work
seen, first, in the entire literary output of the author, as a particular
transformation of her "structure of imagery," and second, in the literary tradition of which the author is a part, arguing that we must
identify the factors of a tradition that "make possible the creation of
new works of literature out of earlier ones" (p. 23). While the kinds
of transformations possible and the factors that influence them will
likely vary more greatly between possession and literature than between any given pair of literary traditions, the line of inquiry re-

mains significant. These sorts of questions have been successfully applied to religion and can be applied to possession as well.[12]

Of course, any given instance of possession activity is more than an inscribed, completed text. Our analysis cannot be restricted to inscribed content. "Author" and "reader" confront one another in direct social interaction; no one is left to grapple with the issues alone in her armchair, no one is left unchanged. As with contemporary "narcissistic narrative" (Hutcheon, 1980), the "reader" is forced to define her relationship to the "text." Relations among the possessed and between the possessed and nonpossessed can also be transformed. Possession is a social activity: The work is also a life. The parody can be bitter and the pain severe when ordinary life is intolerable. This vulnerability of our subjects must also call forth an appropriate response in our models.

In focusing on the product rather than the process of production, the text model may be faulted for being too static and for the tendency to isolate, unduly limit, and reify the subject of analysis. Without losing the benefits of the measured distance provided by the text model, it may be possible to incorporate some of the vitality of possession by viewing it either as performance or as discourse. Like the text model, neither of these perspectives would be sufficient to comprehend possession in its entirety, but each would add to our comprehension of certain moments, phases, or dimensions. The comments that follow, the tail end of a long paper, are merely suggestive.

To view possession as performance is to focus upon the relatively formal enactments in which it is realized. The model focuses on the experience of the participants, whether those actually entering trance (the "performers") or those observing it (the "audience"), who must be *moved* in some way.[13] This movement may refer to a submission to authority (Bloch, 1986; Turner, 1967), a transcending of unconscious conflict, an enlargement of the self, a deeper understanding of the cosmos, or merely a resituation of participants in their social context. This is to view possession as ritual, but ritual that does not merely speak, in symbolic language, about society, but actively constructs it. In ritual performance real things happen to real people. Performance has a vital quality to it; as Schieffelin (1985) puts it, "Participants are engaged with the symbols in the interactional creation of a performance . . . rather than merely being informed by them as knowers" (p. 707).[14] To understand how this engagement works requires attention to the rhetorical, performative, aesthetic, and emergent qualities of the event. A successful performance is a compelling one, urgent, unified, carrying a certain momentum. Kapferer (1983) provides an innovative analysis of the elaborate Sri Lankan exorcisms from this point of view, examining the experiential and aesthetic qualities and consequences of trance, dance, music, and comedy above and beyond their narrative meanings. Analysis of the formal properties of ritual (Rappaport, 1979; Tambiah, 1979) is also necessary in accounting for the transformations engendered through its action. Finally, performance suggests consideration of the relationship of the performer to her role as the latter is displayed to a public (Lambek, 1987; Lee, this volume; Leiris, 1958/1980).

Schieffelin (1985) emphasizes both that in Kaluli seances reality is constructed through the dialogue between the spirit/medium and the "audience" and that "heterogeneity is part of the system no less than [are] its underlying shared cultural assumptions" (p. 720). Both the dialogical quality and the heterogeneity I take to be features of discourse. A discourse model transcends performance, because it directs us to look beyond the immediacy of specific, highly formal events (performances) to broader, more pervasive processes and less discrete or formal occasions. Thus, I have argued (1980) that to focus exclusively on the flamboyant aspects of public performances is to miss the more subtle ways in which spirit possession in Mayotte can articulate, for example, the relationship of a medium with her spouse in informal domestic settings.

As a particular kind of system of communication, possession establishes channels, senders, receivers, and information. It constructs new things to think and talk about and new ways to do so, new forms of experience. Some of the implications of this have been mentioned in earlier sections of the paper. Possession can "thicken," i.e., add new levels of meaning to, social relationships (Lambek, 1980) and it allows for "privileged discourse" (Lambek & Antze, 1983), providing a certain quality of social space in which therapy is implemented. Possession demands both reflexivity and the engagement of onlookers, but it is neither injurious nor therapeutic per se. Not intrinsically functional, possession is simply a discursive practice. Here we move beyond the dominance of the external, collective models for possession behavior in order to account for its open-endedness, the unexpected outcome, the continuing conversation. The discourse operates in the personal, interpersonal, and public domains, constructing a multiplicity of ongoing, overlapping, emergent "objects." More than an idiom for the articulation of personal experience (Crapanzano, 1977; Firth, 1967; Obeyesekere, 1970), possession provides means and procedures that contribute to an on-going, historically located process constituting the self and subjectivity (Boddy, 1988, in press; cf. Foucault, 1980).

Discourse models are also appropriate for dealing with the political aspects of possession activity.[15] As Lewis (1971) notes, though he probably overestimates the distance between these functions, spirit possession can be embedded in a system of traditional authority or can form a protest against one. Bloch (1986) analyzes Merina possession as the virtually inevitable consequence of a larger ritual process that establishes the collective and timeless authority of the deme, thereby suppressing individual action. However, in the same work he notes a popular protest movement expressed through possession. Among the neighboring Sakalava, mediums had greater flexibility and played a significant role in succession disputes and legitimation (Baré, 1977); in the colonial period, the spirits' rules about work formed a means of passive resistance (Feeley-Harnik, 1984). In Mayotte, possession raised issues of power and morality without, during the 1970s, putting them to explicit, public political ends. Among the Shona, spirit possession played a key role in the Zimbabwean struggle for independence (Lan, 1985), and among the Songhay it formed a means of cultural resistance (Stoller, this volume). In none of these cases are the political contexts (e.g., deprivation) or the motivations of individuals sufficient to explain the phenomena. It is the prior existence of possession as a form of discourse that enables it to be used to carry out a range of functions rather than the reverse. This is particularly clear in Lan's study of the authority of Shona mediums and the shifting uses to which it was put. History is primary here; the discourse is open-ended.

In her comparison of spirit possession and anthropology, Boddy (in press) has argued that possession is, among other things, a vehicle for the expression of otherness, not only an objective, if symbolically embellished, catalogue of its varieties (as in the northern Sudanese *zar* or the Songhay *hauka)*, but an embracing of it, in order to reflect upon and transform the self. As ethnographers, we, too, imaginatively assimilate (and then partially distance ourselves from) new vehicles of thought, much as the possessed do, much as the novelist or reader does. In each case, we act creatively with the forms, within the structural and practical constraints, with which our time and culture, whether that of Mayotte spirit possession or professional anthropology, provide us. Making meaning is not a unilateral enterprise for which social scientists or psychologists have yet cornered the market.

NOTES

1. Ortner (1984), following the masterful articulation by Bourdieu (1977), has pointed to practice as the central anthropological issue of the 1980s.

2. "Trance" implies temporary neurophysiological changes as well as an "altered" state of consciousness characterized by subjectively experienced and possibly varied shifts in reality orientation. Further consideration lies beyond the scope of this paper, but even the term "possession," with its economic connotations, deserves closer examination than can be given here. Although it probably does little violence to the Mayotte view, there is some ambiguity in my own usage concerning whether it is the host who possesses the spirit or vice versa.

3. While part of the Comoro Archipelago, Mayotte remains under the political control of France. The indigenous population, over 60,000 in 1985, is Muslim and composed largely of speakers of Shimaoré, a Bantu language, and Kibushy, a dialect of Malagasy and hence Austronesian. Fieldwork was conducted in two neighboring communities of Kibushy speakers.

4. In an alternate sense, anyone subject to possession could be considered a medium, since direct communication with the spirit is possible.

5. On the symbolism of cloth covering the spirit, see Feeley-Harnik, in press.

6. Lambek (1981) Part II discusses this process in detail and describes a case in which the choice of identity was problematic. Lambek (1988) considers the processes by which spirit identities are passed on and shared among family members.

7. Recent analyses of royal ritual in Madagascar (Bloch, 1986) make this interpretation possible.

8. Considering the emphasis on etiology misplaced, I have taken a different approach to possession history in two recent papers. Lambek (1987) shifts the focus from initial experiences with possession to terminal ones, how and when people *leave* trance. Lambek (1988) changes the critical question from *why* someone is possessed to *by whom*. In this way one can examine the "reproduction" of possession relations from generation to generation.

9. Compare Foucaultian work on sexuality. Criticizing the dominant view of sexuality as an inner essence or essences, "an 'expressive state,' rather than an 'expressive act,'" Padgug (1979, p. 7) argues that "biological sexuality is only a precondition, a set of potentialities, which is never unmediated by human reality, and which becomes transformed in qualitatively new ways in human society" (p. 9).

10. I am linking together here approaches that focus on trance as illness and those that focus on possession as therapy despite the attempts of proponents of the latter (e.g., Ward, 1979) to distinguish their arguments from those of the former. While this forms an important advance in removing possession from natural cause, it does not go far enough. The idea of therapy presupposes a prior condition of illness that it addresses, and possession is still viewed as something to be explained in terms of its *external* relations, in this case, the positive functions it fulfills. Here I agree with Lewis (1971) that possession is much more than the sum of its psychotherapeutic functions.

11. As Paul Antze points out, the strength of motivation necessary for trance may vary with the social and psychological costs that accompany trance behavior in any given society. In Mayotte the social costs (in terms of loss of prestige) are considerably greater for men than for women; hence, psychological factors might be expected to play a more specific role in the etiology of cases of male spirit possession (cf. Lambek, 1981).

12. For example, Wilson (1954) likened ritual to poetry, a theme that was elaborated by Turner, the very title of whose major work, *The Forest of Symbols* (1967), hearkens back to Baudelaire. Perhaps the most complete application of the "poetic analogy" is Fernandez' masterpiece on Fang religion (1982), which refers repeatedly to Coleridge. Becker (1979) provides an approach to transformation within a creative tradition. Transformation is, of course, a major theme in the work of Lévi-Strauss on myth (e.g., 1969), but he is concerned with systems in which no version is ever fully "new."

13. "Audience" is not quite what is meant here, since the distance between performers and observers is often easily bridged and since the latter may be virtually as committed to the truth of what transpires as the "performers."

14. Actually, this is true of readers as well. Critics of the "text" model often attribute to it a static and fixed quality that, with the possible exception of early structuralism, it does not have. The focus on performance, as I see it, is not a categorical alternative to text but a matter of emphasis.

15. Parkin (1984) has argued that performance models (especially as applied by Americans) tend to play down the political effects of speech.

REFERENCES

Ackerman, S. E., & Lee, R. L. M. (1981). Communication and cognitive pluralism in a spirit possession event in Malaysia. *American Ethnologist, 8*, 789-799.

Baré, J-F. (1977). *Pouvoir des vivants langage des morts*. Paris: Maspero.

Becker, A. L. (1979). Text-building, epistemology, and aesthetics in Javanese shadow theatre. In A. L. Becker & A. A. Yengoyan (Eds.), *The imagination of reality* (pp. 211-243). Norwood, NJ: Ablex.

Bloch, M. (1974). Symbols, song, dance and features of articulation. *European Journal of Sociology, 15*, 55-81.

Bloch, M. (1986). *From blessing to violence: History and ideology in the circumcision ritual of the Merina of Madagascar*. Cambridge: Cambridge University Press.

Boddy, J. (1988). Spirits and selves in Northern Sudan: The cultural therapeutics of possession and trance. *American Ethnologist, 15*, 4-27.

Boddy, J. (in press). *Wombs and alien spirits: Women, men, and the zar cult in Northern Sudan*. Madison: University of Wisconsin Press.

Bourdieu, P. (1977). *Outline of a theory of practice* (R. Nice, Trans.). Cambridge: Cambridge University Press.

Bourguignon, E. (1967). World distribution and patterns of possession states. In R. Prince (Ed.), *Trance and possession states*. Montreal: R. M. Bucke Foundation.

Burridge, K. (1969). *New heaven, new earth*. Toronto: Copp Clark.

Crapanzano, V. (1977). Introduction. In V. Crapanzano & V. Garrison (Eds.), *Case studies in spirit possession* (pp. 1-40). New York: John Wiley.

Diamond, S. (1972). Introductory essay. In P. Radin, *The trickster*. New York: Schocken.

Dumont, L. (1975). Preface to the French edition of E. E. Evans-Pritchard's *The Nuer*. In J. H. M. Beattie & R. G. Lienhardt (Eds.), *Studies in social anthropology*. Oxford: Clarendon.

Feeley-Harnik, G. (1984). The political economy of death: Communication and change in Malagasy colonial history. *American Ethnologist, 11*, 1-19.

Feeley-Harnik, G. (in press). Clothing the dead. In J. Schneider & A. Weiner (Eds.), *Cloth in society and history.* Washington, DC: Smithsonian Press.

Fernandez, J. W. (1982). *Bwiti: An ethnography of the religious imagination in Africa.* Princeton: Princeton University Press.

Firth, R. (1967). *Tikopia ritual and belief.* Boston: Beacon.

Foucault, M. (1980). *Power/knowledge: Selected interviews and other writings.* New York: Pantheon.

Frye, N. (1971). *The critical path: An essay on the social context of literary criticism.* Bloomington: Indiana University Press.

Geertz, C. (1973). *The interpretation of cultures.* New York: Basic Books.

Giddens, A. (1982). *Profiles and critiques in social theory.* Berkeley: University of California Press.

Hutcheon, L. (1980). *Narcissistic narrative: The metafictional paradox.* Waterloo: Wilfrid Laurier Press.

Janzen, J. M. (1983a). [Review of *Human spirits*]. *Canadian Review of Sociology and Anthropology, 20,* 493-495.

Janzen, J. M. (1983b). *On the comparative study of medical systems: Ngoma, a collective therapy mode in Central and Southern Africa.* Unpublished manuscript, University of Kansas, Department of Anthropology, Lawrence.

Kapferer, B. (1979). Mind, self and other in demonic illness: The negation and reconstruction of self. *American Ethnologist, 6,* 110-133.

Kapferer, B. (1983). *A celebration of demons: Exorcism and the aesthetics of healing in Sri Lanka.* Bloomington: Indiana University Press.

Kehoe, A. B., & Giletti, D. H. (1981). Women's preponderance in possession cults: The calcium deficiency hypothesis extended. *American Anthropologist, 83,* 546-561.

Kennedy, J. G. (1967). Nubian zar ceremonies as psychotherapy. *Human Organization, 26,* 185-194.

Kleinman, A. (1983). Editor's note. *Culture, Medicine and Psychiatry, 7,* 97-99.

Lambek, M. (1980). Spirits and spouses: Possession as a system of communication among the Malagasy speakers of Mayotte. *American Ethnologist, 7,* 318-331.

Lambek, M. (1981). *Human spirits: A cultural account of trance in Mayotte.* New York: Cambridge University Press.

Lambek, M. (1984). Reply to Janzen. *Canadian Review of Sociology and Anthropology, 21* (1), 105-106.

Lambek, M. (1985). Ecstasy and agony in Sri Lanka [Review article]. *Comparative Studies in Society and History, 27,* 291-303.

Lambek, M. (1987). *Graceful exits: Spirit possession and performance in Mayotte.* Manuscript submitted for publication.

Lambek, M. (1988). *Spirit possession/spirit succession: Aspects of social continuity in Mayotte.* Manuscript submitted for publication.

Lambek, M., & Antze, P. (1983). *Privileged discourse: Self-negation and self-creation in psychoanalysis and spirit possession.* Unpublished manuscript.

Lan, D. (1985). *Guns and rain: Guerillas and spirit mediums in Zimbabwe.* London: J. Currey and Berkeley: University of California Press.

Leacock, S., & Leacock, R. (1975). *Spirits of the deep.* Garden City, NY: Doubleday.

Leiris, M. (1980). *La possession et ses aspects theatraux chez les Ethiopiens de Gondar.* Paris: Le Sycomore. (Originally published 1958.)

Lewis, I. M. (1971). *Ecstatic religion: An anthropological study of spirit possession and shamanism.* Harmondsworth: Penguin.

Lévi-Strauss, C. (1969). *The raw and the cooked.* New York: Harper & Row.

Masud Khan, M. (1974). *The privacy of the self.* London: Hogarth.

Mauss, M. (1954). *The Gift* (I. Cunnison, Trans.). London: Cohen & West. (Original work published 1925.)

Messing, S. (1958). Group therapy and social status in the zar cult of Ethiopia. *American Anthropologist, 60,* 1122-1126.

Needham, R. (1971). Remarks on the analysis of kinship and marriage. In R. Needham (Ed.), *Rethinking kinship and marriage* (pp. 1-34). London: Tavistock.

Obeyesekere, G. (1970). The idiom of demonic possession: A case study. *Social Science and Medicine, 4,* 97-111.

Obeyesekere, G. (1981). *Medusa's hair.* Chicago: University of Chicago Press.

Obeyesekere, G. (1984). [Review of *Human spirits*]. *Comparative Studies in Society and History, 26,* 744-748.

Ortner, S. B. (1984). Theory in anthropology since the Sixties. *Comparative Studies in Society and History, 26,* 126-166.

Padgug, R. A. (1979). Sexual matters: On conceptualizing sexuality in history. *Radical History Review, 20,* 3-23.

Parkin, D. (1984). Political language. *Annual Review of Anthropology, 13,* 345-365.

Rappaport, R. A. (1979). *Ecology, meaning and religion.* Richmond, CA: North Atlantic Books.

Sahlins, M. (1976). *The use and abuse of biology.* Ann Arbor: University of Michigan Press.

Schieffelin, E. L. (1985). Performance and the cultural construction of reality. *American Ethnologist, 12,* 707-724.

Stirrat, R. L. (1977). Demonic possession in Roman Catholic Sri Lanka. *Journal of Anthropological Research, 33,* 33-57.

Tambiah, S. (1979). A performative approach to ritual. *Proceedings of the British Academy, 65.*

Turner, V. (1967). *The forest of symbols: Aspects of Ndembu ritual.* Ithaca: Cornell University Press.

Wallace, A. F. C. (1972). Mental illness, biology, and culture. In F. L. K. Hsu (Ed.), *Psychological anthropology.* Cambridge, MA: Schenkman.

Ward, C. (1979). Therapeutic aspects of ritual trance: The Shango cult in Trinidad. *Journal of Altered States of Consciousness, 5,* 19-29.

Wilson, M. (1954) Nyakyusa ritual and symbolism. *American Anthropologist, 56,* 228-241.

Zempleni, A. (1977). From symptom to sacrifice: The story of Khady Fall. In V. Crapanzano & V. Garrison (Eds.), *Case studies in spirit possession* (pp. 87-139). New York: John Wiley.

PART II

Altered States of Consciousness and Psychopathology

> Must the experiencers of altered states of consciousness continue to see the scientists as concentrating on the irrelevant and the scientists see the experiencers as confused or mentally ill? (Tart, 1973, p. 45)

Accounts of altered states of awareness have proved problematic for behavioral scientists, with the limitations of scientific method and the biases of contemporary paradigms often cited as the prime causes. Our approach to understanding altered states, based on observation and theory testing, is logical, sequential, quantitative, and—whether behavioral, cognitive, or social in nature—largely culture-bound. Extending our scientific observations and theories to diverse cultural contexts entails certain difficulties, since indigenous perspectives on these phenomena are bound to involve divergent explanatory approaches; in short, a clash between scientific paradigms and magical thinking is likely to ensue. Cross-cultural scholars, however, aspire to keep one foot in each world and understand and interpret altered states of consciousness in terms that have both culture-specific and culture-general relevance.

The four papers that follow consider various altered states of consciousness in relation to psychopathology. With the concentration on trance and spirit possession—a condition determined by the indigenous attribution of causality—a mixture of explanatory frameworks arises. Although the contributors rely on a diverse range of psychological theories, including social role enactment, stress and coping analysis, and communication processes, sensitive attempts are made to appreciate and highlight the alternative indigenous explanations.

The section commences with Kemp's analysis of spirit possession in the Middle Ages. The author takes issue with the prevalent
contention that the mentally ill were typically perceived as
"witches or possessed by devils" and examines in depth the alternative medieval medical and legal perspectives on mental illness.
Kemp convincingly argues that, although certain disorders were
more likely to be associated with diabolic possession and treated
by exorcism, these largely excluded schizophrenia and epilepsy
and were the minority of cases. He also distinguishes possession
and obsession, pointing out that the latter was not generally regarded as insane. Drawing cross-cultural comparisons, Kemp suggests that the religious approach to mental illness existed side by
side with medical and legal analyses and that a variety of fairly sophisticated perspectives on altered states of consciousness and
mental health existed in medieval times.

Chandra shekar, by contrast, utilizes field data from India for
the application of psychological theories to the assessment of altered states of consciousness and mental health. With an emphasis
on spirit possession, the author considers definitive qualities of the
condition—such as the source, purpose, and religious or
nonreligious nature of the possession and whether the possession is
manifested in an individual or group—as well as the characteristics of the associated altered states of consciousness. He further ex-
plores various classification schemes, such as central versus peripheral possession; ceremonial, neurotic, and psychotic possession; and genuine, paroxysmal, and lucid possession. Most
important, Chandra shekar discusses possession in relation to
psychopathology, interpreting ASC's alternatively in terms of the
dissociation, communication, and expectancy theories and illustrating the substance of possession with case studies of
psychosocial stress and epidemic hysteria.

Spanos extends some of Chandra shekar's comments on expectancy theory to a sophisticated analysis of three superficially divergent modes of ASC's: hypnosis, multiple personality, and demon
possession. He interprets these phenomena in terms of strategic role
enactment. Paralleling the three phenomena with respect to elements of volition, control, and amnesia, Spanos maintains that
these behaviors are continually shaped and validated by the social

context in which they occur, whether that context is a religious or therapeutic environment. Objecting to the association of spirit possession with mental illness, Spanos argues that the reason these and related conditions have been perceived as problematic is that they have been inaccurately conceptualized as discontinuous from our everyday behaviors. Instead, these activities should be perceived and interpreted in terms of our theoretical accounts of everyday social interaction, which assume that complex behaviors are goal-directed enactments guided by social requirements and shaped by impression management. In short, possession, hypnosis, and multiple personality seem out of the ordinary only because the social roles associated with them are unusual.

Although Ward readily accepts the significance of sociocultural expectations and discusses medical, magical, and psychosocial models of psychopathology, she concentrates on spirit possession within a stress and coping framework. Spirit possession, as defined by the host culture, includes both symptoms of subjective psychological distress and norm violation, and as such it may be analyzed in terms of predisposing and precipitative factors, contingent norms and values, and available coping strategies. The analysis is undertaken from her own fieldwork in the West Indies as well as cross-cultural studies from Hong Kong, India, and North Africa. Ward not only parallels certain forms of spirit possession and neurotic coping attempts but interprets exorcism in terms of the dynamic processes and elements relevant to other therapeutic endeavors, including the nature of the sick role, expectations, and the client-therapist relationship.

All in all, the authors in this section attempt to understand and appreciate the sociocultural significance of various altered states of consciousness while extending psychological theory to account for these phenomena and their relationship to mental health.

REFERENCE

Tart, C. (1973). States of consciousness and state-specific sciences. In R. E. Ornstein (Ed.), *The nature of human consciousness* (pp. 41-66). San Francisco: Freeman.

3

"RAVISHED OF A FIEND"
Demonology and Medieval Madness

SIMON KEMP

Amongst present-day psychologists there seem to be two schools of thought regarding medieval European beliefs in the power of the devil to cause mental illness. The most popular view, which seems to have originated with Zilboorg (1941), is that all, or nearly all, mentally ill people in the Middle Ages were regarded either as witches or as possessed by devils. This view is commonly reiterated in introductory psychology texts. For example:

> During the Middle Ages, treatment for the mentally ill in Europe focussed on *demonology*. Abnormal behavior was attributed to supernatural forces such as possession by the devil or the curses of witches and wizards. As treatment, *exorcism* was used to drive out the devil. (Coon, 1983, p. 501)
>   When the Roman Empire fell, the rational view of mental disorders was displaced in favor of religious demonology. Those who suffered from mental disorders were suspected of having been invaded by a spirit or a devil. (Dworetetzky, 1982, p. 501)

Opposed to this popular view is that of more recent scholars (e.g., Jackson, 1972; Kroll, 1973; Neugebauer, 1978, 1979) who emphasize alternative approaches to mental disorder in medieval Europe and suggest that diabolic causes were ascribed in only a small, rather well-defined minority of cases.

Generally conceded by both schools is that at least some mentally disordered people were regarded as possessed by the devil or devils in medieval Europe. The purpose of this article is to consider the characteristics of mental disorders that were attributed to demonic causes in the Middle Ages and to see how much demonological beliefs related to other possible causes of mental illness.

BIBLICAL AND EARLY CHRISTIAN TRADITION

Medieval beliefs about devils were, of course, heavily influenced by the Bible, and in particular the New Testament, in which there are numerous accounts of demonic possession and its exorcism by Jesus and the apostles. Two such accounts, which seem to have been particularly influential, are worth detailed attention:

> And when he was come out of the boat, straightaway there met him out of the tombs a man with an unclean spirit, who had his dwelling in the tombs: and no man could any more bind him, no, not with a chain ... When he saw Jesus from afar, he ran and worshipped him; and crying out with a loud voice, he saith, "What have I to do with thee, Jesus, thou Son of the God Most High: I adjure thee by God, torment me not." For he [i.e., Jesus] said unto him, "Come forth, thou unclean spirit, out of the man." And he asked him, "What is thy name?" And he saith unto him, "My name is Legion, for we are many." And he besought him [i.e., Jesus] much that he would not send them away out of the country. (Mark 5.2-10)
>
> One of the multitude [said], "Master, I brought unto thee my son which hath a dumb spirit; and wheresoever it taketh him, it dasheth him down: and he foameth, and grindeth his teeth, and pineth away" ... [Jesus] rebuked the unclean spirit, saying unto him, "Thou dumb and deaf spirit, I command thee, come out of him, and enter no more into him." (Mark 9.17-18, 25)

Oesterreich (1966) has defined a possession syndrome, in which "the patient's organism appears to be invaded by a strange soul" (p. 17). Behavior associated with this syndrome includes changes in voice and physiognomy, as well as unusual and often scatological or blasphemous utterances. Characteristically, the condition alternates lucid and disordered intervals: in the lucid intervals the sufferers either report inability to control their behavior in the disordered interval or retain no memory of it. According to Oesterreich, the syndrome appears in a large number of societies. Subsequent anthropological research (e.g., Bourguignon, 1973, 1976) has confirmed that both the syndrome and the attribution of disturbed or deviant behavior to possession are indeed widespread. However, it should be noted, first, that in many societies mental disorders other than Oesterreich's syndrome as well as therapeutic altered states of consciousness are attributed to possession, and, second, that it is often useful to distinguish "central" from "peripheral" possession (Lewis, 1971; Ward, 1980). Briefly, central possession is highly regarded and often accompanied by ritual, while peripheral possession occurs spontaneously and is regarded generally as a disorder both by those possessed and by observers within the society.

The first biblical account given above describes a peripheral possession that closely resembles Oesterreich's syndrome. In addition, this account displays another interesting feature: The "unclean spirit" is apparently prophetic. Throughout the gospels it is the possessed who first recognize Jesus as the Son of God. As is shown below, medieval accounts of demonic possession often follow this biblical prototype.

The second biblical account apparently describes an epileptic. That this case is different from most of the others described in the gospels is also suggested by the disciples' inability to exorcise the spirit and by Jesus's remark that this kind of spirit can be driven out only by "prayer and fasting" (Mark 9.28). The significance of this case is that it suggested to later readers that a rather wide variety of mental disorders, including epilepsy, might be ascribed to demonic possession. Pope Gelasius, in the fifth century, for example, prohibited epileptics from becoming priests on the grounds that epilepsy arose from demonic possession (Reichel, 1896).

Diabolic powers in the Bible are not limited to possession. An influential passage (Matthew 4.1-11) describes Jesus's temptation by the devil. In this account the devil speaks to Jesus and tempts him with worldly power. The devil also appears in person and shows Jesus a vision of the world. This passage is particularly important because in medieval Europe it could be taken to imply that someone who claimed to speak with the devil, for example, might be describing a real rather than an imagined or hallucinated event.

THE MEDIEVAL TRADITION

Medieval Possession and Obsession

There are a number of medieval accounts of people who were believed to be demoniacally possessed. In the main these accounts are given by religious writers who recorded examples of the cure of possession by saints or at religious shrines in order to demonstrate that a particular person or place was genuinely sanctified. The justification for this belief was, again, biblical: Jesus encouraged his apostles and disciples to drive out devils in his name (e.g., Luke 9.49-50,

10.17). Here is a thirteenth-century example from *The Little Flowers of St. Francis of Assisi*:

> When the man saw Brother Rufino [an early Franciscan] from a distance he immediately began to shout and thrash around with such fury that he broke his bonds and leaped away from the men. They were amazed ... and urged him to tell them why he was being tormented more than usual. He answered: "Because that poor little friar ... burns me up and crucifies me by his saintly virtues and humble prayers. And so I cannot remain in this man any longer." And after saying that, the devil left him at once. (Habig, 1973, p. 1479)

In the twelfth-century *Book of the Foundation of St. Bartholomew's Church in London* a knight is described who was "rauashid of a feende and made woid" [mad]. He dismounted, scattered his clothes and money and ran wild, but was later cured after two nights at the church (Moore, 1923, p. 46).

The passage above illustrates that, in the hands of religious writers, possession might be ascribed to a rather wide range of mental disorders, just as it is in the Bible. Also deriving from the biblical account is the distinction between demonic possession and obsession.

In modern Catholic thinking a distinction is drawn between demonic possession, in which the devil "takes up his abode in the human body, which he moves at will as if he were its master" and demonic obsession, which "consists in a series of unusually violent and persistent temptations" (Tanquerey, 1923, p. 718).[1] Obsession may produce visual, auditory, or even tactile hallucination, or stir up disturbing mental images or emotions. Hallucination is not generally characteristic of possession, but then the possessed often retain no memory of the interval of possession. The crucial distinction is that in obsession the individual retains control of his or her behavior, whereas in possession he or she does not (Poulain, 1921; Tanquerey, 1923). The distinction is actually of medieval origin and is found in *Malleus Maleficarum*, which was written in 1484, although the terms used are a little different (Kramer & Sprenger, 1948).

Medieval accounts of obsession frequently follow the biblical example in that the devil appears in person and offers some form of temptation. Many of the saints seem to have been obsessed at one time or another. Probably the best-known example is that of St. Anthony, whose temptations were later vividly portrayed by the painter Hieronymus Bosch. St. Francis of Assisi is recorded as having suffered from a tactile hallucination in which he was severely beaten by devils (Habig, 1973, p. 461). Luther even had some earthy advice for the obsessed:

> When the devil comes at night to worry me, this is what I say to him. If he keeps on nagging me and trots out my sins, then I answer: "Sweet devil, I know the whole list. Also write on it that I have shit in my breeches. Then hang that around your neck and wipe your mouth on it." (Haile, 1980, p. 191)

Occasionally, obsession seems to have developed into possession. One of the St. Bartholomew's cases, a chastely brought-up clergyman's daughter, was tempted by the devil appearing as a handsome young man. On one occasion a nurse saw her talking to no one. The devil came whenever the girl was alone and one day became violent and threatened her, whereupon she "fell down out of her wits" and wallowed and turned on the floor. She was regarded with horror by her neighbors while she foamed at the mouth. Later she recovered and told what had happened. After further attacks she was taken to the church, where the prayers of the clergy were successful (Moore, 1923, pp. 49ff).

Perhaps the most interesting feature of medieval obsession is that those suffering from it do not usually seem to have been regarded as insane or mad at all. Such a finding serves to emphasize the significance of culture-specific (emic) factors in the evaluation of health and illness (e.g., Ward, this volume, chap. 1). Thus, no action was taken when the clergyman's daughter was overheard talking to the devil but only when she went into paroxysm. Kroll and Bachrach (1982), who reviewed a large sample of medieval visionary experiences, concluded that, while these were not always accepted as bona fide visions, they were not regarded as evidence of psychopathology. (See Zusne, this volume, for an early-twentieth-century parallel.) One might add, in this context, that it would probably be a difficult task today to argue convincingly that St. Francis was mentally ill.

Treatment

Jesus's use of exorcism was imitated both by his disciples and by the early church. From the third century the church counted exorcists among the four lower orders of clergy. They were required to memorize the forms of exorcism and to lay hands on those possessed with evil spirits (Reichel, 1896). Successful exorcisms were also attributed to many of the medieval saints, partly with the object of demonstrating their sanctity. St. Francis of Assisi, for example, was credited with several times interrogating and casting out devils (Habig, 1973). Various forms of exorcism seem to have been employed by different exorcists. The elaborate Roman Catholic ritual of exorcism was not developed until the seventeenth century, and its form then probably owed as much to considerations of combatting Protestantism as to relieving the mentally ill (Kelly, 1968; Thomas, 1971). In *Malleus Maleficarum*, however, Kramer and Sprenger (1948) do suggest a formal service of exorcism.

There is some indication that in medieval Europe exorcism was sometimes used as a means to detect as well as to expel demons. Constantine of Africa and John of Gaddesden both suggest a means for distinguishing epilepsy from demonic possession that involved commanding the devil to leave. If the patient was unaffected, epilepsy was suggested, while if the patient fell into a coma, he was presumed possessed (Lennox, 1970; Temkin, 1945).

While exorcism seems to have been commonly used as a treatment for possession in medieval Europe, as indeed it is today in a variety of cultures (Ward, this volume, chap. 6), it was by no means the only treatment used, even by the clergy. Bede describes a man who was cured of his apparent possession—the symptoms described are actually those of epilepsy—by the dust over which the water that had washed the blessed Oswald's bones had been poured (Bede, 1890). None of those cured at St. Bartholomew's shrine appear to have been formally exorcised; rather, the demons appear to have departed in response to the prayers of the resident clergy (Moore, 1923). At first sight the distinction between treatment by exorcism and treatment by relics or prayer may appear a rather minor one, since both treatments are of a religious nature. The key point, however, is that relics and prayers were generally believed to be effective against any kind of disorder, not just those attributed to devils. Most of the St. Bartholomew's cases, for instance, describe the cure of illnesses with a recognized physical cause, not a diabolic one (Moore, 1923). The indication, then, is that demonic and physical causes were not necessarily regarded as completely separate, but might interrelate to some degree.

It is unsurprising, when these considerations are borne in mind, to find that physical means might be used to treat demonic possession. An Anglo-Saxon leechbook, for example, prescribes "For witlessness, that is, for devil sickness, or demoniacal possession, take from the body of this same wort mandrake, by weight of three pennies, administer to drink in warm water" (Cockayne, 1864, p. 249). In *Malleus Maleficarum*, it is suggested that "a man possessed by a devil can indirectly be relieved by the power of music, as was Saul by David's harp, or of a herb, or of any other bodily matter in which there lies some natural virtue" (Kramer & Sprenger, 1948, p. 178).

Alternative Approaches to Mental Illness

So far we have considered the religious approach to mental illness in the Middle Ages. This approach, however, existed not in isolation but, at least from the eleventh century onward, side by side with both a medical and a legal approach.

The medical approach was predominantly a physiological one. The approach originated in Greek and Roman medicine with writers like Galen (A.D. 122-199) and was widely disseminated in medieval Europe by a number of translators and commentators. Mental illness, in this tradition, was presumed to arise chiefly from a humoral imbalance in which black bile was produced and was termed "melancholy." Melancholy could produce a range of symptoms wide enough to cover most present-day psychoses and was not simply restricted to depressive illnesses. Other humoral imbalances or physiological mechanisms could produce epilepsy and other nonmelancholic disorders. Treatment of melancholy and other disorders occasionally included surgery but more normally employed dietary means to restore the humoral balance (Flashar, 1966; Jackson, 1969; Kroll, 1973; Temkin, 1945).

At least in medieval England, a legal approach can also be distinguished whose main consideration was the determination of the competence or responsibility of individuals for their actions. In both Anglo-Saxon and Norman law, insanity could be used as a defense, although this probably occurred rather rarely (Walker, 1968). The medieval Chancery occasionally had to decide on the competence of individuals to administer their estates. Idiocy—that is, mental deficiency present from birth—seems to have been determined by the court using commonsense measures, for example, the ability to count. The determination of lunacy—disorder that commenced postnatally—seems to have involved both tests of cognitive function and a search for behavioral abnormality (Neugebauer, 1978, 1979).

The Court of Chancery not only judged on the fact of mental incompetence but also frequently assigned a cause for it. In only one case did the court attribute lunacy to "the snares of evil spirits" (Neugebauer, 1979, p. 481). Instead the explanations offered were generally environmental: the effect of an illness or a blow on the head, "induced by fear of his father" (p. 481). Thus, neither the religious nor the medical approaches seem to have had much impact on the court.

Relative Use of the Different Approaches

Generally, the religious, approach to mental disorder seems to have had little impact on either the medical profession or the courts. It is not clear, however, whether this is because doctors and lawyers rejected demonological explanations of mental disorder or because they simply regarded such explanations and spiritual healing as outside their area of competence. That the Chancery found one demonic cause in a case of mental disorder, and that the medical writers Constantine of Africa and John of Gaddesden found it necessary to distinguish epilepsy and demonic possession, suggest the latter possibility, but the evidence is not strong.

Religious writers, on the other hand, consistently acknowledged that the medical approach had validity. That epilepsy, for example, was generally due to physical causes is clearly acknowledged in *Malleus Maleficarum* (Kramer & Sprenger, 1948) and also in the records of medieval shrines (Clarke, 1975). Luther, when asked for his advice in a case of mental illness, prefaced his suggestion of prayer with the remark "If the physicians are at a loss to find a remedy, you may be sure that it is not a case of ordinary melancholy" (Hoffman, 1976, p. 199). Johan Busch, a fifteenth-century German clergyman, recounted that a man "ran forth from the field and said that his wife was possessed with a devil ... I found she had many fantasies, for that she was wont to sleep and eat too little, whence she fell into feebleness of brain and thought herself possessed by a demon; yet there was no such thing in her case" (Coulton, 1928, pp. 231-232).

Thomas of Celano also recorded an attempt by St. Francis of Assisi to determine whether an actual possession had occurred. A woman "observed by the devil" had been brought to the saint's lodging to be healed by him, but he "sent to her a brother who was with him, wishing to discover whether it was really a devil or deception on the part of the woman. When that woman saw him, she began to

deride him, knowing that it was not Francis who had come out"
(Habig, 1973, p. 287).

In practice, the diagnosis of a physiological or a demonic cause
must have sometimes been very difficult indeed. A late-fifteenth-
century account of the illness of Hugo van der Goes illustrates
this point:

> Certain people talked of a peculiar case of *frenesis magna*, the great
> frenzy of the brain. Others, however, believed him to be possessed of
> an evil spirit. There were, in fact, symptoms of both unfortunate dis-
> eases present in him, although I have always understood that through-
> out his illness he never once tried to harm anyone but himself. This,
> however, is not held to be typical of either the frenzied or the pos-
> sessed. In truth, what it really was that ailed him only God can tell.
> (Rosen, 1968, p. 145).

Despite the difficulties of differential diagnosis, it appears that
certain kinds of mental disorder were more likely to be labeled possession than others. Oesterreich's (1966) syndrome clearly fell into
this category; at least one of the St. Bartholomew's cases describes
"an apparent invasion" of this type attributed to demonic possession (Moore, 1923, case 2-19). Although such disorders are rather
rare in modern psychiatric practice (Enoch & Trethowan, 1979),
they may not have been so rare in medieval Europe. It is generally
agreed that behavior giving the appearance of possession occurs
more frequently in a culture or subculture that believes in the possibility of an actual possession (Lambek, this volume; Spanos, this
volume). On the other hand, other kinds of disorder were not generally attributed to demonic possession. Epilepsy, for example, seems
to have been generally attributed to physical causes after the eleventh century. The present-day diagnosis of schizophrenia was generally called melancholy and attributed to a humoral imbalance.

CONCLUSIONS

Although some features of medieval attribution of mental disorder to demonic possession remain unclear, some general conclusions can also be drawn. It seems safe to presume, for example, that
the possibility of diabolically caused mental disorder was generally
accepted in medieval Europe. However, not all mental disorder was
attributed to demonic influences; physiological and environmental

causes were also conceded, even by religious writers. No real esti-
mate can be made of the relative frequency of demonic diagnoses.
The case descriptions given above suggest that religious chroniclers
were rather more ready to perceive demonic influence than doctors
or lawyers, but this may reflect the type of cases they dealt with as
much as biases in perception. It also appears that certain kinds of
disorder were more likely to be diagnosed as due to demonic possession than others. Thus, radically different approaches to mental disorder existed side by side in medieval Europe, as indeed they do
today—in parts of Africa, for example. It is not uncommon in some
locales to find both the traditional shaman and Western-oriented
practitioners, sometimes even working with the same patient
(Rappaport & Rappaport, 1981).

To the twentieth-century observer, the apparent willingness of
medieval clergymen, doctors, and lawyers to concede demonic
explanations of mental illness, as well as, and alongside, physical
and environmental ones may appear a peculiar mixture of igno-
rant superstition and science. It might also appear that medieval
thinking about mental illness was rather a patchwork affair
made up of assorted irreconcilable beliefs. Such a view, however,
is not completely accurate: at least two common threads served
to unite the demonological with the medical and legal accounts
of mental illness.

In the first place, a rather strict definition of insanity, that it was a
state in which the rule of reason was overthrown, was common to all
three approaches. Hence, for example, the curious fact that the
demonically obsessed were not usually regarded as insane by their
contemporaries, regardless of the nature of their visions. Hence also
the reliance of the Court of Chancery on tests of reasoning ability in
determining legal competence.

Second, it was acknowledged that mental illness might reflect the
interaction of a number of possible causes. In *Malleus Maleficarum*,
for example, Kramer and Sprenger (1948, p. 178) remarked that
"according to physicians, mania very much predisposes a man to
dementia and consequently to demonic obsession." They also produced physical mechanisms for diabolic involvement: "The devils
can stir up and excite the inner perceptions and humours" (p. 50).
To the present-day observer this may seem a bizarre mixture of
causes of quite different kinds, although this is quite common in a
cross-cultural context (see Chandra shekar, this volume). The theoretical difficulties of reconciling the different causes, however, were

probably no greater than the problem of trying to integrate genetic and environmental influences on behavior.

Overall, it is clear that the popular view of mental illness and its treatment in medieval Europe is quite inaccurate. Although demonological explanations of mental illness were employed, they were by no means the only explanations used. Nor does there appear to be any good reason for regarding the explanations as irrational. On the contrary, the demonic account appears to have been deeply considered, as was its place alongside other possible accounts of mental illness.

NOTE

1. A similar distinction is made by healers in the Kardecismo spiritist movement in Brazil (Krippner, this volume).

REFERENCES

Bede (1890). *Ecclesiastical history of the English people.* London: Trubner.

Bourguignon, E. (1973). Introduction: A framework for the comparative study of altered states of consciousness. In E. Bourguignon (Ed.), *Religion, altered states of consciousness, and social change* (pp. 3-35). Columbus: Ohio State University.

Bourguignon, E. (1976). *Possession.* San Francisco: Chandler and Sharp.

Clarke, B. (1975). *Mental disorder in earlier Britain.* Cardiff: University of Wales.

Cockayne, O. (1864). *Leechdoms, wortcunning and starcraft of early England.* London: Longmans

Coon, D. (1983). *Introduction to psychology: Exploration and application.* St. Paul: West.

Coulton, G. G. (1928). *Life in the middle ages* (Vol. 1). Cambridge: Cambridge University Press.

Dworetetzky, J. P. (1982). *Psychology.* St. Paul: West.

Enoch, M. D., & Trethowan, W. H. (1979). *Uncommon psychiatric syndromes* (2nd ed.). Bristol: John Wright and Sons.

Flashar, H. (1966). *Melancholie und Melancholiker in den Medizinischen Theorien der Antike.* Berlin: Walter de Gruyter.

Habig, M. A. (Ed.). (1973). *St. Francis of Assisi: Writings and early biographies.* London: Society for Promoting Christian Knowledge.

Haile, H. G. (1980). *Luther: An experiment in biography.* New York: Doubleday.

Hoffman, B. R. (1976). *Luther and the mystics.* Minneapolis: Augsburg.

Jackson, S. W. (1969). Galen on mental disorders. *Journal of the History of the Behavioral Sciences, 5,* 365-384.

Jackson, S. W. (1972). Unusual mental states in medieval Europe. I. Medical syndromes of mental disorder: 400-1100 A.D. *Journal of the History of Medicine and Allied Sciences, 27,* 262-297.

Kelly, H. A. (1968). *The devil, demonology, and witchcraft.* New York: Doubleday.

Kramer, H., & Sprenger, J. (1948). *Malleus Maleficarum* (M. Summers, Trans.). London: Pushkin.

Kroll, J. (1973). A reappraisal of psychiatry in the middle ages. *Archives of General Psychiatry, 29,* 276-283.

Kroll, J. & Bachrach, B. (1982). Visions and psychopathology in the Middle Ages. *The Journal of Nervous and Mental Disease, 170,* 41-49.

Lennox, W. G. (1970). *Epilepsy and related disorders* (Vol. 1). London: Churchill.

Lewis, I. M. (1971). *Ecstatic religion.* Middlesex: Penguin.

Moore, N. (Ed.). (1923). *The book of the foundation of St. Bartholomew's Church in London.* London: Early English Text Society, O.S. 163.

Neugebauer, R. (1978). Treatment of the mentally ill in medieval and early modern England. *Journal of the History of the Behavioral Sciences, 14,* 158-169.

Neugebauer, R. (1979). Medieval and early modern theories of mental illness. *Archives of General Psychiatry, 36,* 477-483.

Oesterreich, T. K. (1966). *Possession: Demoniacal and other* (D. Ibberson, Trans.). New York: University Books.

Poulain, A. (1921). *The graces of interior prayer.* London: Kegan Paul.

Rappaport, H., & Rappaport, M. (1981). The integration of scientific and traditional healing. *American Psychologist, 36,* 774-781.

Reichel, O. J. (1896). *A complete manual of canon law: Vol 1. The sacraments.* London: John Hodges.

Rosen, G. (1968). *Madness in society.* London: Routledge and Kegan Paul.

Tanquerey, A. (1923). *The spiritual life: A treatise on ascetical and mystical theology* (2nd ed., H. Branderis, Trans.). Tournai: Society of St. John the Evangelist.

Temkin, O. (1945). *The falling sickness.* Baltimore: Johns Hopkins University Press.

Thomas, K. (1971). *Religion and the decline of magic.* London: Weidenfeld and Nicolson.

Walker, N. (1968). *Crime and insanity in early England: Vol 1. Historical perspective.* Edinburgh: University.

Ward, C. (1980). Spirit possession and mental health: A psycho-anthropological perspective. *Human Relations, 33*(3), 149-163.

Zilboorg, G. (1941). *A history of medical psychology.* New York: Norton.

4

POSSESSION SYNDROME IN INDIA
C. R. CHANDRA SHEKAR

Spirit possession is a phenomenon long known to humankind. Primitive folk believed that evil spirits and angry gods caused most difficulties and misfortunes, including ill health, a view that had some currency in the Middle Ages (see Kemp, this volume). Mora (1975) notes that possession by an evil spirit, resulting in verbal manifestations of abnormal behavior, came to be seen as a common cause of mental disorder, and the exorcising of persons allegedly possessed by harmful intruders became a frequent practice in medieval times. Despite the march of civilization and advances in scientific knowledge, the possession syndrome still exists in both underdeveloped countries and technologically advanced nations (though there has been a considerable decline in its incidence). It has been reported not only from Africa and Asia but also from other continents (Kiev, 1961; McAll, 1971; Spanos, this volume). Bourguignon and Evascu (1977) found that 90% of a worldwide sample of 488 societies displayed trance and/or possession. This phenomenon, associated with mythology, cultural tradition, and specific rituals in different societies, has been a popular subject for discussion among anthropologists, psychiatrists, writers, and people in general. Ward (1980) wrote, "Possession represents just one aspect of a particular world-view, an overall attempt to explain the cosmos and man's place in it—the meaning of good and evil, human and divine, mystical and mundane" (p. 150). Anthropologically, possession is viewed as a stylized performance serving the purpose of linking humans with natural and supernatural forces, creating solidarity in public ceremonies and explaining the panoramic cosmos (Walker, 1972). Psychiatrically, possession is described as an ultraparadoxical state of emotional excitement that disrupts previously learned responses and eventually results in a transmarginal collapse (Sargant, 1974). Possession is also described as a dissociative state in which unconscious issues and conflicts surface in different forms. Though such a variety of explanations is available in the literature, none is satisfactory and the possession syndrome has remained an enigma.

THE POSSESSION SYNDROME

The dictionary (Oxford) defines possession as "A state of possession (ownership) and a state of being possessed by a deity, demon, idea and the like." Though the phenomenon of spirit possession is an age-old one, it was introduced into modern psychiatric literature by P. M. Yap in 1960 and was called "Possession Syndrome." Oesterreich (1966) defined it as "a state in which the organism appears to be invaded by a new personality and governed by a strange soul" (p. 17). Wintrob (1973) and Wijesinghe, Dissanayake, and Mendis (1976) described possession as an episodic disruption of behavior during which it is presumed that the subject's personality has been replaced by that of a spirit or God, whose characteristics are well-known within the subject's culture, and after which the subject claims either partial or total amnesia for his or her behavior.

With such vague and ambiguous definitions of possession, the situation becomes confusing for the mental health clinician. Since many types of deviant behavior are attributed to spirit possession, and since culture-specific elements have an important pathoplastic effect on mental illnesses (Wittkower & Rin, 1965), possession becomes part of clinical manifestations of many known psychiatric illnesses. As authors seem to have described a wide variety of cases, a uniform picture is lacking.

Magnitude of the Possession Syndrome

Though literature on possession syndrome is abundant, there are only a few epidemiological studies on the topic. Wijesinghe et al. (1976) quoted a prevalence rate of 0.5% in a semi-urban population of Sri Lanka. Carstairs and Kapur (1976) reported a period prevalence (6 months) of 2.8% in a rural population in the west coast of South India, and Venkataramaiah, Mallikarjunaiah, Chandrashekar, Rao, and Reddy (1981) cited a prevalence (1 year) of 3.7% in another rural population of South India.

Although the possession syndrome is widely prevalent and constitutes a significant health problem, the majority of the victims seek the help of traditional healers, and only a minority seek psychiatric assistance (Chandra shekar, Venkataramaiah, Mallikarjunaiah, Rao, & Reddy, 1982; Pradeep, 1977).

TABLE 4.1. Comparison of Three Epidemiological Studies

Item	Wijesinghe et al. (1976)	Carstairs & Kapur (1976)	Venkataramaiah et al. (1981)
Area surveyed	Semi-urban	Rural	Rural
Population studied	7653	1233	1158
Possession cases	40	34	43
Prevalence rate	0.52%	2.76%	3.7%
Religion (cases)	—	All Hindu	All Hindu
Main Caste (cases)	—	Fishing	Farming
Female sex (cases)	73%	77%	74.4%
Education:			
nil	14%	—	20%
1 to 10 years	86%	—	80%
above 10 years	—	—	—
Low income (<Rs. 300/-PM)	80%	—	33%
Belief in possession	—	60% of population	90%

Characteristics of Possession

From the available literature it is evident that the characteristic features of this phenomenon differ widely in a cross-cultural context (see Lambek, Kemp, Ward, Spanos, this volume). The clinical manifestations and interventions differ depending on the following factors.

(1) Possessing element: Possessing agents may be spirits or God. The spirits are usually of dead relatives or others who have died unnaturally and become ghosts. Salisbury (1968), for example, has observed that the onset of possession syndrome commonly occurs within two weeks of such deaths. Occasionally spirits of national heroes or holy persons possess their followers. Usually one spirit possesses an individual throughout his or her possession history. It is rare to be possessed by more than one spirit, and such multiple possessions never occur simultaneously. If there is a history of more than one element possessing an individual, it is usually a semigod or God replacing another type of spirit. Very rarely are individuals possessed alternately by spirits and Gods (Chandra shekar 1981; Chandra shekar et al., 1982).

(2) Purpose of possession: Possession may occur to assist or harm.

(3) Number of individuals involved in possession: Individual or group.

(4) Religious or nonreligious nature of the possession.

(5) Voluntary or involuntary nature of the possession.

But in all these cases some common features have been observed to be present. They are

(1) Alterations in consciousness.

(2) Alterations of facial expression and quality and content of speech.

(3) Change of behavior.

(4) Physical changes: Anaesthesia to pain and heat, tonic spasms of the muscles.

(5) Common link with hysterical personality (Okasha, 1966; Teja, Khanna, & Subramanyam, 1970; Yap, 1960).

Classificatory Systems of Possession Syndrome

Different workers have classified the possession syndrome in different ways.

(A) P. M. Yap (1960) classified the possession syndrome according to the depth of consciousness.

(1) First degree, or complete: The first-degree syndrome consists of clouding of consciousness, skin anaesthesia to pain, a changed demeanor and tone of voice, impossibility of recall to reality, and subsequent amnesia.

(2) Second degree, or partial: The second-degree syndrome consists of mild clouding, partial amnesia, and no change in voice or demeanor. While the possibility of recall to reality is present, partial amnesia follows.

(3) Third degree, or histrionic: The third-degree syndrome is marked by an absence of clouding and anaesthesia, no change in voice or demeanor, the possibility of immediate recall to reality, and the gaining of attention and mannerisms such as giggling and other attention-seeking devices.

(B) Dr. Jean L'Hermitte (1963) classified the possession syndrome into three types:

(1) Genuine type: There is a full replacement of the personality by the possessor, with a full retention of insight.

(2) Paroxysmal hysterical or mythomaniacal types: These exhibit a clouding of consciousness and regression to an earlier stage of morality, with a dissociation of personality.

(3) Lucid possession: There is a battle going on within the person as to which force is going to take control.

(C) Wittkower (1970) has classified such cases, depending on the symptoms, into

(1) Ceremonial possession.
(2) Neurotic possession.
(3) Psychotic possession.

(D) Extending Lewis's (1971) model, Ward (1980) classified possession into ritual and peripheral possession.

(1) Ritual possession is said to be generally voluntary, reversible, and short-term. It is supported and encouraged by cultural beliefs and induced in ritual ceremonies. It often functions as a defense mechanism and is irrelevant to cultural concepts of illness. No curatives are sought.
(2) Peripheral possession is involuntary, long-term, and evaluated negatively by the host culture. It is generally induced by an individual's stress and constitutes a pathological reaction. It is connected with physical and mental illness, and curatives are sought.

(E) Psychiatric classification: Many psychiatrists have attempted to classify persons with the possession syndrome into known psychiatric diagnostic categories. McAll (1971) quotes a sample of psychiatric diagnoses in earlier records of demon possession:

Kirchoff (1888): Many cases of demon possession are cases of senile dementia.
O. Snell (1894): Many are melancholics, epileptics, paranoids, manics, hysterics.
Freud (1923): Seventeenth-century demon possessions—all schizophrenics.
Jarce (1944): Diagnosis of compulsive neurotics.
Stainbrook (1952), Bowers (1968), Bowers & Freedman (1968): Possession is indicative of schizophrenia.

Verma, Srivastava, and Sahay (1970) and Teja et al. (1970) found that many possessed individuals were either schizophrenics or hysterics. Okasha (1966) reported that 40% of the zar ceremony attenders were hysterics. Since possessed individuals were in distress in some way, it would appear that they could fit into psychiatric categories, but a satisfactory classification that incorporates all types of possession meaningfully has yet to be established.

Possession and Psychopathology

Different theorists have offered different explanations for the possession phenomenon and psychopathology. These explanations can be broadly grouped into three categories:

(1) Dissociation Theory.
(2) Communication Theory.
(3) Expectation Theory or Sociocultural Theory.

1. Dissociation Theory. Fundamentally it is argued that the possession syndrome is a manifestation of hysterical dissociation. The French workers (Teja et al., 1970) believe that the process of dissociation facilitates mythopoeic thinking and that the theme of the conflictual situation is played out in a dramatic way in possession. Possession is explained as a return of the repressed conflicts or desires where id representatives overwhelm the ego in a state of dissociation. Thus, there is a primary gain of relief from intrapsychic tension and a secondary gain in the form of attention and sympathy (Freed & Freed, 1964). Dissociation is recognized as occurring by the native ideology, in which actions displayed in possession are not considered to be performed by the patient but by the possessing element. Thus the individual can do many things, such as scolding the mother-in-law or husband, that could not be done otherwise (see also Lambek, this volume). A few workers, such as Carstairs (1958) and Wittkower (1970), argue that there are many similarities between the possession syndrome and hypnotic trance states seen in the West (see Spanos, this volume). For example:

(1) Both are states of altered consciousness.
(2) Both are induced by an authoritative person.
(3) Both states allow for the discharge of basic drives, repressed impulses, and inhibitions in a goal-directed manner.
(4) Alterations in identity in both states provide freedom from superego pressures, inhibition, and guilt.
(5) States may be harmful or beneficial.

Some others, however, argue that the possession syndrome is not a hysterical dissociation (Claus, 1979; McCall, 1971). Claus writes that the dissociation terminology merely shifts the identification of the patient's behavioral traits from one label to another— possession to hysteria—and the explanation from one paradigm (spiritual) to another (psychological). Wig and Narang (1969) and Teja (1971) nevertheless argue that the possession syndrome is hysterical psychosis and plead that it is a type of reactive psychosis.

2. *Communication Theory.* Here it is argued that some people use the possession syndrome as a distress signal to communicate with others. Possessed individuals assume the sick role and attempt to obtain attention and benefits. Many authors have reported that psychological precipitating factors were present in the majority of their cases (Chandra shekar et al., 1982; Teja et al., 1970; Ward, this volume; Wijesinghe et al., 1976; Yap, 1960). But why individuals select this painful method of communication is difficult to understand.

Explaining why women become possessed more frequently than men, Verma et al. (1970) and Lewis (1971) say that women in many societies are underrepresented in authority structures. They have less opportunity to gain esteem through personal achievement, and they are excluded from authority positions in male-dominated societies (Walker, 1972). Possession may satisfy their desires for a variety of material and emotional gains. But Carstairs and Kapur (1976) did find a high incidence of possession in Moger women, who enjoy better rights and status in the matrilineal system. Ward (1982) argues that in most instances women have minimum control over their failures in the roles society deems valuable and that possession reactions in women of traditional and syncretic societies may constitute a culture-based neurosis, linked to psychosocial stresses and the nature of the female role.

3. *Expectation or Sociocultural Theories.* Ari Kiev (1961) maintains that spirit possession is a culturally sanctioned, heavily institutionalized phenomenon (see Lambek, Lee, Krippner, this volume). He observed that from an early age the peasant child in Haiti was exposed to ceremonial possessing and was made aware of the prestige of the "Hungan" (voluntary possession) and the possessed. The child then grew up with the hope of some day experiencing possession. Carstairs (1958) made similar observations in Rajastan, India: "Everyone sees it happen to others and expects without question that in similar circumstances it will happen to oneself, and it does"

(p. 1218). Claus (1979) notes that "the psychological and sociological pre-conditioning sometimes identified as the causes of possession may only be secondary features. There is the strong suggestion that possession behavior is expected behavior. Because it is expected, it may actually be performed although never perhaps consciously or deceptively" (p. 50).

Lewis (1971) and Wittkower (1970) also opine that possession is a culturally sanctioned behavior that has an adaptive function. In general, the individual and group possession by "God" or good spirits is a sanctioned and institutionalized phenomenon, whereas possession by evil spirits is considered to be an affliction and treatment is sought. Though some (Sethi, 1978; Teja et al., 1970) call the possession syndrome a culture-bound syndrome, many, such as Wittkower (1970), Wittkower and Rin (1965), and L'Hermitte (1963), argue the opposite: the possession syndrome is not specific to one culture, and its manifestations may differ from one culture to another. Although it may be graced with a local name and imbued with exotic-sounding symbolism, it is basically the same in all the cultures.

Treatment

Exorcists, traditional healers, and religious persons are believed to be capable of treating people with the possession syndrome, and they are consulted often. The treatment generally occurs in the form of exorcism/prayer, incantation, and induction of physical pain by branding, beating with neem leaves, and consumption of assorted purgatives. When these fail to give relief, as a last resort and rarely psychiatrists are consulted (Chandra shekar et al., 1982; Okasha, 1966). This is specifically seen in countries like India, where existing meager psychiatric services are limited to big cities, and no modern mental health care services are available in the rural areas, where 76% of the population live. Psychiatrists do not have any specific treatment method apart from drug abreaction and counseling. "Modern therapists therefore require an understanding of folk medicine to deal successfully with these cases" (Ward, 1980, p. 160).

POSSESSION: THE INDIAN SCENE

The phenomenon of possession is very common in India, especially in rural areas. Every person believes in possession, and in every village one or two persons are said to experience possession by either spirits or God. There are many shrines where the priests become possessed by God for the benefit of the masses. Large numbers of people gather on that day and seek advice, guidance, solutions for their problems, and treatment for their ailments. The exorcists are popular healers who are frequently consulted for the treatment of various types of physical and mental ailments, as well as various problems and hardships believed to be the result of mischievous evil spirits. Generally it is accepted that young people who die accidentally or unnaturally (suicide/homicide), and people who die before their desires are fulfilled, become ghosts. They possess their relatives for fun or in order to trouble them.

Individual Spirit Possession

Individual spirit possession is commonly seen and is reported by Verma et al. (1970), Teja et al. (1970), Carstairs and Kapur (1976), Chandra shekar, Channabasavanna, and Venkataswamy (1980), and many others. Possession of this type is sudden in onset, whether it is expected or unexpected. The individual behaves as if he or she is a "different person." The person is usually possessed by the spirit of a dead relative and exhibits an altered state of consciousness. There is a change in the quality and content of both speech and behavior; most of the time these resemble those of the deceased to such an extent that people often readily recognize the spirit. The possessing spirit, through the medium of the patient, makes different demands on the surrounding people, usually the family members. The relatives typically conduct themselves in accordance with the demands made. Spirit possession is considered to be an affliction, and necessary measures are taken immediately for cure. When the exorcism-cure is completed, the victim abruptly falls to the ground, totally exhausted. When consciousness is regained, the individual usually claims amnesia for the entire episode.

In most of the cases, the victim is a young woman who suffers severe psychosocial problems. These cases typically fit into the diagnostic category of Hysterical Dissociation States. Because of conflicts in interpersonal relationships, sexual matters, and her status in the family, the victim suffers from severe anxiety, which is relieved through possession (primary gain). After being possessed, she receives attention, sympathy, and concern from others, as well as relief from responsibilities (secondary gains).

A good illustration is presented by the case of Sita, a 20-year-old only daughter who was married to a man from a large extended family. When she moved to her in-laws' house, Sita was just one among 25 family members and felt no one paid any attention to her. Her husband was a timid individual who had no status in the family; he did not bother to inquire into the needs of his wife. Sita was treated like a servant by others, including the mother-in-law. Although Sita sought the assistance of her parents, they expressed their helplessness in this regard and advised her to be patient and wait for good days. Two years passed, and things did not improve. One day Sita became possessed by her grandmother's spirit. She spoke in a different tone that was very authoritative. The spirit blamed those who were ill-treating Sita and warned them that if they did not change, they would be punished. Family members became alarmed and talked about the possession. Attention was given to Sita, and she was taken to temples and healers. Her situation improved. Later attacks and possession became infrequent, and now she becomes possessed about once a year.

Another example is provided by Gowri, a 28-year-old housewife, who was discontent because her husband had many bad habits, such as drinking and visiting prostitutes. He was very stubborn and did not listen to her. He often berated her, saying, "I will do whatever I want to. You are nobody to advise me. If you want to stay with me, stay or get lost." Gowri cursed her fate and mourned that there was nobody to support her. (She had lost her parents when she was quite young.) At one point Gowri became possessed by her mother's spirit when there was a ceremonial function at home. She declared openly that her son-in-law was purposefully neglecting her daughter, behavior for which he would pay dearly. Gowri's husband became panicky and assured the spirit in front of relatives that from then onward he would look after Gowri properly. Although he did not change totally, he did care more for his wife. Once in a while the mother's spirit descends on Gowri and talks about protecting her due rights and warns the son-in-law.

Individual God Possession

This form of possession differs from those reported so far, as it is a voluntary possession and sought by one and all for different reasons. The possessed individual assumes the role of a known traditional healer, medium, or counselor. Possession takes place on ceremonial days (such as Fridays or Saturdays), which are said to be auspicious times. This possession requires preparation, and the medium observes abstinence from non-vegetarian food, smoking, alcohol, and sex, and keeps himself or herself "pure." In the morning after bathing, he or she worships the deity, often in a ceremonial context; then, suddenly, the God descends. The individual exhibits an altered state of consciousness, with trembling movements, and may shout, abuse, curse, and bless, according to the mood. Overall, the state is characterized by restlessness and hyperactivity; the audience reacts with fear and deference, seeks the medium's predictions, and carries out orders faithfully. The ritual possession terminates abruptly when the individual falls to the ground, exhausted.

During possession, mediums may perform certain tasks that appear to be superhuman. Some are known to beat themselves with swords without any sign of pain. Others walk on red-hot charcoal. Still others may carry heavy rocks that cannot be lifted by three or four people. Mediums may also eat and drink enormous quantities of food, and identify the problems of devotees and suggest solutions offhand. Thus the medium proves access to supernatural powers through the possession.

When a few such healers were examined by the author, they appeared quite conscious during this so-called possession state. They could see and understand the proceedings of the session and consciously responded to the stimuli. The healers' assistants had collected information about the devotees' problems earlier; predictions were vague and could be interpreted in any way. When predictions became true or suggestions gave good results, the medium was highly praised. Everyone would talk about the feat, and more people in distress would seek help. If predictions were false, and suggestions did not not yield good results, the medium was not blamed. People blamed their own fate and went to another, more powerful healer or shrine. Failures were not highlighted. Thus, in spite of many failures, these healers thrive on occasional successes and maintain their reputations through active propaganda. Only a few healers go into a dissociative state during possession and exhibit unusual behavior or powers. Wijesinghe et al. (1976) from Sri Lanka, Salisbury (1968) from New Guinea, McAll (1971) from Britain, Ludwig (1965) from the United States, and Krippner (this volume) from Brazil, have also reported individual God possession.

Group Possession

Possession syndrome occurring in a group setting, involving many individuals simultaneously, also occurs in the cross-cultural context, most commonly in religious ceremonies. In India, it is a common scene in many popular shrines and traditional healing centers, and in religious prayer meetings (Carstairs, 1958; Carstairs & Kapur, 1976). Examples of group possession include the Sirr cult in Karnataka, South India (Claus, 1979) and Balaji Temple in Rajastan, North India (Kakar, 1980); similarly the Voodoo services in Haiti (Kiev, 1961; Wittkower, 1970), the prophet healing services in Liberia, the Candable cult in Brazil (Wittkower, 1970), and the Zar ceremony in Egypt, Ethiopia, Muslim Sudan, North Africa, and Arabia (Messing, 1958; Nelson, 1971; Okasha, 1966; Sendiony, 1977). The common features of group possession are

(1) The strong expectation of possession at such ceremonies.
(2) Particular ritualistic arrangements made for the ceremony.
(3) Monotonous but rhythmic music (from drums and other percussion instruments that make loud rhythmic sounds), songs, and dances (see Jilek, Krippner, this volume).
(4) Provocative songs and dances.
(5) Impressively dressed healers with personal charisma (see Lee, Ward, this volume).

Many authors also feel that such an atmosphere encourages many highly suggestible individuals to go into a "trance state" and behave as though they were possessed, in accordance with the local beliefs.

Possession, however, sometimes is reported to occur in an epidemic form outside of the ritual setting (Chandra shekar et al., 1982; Narayanan & Mahal, 1977; Verma et al., 1970). The following is a description of an epidemic of possession in a school of Karnataka in South India.

One day, the children of Thyavana primary school assembled as usual for prayer. Miss S., a seventh-standard student, fell down and was shifted to the shade. She recovered soon and reported that she felt giddy and that her vision was blurred. She was given milk to drink and was sent home to rest. Two days later, two girls from fifth standard had similar attacks. Their parents and the villagers concluded that these attacks were due to evil spirits. An elderly man recollected that fifteen years ago, two dead bodies were buried in the ground where later the school was built. He suggested that these spirits were angry about their territory being occupied. Arrangements were made to drive away the spirits. Special prayers, rituals, and offerings were made in vain. To the villagers' alarm, more and more children experienced the attacks. During such attacks, a few children declared that they were "God of Strength" (Kantibale, Balevathe). All of them would beat their chests and stomachs, demanding and receiving fruits, milk, and meat. After recovery they would claim amnesia except of having initial symptoms like giddiness and blurring of vision. This continued for more than one year.

On examination, the children who had attacks for one year were found to be highly suggestible and exhibited dissociative states on suggestion. Under abreaction, two girls reported that they performed the acts as they were suggested by the elders. Later they continued to have the attacks because they were given food, had no need to attend the classes, and were awarded a special status. Among other affected children, some said that they were amused by the talk and behavior that were rewarded and that they had desired to show the same behavior.

In summary, possession in India is a socioculturally sanctioned phenomenon used by people for different purposes. Some use it to earn their livelihood; they become faith healers and counselors and enjoy high status in the society. Some people, mainly women, use it to communicate their problems and to get the attention of others; they take up either the sick role by often becoming possessed by a spirit or take up an alternative, respectable role by displaying possession by God and trying to get things done according to their desires and requirements. Some people who are highly suggestible also become possessed in group settings, often without understanding the basis of the experience. The phenomenon exists because there is a strong belief in the community as well as in the person possessed.

POSSESSION SYNDROME AND MENTAL HEALTH IN THE INDIAN CONTEXT

The possession syndrome is closely associated with mental health in India. Individuals who are poor in communication, like children, illiterate young men and women, and women who are oppressed by men and who are afraid to communicate directly, instead of developing neurotic symptoms, use possession phenomena for their benefit. Their conflicts and problems are expressed through possession, and a mental equilibrium is sought.

The healer who is possessed by God becomes the source of inspiration and a source of support to people in distress. Such healers are located in many popular shrines and attract many people. The majority of mentally ill people are taken to these centers for help. The group possession sessions in the shrines and religious meetings provide an opportunity for persons to abreact and maintain their mental equilibrium. When patients with reactive psychosis, mania, or depression recover spontaneously, the credit goes to the healer. Improvement of neurotics with suggestion and support also helps to increase the popularity of the healer. Thus, mental hospitals and psychiatric departments fail to attract the mentally ill and are underutilized. People generally find it easier to blame evil spirits for the illness than to accept the biopsychosocial causation of the illness. The patient who is considered to be the victim of evil spirits is offered sympathy and is not held responsible for the accompanying symptoms or behavior. Thus, mentally ill people often seek shelter under the banner of possession syndrome.

SUMMARY

(1) Possession phenomenon is not restricted to one culture but is widely prevalent.

(2) Its manifestations, purpose, and consequences differ across cultures.

(3) Possession may occur in individuals or groups and may be voluntary or involuntary.

(4) Possession usually occurs sporadically but rarely in epidemic form.

(5) Possession is seen in both religious and nonreligious groups. Ceremonial possession provides a source of esteem and subcultural prestige and possibly emotional catharsis for the group as a whole.

(6) Altered states of consciousness, alteration in quality and content of speech and behavior, and amnesia are usual presenting features of possession.

(7) Possessing elements may be spirits, demons, or gods.

(8) In India, spirit possession is considered to be an affliction, whereas God possession is helpful and esteemed.

(9) Spirit possession in India is more common in young, married

women with low educational levels and with low socioeconomic status.

(10) Many of the possessed individuals receive psychiatric diagnoses such as anxiety and hysterical neuroses and schizophrenia.

(11) Possession syndrome may be interpreted as

(a) Hysterical dissociation/ hysterical psychosis.
(b) Communication of distress.
(c) Culturally sanctioned, socially institutionalized expected behavior.

(12) In India, possession syndrome is a common, socioculturally sanctioned phenomenon and is used for different purposes, such as

(a) To provide a source of livelihood (by priests and healers).
(b) To gain attention, to protest, to communicate distress (e.g., by women).
(c) To be one with the others (religious group possession).

In the majority of cases, possession is manifested as an altered state of consciousness and is closely related to mental health.

REFERENCES

Bourguignon, E., & Evascu, T. (1977). Altered states of consciousness within a general evolutionary perspective: A holo-cultural analysis. *Behavior Science Research, 12*(3), 197-216.

Carstairs, G. M. (1958). Some problems of psychiatry in patients from alien cultures. *The Lancet, 1*, 1217-1220.

Carstairs, G. M., & Kapur, R. L. (1976). *The great universe of Kota*. London: Hogarth Press.

Chandra shekar, C. R. (1981). A victim of an epidemic of possession syndrome. *Indian Journal of Psychiatry, 23*, 370-372.

Chandra shekar, C. R., Channabasavanna, S. M., & Venkataswamy, M. (1980). Hysterical possession syndrome. *Indian Journal of Psychological Medicine, 3*, 35-40.

Chandra shekar, C. R., Venkataramaiah, V., Mallikarjunaiah, M., Rao, C. K., & Reddy, G. N. (1982). An epidemic of possession in a school of South India. *Indian Journal of Psychiatry, 24*, 295-299.

Claus, P. J. (1979). Spirit possession and spirit mediumship from the perspective of Tulu oral traditions. *Culture, Medicine & Psychiatry, 3*, 29-52.

Freed, S. A., & Freed R. R. (1964). Spirit possession as an illness in a North Indian village. *Ethnology, 3*, 52-72.

Kakar, S. (1980, March). The myth of faith healing. *Imprint*, pp. 74-91.

Kiev, A. (1961). Spirit possession in Haiti. *American Journal of Psychiatry, 118*, 133-138.

Lewis, I. M. (1971). *Ecstatic religion: An anthropological study of spirit possession and shamanism.* Boston: Penguin.

L'Hermitte, J. (1963). *Diabolical possession, true or false?* Paris: Burns and Oates.

Ludwig, A. (1965). Witchcraft today. *Diseases of the Nervous System, 26,* 288-291.

McAll, R. K. (1971). Demonosis, or the possession syndrome. *International Journal of Social Psychiatry, 17,* 150-158.

Messing, S. (1958). Group therapy and social status in the Zar cult of Ethiopia. *American Anthropologist, 60,* 1120-1127.

Mora, G. (1975). Historical and theoretical trends in psychiatry. In A. M. Freedman, H. I. Kaplan, & B. J. Sadock (Eds.), *Comprehensive textbook of psychiatry.* Baltimore: Williams and Wilking.

Narayanan, H. S., & Mahal, A. S. (1977). A clinical report of epidemic hysteria in six members of a family. *Indian Journal of Psychiatry, 19*(3), 39-42.

Nelson, C. (1971). Self, spirit possession and world view: An illustration from Egypt. *International Journal of Psychiatry, 17,* 194.

Oesterreich, T. K. (1966). *Possession: Demonical and other.* New York: University Books.

Okasha, A. (1966). A cultural psychiatric study of El zar cult in UAR. *British Journal of Psychiatry, 112,* 1217-1221.

Pradeep, D. (1977). *A study of clientele and practice of a traditional healer.* Unpublished doctoral dissertation, Bangalore University, India.

Salisbury, R. F. (1968). Possession in the New Guinea highlands. *The International Journal of Social Psychiatry, 14,* 85-94.

Sargant, W. (1974). *The mind possessed.* New York: Lippincott.

Sendiony, M. F. (1977). The problem of cultural specificity of mental illness: A survey of comparative psychiatry. *The International Journal of Social Psychiatry, 23,* 223-229.

Sethi, B. B. (1978). Culture bound symptoms in India. *Indian Journal of Psychiatry, 20,* 295-296.

Teja, J. S. (1971). Proposed classification of other psychosis for use in India. *Indian Journal of Psychiatry, 13,* 7-13.

Teja, J. S., Khanna, B. S., & Subramanyam, T. B. (1970). Possession states in Indian patients. *Indian Journal of Psychiatry, 12,* 71-87.

Venkataramaiah, V., Mallikarjunaiah, M., Chandra shekar, C. R., Rao, C. K., & Reddy, G. N. (1981). Possession syndrome: An epidemiological study in West Karnataka. *Indian Journal of Psychiatry, 23,* 213-218.

Verma, L. P., Srivastava, D. K., & Sahay, R. N. (1970). Possession syndrome. *Indian Journal of Psychiatry, 12,* 58-70.

Walker, S. (1972). *Ceremonial spirit possession in Africa and Afro-America.* Leiden: Brill.

Ward, C. (1980). Spirit possession and mental health: A psycho-anthropological perspective. *Human Relations, 33,* 149-163.

Ward, C. (1982). A transcultural perspective on women and madness: The case of the mystical affliction. *Women's Studies International Forum, 5*(5), 411-418.

Wig, N. N., & Narang, R. L. (1969). Hysterical psychosis. *Indian Journal of Psychiatry, 11,* 93-100.

Wijesinghe, C. P., Dissanayake, S. A. W., & Mendis, N. (1976). Possession trance in a semi-urban community in Sri Lanka. *Australian & New Zealand Journal of Psychiatry, 10,* 135-142.

Wintrob, R. M. (1973). The influence of others, witchcraft and root work as explanations of behavior disturbance. *Journal of Nervous and Mental Diseases, 156,* 318-326.

Wittkower, E. D. (1970). Trance and possession states. *International Journal of Social Psychiatry, 16,* 153-160.

Wittkower, E. D., & Rin, H. (1965). Transcultural psychiatry. *Archives of General Psychiatry, 13,* 389-394.

Yap, P. M. (1960). The possession syndrome. *Journal of Mental Science, 106,* 114-137.

5

HYPNOSIS, DEMONIC POSSESSION, AND MULTIPLE PERSONALITY
Strategic Enactments and Disavowals of Responsibility for Actions

NICHOLAS P. SPANOS

This chapter discusses hypnosis, demonic possession, and multiple personality. The historical links among these phenomena have been described in some detail elsewhere and will not be reiterated here (Ellenberger, 1970; Sarbin & Coe, 1979; Spanos & Gottlieb, 1979). Instead, the chapter focuses on several behavioral commonalities among these phenomena. All three of these phenomena have been associated with the following notions: (1) Actors temporarily lose control over their behavior, and voluntary actions become transformed into involuntary happenings. (2) Control for actions is transferred from the self to indwelling but "hidden" mental parts, selves, or agencies. With appropriate procedures these "hidden agencies" can be made manifest as secondary selves or personalities. (3) Actors are often amnesic for information that is accessible to their hidden selves. I will argue that these notions are misleading and that hypnotic responding, demonic possession, and multiple personality can be more usefully conceptualized as social role enactments.

The term *role enactment* refers to patterns of action that are linked to and identified with a particular social status (e.g., Priest), an informally defined social position (e.g., class clown), or a social value (e.g., concerned citizen; Biddle & Thomas, 1966; Zurcher, 1983). Role enactments may involve prescribed patterns of subjective experience as well as overt behavior. Moreover, this notion does *not* imply that enactments involve a lack of personal conviction or a superficial "going through the motions" without subjective involvement (Goffman, 1961; Sarbin & Allen, 1968). On the other hand, a

AUTHOR'S NOTE: Preparation of this article was supported by grants from the Natural Science and Engineering Research Council of Canada and the Social Sciences and Humanities Research Council of Canada.

I thank Lorne D. Bertrand and John R. Weekes for critically commenting on earlier drafts of this article.

role theory perspective does not preclude analysis of such phenomena as faking or disinterested enactment (Goffman, 1974). This perspective attempts to account for variations in the credibility that actors assign to their enactments by delineating contextual and other variables that differentially affect such assignments.

Hypnotic responding, demonic possession, and multiple personality are here conceptualized as role enactments in which contextual factors lead actors to interpret their goal-directed actions as involuntary happenings (Sarbin, 1983; Spanos, 1982a, 1983a, 1986a). From this perspective, people who enact the roles of being hypnotized, possessed, or suffering from multiple personality have not lost control over their behavior. On the contrary, only by maintaining the behavioral control necessary to guide their actions in terms of culturally defined role prescriptions can they convincingly present themselves as the victims rather than the perpetrators of their own actions.

HYPNOSIS

Historically, hypnosis has been conceptualized as an altered state of consciousness that greatly increases responsiveness to suggestion and, at least in "susceptible" subjects, produces remarkable enhancements and distortions in sensory functioning, perception, and memory (Sarbin, 1962). In the last few decades, however, a great deal of empirical evidence has challenged this traditional view (for recent reviews, see Spanos, 1982a, 1986b). For example, despite much effort, physiological evidence to support the view of hypnosis as an altered state has not been forthcoming (Barber, 1970; Wagstaff, 1981). Moreover, a large number of studies indicate that even the seemingly dramatic behaviors of highly susceptible hypnotic subjects (e.g., displays of analgesia) can be accomplished by motivated control subjects who have not been administered a hypnotic induction procedure (Barber, 1969, 1979; Diamond, 1974; Wagstaff, 1981). Alternatively, a good deal of data support the contention that hypnotic behavior reflects goal-directed striving and that susceptible hypnotic subjects are cognizing individuals attuned to interpersonal cues, even subtle ones, and strongly invested in presenting themselves as "good" subjects (Sarbin & Coe, 1972; Spanos, 1986a; Wagstaff, 1986).

Hypnosis and Reports of Nonvolition

Susceptible hypnotic subjects frequently report that their responses to suggestions occurred effortlessly and involuntarily (Spanos, Rivers, & Ross, 1977). A number of investigators have interpreted these reports literally and have posited a variety of hypothetical psychological processes to explain how "hypnotized" subjects become transformed from "active doers" to passive observers of their own automatically occurring behaviors. According to Hilgard (1977), for example, the mechanisms that control responding become dissociated from conscious control during hypnosis. Consequently, "hypnotized" subjects are described as *unable* (as opposed to unwilling) to resist or counter suggested effects. Thus, despite serious efforts, hypnotically amnesic subjects are purportedly *unable* to recall, and those given suggestions for limb rigidity are *unable* to bend their arms (Hilgard, 1977).

Alternatively, social psychological formulations hold that the positing of special psychological mechanisms to account for reports of involuntariness is unnecessary, because such reports do not reflect a transformation of actions into happenings. Instead, reports of involuntariness reflect an interpretation made by subjects about their own behavior. Suggested behaviors are strategic or goal-directed enactments that hypnotic subjects often interpret as involuntary happenings (Spanos et al., 1977; Spanos, 1982b). From this perspective, understanding why hypnotic subjects proffer reports of involuntariness requires examination of the context in which these reports are generated.

The Structure of the Hypnotic Situation

In experimental contexts the hypnotic situation usually consists of a hypnotic induction procedure followed by a series of test suggestions. From a social psychological perspective, hypnotic inductions are cultural rituals that define the situation as hypnosis and that reinforce the general expectation that hypnosis involves a transformation from actions to happenings. For instance, although inductions frequently begin with direct instructions (e.g., "Relax the muscles in your legs"), these are gradually transformed to imply the occurrence of happenings (e.g., "Your legs are becoming heavy and limp"). Test suggestions are even more explicit in communicating the expectation that hypnotic responses are to occur involuntarily.

Hypnotic test suggestions do not explicitly direct subjects to enact overt behaviors. Instead, they foretell the occurrence of behavioral events and invite subjects to become involved in imaginings that are consistent with the involuntary occurrence of these behaviors (Spanos, 1971). Several studies (Spanos & Barber, 1972; Spanos & de Groh, 1983; Spanos & Gorassini, 1984; Weitzenhoffer, 1974) have found that responses to suggestions (e.g., "Your arm is rising") are rated by subjects as significantly more involuntary than are responses to instructions that imply voluntary behavior (e.g., "Raise your arm").

Although test suggestions inform subjects that their responses are to be defined as involuntary, not all subjects accept this interpretation of the situation. Numerous studies that included posttest assessments of experience (reviewed by Spanos, 1986a) indicate that subjects who succeeded in defining their responses as involuntary were actively involved in generating cognitive activity that sustained that interpretation. For instance, subjects who rated suggested behavior as involuntary were much more likely than nonresponsive subjects to become absorbed in carrying out thoughts and imaginings that were consistent with a nonvoluntary interpretation (e.g., subjects informed their arm was rising might imagine a pulley lifting it; Spanos & McPeake, 1977; Spanos et al., 1977). Thus, instead of simply happening passively, hypnotic responses are goal-directed enactments.

Hypnosis and Hidden Selves

Under some circumstances hypnotic subjects interpret their actions as stemming from the activities of multiple indwelling selves and present themselves in a manner consistent with this interpretation. Kampman (1976), for example, found that 41% of highly susceptible subjects manifested evidence of a new identity and called themselves by a different name when given hypnotic suggestions to regress beyond their birth and become a different person. Along similar lines, Watkins and Watkins (1980) found that 60% of highly susceptible hypnotic subjects indicated that they possessed a hidden part and called themselves by a new name while enacting the role of this "part" in a study of suggested deafness.

When exposed to noxious stimulation following a hypnotic suggestion for analgesia, highly susceptible subjects often report large reductions in pain. This finding is noncontroversial and has been replicated consistently across laboratories (e.g., Barber & Hahn, 1962; Evans & Paul, 1970; Spanos, Radtke-Bodorik, Ferguson, &

Jones, 1979). According to Hilgard (1977), however, only the "conscious part" of the subject experiences reduced pain under these circumstances. Supposedly, intense pain continues to be felt by a "hidden part" of the subject, and hidden reports reflect the intrinsic functioning of this dissociated cognitive subsystem.

Hilgard (1977) and Watkins and Watkins (1980) maintain that hidden reports are not shaped by the experimental instructions administered to subjects in "hidden part" studies. On the other hand, Spanos and Hewitt (1980) argued that hidden reports were part of a strategic role enactment engendered and shaped by the communications transmitted in these experiments. To test this hypothesis, high susceptibles were divided into two groups, and subjects in both groups were told that they possessed a hidden part (Spanos & Hewitt, 1980). The instructions given to one group were modeled after those used by Hilgard (1977) and implied that during hypnotic analgesia subjects' hidden part would feel more pain than their conscious part. Alternatively, the instructions given to the second group implied that their hidden part would feel even *less* pain than their conscious part during hypnotic analgesia. Subjects in the two groups behaved as if they had hidden parts with opposite characteristics: high sensitivity to pain in one case, reduced sensitivity in the other. In a related study, Spanos, Gwynn, and Stam (1983) found that the same subjects generated hidden pain intensity ratings that changed from being the same as conscious ratings, to being higher than conscious ratings, to being lower than conscious ratings as they obtained changing information about the characteristics of their hidden parts. Clearly, "hidden part" instructions do not simply "set the stage" for the emergence of a preexisting dissociated subsystem. Instead, they provide sentient subjects with the information needed to build a self-presentation that is congruent with perceived role demands. The "hidden selves" enacted in these experiments are social constructions. Subjects act as if they have hidden selves because their instructions lead them to interpret their experiences in these terms and to enact behaviors that are congruent with this interpretation (Spanos, 1983a).

Hypnotic Amnesia

From a social psychological perspective, hypnotic amnesia, like other hypnotic behaviors, involves goal-directed action. Hypnotically amnesic subjects retain control over memory processes and enact recall failures strategically in order to meet the role demands of the amnesia test situation (Coe, 1978; Spanos & Radtke, 1982). In support of this hypothesis, several studies indicate that "good" hypnotic subjects alter the cognitive strategies they employ in accordance with changes in amnesia suggestion task demands (Bertrand & Spanos, 1985; Spanos & de Groh, 1984). For instance, most amnesia suggestions ask subjects to forget a "chunk" of information in its entirety (e.g., an entire list of previously learned words). Highly susceptible hypnotic subjects usually meet these task demands by shifting attention away from target recall during the amnesia test period. When later informed that amnesia is "canceled" and that they can again remember, they focus on retrieval cues and thereby easily recall the "forgotten" material (Spanos & D'Eon, 1980; Spanos & Radtke, 1982). In short, hypnotic amnesia is an achievement rather than a happening. It is brought about by cooperative subjects who strategically modify their cognitive activities in order to meet the task demands that constitute "being amnesic."

Frequently, highly susceptible hypnotic subjects maintain their amnesia in the face of repeated exhortations to be honest and to try their best to recall (e.g., Howard & Coe, 1980). Some investigators (e.g., Kihlstrom, Evans, Orne, & Orne, 1980) interpret such failures to "breach" amnesia as meaning that hypnotically amnesic subjects are *unable* to recall. Alternatively, Spanos, Radtke, and Bertrand (1984) suggested that failing to breach amnesia in the face of strong and repeated exhortations constitutes a role-validating maneuver. Each failure to breach adds legitimacy to the subject's self-presentation as "truly unable to remember" and therefore as deeply hypnotized.

Spanos et al. (1984) tested these ideas with eight very highly susceptible hypnotic subjects who had previously failed to breach amnesia despite repeated exhortations to be honest and to try their best to recall. Subjects were taught a list of three concrete and three abstract words and were then informed that concrete words were stored in one cerebral hemisphere and abstract words in the other. They were further informed that each hemisphere had a "hidden part" that remained aware of the information in its own hemisphere but was unaware of information in the opposite hemisphere. Following a suggestion to forget, all subjects showed high levels of amnesia for both the concrete and abstract words. Before canceling amnesia, the experimenter "contacted" each subject's two hidden parts in succession. Under these circumstances, each subject recalled all of the words associated with the "appropriate" hemisphere, but none of the words associated with the opposite hemisphere. In other words, all subjects breached amnesia in a two-stage sequence that validated their self-presentations as deeply hypnotized and in possession of hidden selves.

In summary, the available data strongly indicate that hypnotic behavior is goal-directed action. Good hypnotic subjects are invested in meeting the role demands of the hypnotic situation, and they use whatever information they can glean to guide their behavior in conformance with these demands. However, a central demand of the hypnotic situation is that subjects define their responses as involuntary "happenings" rather than as self-initiated actions. Thus, subjects are required to guide their actions in terms of role requirements while, at the same time, conveying the impression (to themselves as well as the experimenter) that they have lost control over their behavior. The notion that hypnotic subjects possess dissociated "parts" of "selves" extends the idea that hypnotic responses are involuntary. Responsibility for behavior is attributed to the dissociated parts, while subjects themselves are defined as passive observers of their own nonvoluntary behavior.

As with other hypnotic behaviors, the enactment of "dissociated parts" involves strategic self-presentation. In hypnotic contexts information about the characteristics of the "dissociated selves" role is provided by experimental instructions, and subjects guide the impression they create in terms of these role prescriptions. The "dissociated self" role usually requires displays of amnesia as a central component. To enact this aspect of the role successfully, subjects must maintain control over memory and guide their recall according to the particular "self" being presented.

DEMONIC POSSESSION

The notion that demons can enter into people and take control of their functioning emerged in Western Europe as an accompaniment of Christianity, although the beliefs have a much earlier origin and cross-cultural relevance (Lewis, 1971; Ward, 1980).[1] This notion is made explicit in the New Testament, where the Synoptic Gospels provide numerous examples of possession and of Christ successfully exorcising the possessed. Among the most prominent symptoms displayed by the New Testament demoniacs (i.e., possessed persons) were convulsions, sensory and motor deficits, displays of alternate identities that were defined as indwelling demons, loss of voluntary control over behavior, and amnesia (Catherinet, 1972). In the New Testament descriptions, individual demoniacs usually displayed only one or sometimes a few of these symptoms. By the medieval and late medieval period, however, individual demoniacs consistently displayed all or most of these behaviors (Oesterreich, 1966; see Kemp, this volume, for a discussion of possession and mental illness in the Middle Ages). The hodgepodge of odd and isolated behaviors described in the New Testament as indicators of possession coalesced into a relatively stereotypic social role that persisted (albeit with important local variations) for over a millenium (Spanos, 1983a).

Psychiatric historians usually contend that the demonically possessed of earlier centuries were suffering from one or another mental illness (e.g., Zilboorg & Henry, 1941). Hysteria is the most common diagnosis applied to these cases, and the practice of labeling demoniacs as hysterics had gained widespread acceptance by the late nineteenth century (e.g., Cesborn, 1909). Charcot and Marie (1892), for example, argued that demonically possessed seventeenth century French nuns were hysterics and supported this contention by pointing to similarities between the behavior of the possessed and the symptoms of their hysterical patients. Similar parallels have been drawn by modern psychiatrists and historians (Thompson, 1972; Veith, 1977), and hysteria remains a common interpretation of possession in the cross-cultural context (Chandra shekar, Ward, this volume).

Using the concept of hysteria to explain possession is problematic for a number of reasons. For one, the term *hysteria* has been used in different ways by different authors and historically has been associated with a vast array of behaviors that appear to have little in common (e.g., Slater, 1965). Even more serious are the misleading implications that accrue when deviant behaviors are labeled symptoms of a mental illness. As pointed out by Szasz (1961), mental illness labels like hysteria carry the implication that the behaviors labeled as symptoms are involuntary happenings rather than goal-directed actions. Behavioral "symptoms" are robbed of their intentional character, and attempts to explain these "symptoms" usually focus on bygone etiological happenings (e.g., exposure to inconsistent or abusive parents), rather than on the meanings attached to these behaviors in the context of the person's current construals, goals, and interpretations.

As an alternative to mental illness formulations, demonic possession is construed here as having been a learned pattern of interpersonal behavior that was shaped and maintained by elements of the social context in which it occurred. Thus, the demonically possessed, like modern "good" hypnotic subjects, were actively engaged in enacting a socially structured self-presentation that conformed to implicitly and explicitly held beliefs about what constituted "being possessed" (see Lambek, this volume). Like "being hypnotized," the enactments that constituted "being possessed" were legitimated by significant others as happenings outside the actor's sphere of control (Lee, this volume; Spanos, 1983a).

Socialization into the Demonic Role

The idea that people could be possessed by demons was taken for granted by the average person in late medieval Europe (Baroja, 1964; Thomas, 1971). The major components of the demonic role were well known, and the potential demoniac's exposure to clerical experts defined the more subtle aspects of the role in great detail (Spanos, 1983b). Demonic possession was used as one explanation for certain physical illnesses and/or for behavior that became socially disruptive or defined as abnormal (Kemp, this volume). During the initial stages of possession the demoniac's symptoms were often quite ambiguous. However, these symptoms frequently began to correspond to "official" stereotypes of demonic possession as the demoniac gained information about those stereotypes (Spanos & Gottlieb, 1979; Walker, 1981). For example, the afflicted (i.e., demoniac) children in the famous Salem witch trials initially enacted an odd array of behaviors, such as running about the house, adopting odd postures, and creeping under chairs. After several weeks of close observation by and interaction with concerned neighbors and clergy, however, their symptoms became much more uniformly diabolical and included convulsions, reports of being bitten and pinched, and "seeing" the spectres of witches attack them and others (Spanos & Gottlieb, 1976). The particular behaviors that constituted the possessed role sometimes varied as a function of local beliefs and practices. For instance, along with convulsions and sensory/motor deficits, Catholic demoniacs frequently exhibited evidence of an indwelling "demon self" (e.g., they often spoke in a different voice that identified itself as an indwelling demon with its own name), whereas Protestant demoniacs of the same period rarely did so (Walker, 1981).

Catholic/Protestant variation in the frequency of "demon self" enactments can be understood by examining the different practices of these religions toward the possessed. Catholic exorcism procedures were standardized and involved the priest's communicating directly with the indwelling demon. Exorcists made a clear distinction between questioning indwelling demons and talking with the person possessed by those demons. When questioning a demon, the exorcist expected to be answered by the demon and not by the person possessed (Oesterreich, 1966). As preliminaries to the exorcism rite, the priest was required to question the demons in order to obtain their names, number, reasons for possessing the person, hour they entered the body, and length of time they proposed to stay (The Roman Ritual of Exorcism, 1614/1976; Kelly, 1974). During the exorcism, the demons were often questioned repeatedly and at great length about their motives, earthly accomplices, status in the social structure of Hell, and so on (e.g., Michaelis, 1613). In short, Catholic exorcism procedures strongly cued "demon selves" as a central feature of the demonic role. In contrast, Protestants rarely employed formal exorcism procedures, and direct communication with indwelling demons was usually shunned by Protestants as a sinful practice (Thomas, 1971). Thus, Catholic demoniacs were exposed to a structured social ritual that strongly demanded and legitimated the enactment of "demon selves." Protestant demoniacs were much less likely to be taught this aspect of the demonic role.

Detailed information concerning role prescriptions was conveyed to both Catholic and Protestant demoniacs outside of exorcism situations. The sources of this information sometimes included (1) explicit coaching by parties with vested interests in the demoniac's giving a convincing performance, (2) exposure to the performances of other, more practiced demoniacs, and (3) conversing in the demoniac's presence about the occurrence, timing, and termination of expected symptoms (Harsnett, 1599, 1603; Hutchinson, 1720; Thomas, 1971; Walker, 1981). An example of indirect instruction that conveyed much information about role prescriptions is provided in the following confession given by a demoniac:

> It was the ordinary custom of the Priests to be talking of such, as had been possessed beyond the seas, and to tell the manner of their fits, and what they spake in them . . . and how when reliques were applyed unto them, the parties would roare: how they could not abide holy

water, nor the sight of the sacrement ... how the devills would complaine, when the Priests touched the parties, that they burned ... (Harsnett, 1603, p. 36)

In short, demonic enactments did not occur in a social vacuum. They were continually shaped and validated by the social context in which they occurred (Spanos, 1983b).

A number of important social psychological factors converged in leading potential demoniacs to define themselves as possessed (Oesterreich, 1966; Spanos, 1983b; Thomas, 1971). These individuals shared the same cultural frame of reference as the community that labeled them and, therefore, were likely to interpret their own illness or behavioral deviations in the same terms as their neighbors and clerical superiors. In some cases, demoniacs were made dependent on those who labeled them for the satisfaction of physical and social needs. The labelers consistently interpreted the experiences of demoniacs in terms of possession and isolated the demoniacs from others who might offer nondemonic interpretations of these events (Spanos, 1983b).

Denials of being possessed sometimes occurred, but these were routinely construed by authorities as indications of a wily demon attempting to escape divine punishment. Continued refusal to enact the role properly frequently led to punishment administered in the guise of benevolently motivated attempts to free a helpless victim from demonic control (Aubin, 1716; Harsnett, 1599; Michaelis, 1613). It is important to emphasize that harsh treatment was meted out to demoniacs, not for adopting the possessed role, but, instead, for refusals to enact it properly, or for premature attempts to give up the role by denying that they were possessed.

The role of demoniac was most commonly adopted by individuals with little social power or status, and few sanctioned avenues for protesting the dissatisfactions that stemmed from their lowly status (Oesterreich, 1966). For such people the demonic role offered numerous advantages. Frequently, its adoption led to a dramatic rise in social status. On the one hand, demoniacs were viewed as helpless victims of satanic influence and consequently received sympathetic attention and a lightened work load. On the other hand, they were often treated as awesome seers whose affliction placed them in direct contact with the supernatural and whose performances commanded fearful respect and attention. Demoniacs often became the star attractions in what the community considered a deadly serious combat between the forces of Heaven and Hell (Spanos, 1983b;

Walker, 1981). In short, adoption of the demonic role was often associated with increases in social position, power, and respect that would have been unavailable in other ways (Spanos & Gottlieb, 1976; Thomas, 1971). The same has been argued for the instances and consequences of possession in a cross-cultural context (Crapanzano & Garrison, 1977; Lewis, 1971).

Demonic Enactments as Strategic

Demonic possession was defined by society at large as an involuntary occurrence. Medieval canon law classified possession as a species of demonically induced insanity, and the possessed, like other insane, were not considered responsible for their actions (Pickett, 1952). Possessed people often accounted for their own deviant behavior by using the same explanations as the rest of their community: They disavowed responsibility for their demonic behavior by attributing it to the machinations of indwelling demons. Thus, like modern "good" hypnotic subjects, demoniacs enacted complex, goal-directed behavior but interpreted this behavior as occurring involuntarily. The strategic nature of demonic enactments is sometimes obscured by the treating of convulsions, sensory/motor deficits, hallucinations, and other behaviors as isolated symptoms of disease. When demonic enactments are viewed within their social context, however, their strategic nature becomes clear.

Convulsions were among the most dramatic "symptoms" of possession, and they are still commonly observed in cross-cultural possession cases (Jilek, this volume). Although epileptic convulsions may have been misinterpreted as possession in some cases, the convulsions associated with possession were frequently *not* epileptic in nature (Oesterreich, 1966). They were instead, socially cued role enactments (Spanos, 1983a). For instance, demoniacs commonly convulsed on cue when presented with the witch that supposedly caused their possession (e.g., Glanvill, 1689). Thus, in an English case involving three possessed children, "no sooner had [the accused] entered the hall but at one moment the said three children fell down upon the ground strangely tormented" (The Most Strange and Admirable Discovery, 1593/1972, p. 246). The Salem demoniacs were responsive to social cues from one another as well as from the accused and were therefore able to predict the occurrence of one another's fits. In these cases one of the demoniacs would cry out that she saw the spectre of an accused witch about to attack another demoniac. The other demoniac would then immediately enact a convulsive fit (Spanos, 1983c).

Convulsions were not, of course, the only demonic "symptoms" that were socially cued. For instance, during the Salem trials the demoniacs sometimes mimicked the accused. When an accused witch rolled up her eyes, the demoniacs followed suit and cried that their eyes were stuck. When rag puppets supposedly used for black magic were burned in their presence, the demoniacs screamed that they were burned (Spanos & Gottlieb, 1976). Spitting up the pins or nails purportedly used by indwelling demons to torture the demoniac internally was a fairly regular feature of English and Continental possession cases (Notestein, 1911; Oesterreich, 1966). Equally common was the tendency of Catholic demoniacs to scream that they were tortured and burned when sprinkled with holy water or touched with the relics of Catholic saints (Harsnett, 1599; Oesterreich, 1966).

Possessions and exorcisms often functioned as propaganda vehicles used to affirm parochial religious values and to debase competing religious beliefs. For instance Catholic exorcists commonly held that, when confronted by an ordained priest during an exorcism, indwelling demons were constrained to tell the truth (Michaelis, 1613). Thus, while enacting "demon selves," Catholic demoniacs frequently affirmed the truths of the Catholic Church, indicated that they hated the Pope (thereby legitimating him as holy), and claimed to love Calvin and other Protestants (Aubin, 1716; Michaelis, 1613). On the other hand, Puritan demoniacs in Boston, Salem, and England affirmed Puritan doctrines by enacting an inability to read the writings of Calvin (indicating that demons could not tolerate sacred writings). However, these same demoniacs read the sacred writings of Quakers, Catholics, and Anglicans with ease (Calif, 1700/1914; Mather, 1693/1914; Thomas, 1971).

In short, demonic behaviors were not the involuntary symptoms of disease. Instead, they constituted coordinated, goal-directed self-presentations aimed at conveying and sustaining the impression that the actors were possessed by evil spirits (Spanos, 1983b, 1983c). As with the hypnotic role, a central feature of the demonic role involved conveying the impression that behaviors were no longer governed by the actor. However, conveying this impression convincingly required that demoniacs retained behavioral control and geared their enactments to contextual demands in a manner consistent with their audience's conception of what it meant to be possessed.

MULTIPLE PERSONALITY

The Psychiatric Disease Perspective

Multiple personality is usually conceptualized as a mental disease that involves the alternating of two or more personalities within the same individual (Greaves, 1980). According to traditional psychodynamic formulations, the most important antecedents of this disorder involve early developmental traumas such as physical and sexual abuse, and ambivalent and inconsistent treatment by parents during "preoedipal" development (Allison, 1974; Gruenewald, 1977, 1984; Saltman & Solomon, 1982). According to this view, adult stress may exacerbate some manifestations of the disorder, but is insufficient to produce multiple personality. From this perspective, multiple personality patients (i.e., multiples) are implicitly conceptualized as the victims of unconscious processes that temporarily displace the "normal self" and become manifest as new identities.

Cases of multiple personality were relatively common around the turn of the present century (Sutcliffe & Jones, 1962; Taylor & Martin, 1944). Between 1920 and 1970, however, such cases were reported only infrequently. Since the mid-seventies the number of multiple personality cases has skyrocketed (Boor, 1982; Greaves, 1980; Orne, Dinges, & Orne, 1984; Rosenbaum, 1980). For example, Bliss, Larson, and Nakashima (1983) reported that 27 out of 45 patients (60%) admitted to a single inpatient psychiatric service with auditory hallucinations were discovered to be multiple personalities. That is more than twice as many multiples as were reported in the United States between 1934 and 1971 (Rosenbaum, 1980). Some psychotherapists seem much more likely than others to make contact with multiple personality patients. According to Gruenewald (1971), most psychotherapists do not see even one such patient throughout their entire career. Nevertheless, Bliss (1980, 1984a), Allison (Allison & Schwarz, 1981), and Kluft (1982) have each dealt with over 50 such patients.

The Social Role Perspective

Our social role perspective suggests that people learn to enact the multiple personality role in the same sense that "good" subjects learn to enact the hypnotic role and earlier demoniacs learned to enact the demonic role. Thus, multiples are conceptualized as actively involved in using available information to create a social impression that is congruent with their perceptions of situational demands and with the interpersonal goals they are attempting to achieve (Spanos, Weekes, & Bertrand, 1985; Sutcliffe & Jones, 1962). According to this perspective, psychotherapists play a particularly important part in the generation and maintenance of this role enactment. Therapists sometimes encourage patients to adopt the role of being a multiple, provide them with information about how to enact the role convincingly, and, perhaps most important, provide "official" validation for the different identities that their patients enact (Spanos et al., 1985; Spanos, Weekes, Menary, & Bertrand, 1986; Sutcliffe & Jones, 1962). Thus, differences in the frequency with which psychotherapists in diagnose multiple personality may stem not so much from differences in diagnostic acumen as from the differential use of diagnostic and therapeutic practices that unwittingly encourage patients to adopt the role of being a multiple.

Hypnotic procedures have been of central importance in the diagnosis of multiple personality. In many cases, the initial manifestations of secondary personalities occurred during hypnotic treatment, and a number of modern investigators strongly advocate hypnotic procedures for discovering, communicating with, and eventually eliminating patients' secondary identities (Allison & Schwarz, 1981; Bliss, 1980, 1984a). From a social role perspective, hypnotic procedures do not have intrinsic properties that facilitate the discovery of hidden personalities. As seen in our discussion of "hidden part" experiments, however, these procedures can be easily adapted to encouraging and legitimating the enactment of hidden selves (Spanos, 1983a). It is not surprising, therefore, that the extensive use of such procedures in clinical settings leads to the enactment of secondary personalities (Spanos et al., 1985; Sutcliffe & Jones, 1962).

When viewed from a social role perspective, the similarities between the "demon self" enactments of Catholic demoniacs and the enactments of secondary selves by modern multiples are striking. Multiples, like earlier demoniacs, convey the impression that their "normal self" is temporarily but periodically displaced by foreign identities. Typically, the foreign identities each have their own name and manifest attributes that are very different from the patient's "normal" dispositions, habits, and preferences (Sutcliffe & Jones, 1962). Like demoniacs, multiples often display amnesia for periods during which their secondary personalities are "in control" and invariably disavow responsibility for the actions carried out at these times. Just as the enactment of "demon selves" could be orchestrated by the exorcist, so the enactment of secondary personalities is often brought under the control of the hypnotherapist (Bliss, 1980).

There are, of course, differences as well as similarities between the role enactments of multiples and demoniacs. The multiple personality role has been thoroughly secularized to the requirements of a modern, technologically oriented society. The convulsing at witches and abhorrence of the sacred so central to demonic enactments are gone, and the invading demons have been replaced by secular secondary personalities. The religious rite of exorcism, so impressive in a theologically oriented age, has been replaced with "scientific exorcisms" like hypnotherapy that resonate more comfortably with the psyches of modern psychotherapists.

Socialization into the Multiple Personality Role

Information about multiple personality is widespread in our culture, and, as a result, the major components of the role are probably rather well known. For instance, popular movies and television shows, such as *The Three Faces of Eve* and *Sybil*, and a number of popular biographies, such as *Sybil* (Schreiber, 1973), *The Minds of Billy Milligan* (Keyes, 1981), *The Five of Me* (Hawksworth & Schwarz, 1977), and *Prism* (Bliss & Bliss, 1985), provide extensive information about the symptoms and course of multiple personality. For example, Gruenewald (1971) described a 17-year-old hospitalized patient whose first enactment of a secondary personality occurred the day after seeing the movie *The Three Faces of Eve*.

Popular sources typically make the role of multiple personality appear in a relatively attractive light by portraying the protagonist as a person with a dramatic set of symptoms who surmounts numerous obstacles and eventually gains esteem, dignity, and much sympathetic attention and affection from significant, high-status others. Thus, the idea of being a multiple personality may provide some people with a viable and face-saving account for personal failings and problems, as well as a dramatic means of gaining concern and sympathetic attention from valued others. Nevertheless, people are unlikely to enact as deviant and complex a role as multiple personality without assurances that their enactments will be treated seriously. Even in the case of Gruenewald's (1971) patient, the initial enactment of a secondary personality was legitimated by the therapist, who agreed to call the patient by a different name during her enactments of the secondary personality.

The Role of Therapeutic Context. According to our social role hypothesis, psychotherapists constitute a major source of legitimation for the enactment of the multiple personality role. Psychotherapists are usually seen by patients as competent experts whose opinions are highly valued and whose suggestions are treated very seriously. Furthermore, clients are frequently unhappy, insecure people who are concerned about the status of their relationship with their therapist and who are invested in presenting themselves in a manner that will win their therapist's concern, interest, and approval. Given these circumstances, mutual shaping between therapists "on the lookout" for signs of multiple personality and clients involved in conveying an appropriate impression may lead to enactments of multiple personality that confirm the initial suspicions of the therapists and that, in turn, lead the therapists to encourage and to validate more elaborate displays of the disorder (Sutcliffe & Jones, 1962).

Even the limited case report data available support the hypothesis that some therapists subtly encourage and then validate manifestations of multiple identity. Allison and Schwarz (1981), for example, contend that patients are frequently reluctant to accept that they are multiples and, under these circumstances, should be actively persuaded by the therapist to accept this diagnosis. A number of investigators (Allison & Schwarz, 1981; Bliss, 1980, 1984b; Brandsma & Ludwig, 1974) recommend that hypnotic procedures be used to explicitly "call forth" and identify secondary personalities.

From a social role perspective, persuading patients to accept the diagnosis of being multiple, or using hypnotic procedures to "call forth" hidden personalities, serves to encourage and validate patients' self-presentations as multiples. Validation is extended further by the common therapeutic practice of conversing at length with the various "personalities" and obtaining from each information about their origins, functions, and habits, as well as information about what "they" know and do not know about each other. Once patients are publicly identified as multiples, their enactments of secondary personalities will often be repeatedly validated by others who become aware of their diagnosis. Kohlenberg (1973), for example, commented that the staff of a ward that housed a multiple were sensitized to his three different personality enactments and interacted with each "personality" in a different manner.

Kohlenberg (1973) also demonstrated the importance of contextual variables in maintaining enactments of multiple identity. Baseline rates of occurrence were assessed for the behaviors associated with each of the patient's three personalities and afterward the behaviors associated with one of the personalities were selectively reinforced. The behaviors associated with the reinforced personality showed a dramatic increase in frequency. On later extinction trials the frequency of these behaviors decreased to baseline levels.

A Case Example and Experimental Demonstration. In 1979 Kenneth Bianchi was implicated in the rape-murders of several Californian women. Despite physical evidence of guilt, Bianchi maintained his innocence and was remanded for pretrial psychiatric evaluation. As part of his evaluation, Bianchi underwent a hypnotic interview and during this procedure manifested evidence of multiple personality. Bianchi's interview was videotaped and transcribed and thereby provides an unusual amount of information about the clinician/patient negotiations that lead to the enactment of a "new" identity (see Schwarz, 1981).

Recently, Spanos et al. (1985) used the Bianchi case as a model for exploring the role of therapeutic communications in encouraging and legitimating enactments of multiple personality. College students were instructed to play the role of an accused murderer who had pleaded innocent and had been remanded for psychiatric evaluation. Subjects were informed that they would be interviewed by an experimenter who was role-playing a psychiatrist. They were instructed to role-play the accused murderer throughout the psychiatric interview and to use whatever cues they could glean from the situation to give a convincing performance. Subjects in one group were exposed to a hypnotic interview that was modeled very closely on the interview employed with Bianchi. For example, as in the Bianchi interview the "psychiatrist" informed subjects that there might be another part of them and that he would like to communicate with that other part. The "psychiatrist" then addressed the subject's "part" directly. Role-playing control subjects were informed that personality was complex and involved walled-off thoughts and feelings "almost like there are different people inside" (Spanos et al., 1985, p. 368). However, nothing was said to the controls about hypnosis or about the "psychiatrist" contacting part of them.

In a second session the "psychiatrist" again "contacted" the secondary personalities of the role-playing multiples and administered the secondary personalities a sentence-completion test and a semantic differential. Later the primary personalities of these role-playing multiples were administered the same tests. Role-playing nonmultiple controls simply took these tests twice in succession.

Most of the subjects in the Bianchi interview treatment enacted the "symptoms" of multiple personality by (1) adopting a different name, (2) referring to their primary personality in the third person, (3) confessing to the murders, and (4) displaying amnesia for their secondary personality enactments after termination of the hypnotic procedures. None of the role-playing controls adopted a different name, confessed, or displayed amnesia. Role-playing multiples maintained their role successfully in their second session. Like actual patients given this diagnosis, the role-playing multiples exhibited marked and consistent differences between personalities on the semantic differential and word association tests. Role-playing controls performed similarly on the two administrations of these tests. In short, when people are provided with information about role requirements in the context of a patient/clinician interaction, they can easily learn to give convincing enactments of multiple personality.

Spanos, Weekes, Menary, and Bertrand (1986) replicated these findings in all important respects. Furthermore, these investigators exposed role-playing multiples to detailed interviews that focused on childhood experiences. The task of the role players was not, of course, to accurately describe their own childhoods, but instead to provide the kinds of descriptions that they believed would be proffered by actual multiples. Like actual multiples, the role-playing multiples in the Spanos, Weekes et al. (1986) study gave negatively toned descriptions of childhood, described their parents as punitive and rejecting, described an early onset (before age 10) for their secondary personalities, and described their secondary personalities as "taking over" in order to handle difficult situations and express strong emotions.

The findings of the Spanos, Weekes et al. (1986) study do not, of course, mean that patient multiples simply fabricate the childhood histories that they and their therapists "uncover" in the course of therapy. On the other hand, these findings do suggest that the retrospective descriptions of such patients may be influenced by commonly held conceptions of the traumatic childhood origins of psychopathology. Thus, memory fragments of what actually happened and fantasies of what "should" have happened given their current predicament may become indistinguishably interwoven. With the tacit encouragement and unwitting guidance of their psychotherapists, such memory/fantasies may be organized and elaborated into biographical accounts that serve to buttress an ongoing self-presentation as a multiple personality patient.

Extreme Personality Differences. Numerous clinical reports (Ludwig, Brandsma, Wilbur, Benfeldt, & Jameson, 1972; Smith, Buffington, & McCord, 1982; Thigpen & Cleckley, 1957; Watkins & Johnson, 1982) indicate that the identities of multiples are typically extreme opposites in terms of preferences, moods, and behavior. If personality A is a frigid personality, B is seductive; if A is passive, B is aggressive; and so on. This tendency toward opposites was clearly evident in the personality test data obtained from the role-playing multiples in the Spanos et al. (1985) study. The tendency is also evident in descriptions of Catholic demoniacs. In these cases the people possessed were often described as being innocent, demure, loving, and religious, while the indwelling demons were described as vicious and taunting, and as hating religion (Aubin, 1716; Michaelis, 1613).

The tendency of multiples to display personalities that are markedly different from one another is usually explained by contending that wishes unacceptable to the primary personality are expressed by secondary personalities (e.g., Allison & Schwarz, 1981). Certainly, those who adopt the multiple personality role are afforded a convenient way of gratifying wishes and intentions that they publicly disavow. However, the tendency to display opposite characteristics may also be motivated by more basic considerations of cognitive economy.

Successfully self-presenting as a multiple requires remembering which experiences, preferences, and behaviors go with personality A and which go with personality B. The memory load involved in this task can be substantially lightened by making personality A and personality B stereotypical opposites. Under these conditions, interactions can be guided in terms of relatively straightforward decision rules: e.g., as personality A, act like a prototypical "sweet angel"; as personality B, act like a prototypical "bitch." As long as personality A differs dramatically from personality B, the person will have little difficulty differentiating the experiences and memories that go with each.

Amnesia. Displays of amnesia, usually by the "primary personality" for the enactments of one or more "secondary personalities," is a typical feature of the multiple personality role. From a social role perspective these amnesic displays, like the amnesic displays of "good" hypnotic subjects, are contextually supported strategic enactments. Displays of memory failures between personalities are an important means of conveying the impression that different identity enactments reflect the operation of distinct indwelling selves. Furthermore, displays of amnesia provide a means by which patients can disavow responsibility for actions that are incongruent with how they wish to see themselves or be seen by others (Sarbin & Coe, 1979; Spanos et al., 1985). Far from being "uncontrolled happenings," displays of amnesia by multiples, like those of "good" hypnotic subjects, require that control over memory processes be retained. As indicated above, multiples can enact their role convincingly only by selectively recalling and failing to recall the appropriate memories under the appropriate identity enactments.

Our analysis of the Bianchi interview and the results of the Spanos et al. (1985, 1986) role-playing experiments support the hypothesis that displays of amnesia between personalities are cued and then legitimated by aspects of the therapeutic context. The importance of contextual variables in influencing displays of psychogenic amnesia was also demonstrated in an early but neglected clinical study by Parfitt and Gall (1944). When therapists in that study clearly and consistently communicated the expectation that successful recall was a requirement of the situation and that continued amnesic displays were inappropriate, almost all patients recalled the events for which they had earlier claimed amnesia. These clinical findings seem quite analogous to Spanos et al.'s (1985) experimental demonstration that hypnotic amnesia was completely breached when remembering rather than forgetting was convincingly legitimated as the role-appropriate behavior.

Numerous clinical anecdotes (e.g., Allison & Schwarz, 1981; Bliss, 1980; Schwarz, 1981) suggest that contextual interventions that legitimate remembering without discrediting earlier enactments of amnesia can induce a "sharing" of memories among the several identities enacted by multiple personality patients. For instance, posthypnotic suggestions that the primary personality will gradually become aware of a previously "hidden" secondary personality, or hypnotic suggestions encouraging the various "personalities" to share their memories with one another, are sometimes associated with increased recall by the primary personality of previously "hidden" memories. From a social role perspective, of course, hypnotic procedures do not possess any intrinsic properties for enhancing recall or for promoting the "fusion" of "dissociated identities." Instead, such interventions provide a legitimating context for redefining the situation as one in which at least some display of "cross personality" remembering is now considered role-appropriate.

Believed-In Enactments. In cases like that of Bianchi (see also the case of Billy Milligan, in Keyes, 1981), possible escape from legal punishment probably serves as an important inducement for adoption of the multiple personality role. From a social psychological perspective, the salience of an inducement may affect the causal attributions that actors apply to their behavior (e.g., Jones, 1979; Nisbett & Ross, 1980). Because escaping punishment is so salient, people who adopt the role of being multiple under the threat of legal prosecution are unlikely (at least initially) to privately assign much credibility to their enactments. They, like many observers who are aware of their predicament, are likely to (privately) explain their enactments as an attempt to "beat the system." In more typical cases, however, where external inducements for adopting the role of a multiple are a good deal more subtle, many patients probably become convinced by their own enactments and come to believe that they possess multiple selves.

People tend to obey legitimate authority (Milgrim, 1974). Therapists, of course, constitute legitimate authorities with whom most patients develop strong ties of trust and dependence (Krippner, Katz, this volume). Typically, therapists are involved (often subtly and indirectly) in influencing the way in which patients learn to conceptualize themselves, their problems, and their pasts, and the way in which they "make sense" out of their current predicaments. Relatedly, patients are frequently willing to adopt and utilize the conceptual categories for self-construal and self-examination that their therapists provide. In short, psychotherapy patients regularly come to construe themselves and their problems in the same terms as do their therapists. In fact, the tendency for patients to do so is often considered a sign of progress, while their failure to do so is often interpreted as resistance to treatment (e.g., Frank, 1973).

In many psychotherapies patients learn to conceptualize their problems as the result of unconscious forces or unconscious "parts" of their personalities. They also learn that these hidden parts must be uncovered if therapeutic progress is to ensue. When hypnotic procedures are introduced into such therapies, they are often described as techniques for facilitating the discovery of hidden memories and repressed "fragments" of personality (Gill & Brenman, 1959; Raginsky, 1967). To all of this, some therapists add explicit encouragement to conceptualize some remembrances as belonging to quasi-independent selves, and to enact these "selves" when they are "called forth" during hypnosis (Allison & Schwarz, 1981; Bliss, 1980; Watkins & Johnson, 1982).

From a social psychological perspective, the procedures that constitute psychotherapy serve to socialize the person into the role of psychotherapy patient. One variant of this role is "hypnotherapy patient," and one way in which hypnotic procedures may be employed is for legitimating transitions from manifestations of the patient's "normal identity" to manifestations of secondary personalities. Under these circumstances patients are probably led not only to enact the overt behaviors that constitute the social role of multiple personality, but also to adopt the same conceptual schemas for understanding and interpreting their behavior as are held by their therapists. In short, patients come to see themselves as having "multiple personalities."

A social role perspective on multiple personality is not inconsistent with the notion that long-standing attributes and cognitive styles may predispose some people to adopt this self-presentation more easily and convincingly than others. For instance, a number of clinical reports describe multiples as highly imaginative people with rich fantasy lives who, as children, created imaginary companions (Allison & Schwarz, 1981; Greaves, 1980; Keyes, 1981). Moreover, recent studies also indicate that multiples are relatively high in hypnotic susceptibility (Bliss, 1984a, 1984b). These findings seem to describe people who have spent a good deal of time covertly rehearsing and becoming absorbed in a range of fantasized roles and activities. It does not seem particularly surprising that such people are adept at enacting the role of a secondary personality when contextual inducements call for such an enactment.

OVERVIEW AND CONCLUSIONS

Hypnotic responding, demonic possession, and multiple personality have traditionally been viewed as phenomena that resist explanation in terms of the theoretical accounts used by social scientists to "make sense" out of more mundane forms of social behavior.

Theoretical accounts of everyday social action are usually premised on the assumption that complex behaviors are goal-directed enactments guided by people's tacit understandings of social requirements and shaped by the impressions they wish to convey about themselves (e.g., Zurcher, 1983). On the other hand, hypnotic responding, possession, and multiple personality are usually conceptualized as being discontinuous from everyday social behavior. Typically, the behaviors associated with these phenomena are seen as "happenings" over which actors have lost voluntary control. According to this perspective, control over behavior has been transferred from the person to indwelling but associated agencies, forces, or selves (e.g., Bliss, 1984a, 1984b; Hilgard, 1977).

This article had suggested that traditional perspectives toward these phenomena are misleading and that hypnotic responding, possession, and multiple personality can be more usefully conceptualized as strategic role enactments than as dissociated happenings. According to this perspective, people who enact these roles convincingly maintain control over their behavior and actively process and interpret changing contextual information in order to strategically guide their enactments in terms of socially defined role requirements. Hypnotic, demonic, and multiple personality enactments appear to be out of the ordinary because the requirements associated with these social roles are unusual. Unlike the demands associated with most social roles, a central requirement of the roles of being hypnotized, possessed, or multiple is that actors convey the impression that their enactments are non-self-guided happenings. In short, actors are required to maintain behavioral control in order to self-present as passive participants in a drama in which they have lost behavioral control.

Hypnosis, demonic possession, and multiple personality are interpersonal phenomena that are enacted within a social matrix and guided by social rules. For each of these social roles knowledge about the behaviors expected from actors is fairly widespread. Moreover, in each case high-status experts (i.e., experimenter, cleric, psychotherapist) function to continually define subtle aspects of the role, encourage and shape enactments, and provide official legitimation for role-appropriate self-presentations. In each case, communications from experts shape not only overt behaviors, but also the conceptual categories employed by actors to understand and interpret their own role behavior. When the shaping process is successful, the causal interpretations employed by actors and experts converge. Both come to construe the actor's strategic role enactments as involuntary occurrences.

NOTE

1. Kelly (1974) provides an interesting synopsis of pre-Christian influences on Western European demonology. Standard histories of psychiatry frequently confuse demonic possession with witchcraft. It is important to emphasize that these were very different phenomena and were rarely associated with one another before the fifteenth century (Spanos, 1978). After this period the demoniac was often construed as the victim of witchcraft and was encouraged to name the witch that caused her to be possessed. The accused witch was often tried and sometimes executed on the basis of accusations made by demoniacs (Kelly, 1974; Spanos, 1978).

REFERENCES

Allison, R. B. (1974). A new treatment approach for multiple personalities. *American Journal of Clinical Hypnosis, 17,* 15-32.
Allison, R. B., & Schwarz, T. (1981). *Minds in many pieces.* New York: Rawson, Wade.
Aubin, N. (1716). *Cruels effets de la vengeance du Cardinal de Richelieu ou histoire des diables de Loudun.* Amsterdam: E. Roger.
Barber, T. X. (1969). *Hypnosis: A scientific approach.* New York: Van Nostrand Reinhold.
Barber, T. X. (1970). *LSD, marijuana, yoga and hypnosis.* Chicago: Aldine.
Barber, T. X. (1979). Suggested ("hypnotic") behavior: The trance paradigm versus an alternative paradigm. In E. Fromm & R. E. Shor (Eds.), *Hypnosis: Developments in research and new perspectives.* Chicago: Aldine-Atherton.
Barber, T. X., & Hahn, K. W., Jr. (1962). Physiological and subjective responses to pain producing stimulation under hypnotically-suggested and waking-imagined "analgesia." *Journal of Abnormal and Social Psychology, 65,* 411-418.
Baroja, J. C. (1964). *The world of witches.* London: Weidenfeld & Nicolson.
Bertrand, L. D., & Spanos, N. P. (1985). The organization of recall during hypnotic suggestions for complete and selective amnesia. *Imagination, Cognition and Personality, 4,* 249-261.
Biddle, B. J., & Thomas, E. J. (1966). (Eds.). *Role Theory: Concepts and research.* New York: John Wiley.
Bliss, E. L. (1980). Multiple personalities: A report of 14 cases with implications for schizophrenia and hysteria. *Archives of General Psychiatry, 37,* 1388-1397.
Bliss, E. L. (1984a). A symptom profile of patients with multiple personalities, including MMPI results. *Journal of Nervous and Mental Disease, 171,* 197-202.
Bliss, E. L. (1984b). Hysteria and hypnosis. *Journal of Nervous and Mental Disease, 172,* 203-206.
Bliss, E. L., Larson, E. M., & Nakashima, S. R. (1983). Auditory hallucinations and schizophrenia. *Journal of Nervous and Mental Disease, 171,* 30-33.
Bliss, J., & Bliss, E. (1985). *Prism.* New York: Stein & Day.

Boor, M. (1982). The multiple personality epidemic: Additional cases and inferences regarding diagnosis, etiology, dynamics and treatment. *Journal of Nervous and Mental Disease*, *170*, 302-304.

Brandsma, J. M., & Ludwig, A. M. (1974). A case of multiple personality: Diagnosis and treatment. *International Journal of Clinical and Experimental Hypnosis*, *22*, 216-233.

Calif, R. (1700/1914). More wonders from the invisible world. In G. L. Burr (Ed.), *Narratives of the witchcraft cases, 1648-1706*. New York: Scribner's.

Catherinet, F. M. (1972). Demoniacs in the Gospel. In F. J. Sheed (Ed.), *Soundings in Satanism*. New York: Sheed & Ward.

Cesborn, H. (1909). *Histoire critique de l'hysterie*. Paris: Asseline et Houzeau.

Charcot, J. M., & Marie, P. (1892). Hysteria. In D. Hack Tuke (Ed.), *Dictionary of psychological medicine*. London: Churchill.

Coe, W. C. (1978). The creditability of posthypnotic amnesia: A contextualist's view. *International Journal of Clinical and Experimental Hypnosis*, *26*, 218-245.

Crapanzano, V., & Garrison, V. (Eds). (1977). *Case studies in spirit possession*. New York: John Wiley.

Diamond, M. J. (1974). Modification of hypnotizability: A review. *Psychological Bulletin*, *81*, 180-198.

Ellenberger, H. (1970). *The discovery of the unconscious*. New York: Basic Books.

Evans, M. B., & Paul, G. L. (1970). Effects of hypnotically suggested analgesia on physiological and subjective response to cold. *Journal of Consulting and Clinical Psychology*, *35*, 362-371.

Frank, J. D. (1973). *Persuasion and healing*. New York: Schocken.

Gill, M. M., & Brenman, M. (1959). *Hypnosis and related states*. New York: International University Press.

Glanvill, J. (1689). *Saducimus triumphatus*. London: J. Collins & S. Lownds.

Goffman, E. (1961). *Encounters: Two studies in the sociology of interaction*. Indianapolis: Bobbs-Merrill.

Goffman, E. (1974) *Frame analysis*. New York: Harper & Row.

Greaves, G. (1980). Multiple personality 165 years after Mary Reynolds. *Journal of Nervous and Mental Disease*, *168*, 577-595.

Gruenewald, D. (1971). Hypnotic techniques without hypnosis in the treatment of a dual personality. *Journal of Nervous and Mental Disease*, *153*, 41-46.

Gruenewald, D. (1977). Multiple personality and splitting phenomena: A reconceptualization. *Journal of Nervous and Mental Disease*, *164*, 385-393.

Gruenewald, D. (1984). On the nature of multiple personality: Comparisons with hypnosis. *International Journal of Clinical and Experimental Hypnosis*, *32*, 170-190.

Harsnett, S. (1599). *Discovery of the fraudulent practices of John Darrel*. London: John Wolfe.

Harsnett, S. (1603). *A declaration of egregious popish impostures*. London: I. Roberts.

Hawksworth, H., & Schwarz, T. (1977). *The five of me*. Chicago: Henry Regnery.

Hilgard, E. R. (1977). *Divided consciousness*. New York: John Wiley.

Howard, M. L., & Coe, W. C. (1980). The effects of context and subjects' perceived control in breaching posthypnotic amnesia. *Journal of Personality and Social Psychology*, *46*, 342-359.

Hutchinson, F. (1720). *A historical essay concerning witchcraft*. London: R. Knaplock.

Jones, E. E. (1979). The rocky road from acts to dispositions. *American Psychologist*, *34*, 107-117.

Kampman, R. (1976). Hypnotically induced multiple personality: An experimental study. *International Journal of Clinical and Experimental Hypnosis, 24*, 215-227.

Kelly, H. A. (1974). *The devil, demonology and witchcraft.* New York: Doubleday.

Keyes, D. (1981). *The minds of Billy Milligan.* New York: Bantam.

Kihlstrom, J. F., Evans, F. J., Orne, M. T., & Orne, E. C. (1980). Attempting to breach posthypnotic amnesia. *Journal of Abnormal Psychology, 89,* 603-616.

Kluft, R. P. (1982). Varieties of hypnotic interventions in the treatment of multiple personality. *American Journal of Clinical Hypnosis, 24,* 230-240.

Kohlenberg, R. J. (1973). Behavioristic approach to multiple personality: A case study. *Behavior Therapy, 4,* 137-140.

Lewis, I. M. (1971). *Ecstatic religion: An anthropological study of spirit possession and shamanism.* Boston: Penguin.

Ludwig, A. M., Brandsma, J. M., Wilbur, C. B., Benfeldt, F., & Jameson, D. H. (1972). The objective study of a multiple personality: Or, are four heads better than one? *Archives of General Psychiatry, 26,* 198-310.

Mather, C. (1693/1914). A brand pluck't out of the burning. In G. L. Burr (Ed.), *Narratives of the witchcraft cases, 1648-1706.* New York: Scribner's.

Michaelis, S. (1613). *The admirable history of the possession and conversion of a penitent woman.* London.

Milgram, S. (1974). *Obedience to authority.* New York: Harper & Row.

The most strange and admirable discovery of the Witches of Warboys ... (1593/1972). In B. Rosen (Ed.), *Witchcraft.* New York: Taplinger.

Nisbett, R., & Ross, L. (1980). *Human inference: Strategies and shortcomings of social judgment.* Englewood Cliffs, NJ: Prentice-Hall.

Notestein, W. (1911). *A history of witchcraft in England.* New York: Crowell.

Oesterreich, T. K. (1966). *Possession: Demoniacal and other.* Secaucus, NJ: Citadel Press.

Orne, M., Dinges, D. F., & Orne, E. C. (1984). On the differential diagnosis of multiple personality in the forensic context. *International Journal of Clinical and Experimental Hypnosis, 32,* 118-169.

Parfitt, D. N., & Gall, C. M. C. (1944). Psychogenic amnesia: The refusal to remember. *Journal of Mental Science, 90,* 511-531.

Pickett, R. (1952). *Mental affliction and church law.* Ottawa: University of Ottawa Press.

Raginsky, B. (1967). Rapid regression to the oral and anal levels through sensory hypnoplasty. *International Journal of Clinical and Experimental Hypnosis, 15,* 19-30.

The Roman Ritual of Exorcism (1614/1976). Translated and reprinted as an appendix in M. Malachi, *Hostage to the devil.* New York: Reader's Digest Press.

Rosenbaum, M. (1980). The role of the term schizophrenia in the decline of diagnoses of multiple personality. *Archives of General Psychiatry, 37,* 1383-1385.

Saltman, V., & Solomon, R. S. (1982). Incest and multiple personality. *Psychological Reports, 50,* 1127-1141.

Sarbin, T. R. (1962). Attempts to understand hypnotic phenomena. In L. Postman (Ed.), *Psychology in the making.* New York: Knopf.

Sarbin, T. R. (1983, August). *A contextual analysis of nonvolition in hypnosis.* Paper presented at the annual meeting of the American Psychological Association.

Sarbin, T. R., & Allen, V. L. (1968). Role theory. In G. Lindzey & E. Aronson (Eds.), *The handbook of social psychology* (Vol. 1). Reading, MA: Addison-Wesley.

Sarbin, T. R., & Coe, W. C. (1972). *Hypnosis: A social-psychological analysis of influ-*

ence communication. New York: Holt, Rinehart & Winston.

Sarbin, T. R., & Coe, W. C. (1979). Hypnosis and psychopathology: Replacing old myths with fresh metaphors. *Journal of Abnormal Psychology, 88,* 506-562.

Schreiber, F. R. (1973). *Sybil.* New York: Warner.

Schwarz, T. (1981). *The hillside strangler: A murderer's mind.* New York: New American Library.

Slater, E. (1965). Diagnosis of "hysteria." *British Medical Journal, 29,* 1395-1399.

Smith, R. D., Buffington, P. W., & McCord, R. H. (1982). *Multiple personality: Theory, diagnosis and treatment.* New York: Irvington.

Spanos, N. P. (1971). Goal-directed fantasy and the performance of hypnotic test suggestions. *Psychiatry, 34,* 86-96.

Spanos, N. P. (1978). Witchcraft in histories of psychiatry: A critique and an alternative conceptualization. *Psychological Bulletin, 85,* 417-439.

Spanos, N. P. (1982a). A social psychological approach to hypnotic behavior. In G. Weary & H. L. Mirels (Eds.), *Integrations of clinical and social psychology.* New York: Oxford.

Spanos, N. P. (1982b). Hypnotic behavior: A cognitive social psychological perspective. *Research Communications in Psychology, Psychiatry and Behavior, 7,* 199-213.

Spanos, N. P. (1983a). Demonic possession: A social psychological analysis. In M. Rosenbaum (Ed.), *Compliance behavior.* New York: Free Press.

Spanos, N. P. (1983b). Ergotism and the Salem witch panic: A critical analysis and an alternative conceptualization. *Journal of the History of the Behavioral Science, 19,* 358-369.

Spanos, N. P. (1983c). The hidden observer as an experimental creation. *Journal of Personality and Social Psychology, 44,* 170-176.

Spanos, N. P. (1986a). Hypnosis, nonvolitional responding and multiple personality: A social psychological perspective. In B. Maher & W. Maher (Eds.), *Progress in experimental personality research* (Vol. 14, pp. 1-62).

Spanos, N. P. (1986b). Hypnotic behavior: A social psychological interpretation of amnesia, analgesia and "trance logic." *Behavioural and Brain Sciences, 9,* 449-502.

Spanos, N. P., & Barber, T. X. (1972). Cognitive activity during hypnotic suggestion: Goal-directed fantasy and the experience of nonvolition. *Journal of Personality, 40,* 510-524.

Spanos, N. P., & D'Eon, J. L. (1980). Hypnotic amnesia, disorganized recall and inattention. *Journal of Abnormal Psychology, 89,* 744-750.

Spanos, N. P., & de Groh, M. (1983). Structure of communication and reports of involuntariness by hypnotic and nonhypnotic subjects. *Perceptual and Motor Skills, 57,* 1179-1186.

Spanos, N. P., & de Groh, M. (1984). *Effects of active and passive wording on response to hypnotic and nonhypnotic instructions for complete and selective forgetting.* Unpublished manuscript, Carleton University.

Spanos, N. P., & Gorassini, D. R. (1984). Structure of hypnotic test suggestions and attribution of responding involuntarily. *Journal of Personality and Social Psychology, 46,* 688-696.

Spanos, N. P., & Gottlieb, J. (1976). Ergotism and the Salem Village witch trials. *Science, 194,* 1390-1394.

Spanos, N. P., & Gottlieb, J. (1979). Demonic possession, mesmerism and hysteria: A social psychological perspective on their historical interrelations. *Journal of Abnormal Psychology, 88,* 527-546.

Spanos, N. P., Gwynn, M. I., & Stam, H. J. (1983). Instructional demands and ratings of overt and hidden pain during hypnotic analgesia. *Journal of Abnormal Psychology, 92,* 479-488.

Spanos, N. P., & Hewitt, E. C. (1980). The hidden observer in hypnotic analgesia: Discovery or experimental creation? *Journal of Personality and Social Psychology, 39,* 1201-1214.

Spanos, N. P., & McPeake, J. D. (1977). Cognitive strategies, goal-directed fantasy and response to suggestion in hypnotic subjects. *American Journal of Clinical Hypnosis, 20,* 114-123.

Spanos, N. P., & Radtke, H. L. (1982). Hypnotic amnesia as a strategic enactment: A cognitive, social-psychological perspective. *Research Communications in Psychology, Psychiatry and Behavior, 7,* 215-231.

Spanos, N. P., Radtke, H. L., & Bertrand, L. D. (1984). Hypnotic amnesia as a strategic enactment: The successful breaching of hypnotic amnesia in high susceptible subjects. *Journal of Personality and Social Psychology, 47,* 1155-1169.

Spanos, N. P., Radtke-Bodorik, H. L., Ferguson, J., & Jones, B. (1979). The effects of hypnotic susceptibility, suggestions for analgesia and the utilization of cognitive strategies on the reduction of pain. *Journal of Abnormal Psychology, 88,* 282-292.

Spanos, N. P., Rivers, S. M., & Ross, S. (1977). Experienced involuntariness and response to hypnotic suggestions. *Annals of the New York Academy of Sciences, 296,* 208-221.

Spanos, N. P., Weekes, J. R., & Bertrand, L. D. (1985). Multiple personality: A social psychological perspective. *Journal of Abnormal Psychology, 94,* 362-376.

Spanos, N. P., Weekes, J. R., Menary, E., & Bertrand, L. D. (1986). Hypnotic interview and age regression procedures in the elicitation of multiple personality symptoms: A simulation study. *Psychiatry, 49,* 298-311.

Sutcliffe, J. P., & Jones, J. (1962). Personal identity, multiple personality and hypnosis. *International Journal of Clinical and Experimental Hypnosis, 10,* 231-269.

Szasz, T. S. (1961). *The myth of mental illness.* New York: Harper & Row.

Taylor, W. S., & Martin, M. F. (1944). Multiple personality. *Journal of Abnormal Psychology, 39,* 281-300.

Thigpen, C. H., & Cleckley, H. M. (1957). *The three faces of Eve.* New York: McGraw-Hill.

Thomas, K. (1971). *Religion and the decline of magic.* New York: Scribner's.

Thompson, R. (1972). Salem revisited. *Journal of American Studies, 6,* 317-336.

Veith, I. (1977). Four thousand years of hysteria. In M. J. Horowitz (Ed.), *Hysterical personality.* New York: Aronson.

Wagstaff, G. F. (1981). *Hypnosis, compliance and belief.* New York: St. Martin's Press.

Wagstaff, G. F. (1986). Hypnosis as compliance and belief: A socio-cognitive view. In P. L. N. Naish (Ed.), *What is hypnosis?* Philadelphia: Open University Press.

Walker, D. P. (1981). *Unclean spirits.* Philadelphia: University of Pennsylvania Press.

Ward, C. (1980). Spirit possession and mental health: A psycho-anthropological perspective. *Human Relations, 33*(3), 149-163.

Watkins, J. G., & Johnson, R. J. (1982). *We, the divided self.* New York: Irvington.

Watkins, J. G., & Watkins, H. (1980). Ego states and hidden observers. *Journal of Altered States of Consciousness, 5,* 3-18.

Weitzenhoffer, A. M. (1974). When is an "instruction" an "instruction"? *International Journal of Clinical and Experimental Hypnosis, 22,* 258-269.

Zilboorg, G., & Henry, G. W. (1941). *A history of medical psychology.* New York: Norton.

Zurcher, L. A. (1983). *Social roles.* Beverly Hills, CA: Sage.

6

POSSESSION AND EXORCISM
Psychopathology and Psychotherapy in a
Magico-Religious Context

COLLEEN A. WARD

MODELS OF PSYCHOPATHOLOGY

The Magical Model

> In the past, most people believed in sorcery, sympathetic magic and witchcraft. Men have a powerful need to perceive the causes of natural disasters, epidemics and personal misfortunes and death. Magic and witchcraft supply a primitive theory for explaining such occurrences and methods for coping with them. (Szasz, 1970, p. 3)

The way in which people respond to illness or misfortune in any culture is related to the entire religious and philosophical framework in which existence is perceived. Initial attempts to explain ill health were intuitive, and when organic or other natural causes were not recognized, suspicions were often aroused about the operation of spiritual forces. In this context, personal misfortunes and maladies were most often attributed to malignant influences based on soul loss, spirit intrusion, or imitative magic and were dealt with in the realm of sorcery.

While a strong mythological link exists between human affliction and supernatural forces, the precise relationship between spirit possession and mental health has not been adequately clarified by psychologists, psychiatrists, or anthropologists. In many instances, both historically and cross-culturally, spirit possession has been encouraged as a mystical and divine experience, interpreted within a religious framework as uniting humans with gods, supporting cultural cosmology, and offering positive psychological and social benefits (Chandra shekar, this volume; Jilek, this volume; Kiev, 1966; Krippner, this volume; Mischel & Mischel, 1958; Prince, 1966; Ward, 1979, 1980). In other circumstances, however, possession has been perceived as a malevolent intrusion of spiritual beings that perpetuates illness, misfortune, or even death, reiterating the association between natural events and supernatural influences (Chandra shekar, this volume; Kemp, this volume; Spanos, this volume). In these cases, a culture generally recognizes the maladaptive nature of possession, including its relation to physical and psychological disorders, and attempts to treat the condition with various folk remedies, particularly exorcism (Freed & Freed, 1964; Galvin & Ludwig, 1961; Lewis, 1971; Ludwig, 1965; Warner, 1977; Yap, 1960).

Malevolent spirit possession of this kind has been documented over time and across cultures. Perhaps the earliest examples occurred in the Stone Age when primitive psychiatrists attributed the cause of psychological disturbances to seizure by demons and implemented a cure in the form of trephining—chipping away of one area of the skull to provide a small escapeway for mischievous evil spirits (Coleman, 1964). Ancient records of the Egyptians, Babylonians, Hebrews, and Greeks demonstrated the attribution of assorted disorders to demons. Likewise, in Asia, early Chinese medical systems implicated ghosts and devils in diverse forms of insanity, and Vedic priests in India often assumed the role of therapists, exorcising angry demons who inhabited various parts of the body. Historically, however, the European Middle Ages is perhaps most infamous for its preoccupation with possession, including epidemics of mass hysteria and cruel, inhumane exorcism practices (Zilboorg, 1941).

While instances of spirit possession have been amply documented over time, it is less apparent to many that it is also widespread over cultures. A 1977 study by anthropologists Bourguignon and Evascu revealed that in a worldwide sample of 488 societies, 90% displayed evidence of trance and/or possession states. Interdisciplinary cross-cultural research has also verified malevolent spirit possession in Asia, including Sri Lanka (Obeyesekere, 1970; Wirz, 1954), India (Chandra shekar, this volume; Freed & Freed, 1964), Burma (Spiro, 1967), Indonesia (Freeman, 1965), Hong Kong (Yap, 1960), Malaysia (Ackerman & Lee, 1978), and the Philippines (Guthrie & Szanton, 1976); in Africa, including Ethiopia, Egypt, and Sudan (Messing, 1958), Kenya (Whisson, 1964), Nigeria, (Uyanga, 1979), Zambia (Sargant, 1973), Transkei (O'Connell, 1982), and Tribal East Africa (Harris, 1957); in North America, including the United States (Ruiz & Griffith, 1977; Warner, 1977) and Canadian tribal people (Jilek, 1976); in Central and South America (Finkler, 1980), including the Caribbean (Ward

& Beaubrun, 1980); and in Europe (L'Hermitte, 1944), Australasia, and the Arctic regions (Lewis, 1971).

Medical and Sociocultural Models in the Cross-Cultural Context

> Both demon possession and psychopathology are attributional statements about inferred causal entities based on observation of an individual's behavior. Both are acceptable and meaningful in the realm of discourse and in the culture in which the statement is made. The essential difference is that possession infers a supernatural causal agent ... Pathology infers a neurological causal agent. (Bach, 1979, p.25)

With the rise of transcultural psychiatry, broader theoretical issues concerning the relationship between culture and psychopathology as well as "exotic" phenomena such as trance and spirit possession have become the focus of much social and behavioral research (Kiev, 1972; Opler, 1967). The majority of such investigations have been concentrated on cultural influence on the form and frequency of psychological irregularities in varied societies but have been based on the implicit assumption that mental disorder is universal—that each culture recognizes its existence but attributes to it different names, symptoms, explanations, and theories of causality (DeVos, 1976; Wallace, 1972). In instances of culture-bound reactive syndromes, such as malevolent forms of possession, Arctic hysteria, *susto*, etc., the same underlying dynamic response patterns and the causal relationship between organic factors or stress and psychopathology are assumed to exist.[1] In short, from the perspective of transcultural psychiatry, the essence of psychopathology is universal, but the trappings may vary in accordance with significant cultural factors (Kiev, 1972; Yap, 1969).

As cross-cultural trends in mental health have become a topical area for interdisciplinary investigation, objections have arisen to sole reliance on the medically oriented psychopathology model and its principal assumption that culture and mental disorder are objective givens from which the form and frequency of psychopathology can be analyzed, predicted, and controlled. It has also been argued that the medical model is unduly restrictive and fails to capture the dynamic character of the culture-bound syndrome by dismissing the relativistic nature of deviance and ignoring the impact of norm violation on the definition of mental illness (Scheff, 1966; Szasz, 1970). In practical terms, psychological disturbances generally encompass both a disordering of psychological processes and an element of norm violation, impinging on both the medical and sociocultural models of psychopathology. What is significant about the phenomenon of malevolent spirit possession is that, although interpreted within a magical framework, its manifestation retains elements of both psychiatric symptoms and norm violation. These bipartite deviations are recognized by the host culture, which offers indigenous therapies for the condition's alleviation and cure. In this context, the dynamics of the possession response can be legitimately analyzed in terms of other maladaptive forms of behavior—that is, in a psychosocial framework, by focusing on predisposing and precipitating factors, contingent social norms and values, available coping strategies, and consequences. Similarly, its cure, exorcism, may be assessed as other therapies, with reference to dynamic processes in the therapeutic session, client-therapist relationship, and effectiveness of the technique. Viewed from a more global perspective, the dynamics of possession and exorcism may reflect a cycle of sickness behavior, help seeking, and cure displayed universally but patterned by cultural constraints and cosmologies.

POSSESSION: THE DISORDER

Problems of Definition

Psychopathology is but a formal and general term for the study of human suffering, but the experience of suffering can better be allotted to the presence of demonic images which arcanely and uncannily haunt us. (Grotstein, 1978, p. 4)

Whereas mental illness is largely identified and classified in terms of psychological, behavioral, or organic symptoms viewed as unhealthy, socially unacceptable, and requiring treatment, possession is interpreted by cultural beliefs and traditions and applied to a wide range of positive and negative activities and behaviors. Consequently, clarification of the precise relationship between possession and mental health is confounded by problems of definition. The difficulties have been exacerbated by a number of researchers who have overlooked the cultural interpretation of the possession event and neglected to recognize the additional significance of social norms in the assessment of psychopathology. In this context, a fun-

damental distinction between central (ritual) and peripheral possession proposed by Lewis (1971) and expanded by Ward (1980) serves
as a useful framework for the analysis of possession and
psychopathology.

In anthropological terms, Lewis maintains that central possession is
distinguished by its social function: to uphold official morality, religious traditions, and established power. Incorporating a psychological
dimension into the definition, this ritual possession may be viewed as a
temporary, generally voluntary, and usually reversible form of trance
(altered state of consciousness) exhibited in the context of religious ceremonies and attributed to the power of sympathetic spirits (Walker,
1972). Conversely, peripheral possession provides no direct support of
the moral code and typically plagues low-status group members or
those who occupy marginal positions in society (Lewis, 1971). It may
be further characterized as a relatively stable and long-term state in
which the individual believes that he or she is unwillingly possessed by
one or more intruding demons and involuntarily exhibits contingent
behavioral responses that are attributed to the spirits' influence (Ward
& Beaubrun, 1980). This condition may be punctuated by altered
states of consciousness, although the individual spends large periods of
time in a lucid state. Recent literature on ritual possession has empha
sized its therapeutic and adjustive nature in physiological, psychological, and social terms (Jilek, this volume; Kiev, 1966; Lex, 1975; Prince,
1966; Sargant, 1973; Ward, 1980, 1984). In contrast, peripheral possession has been characterized as indicative of neurosis (Freed &
Freed, 1964; Ward & Beaubrun, 1980, 1981), psychosis (Ludwig,
1965; Yap, 1960) and personality disorders (Ludwig, 1965), and a
combination of diagnoses, such as Langness's (1976) hysterical
psychosis.[2] This paper deals specifically with peripheral possession,
which may be referred to in other literature as diabolical mysticism
(James, 1958), involuntary possession (Oesterreich, 1966), sickness
possession (Mars, 1954) or negative possession trance (Peters, 1988).

The Possession Experience   •

> Mental illness is but a way of expressing the experience of being kid-
> napped, ensorcelled or possessed by a state of mind whose personi-
> fied imagery is diabolical, preternatural, uncanny. (Grotstein, 1978,
> p. 2)

Data on the phenomenon of peripheral spirit possession originate from anthropological, psychological, and psychiatric sources and include macro-description, case studies, and clinical overviews. From an anthropological perspective, Lewis (1971) has taken an epidemiological approach, isolating the societies where illness is interpreted as malignant possession and subsequently analyzing the categories of individuals at risk and the circumstances under which they most frequently succumb to possession. Surveying cross-cultural literature, Lewis discovered that possession occurs most frequently in low-status marginals, particularly women, and is interpreted as a psychological maneuver exemplifying social protest against the pressures of subordinate and restrictive roles.

A good example is found in Muslim Somalia, where spirit possession is regarded as a prime cause for complaints ranging from slight malaise to acute organic disorders. Conditions are such that men dominate sociopolitical spheres and women are segregated into subordinate roles. A common reaction is observed in women rejected by their suitors: having no means traditionally available to express their emotions, recover their pride, or even replace their traitorous lovers, they have recourse to the possession experience. Similarly, Zar possession, described by Messing (1958) as a "catch all for many psychological disturbances" with accompanying symptoms ranging from mild hysteria and light depression to actual organic disorders, is found in Sudan, Egypt, North Africa, and Arabia as a more common complaint of women. Living under harsh nomadic conditions and forced to compete for attention in a polygamous situation, married women are particularly susceptible to possession, especially in relation to wife beating and the threat of additional bride purchase (Leiris, 1958). The Muslim Hausa women also succumb to mystical afflictions caused by pathogenic spirits in situations of domestic conflict and strife, and parallel cases, involving hysterical and other symptoms, frequently occur in tribal Africa (Lewis, 1971).

In Asia, similar patterns transpire in which malevolent spirits haunt the weak and vulnerable. In India, for example, possession occurring in the form of bride sickness is common when young women are moved to their husbands' homes and experience anxiety over the new location, family relationships, sexual relations, and childbearing. Chandra shekar, Channabasavanna, and Venkataswamy (1980) reported involuntary possession most common in married women (aged 20–35 years) with little education and relatively impoverished backgrounds. Older and infertile women are also occasionally overcome by spirits (Lewis, 1971). Typically, the possession reaction is disturbing and traumatic and not uncommonly is a response to personal affliction and adversity.

Perhaps a more substantial explanation of the dynamics of possession can be achieved by analyzing case studies in a cross-cultural context. Ward and Beaubrun (1980) reported a case of a 17-year-old Trinidadian boy who exhibited periods of dissociation, selective amnesia, general malaise, and depression, accompanied by psychosomatic complaints. The boy had been exposed to considerable domestic tension centering on his stepfather, who vacillated between violent outbursts of alcoholic intoxication and tender paternal concern. Removed from the family home at his stepfather's insistence, the boy had experienced severe emotional stress over the separation and anxiety over his mother's welfare. He responded with depression and periods of dissociation during which he failed to recognize family members but believed himself to be possessed by demons invoked by his stepfather's first wife. The reaction was interpreted as a neurotic coping strategy influenced by cultural traditions, precipitated by domestic conflict and reinforced by impediments to constructive coping alternatives and lack of external supports. The case was treated by exorcism in a Pentecostal church.

Freed and Freed (1964) documented a case of trance and possession in a 15-year-old Indian bride who suffered from dissociation, malaise, giddiness, apathy, and oversleeping. The girl had been moved to her husband's village but was uncomfortable in the new situation, feeling lonely and restricted. She was terrified of sexual relations and also experienced difficulties in her interactions with household members. The young bride and her family believed that a dead girl from a neighboring village was responsible for the possession, but Freed and Freed interpreted this as a hysterical reaction precipitated by cultural events, domestic tensions, and situational difficulties where expectations for aid and support were low. The girl's case was referred to a shaman.

Yap (1960) recounted a case of a 27-year-old illiterate Hong Kong Chinese widow who believed herself to be possessed by spirits of her dead husband and mother and who displayed symptoms of agitation, sleeplessness, and depression, culminating in attempted suicide. The woman was described as unintelligent and superstitious, and overwhelmed with the difficulties of bringing up two children in an urban environment. She experienced conflict over a marriage proposal from a fellow worker and anxiety over her change of religion. In addition, financial difficulties arose immediately before her hospital admission. Yap diagnosed the case as hysteria and interpreted it as the working out and dramatization of guilt conflicts.

While the incidences of possession documented here reflect culture-bound neurotic coping mechanisms in reaction to severe emotional stress or conflict, the dynamic process may afford certain secondary gains, such as escape from unpleasant reality, fantasized wish fulfillment, diminution of guilt and responsibility for maladaptive behavior, manipulation of others, and assertion of rights by marginals (Crapanzano & Garrison, 1977; Lewis, 1971; Spanos, this volume; Ward & Beaubrun, 1980; Yap, 1960). In this sense, possession, rather than other psychological defenses, is ideally suited for coping with crises. Initially, the dissociation and conversion associated with possession furnish a direct means of escaping unpleasant realities. In the case of the young Trinidadian boy, he was able to avoid stressful household relationships and gain momentary relief from domestic constraints by dissociation and denial of painful family bonds. In other instances, psychosomatic symptoms induced by hysterical conversion may diminish emotional tension by shifting focus from fundamental stress factors to secondary somatic complaints. With the individual's attention (as well of that of family and friends) concentrated on somatic problems and possession, the primary source of emotional conflict may be largely ignored.

Possession also allows for diminution of guilt by the projecting of blame onto an intruding agent and the opportunity to manipulate individuals, gaining their attention and affection and even controlling some aspects of their behavior (see Chandra shekar's case discussion of Gowri, this volume). This pattern is found in Zar possession, where women often succeed in influencing their husbands against taking further wives by making demands while under the influence of a possessing spirit. Possession may also be a vehicle for the assertion of rights by minority groups. Ackerman and Lee (1981) have produced an impressive analysis of mass hysteria in Malaysian factories, where, in response to low wages, strict rules, lack of subsidies, and fear of supervisors, disruptive possession behavior defeated the management's production goals.

It must be conceded that not all recorded instances of spirit possession reflect neurotic coping attempts. In particular, Yap's (1960) investigation of 66 Hong Kong patients institutionalized with possession beliefs revealed that the syndrome, manifesting itself in varying degrees of completeness, was distributed among discrete psychiatric diagnoses, including hysteria (48.5%), schizophrenia

(24.3%), and depression (12.2%), with rarer incidences of mania, delirium, general paresis, and postepileptic, lactational, and senile confusion. In an unpublished study of possession cases in a Trinidadian mental hospital, Ward and Beaubrun reported that among 58 patients, schizophrenia accounted for 63.8% of the cases, combining with additional incidences of acute psychotic reaction (8.7%) and drug-induced psychosis (7.0%) to compose the majority of these first admissions. Examples of psychotic possession and bewitchment have also been reported in the United States, particularly amongst Spanish-American clients (Ludwig, 1965; Warner, 1977), and Peters (1988) forcefully argues that possession relates to borderline personality disorders. In these instances cultural beliefs and traditions add picturesque coloration to psychotic symptoms and function as an alternative explanation for the disordered behavior.

EXORCISM: THE CURE

> Whether the issue is demon possession, a paranoid attack or a catatonic seizure, the change agent (therapist or exorcist) assumes that the causal agent (pathology or demon) is not identical with the disturbed person, that the maladaptive or malevolent part of the person is dispensable, and he seeks to move the person to a way of living in which the troublesome part is unnecessary and can be done away with. (Bach, 1979, p. 26)

The classical treatment for possession has been exorcism: ridding the corporal being of unclean spirits. Techniques have varied considerably through the ages but generally have included prayer and incantation as well as the use of assorted purgatives. In extreme cases, flogging, starving, and more severe measures have been employed to make the body of the afflicted individual so unpleasant that the evil spirit would necessarily be driven out. Over time and across cultures, societies have provided indigenous healing techniques for illnesses and disorders in accordance with the cultural cosmology (Katz, this volume; Kiev, 1972; Krippner, this volume; Lee, this volume).

Because the culturally prescribed cure for possession is exorcism, treatment by indigenous therapists is pursued, in preference to standard psychiatric techniques. This reflects fundamental patterns of health care utilization in members of traditional and syncretic cultures. Clark (1970) estimated that half of the Spanish-speaking clients in one California clinic consulted traditional healers before requesting psychiatric assistance. This has been corroborated by Ruiz and Langrod (1976), who reported that approximately one half of the Chicana females and one-third of the males were treated by mediums and spiritual healers concurrent with their clinic attendance. Substantial proportions have been found in Erinosho's (1977) study of pre-admission patients in Nigeria (63.3%) and in Kinzie, Teoh, and Tan's (1976) investigation in Malaysia (33%).

While the "evil spirit" theory of illness and affliction may be scientifically unsound, the resultant therapy is not entirely ineffective, and several researchers have emphasized the therapeutic processes and benefits of indigenous healing techniques. There has been ample anthropological evidence corroborating the success of indigenous therapies with emotionally based psychosomatic disorders, psychogenic organic malfunctions precipitated by emotional stress and conflict, and neuroses (Boyer, 1964; De Rios, 1976). Jilek (1976) has noted the positive impact of indigenous remedies on anxiety, somatic complaints, and substance abuse, while Chen (1979) has discussed the dynamics of traditional medicine in the treatment of depression. Finkler's (1980) more comprehensive study of Mexican spiritualists revealed the greatest success rate in alleviating somatized syndromes and minor psychiatric complications, while Sasaki's (1976) investigation of religious healings in Japanese cults demonstrated consistent improvements in neurotic disorders (80%) and a notable decrease in schizophrenic and psychosomatic symptomology. Finally, Ward (1981) documented personality stabilization in a group of exorcised West Indian Pentecostals. Frank (1973) has postulated that, in contrast to modern medicine, prescientific systems are based on different aspects of the healing process and that indigenous therapists concentrate primarily on the anxiety associated with a particular illness or affliction. If so, an explanation is offered for the particular efficacy of native therapies in the treatment of neuroses and psychosomatic disorders (Kiev, 1964).

Ruiz and Langrod (1976) have noted that when individuals are socially deprived of economic or status achievements, they are likely to revert to strong identification with their original ethnic traditions in order to neutralize the effects of a harsh and repressive environment. In the context of magical beliefs, the possession reaction is understood by the indigenous healer, who is more tolerant of such disorders and offers greater sympathy to the afflicted individual,

strengthening the bond between therapist and patient. The significance of this bond cannot be overestimated, as empirical investigations have indicated that the effectiveness of therapy may depend
less on specific theory and practice than on the quality of the relationship between therapist and client (Phares, 1979; Strupp &
Bergin, 1969).

The therapeutic mechanisms of exorcism are similar to those in
conventional psychotherapy. To a large extent the efficacy of the
treatment rests on placebo power: Exorcism, like most folk medicine
and much of psychotherapy, works because people believe it will
work (Shapiro, 1964). In this context, the therapeutic results are influenced by psychological factors and processes, such as perception,
belief, expectancy, motivation, role playing, demand characteristics,
and reinforcement (Guthrie & Szanton, 1976; Witkins, 1973). As
approaches to healing, exorcism and psychotherapy share common
features and may be analyzed within similar conceptual frameworks. The following five factors/processes warrant consideration in
the therapeutic milieu.

1. *The sick role and therapeutic process*: Distressed individuals
approach therapists primarily for remedial treatment; however, anxiety reduction typically ensues from the process (per se) of seeking
and accepting expert intervention. Subsequently, a diagnosis is
made, and therapeutic instructions are offered. Kleinman (1980) refers to this as the therapeutic mechanism: the sickness is labeled
(e.g., depression, possession), the label is manipulated (therapeutic
intervention), and a new label is applied (e.g., cured, exorcised,
well). Maclean (1977) insightfully notes that if the prescribed cure is
not immediately effective, the afflicted individual rarely loses faith
in the entire therapeutic system but rather places the blame elsewhere, e.g., on an impotent healer or remedy.

2. *The dynamics of the therapist-client relationship*: The quality
of the patient-healer bond is of prime importance in the treatment
process. In clinical settings it has been demonstrated that warm, em-
pathetic, and genuine therapists produce better results (Rogers,
Gendlin, Kiesler, & Truax, 1967; Sloane, Staples, Christol,
Yorkston, & Whipple, 1975). In the magical milieu the significance
of dyadic dynamics has not been highlighted as much as the charismatic and omnipotent manner of the indigenous healer. Tseng
(1976) and Lambo (1978), in Taiwan and Nigeria, respectively, have
emphasized that the native therapist's self-presentation as powerful,
self-confident, omnipotent, and authoritarian energizes the thera-

peutic process, transforming the patient's hope for cure into a concrete reality (see also Lee, this volume).

3. *Placebo effect*: The efficacy of both physical and psychological therapies is often extrinsic to the "actual" potency of the remedy, and treatment is frequently effective because people expect it to be (Beecher, 1956). The concept of placebo effect has been incorporated into psychology and medicine and elaborated in terms of sociopsychological factors such as perception, attention, expectation, motivation, role playing, demand characteristics, and reinforcement. The significance of placebo power has been noted in both modern psychotherapies (Guthrie & Szanton, 1976; Witkins, 1973) and traditional exorcisms (Ward, 1981).

4. *Personality traits and types of disorders*: Individual personality characteristics affect the use of and satisfaction with services, compliance to therapeutic regimens, and, ultimately, prognosis (Gatchel & Baum, 1983; Pattison, Nikolajs, & Doerr, 1973). Cromwell, Butterfield, Brayfield, and Curry (1977) have also argued that in medical settings personality styles and coping predict an individual's suitability for various types of health care. Furthermore, Lindstrom (1978) has noted that placebo reactors have been depicted as religious, hypochondriacal, disturbed, depressed, neurotic, and dependent, but most specifically are characterized by manifest free-floating anxiety—a composition of traits frequently found in possessed individuals. In addition, in both exorcism rites and modern clinical psychology, the greatest improvement is observed in cases of neurotic and psychosomatic disorders, in contrast to psychotic disturbances. Effective treatment of personality disorders probably falls somewhere between these two extremes (Finkler, 1980; Jilek, 1976; Sloane et al., 1975).

5. *Spontaneous remission of psychological symptoms*: While the author is unaware of empirical investigations of spontaneous remission in relationship to exorcism, Bergin (1971) has estimated a median rate of 30% in clinical psychology settings. Prince (1976), however, has given evidence of psychological restoration by endogenous mechanisms alone in a number of traditional settings.

In addition to social and psychological factors, exorcism may also sustain therapeutic effects on a physiological level, functioning as a form of psychiatric abreaction (see Jilek, this volume). In a more conventional psychiatric setting, the abreactive technique allows patients, with the aid of hypnosis or excitatory drugs, to relive an intense emotional experience in an attempt to solve a psychological problem and to release pent-up emotion by cathartic discharge

(Sargant, 1973). In later research it was demonstrated that patients need not revive the specific emotional reminiscence that precipitated the illness, but may even substitute imaginary experiences. As certain extrinsic similarities typically exist between exorcism and abreaction—e.g., periods of dissociation, intense emotional arousal and excitement, and contingent inhibitory collapse followed by subjective reports of exhaustion and relief—it may be suggested that therapeutic effects are also similar.[3]

If exorcism does constitute abreactive therapy, the power of the technique lies in the oscillation of the sympathetic/parasympathetic balance in the autonomic nervous system and the establishment of a new, relatively long-lasting level of balance (Gellhorn & Kiely, 1972). More specifically, under controlled conditions abreaction permits an individual to experience intense emotional responses to stress-provoking stimuli, and thus discharge of affect with accompanying physiological adjustments. As exorcism practices involve processes of excitation and inhibition, maladaptive behaviors may be alleviated by ritual therapies that restore emotional and physiological equilibrium. The performance is primarily effective for the individual but may also provide catharsis for the group (Kiev, 1972).[4]

CONCLUSION

A growing amount of cultural and psychiatric research is showing that illness experience is an interpretive enterprise which is constructed in social situations according to the premises of cultural theories about illness and social behavior generally. (White & Marsella, 1984, p. 3)

Lambek (this volume) has noted that possession is an "indigenous hypothesis" put forward to account for trance behaviors and altered states of consciousness. In the cross-cultural context this hypothesis is applied to assorted deviant and unconventional behaviors; in particular, cross-cultural research indicates that indigenous theories often describe disordered behaviors as spirit possession and attribute supernatural causality—i.e., the intrusion of malevolent forces—to such conditions.

Medical, psychosocial, and sociocultural frameworks offer alternatives to these magical models of illness, but nonetheless represent indigenous or emic theories. Medical approaches assume a universality in pathology, interpret disturbed behaviors as illnesses, and attribute the states to neurological factors. Psychosocial paradigms concentrate on psychological or behavioral problems and attribute their origins to a combination of individual differences such as personality, socialization, and life events, or situational stressors. Sociocultural approaches highlight the importance of social norms in defining or creating mental "illness." Each model, therefore, provides an explanatory framework for human "dis-ease."

As a primary aim of cross-cultural psychology has been the search for universals or derived etics (Berry, 1969), this paper has attempted to demonstrate the cross-cultural utility of psychosocial models of mental disorders and therapeutic mechanisms (see Figure 6.1). In a global context it has been argued that the terms "possession" and "exorcism" may be used interchangeably with "psychopathology" and "psychotherapy." The paper has emphasized the importance of indigenous definitions of health/illness, adjustment/maladjustment, and normal/deviant behaviors; and, given the social interpretation of certain conditions (possession/psychological problems) as requiring treatment (exorcism/therapy), parallels have been drawn between the illness and health-seeking behaviors in a variety of cultural contexts.

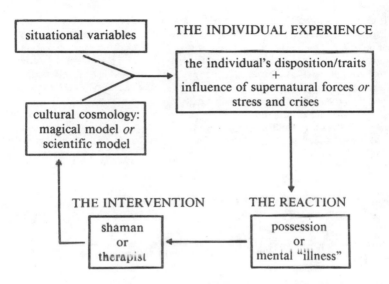

THE SOCIO-CULTURAL
CONTEXT

situational variables

THE INDIVIDUAL EXPERIENCE

the individual's disposition/traits
+
influence of supernatural forces *or*
stress and crises

cultural cosmology:
magical model *or*
scientific model

THE INTERVENTION

shaman
or
therapist

THE REACTION

possession
or
mental "illness"

SOURCE: adapted and expanded from De Rios (1976)

Figure 6.1 The Illness Experience

NOTES

1. Culture-bound reactive disorders include various "exotic" forms of inappropriate behaviors usually recognized by a society as being maladjusted; they are assumed to be representative of universal categories of psychopathology, although the overt symptoms are often bizarre and culture specific.

2. It should be noted that Ludwig refers to his cases as "bewitchment."

3. Exorcisms may vary in form and fashion but often involve repeated sensory stimulation of the possessed individual, resulting in partial or complete dissociation. Emotional arousal is typically present, as well as frequent gross motor activity as the individual struggles to resist the exorcism. The excitatory phase is usually followed by a brief period of emotional collapse, after which the individual recovers consciousness and subjectively experiences psychological rejuvenation (Ward, 1981).

4. It is interesting to note that a number of scholars have drawn comparisons between ritual possession and exorcisms and the therapeutic use of groups in conventional psychotherapy (e.g., Prince, 1964, Ward; 1985) and psychodrama (Chen, 1979).

REFERENCES

Ackerman, S. E., & Lee, R. L. M. (1978). Mass hysteria and spirit possession in urban Malaysia: A case study. *Journal of Sociology and Psychology, 1*, 24-34.

Ackerman, S. E., & Lee, R. L. M. (1981). Communication and cognitive pluralism in a spirit possession event in Malaysia. *American Ethnologist, 8*(4), 789-799.

Bach, P. (1979). Demon possession and psychopathology: A theological relationship. *Journal of Psychology and Theology, 7*(1), 22-26.

Beecher, H. K. (1956). Relationship of significance of wound to the pain experienced. *Journal of the American Medical Association, 161*, 1609-1613.

Bergin, A. E. (1971). The evaluation of therapeutic outcomes. In A. E. Bergin & S. L. Garfield (Eds.), *Handbook of psychotherapy and behavioral change* (2nd ed., pp. 139-189). New York: John Wiley.

Berry, J. W. (1969). On cross-cultural comparability. *International Journal of Psychology, 4*, 119-128.

Bourguignon, E., & Evascu, T. (1977). Altered states of consciousness within a general evolutionary perspective: A holocultural analysis. *Behavior Science Research, 12*(3), 197-216.

Boyer, A. (1964). Folk psychiatry of the Apaches of the Mescalero Indian reservation. In A. Kiev (Ed.), *Magic, faith and healing* (pp. 384-419). London: Collier Macmillan.

Chandra shekar, C. R., Channabasavanna, S. M., & Venkataswamy, M. (1980). Hysterical possession syndrome. *Indian Journal of Psychological Medicine, 3*, 29-52.

Chen, P. C. Y. (1979). *Main puteri*: An indigenous Kelantanese form of psychotherapy. *International Journal of Social Psychiatry, 25*, 167-175.

Clark, M. (1970). *Health in the Mexican-American culture: A community study.* Berkeley: University of California Press.

Coleman, J. (1964). *Abnormal psychology and modern life*. Glenview, IL: Scott, Foresman.

Crapanzano, V., & Garrison, V. (Eds.). (1977). *Case studies in spirit possession*. New York: John Wiley.

Cromwell, R. L., Butterfield, E. C., Brayfield, F. M., & Curry, J. J. (1977). *Acute myocardial infarction: Reaction and recovery*. St. Louis: Mosby.

De Rios, M. D. (1976). The relationship between witchcraft beliefs and psychosomatic illness. In J. Westermeyer (Ed.), *Anthropology and mental health* (pp. 11-17). The Hague: Mouton.

DeVos, G. (1976). The interrelationship of social and psychological structures in trans-cultural psychiatry. In W. Lebra (Ed.), *Culture bound syndromes, ethnopsychiatry and alternative therapies* (pp. 278-298). Honolulu: University of Hawaii Press.

Erinosho, O. A. (1977). Social background and pre-admission sources of care among Yoruba psychiatric patients. *Social Psychiatry, 12*, 71-74.

Finkler, K. (1980). Non-medical treatments and their outcomes. *Culture, Medicine and Psychiatry, 4*, 271-310.

Frank, J. D. (1973). *Persuasion and healing*. Baltimore: Johns Hopkins University Press.

Freed, S. A., & Freed, R. R. (1964). Spirit possession as an illness in a North Indian village. *Ethnology, 3*, 152-171.

Freeman, D. (1965). *Shaman and incubus*. Unpublished manuscript, Australian National University.

Galvin, J. A., & Ludwig, A. M. (1961). A case of witchcraft. *Journal of Nervous and Mental Disease, 133*, 161-168.

Gatchel, R., & Baum, A. (1983). *An introduction to health psychology*. London: Addison-Wesley.

Gellhorn, E., & Kiely, W. F. (1972). Mystical states of consciousness: Neurophysiological and clinical aspects. *Journal of Nervous and Mental Disease, 154*, 399-405.

Grotstein, J. (1978, September). Demoniacal possession, splitting and the torment of hope: A psychoanalytic inquiry into the mystique of negation. Paper presented under the auspices of the Interdisciplinary Group for Advanced Studies in Psychiatric, Borderline and Narcissistic Disorders at William A White Foundation, New York.

Guthrie, B., & Szanton, D. (1976). Folk diagnosis and treatment of schizophrenia: Bargaining with spirits in the Philippines. In W. Lebra (Ed.), *Culture bound syndromes, ethno-psychiatry and alternate therapies* (pp. 147-163). Honolulu: University of Hawaii Press.

Harris, G. (1957). Possession hysteria in a Kenyan tribe. *American Anthropologist, 59*, 1046-1066.

James, W. (1958). *The varieties of religious experience*. New York: New American Library.

Jilek, W. (1976). Brainwashing as a therapeutic technique in contemporary Canadian Indian spirit dancing: A case of theory building. In J. Westermeyer (Ed.), *Anthropology and Mental Health* (pp. 201-213). The Hague: Mouton.

Kiev, A. (1964). The study of folk psychiatry. In A. Kiev (Ed.), *Magic, faith and healing* (pp. 3-35). London: Collier Macmillan.

Kiev, A. (1966). The psychotherapeutic value of spirit possession in Haiti. In R. Prince (Ed.), *Trance and possession states* (pp. 143-148). Montreal: R. M. Bucke Memorial Society.

Kiev, A. (1972). *Transcultural psychiatry.* New York: Free Press.

Kinzie, P., Teoh, J. I., & Tan, E. S. (1976). Native healers in Malaysia. In W. Lebra (Ed.), *Culture bound syndromes, ethno-psychiatry and alternate therapies* (pp. 130-146). Honolulu: University of Hawaii Press.

Kleinman, A. (1980). *Patients and healers in the context of culture.* Berkeley: University of California Press.

Lambo, T. A. (1978). Psychotherapy in Africa. *Human Nature, 1,* 32-40.

Langness, L. (1976). Hysterical psychoses and possession. In W. Lebra (Ed.), *Culture bound syndromes, ethno-psychiatry and alternate therapies* (pp. 56-67). Honolulu: University of Hawaii Press.

Leiris, M. (1958). *La possession et ses aspects théâtraux chez les Ethiopiens de Gondar.* Paris: Librairie Plon.

Lewis, I. M. (1971). *Ecstatic religion.* Middlesex: Penguin.

Lex, B. (1975). Physiological aspects of ritual trance. *Journal of Altered States of Consciousness, 2*(2), 109-122.

L'Hermitte, J. (1944). Les psychoses de possession diabolique. *French Medical Review, 4,* 51-54.

Lindstrom, L. (1978). Religious faith healing and its psychological conditions: A methodological study. In T. Kallstad (Ed.), *Psychological studies on religious man* (pp. 219-241). Stockholm: Almqvist & Wiksell.

Ludwig, A. (1965). Witchcraft today. *Diseases of the Nervous System, 26,* 288-291.

Maclean, U. (1977). *Magical medicine: A Nigerian case study.* Middlesex: Penguin.

Mars, L. (1954). Phenomena of possession. *Tomorrow, 3*(1), 61-73.

Messing, S. (1958). Group therapy and social status in the Zar cult of Ethiopia. *American Anthropologist, 60,* 1120-1127.

Mischel, W., & Mischel, F. (1958). Psychological aspects of spirit possession. *American Anthropologist, 60,* 249-260.

Obeyesekere, G. (1970). The idiom of demon possession: A case study. *Social Science and Medicine, 7,* 97-112.

O'Connell, M. C. (1982). Spirit possession and role stress among the Xesibe of Eastern Transkei. *Ethnology, 21*(1), 21-37.

Oesterreich, T. K. (1966). *Possession.* Secaucus, NJ: Citadel Press.

Opler, M. K. (1967). *Culture and social psychiatry.* New York: Atherton Press.

Pattison, E. M., Nikolajs, A. L., & Doerr, H. A. (1973). Faith healing: A study of personality and function. *Journal of Nervous and Mental Disease, 157*(6), 397-409.

Peters, L. G. (1988). Borderline personality disorder and the possession syndrome: An ethnopsychoanalytic perspective. *Transcultural Psychiatric Research Review, 25,* 5-46.

Phares, E. J. (1979). *Clinical psychology.* Homewood, IL: Dorsey Press.

Prince, R. (1964). Indigenous Yoruba psychiatry. In A. Kiev (Ed.), *Magic, faith and healing* (pp. 84-120). London: Collier Macmillan.

Prince, R. (1966). Possession cults and social cybernetics. In R. Prince (Ed.), *Trance and possession states* (pp. 157-165). Montreal: R. M. Bucke Memorial Society.

Prince, R. (1976). Psychotherapy as the manipulation of endogenous healing mechanisms: A transcultural survey. *Transcultural Psychiatric Research Review, 13,* 115-133.

Rappaport, H., & Rappaport, M. (1981). The integration of scientific and traditional healing. *American Psychologist, 36*(7), 774-781.

Rogers, C. R., Gendlin, G. T., Kiesler, D. V., & Truax, C. B. (1967). *The therapeutic relationship and its impact: A study of psychotherapy with schizophrenics.* Madison: University of Wisconsin Press.

Ruiz, P., & Griffith, E. (1977). Hex and possession: Two problematic areas in the psychiatrist's approach to religion. In E. Foulks, R. Wintrob, J. Westermeyer, & A. Favazza (Eds.), *Current perspectives in cultural psychiatry* (pp. 93-102). New York: Spectrum.

Ruiz, P., & Langrod, J. (1976). Psychiatrists and spiritual healers: Partners in community mental health. In J. Westermeyer (Ed.), *Anthropology and mental health* (pp. 77-81). The Hague: Mouton.

Sargant, W. (1973). *The mind possessed.* New York: Lippincott.

Sasaki, Y. (1976). Nonmedical healing in contemporary Japan: A psychiatric study. In W. Lebra (Ed.), *Culture-bound syndromes, ethno-psychiatry and alternate therapies.* Honolulu: University of Hawaii Press.

Scheff, T. (1966). *Being mentally ill: A sociological theory.* Chicago: Aldine.

Shapiro, A. K. (1964). Factors contributing to the placebo effect: Their implications for psychotherapy. *American Journal of Psychotherapy, 18,* 73-88.

Sloane, R. B., Staples, F. R., Christol, A., Yorkston, N. J., & Whipple, K. (1975). *Psychotherapy versus behavior therapy.* Cambridge, MA: Harvard University Press.

Spiro, M. E. (1967). *Burmese supernaturalism.* Englewood Cliffs, NJ: Prentice Hall.

Strupp, H. H., & Bergin, A. E. (1969). Some empirical and conceptual bases for coordinated research in psychotherapy: A critical review of issues, trends, and evidence. *International Journal of Psychiatry, 7,* 18-90.

Szasz, T. (1970). *The manufacture of madness.* New York: Harper & Row.

Tseng, W. (1976). Folk psychotherapy in Taiwan. In W. Lebra (Ed.), *Culture bound syndromes, ethno-psychiatry and alternate therapies* (pp. 164-178). Honolulu: University of Hawaii Press.

Uyanga, J. (1979). The characteristics of patients of spiritual healing homes and traditional doctors in southeastern Nigeria. *Social Science and Medicine, 13,* 323-329.

Walker, S. (1972). *Ceremonial spirit possession in Africa and Afro-America.* Leiden: Brill.

Wallace, A. F. (1972). Mental illness, biology and culture. In F. IIsu (Ed.), *Psychological anthropology* (pp. 363-402). Cambridge, MA: Schenkman.

Ward, C. (1979). Therapeutic aspects of ritual trance: The Shango cult in Trinidad. *Journal of Altered States of Consciousness, 5*(1), 19-29.

Ward, C. (1980). Spirit possession and mental health: A psycho-anthropological perspective. *Human Relations, 33*(3), 149-163.

Ward, C. (1981, July). Magical medicine: Therapeutic aspects of exorcism in the treatment of possession neurosis. Paper presented at World Congress of Mental Health, Manila, Philippines.

Ward, C. (1984). Thaipusam in Malaysia: A psycho-anthropological analysis of ritual trance, ceremonial possession and self mortification practices. *Ethos, 12*(4), 307-334.

Ward, C. (1985). Psychotherapy in traditional and contemporary healing systems. *Singapore Psychologist, 3*(1), 41-65.

Ward, C., & Beaubrun, M. (1980). The psychodynamics of demon possession. *Journal for Scientific Study of Religion, 19*(2), 201-207.

Ward, C., & Beaubrun, M. (1981). Spirit possession and neuroticism in a West Indian Pentecostal community. *British Journal of Clinical Psychology, 20,* 295-296.

Warner, R. (1977). Witchcraft and soul loss: Implications for community psychiatry. *Hospital and Community Psychiatry, 28*(9), 686-690.

Whisson, M. G. (1964). Some functional disorders among the Kenya Luo. In A. Kiev (Ed.), *Magic, faith and healing* (pp. 283-304). London: Collier Macmillan.

White, G. M., & Marsella, A. J. (1984). Introduction: Cultural conceptions in mental health and practice. In A. J. Marsella & G. M. White (Eds.), *Cultural conceptions of mental health and therapy* (pp. 3-38). Boston: Reidel.

Wirz, P. (1954). *The art of healing in Ceylon*. Leiden: Brill.

Witkins, W. (1973). Expectancy of therapeutic gain: An empirical and conceptual critique. *Journal of Consulting and Clinical Psychology, 40*, 69-77.

Yap, P. M. (1960). The possession syndrome. *Journal of Mental Science, 106*, 114-137.

Yap, P. M. (1969). The culture bound reactive syndromes. In W. Caudill & T. Y. Lin (Eds.), *Mental health research in Asia and the Pacific* (pp. 33-53). Honolulu: East-West Center.

Zilboorg, G. (1941). *A history of medical psychology*. New York: Norton.

PART III

Therapeutic Aspects of Altered States of Consciousness

States of nonordinary reality, meaning unusual reality as opposed to the ordinary reality of everyday life ... [are believed] to be the only form of pragmatic learning and the only means of acquiring power. (Castaneda, 1976, p. 21)

A long-standing dispute in cross-cultural research has revolved around the nature of nonordinary states of consciousness and their classification in terms of mental health and illness. There has traditionally been a hazy distinction between the mad and the mystical, and the final appraisal of these phenomena often depends more on dominant sociocultural views than on the specific states themselves. The following papers offer a radical departure from the still prevalent tendency to regard altered states of consciousness per se as evidence of underlying pathology. Rather, therapeutic aspects of altered states of awareness are explored on both the individual and societal levels in a diversity of cultural settings.

The section commences with Valla and Prince's Montreal survey on religious experiences (RE's). Countering the prevailing misconception that RE's are relatively uncommon, the researchers cite cross-cultural data indicating that 20–40% of randomly sampled respondents report these experiences. Valla and Prince hypothesize that RE's are "dynamic and intelligible functions of the psyche that represent reactions to problematic life situations" and review a variety of descriptions of mystical, hallucinatory, and out-of-body experiences. On the basis of case study reports, the authors propose a classification scheme of RE's, including ecstatic, aesthetic, and hallucinatory states. Research findings, however, suggest that RE's are

145

not limited to self-healing mechanisms and should be interpreted in a broader therapeutic context that includes both prophylatic and remedial domains.

Jilek similarly concentrates on therapeutic aspects of ASC's in his discussion of Amerindian ceremonials and parallels the dynamics of these experiences with clinical practices in contemporary psychiatry. Salish spirit dancing initiation, for example, is likened to certain "brainwashing" techniques in that the practices are believed to involve personality depatterning through shock treatment, introduction of vigorous physical training, and indoctrination. Therapeutic benefits are also offered by the Sun Dance ceremonials in terms of acquisition of spiritual and emotional well-being and the enhancement of self-esteem. Although Jilek discusses the altered states of consciousness involved in these rituals, as well as the Gourd dance, in relation to physiological and biochemical parameters, he extends the significance of these rituals to broader cultural concerns. The emphasis on native cultural identity linked to the revival of Amerindian traditions demonstrates the therapeutic aspects of the rituals on both the individual and societal levels.

While sharing an emphasis on therapeutic features of altered states of consciousness, Krippner shifts the perspective by specifically examining ASC's utilized by indigenous healers. This allows for the analysis of altered states of awareness within the context of healing rituals and the appraisal of their significance for afflicted individuals and the community at large; it also allows for the analysis of the significance of the states (on a more fundamental level) for the shaman-medium. Krippner considers the calling to mediumship via routes of dreams and visions, family tradition, assimilation, early identification and selection, and intellectualism. The author emphasizes the importance of role socialization and cultural expectancies, and while acknowledging that mediums may be fantasy prone, he disclaims that the dissociative states are dysfunctional. Altered states of awareness in Condomblé, Kardecismo, and Umbanda healers are described as adaptive and imaginative and offering positive benefits for the medium, the client, and the extended community.

In the last selection, Katz picks up and expands the theme of community-oriented impact of altered states of consciousness in his sophisticated analysis of ritual trance in the !*Kung* bush people. The author describes the enhanced state of consciousness, !*Kia*, that is at the core of !*Kung* healing. The ASC, experienced most intensely by the healer but shared by the community, affects change and transformation in the group. The activation of *n'um*, boiling energy, provides both therapeutic and social significance that Katz interprets in terms of transformation and utilizes as a model for development. What is most noteworthy about this contribution is that the significance of the enhanced state of consciousness extends beyond the individual shaman and the healing ritual itself and encapsulates a !*Kung* worldview that provides a paradigm for transformation, education, and development.

Overall, the papers display cultural awareness and sensitivity to the socially constructed reality of altered states of consciousness while attempting to advance our understanding of these phenomena through mainstream psychological and psychiatric theorizing.

REFERENCE

Castaneda, C. (1976). *The teachings of Don Juan: A Yaqui way of knowledge.* Middlesex: Penguin.

7
RELIGIOUS EXPERIENCES AS SELF-HEALING MECHANISMS

JEAN-PIERRE VALLA
RAYMOND H. PRINCE

In the eighty-odd years since the pioneering work of William James (1902) and R. M. Bucke (1901), the most important advances in the field of religious experience (RE) have had to do with their demystification. Important elements in this demystification have included, on the one hand, the findings of survey research in the United States and in Britain indicating that RE's are relatively common among ordinary people; and on the other, the formulation of a number of interpretations of RE's that, although they continue to be highly speculative and debatable, are nonetheless based upon more or less testable psychological or psychobiological presuppositions rather than supernatural ones (see Zusne, this volume). In this paper we will review these two areas of advance and, on the basis of a recently completed survey of RE's in Montreal, Canada, examine one of the more promising interpretations of their nature, the hypothesis that RE's are examples of the psyche's endogenous healing mechanisms.

THE EPIDEMIOLOGY OF RELIGIOUS EXPERIENCE

Attempts to determine the frequency of RE's among ordinary people are recent phenomena. Pioneer surveys, such as those of Sinclair (1928), Maslow (1959), Laski (1961), and Douglas-Smith (1971), suffered obvious problems of sample representativeness and other methodological difficulties, but they strongly suggested that experiences subjects described as "being in the presence of the divine," "aware of God in a direct manner," "sensations of transcendental ecstasy," and so forth, were much more prevalent than expected. At about the same time, three sophisticated survey groups had also taken up the question. Back and Bourque (1970) intro-

149

duced a question on RE's into the Gallup Poll in 1962 (American Institute of Public Opinion). The question asked was, "Would you say that you ever had a religious or mystical experience—that is, a moment of sudden religious insight or awakening?" Encouraged by the results from this question, they included several further questions in polls conducted during 1966 and 1967. They found a surprisingly high proportion of positive responders—from 20% to 40% of over 3000 randomly selected subjects. They found that RE's were more likely to be reported by low-socioeconomic-status groups, by residents of small cities, by women, and by Blacks. All three surveys were remarkably consistent as regards these patterns.

A second group to undertake such research was the Chicago-based NORC survey team (Greeley & McCready, 1973). Their study was much more detailed and involved some 1400 respondents reported to be representative of the United States population. They inquired about a wide range of experiences, including déja vu and parapsychological phenomena, but their report dealt largely with the question aimed at eliciting religious types of experience, namely, "Have you ever felt as though you were very close to a powerful, spiritual force that seemed to lift you out of yourself?" Of 1467 respondents, 35% answered affirmatively, and 17% stated that they had had the experience "several times" or "often." Comparing those who affirmed with those who denied having had this type of experience, it was found that the former were disproportionately male, Black, over 40, and college-educated, and had higher-level incomes. The researchers also found that their "mystics" reported a state of "psychological well-being substantially higher than the national average" and that the white mystics were significantly less likely to be racist than the national population.

Finally, Hay and Morisy (1978), of the Religious Experience Unit, Oxford, conducted a similar study in Great Britain. In 1976 they placed the question "Have you ever been aware of, or influenced by, a presence or power, whether referred to as God or not, which is different from your everyday self?" in one of the regular omnibus surveys conducted by National Opinion Polls, Ltd. They polled a representative sample of 1865 individuals. They found that 36% of the British population gave a positive response (males 31%; females 41%), and 6% reported the experience as occurring "often" (males 4%; females 7%). The experience was reported significantly more commonly in the higher reaches of the class scale, and there was a significant (1% level) correlation between psychological well-being (Bradburn Scale) and reports of having had RE's.

It is interesting that all three surveys agree that some 20–40% of the population at large report mystical or religious experiences and that such experiences are more commonly reported by Blacks than Whites in the two studies where the question was raised. But, whereas the NORC and Oxford teams found that frequent experiences are linked with higher social class, the Gallup Poll found the reverse. The NORC and Oxford studies also support the view that those who have such experiences enjoy better mental health than those who do not. It is clear that our knowledge of the distribution of RE's is still far from complete, and there are puzzling discrepancies. Still, a good beginning has been made.

SOME BIOPSYCHOLOGICAL INTERPRETATIONS OF RELIGIOUS EXPERIENCE

An early and still prevalent interpretation of RE's in non-supernatural terms has been to regard them as psychopathological (see Ward, this volume). Leuba (1925) was perhaps the most vocal representative of this view, which has recently been reiterated by a group of six prominent American psychiatrists (Group for the Advancement of Psychiatry, 1976). After reviewing the lives of Ramakrishna, Jacob Frank, Ignatius Loyola, and a number of modern subjects of religious experience, their conclusions may be summarized as follows: Such individuals cannot tolerate the stresses of life; they retreat from reality and invest their interest in internally generated fantasy; this retreat results in a state of mind similar to that of infancy; to compensate for the loneliness involved, the subjects join with others of like mind; they claim authority for their retreat and rebellion by asserting the authority of immediate experience of the divine, which supersedes traditional authority.

But a number of other, more positive views of the nature of RE's have also been advanced. They have been seen as regressions in the *service* of the ego (Gill & Brenman, 1959; Maupin, 1972; Prince & Savage, 1972); as representing deautomatization phenomena (Deikman, 1966); as activations of non-dominant hemispheric functions in some way (Deikman, 1980; Ornstein, 1972); or as providing a sense of certainty-of-belonging in the universe, a sense of euphoria and omnipotence (see Jilek, Krippner, this volume), which may be linked to the production under stress of the body's own morphine-like substances, the endorphins (Prince, 1982, 1984). Attitude changes, usually positive in nature, following near-death experiences have also been reported (Noyes, 1980).

A common feature of the more positive explanations of RE's is that they view them as dynamic and intelligible functions of the psyche that represent reactions to problematic life situations. The experiences help solve problems by increasing self-esteem or broadening the base of psychic functioning by increasing its repertoire of coping abilities. As such, RE's take their place alongside the organism's host of other self-righting or self-healing mechanisms. Cannon (1932) spoke of such mechanisms as illustrating the "wisdom of the body."

THE WESTMOUNT SURVEY OF RELIGIOUS EXPERIENCES

In the summer of 1982, an exploratory community survey was conducted in a high-income suburb of Montreal with the following aims: to discover through in-depth interviews what kinds of experiences individuals were referring to when they responded positively to some of the questions previously used in opinion surveys of RE; to determine the triggers and the life contexts of such experiences; to study the personality types of people reporting them (Valla, 1983).

To this end, 770 questionnaires were placed in the mailboxes of residents of the area. A covering letter explained that the researchers were interested in the ways in which people were able to make the best use of their personal resources and in the possible effects upon health of various kinds of RE. The questionnaire contained three items: (1) Have you ever discovered yourself drawing upon sources of inner strength to accomplish things you thought to be beyond your capacity? (2)Have you ever seen or heard anything so beautiful that it made you indescribably happy or sad? (3) Have you ever been aware of or influenced by a presence or power, whether referred to as God or not, which is different from your everyday self? Respondents were also asked to provide their names and phone numbers if they agreed to be interviewed.

It should be noted that the first question was included with the intention of obtaining a control group. It seemed to us to be considerably more general than the other two (which were taken from previous survey questionnaires), and we expected that many people would respond positively to the first question but negatively to the two "genuine" religious experience questions. We would then have identified groups of individuals with and without RE's from a similar quarter of the city. As it happened, this question did not serve this function, since the respondents seemed to view all three questions as different points on a continuum of intensities of experiences of a similar nature, and very few responded positively to only the first question. We therefore did not succeed in identifying a control group.

One hundred and five subjects returned the questionnaire (13.6%). Of these, 57 gave their phone numbers (7.4%). Eight of these ultimately refused to be interviewed or were out of town. Fifty-one individuals were finally interviewed; one was rejected because the tape recorder did not work and it was not possible to interview him again, and another was dropped because he did not report any RE's. The final sample was made up of 49 subjects (29 males, 20 females). The mean age was 50.3 years.[1]

On the basis of the returned questionnaires, the same psychiatrist (Valla) contacted the individuals concerned and interviewed them in their own homes. Interviews lasted for from 1 to 1½ hours. The interviews were semi-structured and focused on the experiences themselves (the accounts were tape recorded), the circumstances of the occurrence of these experiences, and the life stories of the subjects reporting them. One hundred and eighty-three experiences were reported, of which 4 had occurred following psychedelic drug intake and the remaining 179 appeared to be spontaneous. Each of the 49 subjects reported from 1 to 12 experiences. Most of them (22) reported 3 or 4 experiences.

ARE RELIGIOUS EXPERIENCES SELF-HEALING MECHANISMS?

The experiences reported by our subjects were highly diverse, and in a general way a good proportion of them could be seen as self-healing attempts in that they both occurred in stressful life situations and had positive effects on the subjects (a reorientation of values, a firm decision after a period of uncertainty, a reduction of anxiety/depression, or combinations of these outcomes). Some of the experiences were typical out-of-body states; some included visual or tactile hallucinatory elements; some were review-of-life experiences occurring when the subject was confronted by the possibility of death. Only one or two could be seen as classical nature-mystic experiences (that is, experiences in which there was a loss of ego boundaries and a euphoric feeling of all-is-oneness as described by James, 1902). Many of these experiences resulted in positive states of mind during periods of stress, as will be described below. However, there were at least a few that could not be regarded as attempts at self-healing, since they occurred in circumstances that did not call for healing; there seemed to be no obvious life crises or illness at the time of the experience. For example, some respondents reported the euphoriant effects of music and prayer while attending church services when there was no context of excessive life stress. These experiences may, therefore, be seen as prophylactic rather than therapeutic.

After considerable discussion and attempts at generalization, we concluded that previous interpretations of such experiences were not adequate for many of them. Regression or deautomatization explanations did not seem to fit most of the phenomena reported. This led us to attempt a new classification. The three most numerous types of experiences we labeled *ecstatic, aesthetic*, and *hallucinatory*. The remainder of this paper describes these types of experiences and discusses them in terms of their self-healing or prophylactic properties.

I. Ecstatic Experiences

Ecstatic experiences are those in which subjects reported standing outside of themselves, as it were, and seeing themselves, their life situations, or the world in a more or less objective manner. Whereas prior to the experience they were very much enmeshed in the ongoing stream of their lives, during these states they were able, for a brief period, to distance themselves and see themselves from outside of their bodies, or at least from outside of their social situations. Their experiences, in fact, exemplified the common classical designation for these phenomena as ecstatic states (ex-stasis, which means "standing outside of"). As will be seen, this "standing outside" mechanism resulted in a number of different self-perceptions. For some subjects (e.g., case 4 below), looking at themselves in this way was a positive experience; they were very satisfied with what they saw. On the other hand, objective viewing sometimes demonstrated that subjects' present activities and situations in life were not at all what they wished and called for a reevaluation (case 3). In still other cases, subjects perceived themselves in a fairly neutral manner (cases 1 and 2), and the ex-stasis seemed to provide a temporary haven from anxiety, permitting the subject to view his or her distressing situation with equanimity. Such a mechanism can be seen as an attempt to maintain rational control in circumstances in which consciousness might have otherwise become clouded or cognitive processes confused.

Case 1. A 54-year-old woman was returning home to her apartment late one evening. After she entered the building, a man came in behind her and attacked her with a knife. She ran to get to her apartment but could not make it in time. She described her experience as follows:

> I became two people; it was a very strange thing because, when I was there on the floor, struggling, I was not there, right? I was up here, and I was saying to myself: "I don't see how you will get out of that, you are going to be in trouble." I was up here, completely divorced, away from that person who was down there; yet I was there too and, though I knew I was having a problem there, struggling with that person, this other person up here was being very calm about the whole thing, and looking down upon it as much as if betting on whether I [would] get out of the situation. I don't know if this was a normal reaction. I was reading something about people who had died and then who came back to life, and they have a similar feeling of being out of themselves. That is really what happened to me. At that time I was out of myself in a way, and I could see myself, and it is a really weird experience.

Case 2. A 35-year-old woman had had several out-of-body experiences up until the age of 20, and indeed reported that she could bring them on at will up until that age, but not subsequently. She reported her first experience as follows:

> I had to go to the doctor, and I wasn't very happy about it. I was very young, I must have been only about six or seven years old, I remember it so well that the doctor and my mother were sitting at this table and my body was on the table but I wasn't in the body. I was looking down at them all.

Case 3. This 45-year-old artist reported two review-of-life experiences, including one as a child and one as an adult in his late twenties, which he described as follows:

I was learning to swim and I was drowning. I actually drowned. I remember being in very, very deep water—way over my head. I saw my whole life in a flash. The feeling was just amazing. I will never forget it. I was very young. It was as if all of a sudden I saw my entire previous life—all kinds of things that I had never remembered. The same thing happened another time when I was in my late twenties, when I was in an airplane and thought it was going to crash. In fact, it started to really go down. I had the exact same experience as when drowning, but since I was older I saw a lot more that had happened. I said to myself that there were certain things that played back in my life that I felt I wanted to change, and so I said if I survived this I was going to try to be different. I remember I did say to myself, "If I live through this I'm going to really change my life . . . try to do certain things . . . try to devote my life to good things." There was this feeling that you just have so many years to do what you want to do in life, and I came out of the experience feeling that my life was slipping away and that I must do the things that I want to do. It conveys ideals that I have for myself—wishes and ideals and desires that I've developed over the years that I feel I haven't quite fulfilled and that I would like to realize.

Case 4. After several years of travel, this middle-aged woman, who had two daughters, finally found that the right place to live was in Salisbury. She had intended to remarry but had decided that this was not the right thing to do. In Salisbury she had also at last found a congenial occupation. After settling there, she described her habit of rising early in the morning to contemplate the beauty of the town and her newfound situation:

I would just spend this half hour in what I called peaceful contemplation, and on one occasion—I must have been there about a month, at least—I suddenly felt absolutely empty of myself, if I can put it that way, and felt something outside myself that was flowing through me—took me over completely—I can't think of any other way to explain it. And I didn't know if this was God or what influence it was, all I know is it was a glorious, happy experience, completely and absolutely happy. I suppose it lasted perhaps a minute—five minutes—I just don't know.

I don't say that it made me believe in God again—I don't think it was that at all. I still cannot say I believe implicitly in anything, but at the same time I am very conscious of the fact that there is something that we don't know about that may or does influence our lives . . . This absolute knowledge that it was not me inside with reasoning thought or anything like that . . . I just felt no knowledge of myself at all . . . It was something else that had almost taken over my mind as absolutely quiet and still, and it passed, and I can't tell you the length of time—it couldn't have been very long, because I was at my work at the usual time and so on—and all it did for me was make me feel intensely, intensely happy, at peace, no worries. I'd plenty of worries, but no worries at all—absolutely at peace with myself.

II. Aesthetic Experiences

The preceding four examples fall fairly clearly into the ecstatic category as defined above. The next three examples seem to be of a different sort, though perhaps on the same continuum. They were probably in response to the second of our survey questions: Have you ever seen or heard anything so beautiful that it made you indescribably happy or sad? In varying degrees, although they refer to a kind of distancing from present life circumstances that is similar to some aspects of the ecstatic experiences, there is also a viewing of the world for a fleeting moment as a structure of perfection, beauty, or timelessness. In some ways they could better be considered aesthetic experiences; in all three, attention is fixed upon certain concrete images that symbolize an idealized experience of self-in-the-world. All are experiences that deeply impress the subjects to the extent that they are remembered and cherished for life. Whether or not they should be included in the category of ex-stasis experiences is perhaps debatable, but they indicate a rather special ego response of joyful distancing that generates a reconciliation with the pressures and imperfections of mundane existence. In these examples, the subjects were not living in particularly stressful life circumstances, so that the experiences could more accurately be described as prophylactic than self-healing.

Case 5. A middle-aged male went on a walking expedition in Chile. Each evening he found himself exhausted but happy at having achieved his daily trekking goal:

> So you're sitting there and taking all this in, and you've got the time, the inclination, and the inspiration to absorb it. In other words, the same things in a different surrounding, if you don't give yourself the time (you're too busy going to the next appointment or thinking about the last appointment), you might not be able to appreciate it. Here is a setting where you can completely devote yourself to it. I remember once, I saw a couple of eagles—wingspan larger than my arms stretched out. I hadn't seen eagles before, and just to watch how grace-

fully they floated in the air and how they could dive and dance: different, new, beautiful, it does touch you. There is a great feeling of serenity, extreme serenity. Are you familiar with the expression "See Paris and die"? Well, to a certain extent that held true. I haven't finished in my life all the things that I wanted to finish and all the things that I wanted to do, but at that particular point, I could not say that it would have upset me to feel that I was going to sleep and not wake up—at peace, really at peace and relaxed. I had a sort of a tranquility, a peacefulness, where if it all stopped, well so be it, let it stop.

Case 6. A 50-year-old woman had made a journey up the Li-Kiang River, near Kweilin in China.

It was a feeling of real serenity, and I can remember that I thought: "This is truly one of the great wonders of the world, and I'm seeing something that I will never come back to again," and I wanted to take it all in, and I kept very still, letting it all come in and listening to the sounds.

We went on this boat trip. It was incredibly beautiful. I felt like I was going back in time; all the other traffic in the river was the same type. They looked to me from a thousand years ago, timeless, people on them, you couldn't tell their age. It was very much like looking at a movie, it seemed unreal, and the landscape was just something that I had not seen before, the mountains were very, very strange peaks sticking up very high; they almost came over the boat going through a canyon.

I was on a kind of steamer, just the sound of the boat and the sound of the motors in the water, and the water—it didn't create much of a wave at all—the water was just like glass, and the boat was cutting its way through this glass. It was very, very still. In fact, I took a photo of this, and the reflection on the water is sharper and clearer than real life. The water was a perfect mirror, and people were very quiet, people were enjoying it, and what's also important is the feeling inside. You have to have the feeling of empathy.

Case 7. A 60-year-old nurse described an experience in a Montreal park involving her granddaughter.

I have the picture in that album. Candy had a sweater which is a deep, deep, deep sage-green. I took her to the park, and she was climbing on the climbing frame, and she was right on the top of it. The red climbing frame. This was last winter. There were no leaves on the trees, and then, suddenly, some children ran into the park with a red and sage-green kite the same colors as the climbing frame and the sweater, and it flew up behind her. And it is not that sort of feeling where you say:

"Oh, isn't that pretty, look, it is the same colors." You say: "God, I will never forget this." That is why it is so terribly important to live in places where there is either God's beauty, countryside, or there is man-made beauty. Almost every season, not every day, but every week at least, there is some color, some motion of the trees or something which is perfect.

I think after the experience you just feel calmer and happier than usual. I think the capacity to recognize this makes your life what it is. If you are taught to look and think, as a child, then that changes your life from what it would be if you had never been taught, because it means that wherever you go, whatever you do, there will always be these moments of joy.

III. Hallucinatory Experiences

The distinctive feature of the next three examples is that the subjects each experienced a transitory hallucination or illusion. The subjects were under a considerable degree of life stress associated with conflicts over decisions that involved long-term life plans. They had posed questions to themselves, and the experiences provided them with answers that they had had difficulty arriving at on their own, in all three examples, the subjects felt they had received supernatural aid. In many ways these experiences are parallel to divination procedures that are institutionalized in many cultures but that we have abandoned in the Western world (see, for example, Kiev, 1964). These experiences may be considered self-healing mechanisms in that the subjects are assisted in resolving anxiety-laden life decisions.

Case 8. A 36-year-old wife and mother who was sojourning in England with her husband and family was torn between pursuing her career as a painter and devoting herself full-time to being a housewife. At the time of the experience, her art work was on display in an exhibition, and she was somewhat discouraged by its public reception:

I was looking out the window and thinking really seriously: "Should I really do this? Should I give up painting or not?" It seemed to be such a struggle all the time, trying to keep the family together, and what good was it? There was a convent nearby which included a priest's school for children. This day, out the window, I saw the children coming down the street, two by two. I had seen them lots of times before, and they seemed to be going to a little museum across the street. I was thinking: "Should I stop this? Sometimes artists can become very self-ish, maybe it's not really right." As they walked along, just like a flash the children's clothes changed. I saw their headgear, like stocking caps, the kind they used to wear in Quebec—toques—and boots, rubbers, just slopping along. I could even hear the slopping.

It was over in a flash. I knew at the same time as I saw this that these were children going to see the exhibition that I was having. And, suddenly, I knew that I should keep working.

What happened in England is that I really was asking, "Should I continue?" When you are a painter, you can go for years without sell-ing anything, and sometimes it is difficult with a family. Then it came. Just a flash. I saw them in a kind of vision. It was just like that, although something else was there: a wonderful, loving sort of feeling, altogether a good feeling. All my horrible dread just left me. I still had to do the work, but I had that conviction that it was worthwhile.

I couldn't understand it; it was very mysterious, really. It was very clear that I should keep going. I didn't bother about trying to under-stand it. It doesn't matter if I don't understand, I knew what to do now. Just like when you're driving somewhere and you get lost and look up your map and see where to go, you don't worry about it.

I would say it was a religious experience, because I was really ask-ing for help. It was like a camera clicking, with the same scene, the same people in the same position, only they had different clothes. I saw the children, I had three of my own then, and looking at the line of children it sort of mixed up with my love for the children and the fam-ily. It was like everyday life, everything was the same, but the colors were just more intense.

I felt completely at peace afterwards. The whole thing cannot be separated: seeing them and knowing what it meant. It didn't seem strange at the time, and it was enough for me to keep on working. The funny thing was about three years later, when we came back to Can-ada, I was asked to have an exhibition. It was winter. One day the prin-cipal phoned me from the school and said: "I'm sending one of the classes down, would you be there and answer their questions?" I walked over, and as I was walking over, along came this line of stu-dents with caps, scarves, and boots—and that was what I had seen about three years earlier in England.

Case 9. A fifty-year-old male Hungarian shopkeeper had moved to East Germany after World War II and was having difficulty mak-ing up his mind whether to leave the country or remain and con-tinue with his ailing business.

During my days in Germany, it was very hard. I had been in Hungary for the years before and I feared Communists. Business was bad.

Then I used to go to church and to pray to St. Taddeus. And I asked him for an omen: "If you will help me, let me know, give me a sign." Then, the statue moved its head. I was very strained, and it may have been an effect of my imagination, but I saw it moving and I believe that it really moved towards me. I knew then I should leave and come to Canada.

Case 10. A middle-aged businessman was working in England and had fallen in love with an English girl he hoped to marry. His father, at home in Canada, had suffered a heart attack, and he was torn between returning to his father before he died and staying in England to pursue his girlfriend, who was unable to accompany him to Canada. In the midst of this conflict he was struck by a car in London:

The experience was the result of a car accident in which I broke my leg and fractured my skull. I went through the car windshield and made a big mess on the road. I was unconscious for ten days. They gave me an anaesthetic to keep me unconscious because my jaw was broken, and my nose was broken and my teeth, and they stuck them all back in. The waking experience, coming back from—well, I was considered by the doctors as likely to die—coming back from death was a very profound experience in my life, because I felt the tremendous surge of energy, the need, the will to be alive. The other thing was the sense of being in a light tunnel—the tunnel effect I've heard described by other people. In my experience, I got the sense of being in a tunnel and moving towards a light and then the surge of the will to be alive. This was a very deep experience and made me feel that there is purpose in being alive.

It was almost as though there was a battle inside me. I could feel the sides. It wasn't my decision, it wasn't my control, it was something else, something beyond me, and that's part of the joy of coming alive. The gift of life, because I really was a dead man, and it was just that balance on the head of a pin. I could have died, or I could have lived, but I came to the life side. The most important question of that whole thing was that it wasn't something that I had anything to do with. I'm repeating myself, I know, but this is so deep and profound that I really felt the struggle of my own willingness to die, or the willingness to live, and the pressure was that I wanted to live, a force, the force, the energy, not my decision, I didn't decide that, it was decided beyond me. For some reason I knew then I should return to my father before he died.

The next experience should perhaps not be included in the "hallucinatory" category, since it did not quite reach hallucinatory intensity. It was also different from the other three in that the subject was not in the throes of a decision with long-term consequences. We have included it here because it seems to be on a continuum with the other three experiences in some respects.

Case 11. A 30-year-old woman who had long-term conflicts with her family, particularly with her alcoholic father, was somewhat guilty over the fact that she had left home at the age of 18 and abandoned her mother to a very unsatisfactory life with her father.

> The only time I can really say I had a religious experience is when my mother was dying. I knew she was gone before the medical people. I literally sensed the "Presence" taking her soul. She died a terrible death. I happened to be closer to her than anyone. My mother and father's marriage was very bad. Dad had been drinking very heavily for a number of years.
>
> Anyway, Mum just ended up being very sick and going in for a normal operation and never coming out of it. I think her only defense to Dad was to be sick. I've always been between my Mum and Dad, sort of smoothing over the waters, when I was around. I wasn't around that much—I took off when I was 18. When Mum died, it was one of these things where they kept cutting her open and operating, and she was on every life support system in intensive care, and I was horrified.
>
> The nurse said: "Would you mind waiting in the office? We are working on your Mum at this point." They didn't want me around, so I walked into the office and made myself a hot chocolate. I was sitting there with this cup in my hand, and it wasn't anything I saw but something I sensed, maybe it had to do with some paintings I'd seen, but I could sense this Presence with Mum by the hand, leaving, and a minute later the nurse walked in and said: "You can go back now." I went into my mother's room, and they were just covering her up and checking her blood pressure.
>
> I think it was an assurance to me that He had taken her—that Mum had finally earned her peace because she didn't lead a peaceful life. It was a very peaceful feeling. You are right with everyone, something comes to tell you: "I am with you. Everything is going to be all right no matter how bad things are."

DISCUSSION

We have presented 11 examples of the kinds of religious experiences ordinary people referred to when they responded positively to the kinds of questions surveyors have asked in public opinion polls about religious experiences. We have clustered these in three categories on the basis of certain family resemblances. In addition, we have asked the question whether these experiences can be regarded as examples of endogenous healing mechanisms. A number of points warrant further discussion and examination.

What features had these experiences in common? Almost all of them were of very brief duration—from a few moments to a few minutes. But in spite of their brevity, they were almost all of great significance to the subjects. They were extraordinary states of consciousness that had occurred only a few times in a lifetime and were highly memorable. Many of the subjects spoke of their experiences with considerable intensity and affect, even though they had occurred long before.

Although these experiences shared these similarities, in other ways they were quite diverse, and we had great difficulty trying to cluster them in satisfactory categories. We have roughly grouped them in ecstatic, aesthetic, and hallucinatory categories, but there are many intermediate types that share the features of more than one category. Cases 1 and 2, the out-of-body experiences, are clearly ecstatic by our definition. But case 3, the review-of-life experience, is less clearly ex-static, and case 4 even less so; the subject did report a kind of distancing of herself from everyday life, yet she emphasized the feeling of being pervaded by an outside agency— "Something else . . . had almost taken over my mind"—and did not hint at the idea of being outside of her body looking on. Case 10, the tunnel experience, could possibly be labeled ecstatic. The cluster of aesthetic experiences (cases 5–7) seem similar one to the other, and in some ways case 4 is somewhere between an ecstatic and an aesthetic experience. Finally, cases 8–10 are clearly members of a family in which hallucinatory elements are the distinguishing feature. Case 11, on the other hand, is a variant in that the experience of the mother's soul being led away by the hand hardly reached visual intensity.

As has been noted by many authors, our Western worldview does not encourage or institutionalize alternate states of consciousness. The lack of differentiation in our array of Westmount religious experiences may be seen as the result of our Western denigration of such states. Bourguignon (1973) and others have dichotomized alternate states around the world as either trance states (T) or possession-trance states (PT). T states are exemplified by shamanic experiences that include flight-of-the-soul (out-of-body) experiences, hallucinations, and ability to recall the experience; PT states, as exemplified by a wide variety of ritual possession trances, are characterized by emic interpretations of the taking over of the personality by deities and by amnesia for the episode. In reflecting upon our Westmount experiences, we could categorize our out-of-body and hallucinatory experiences as underdeveloped T states that lack institutional support and patterning. The experiences of case 4, the Salisbury mother, could perhaps be seen as a kind of inchoate PT, as suggested by her experience of being pervaded by another personality. Bourguignon (1985) has recently emphasized the idea that all humans are equipotential as regards alternate states of consciousness and that the kinds of religious experiences found in a given culture depend upon which kinds of experiences are expected, rewarded, and institutionalized (see also Lambek, this volume). This view would receive support from our Westmount findings.

Regarding the healing and prophylactic functions of the spontaneous religious experiences reported here, the preceding remarks about their institutionalization support previous suggestions (Prince, 1976) that healers around the world have shaped and developed these spontaneous experiences to arrive at highly elaborated healing systems (Katz, Krippner, and Lee, this volume). Meditation traditions, drum- and dance-related trance systems, and healing practices employing psychedelic drugs are well-known examples.

CONCLUSIONS

In this chapter, we have attempted to explore the view that religious experiences are endogenous psychological healing mechanisms analogous to the host of well-known mechanisms for the preservation of bodily homeostasis as described by Cannon (1932) and many others. Body temperature, blood sugar, and acid base levels, and blood pressure and pulse rate, to mention but a few, are all maintained within strict limits by diverse self-righting mechanisms. We have interpreted religious experiences as similar homeostatic mechanisms for the stabilization of self-esteem. We have examined a number of religious experiences as they were reported by an upper-middle-class population during the course of a community survey. Subjects were interviewed about their personal experiences and the life context in which they occurred. In a goodly proportion of cases, these experiences could be interpreted in terms of this self-healing hypothesis. We conclude that the interpretation of religious experiences as self-healing mechanisms does make sense in a high proportion of cases and that the concept is well worth further exploration.

NOTE

1. Obviously, the present study is not epidemiological, and the experiences reported here are not representative of any given population; nor are they intended to provide any idea of the frequency of such experiences in any given population. We merely provide a tentative answer to the question: When people have responded positively to religious experience questions in previous surveys (reported in this chapter), what types of experiences could they have been referring to?

REFERENCES

Back, K. W., & Bourque, L. B. (1970). Can feelings be enumerated? *Behavioral Science, 15,* 487-496.

Bourguignon, E. (Ed.). (1973). *Religion, altered states of consciousness and social change.* Columbus: Ohio State University Press.

Bourguignon, E. (1985). Multiple personality, possession trance, and psychic unity. In H. P. Duerr (Ed.), *Die wilde Sele.* Frankfurt: Syndikat.

Bucke, R. M. (1901). *Cosmic consciousness.* Philadelphia: Innis.

Cannon, W. B. (1932). *The wisdom of the body.* New York: Norton.

Deikman, A. J. (1966). De-automatization and the mystic experience. *Psychiatry, 29,* 324-338.

Deikman, A. J. (1980). Bimodal consciousness and the mystic experience. In R. Woods (Ed.), *Understanding mysticism* (pp. 261-269). New York: Doubleday.

Douglas-Smith, B. (1971). An empirical study of religious mysticism. *British Journal of Psychiatry, 118,* 549-554.

Gill, M. M., & Brenman, M. (1959). *Hypnosis and related states: Psychoanalytic studies in regression.* New York: John Wiley.

Greeley, A. M., & McCready, W. C. (1973). The sociology of mystical ecstasy: Some preliminary notes. Paper presented at the meeting of the Society for the Scientific Study of Religion, San Francisco.

Group for the Advancement of Psychiatry. (1976). *Mysticism: Spiritual quest or psychic disorder?* (Vol. 9, Publication No. 97). New York: Group for the Advancement of Psychiatry.

Hay, C., & Morisy, A. (1978). Reports of ecstatic, paranormal or religious experience in Great Britain and the United States: A comparison of trends. *Journal for the Scientific Study of Religion, 17,* 225-268.

James, W. (1902). *The varieties of religious experience.* New York: Longmans Green.

Kiev, A. (Ed.). (1964). *Magic, faith and healing.* New York: Free Press.

Laski, M. (1961). *Ecstasy: A study of some secular and religious experiences.* London: Cresset Press.

Leuba, J. H. (1925). *The psychology of religious mysticism.* London: Routledge & Kegan Paul.

Maslow, A. H. (1959). Cognition of being in the peak experiences. *Journal of Genetic Psychology, 94,* 43-66.

Maupin, E. W. (1972). Zen Buddhism: A psychological review. In J. White (Ed.), *The highest state of consciousness* (pp. 204-224). New York: Doubleday.

Noyes, R. (1980). Attitude change following near-death experiences. *Psychiatry, 43,* 234-242.

Ornstein, R. E. (1972). *The psychology of consciousness.* San Francisco: Freeman.

Prince, R. H. (1976). Psychotherapy as the manipulation of endogenous healing mechanisms: A transcultural survey. *Transcultural Psychiatric Research Review, 8,* 115-133.

Prince, R. H. (Ed.). (1982). Shamans and endorphins [Special issue]. *Ethos, 10,* 299-409.

Prince, R. H. (1984). Shamans and endorphins/exogenous and endogenous factors in psychotherapy. In P. B. Pederson, N. Sartorius, & A. J. Marsella (Eds.), *Mental health services: The cross-cultural context* (pp. 59-77). Beverly Hills, CA: Sage.

Prince, R. H., & Savage, C. (1972). Mystical states and the concept of regression. In J. White (Ed.), *The highest state of consciousness* (pp. 114-134). New York: Doubleday.

Sinclair, R. D. (1928). A comparative study of those who report the experience of the Divine Presence and those who do not. *Iowa Studies of Character, 2,* 9-63.

Valla, J. P. (1983). *Survey of spontaneous religious experience in a Montreal community: A pilot study.* Unpublished master's thesis. McGill University, Montreal.

8

THERAPEUTIC USE OF ALTERED STATES OF CONSCIOUSNESS IN CONTEMPORARY NORTH AMERICAN INDIAN DANCE CEREMONIALS

WOLFGANG G. JILEK

In this chapter, observations on sociocultural phenomena are presented in the light of physiological and psychological theories. I hope to demonstrate by the example of three contemporary North American Indian dance ceremonials that traditional therapeutic principles, developed in a specific non-Western cultural and historical context, confirm the transcultural validity of theoretical propositions of modern physiology and psychology regarding altered states of consciousness and their relationship to mental health.

PARADIGM I: SALISH SPIRIT DANCING

The winter spirit dances are the major ritual activity of Salishan-speaking Indians of the Pacific Coast of North America. The Salish Indians regard winter as the appropriate time for ceremonies, a time when vitality is weakened, to be strengthened again by the annual return of the Spirit Powers. While much of traditional Salish Indian culture crumbled, the ceremonial was performed clandestinely by older people and survived in spite of previous efforts by government, church, and school authorities to suppress this "pagan" ritual under the "Law against Potlatch and Tamanawas Dancing" (Section 3, Statutes of Canada, 1884). Spirit dancing was openly revived in the 1960s and today has all the characteristics of a growing nativistic movement.

Prior to suppression of the spirit dance ceremonial, initiation to the winter spirit dances was a necessary test and collective confirmation of powers that the candidate had already acquired as an adolescent in months or years of individual spirit quest. Today, in the revived ceremonial, the initiation itself is the way to acquire power for self-healing. The major purpose of the initiation process is now to cure serious psychosomatic, psychosocial, and behavioral disturbances of young Salish Indian people who are seen as suffering from *spirit illness* due to alienation from traditional "Indian ways." The major purpose of continuing participation in the annual winter dances is to strengthen the self-healing power and to maintain a wholesome state of mind and body.

Salish ritualists consider Amerindian persons suffering from depression, anxiety, and somatic complaints that are unresponsive to Western treatment, as well as young Amerindians with behavioral, alcohol, and drug problems, as candidates for spirit dance initiation. Such persons often manifest the *anomic depression* syndrome of psychic, somatizing, and behavioral symptom formation in the context of cultural and social deprivation (Jilek, 1982). The indigenous diagnosis of this condition as spirit illness permits reidentification of an alienated person with aboriginal culture, as does indigenous treatment via initiation into spirit dancing.

The death-and-rebirth myth is the central theme of the collective suggestions surrounding the spirit-dance initiation. According to contemporary Salish theory, it is the spirit power that acts through the initiator on the initiates, and it is this spirit power, not the initiator, that cures the novices, burying their ailments and conflicts together with the old personality and at the same time giving them rebirth into a new life. As the shaman's healing craft has to be sanctioned by supernatural powers (Jilek, 1971), so the initiator here is a healer by the power of the guardian spirit. As an instrument of the guardian spirit, the initiating ritualist is empowered to "club to death" the initiates' faulty and diseased old selves, to let them awaken with a new potential for total change, and to guide them on the path of Salish tradition through the teaching of their elders. Not only are the "newborn" initiates called "babies," they are also treated as such: bathed, fed, and dressed, constantly attended and guarded by "babysitters." Regression to a state of complete infantile dependency is at first imposed on the initiates, who, in the quasi-uterine shelter of a dark longhouse cubicle, hatch their power, prepared to grow with it into a more rewarding and healthier existence. Henceforth, they will count their spiritual age from the day initiation started.

In the whole process of initiation, three major therapeutic approaches can be discerned: (1) depatterning through shock treatment, followed by (2) physical training, with (3) indocrination.[1] The candidates, young men and women, are kept in the longhouse, secluded in a dark cubicle or "smokehouse tent" for a period of usually 10 days. The length of the seclusion, which after four days of passive endurance is interrupted by frequent strenuous exercises, varies with candidates and ritualists. This is dependent on the novice's motivation and unconscious or conscious cooperation in "finding the song and dance"—the professed aim of the initiation process. The principal therapeutic functions of this process—personality depatterning and reorientation—are not unknown to the ritualists. In the words of a senior participant:

> It is an Indian treatment, it is a kind of brainwashing, four to ten days of torture. Through this torture they soften up, their brain gets soft. During that time you're the weakest and your brain is back to nil, anything you're taught during those ten days is going to stick with you, you'll never forget it.[2]

Personality depatterning starts with an initial shock treatment known as the "clubbing," "grabbing," or "doctoring up" of the candidate, which is aimed at rapid induction of an altered state of consciousness. In the cases I observed, this was performed on male candidates only. The repeated and prolonged treatment included sudden bodily seizure of the allegedly unsuspecting candidate; immobilization of his limbs by physical restraints; blindfolding, hitting, biting, and tickling of exposed body parts (abdomen, sides, foot soles). At the same time the candidate was subjected to kinetic stimulation (lifted up and dropped, hurriedly carried around the longhouse, whirled about and swayed) and to intensive acoustic stimulation (loud drumming and rattling in rapid rhythms, singing and howling close to his ears). This "grabbing" procedure was repeated at least four times; each time the eight "workers" completed four circles around the longhouse hall with their candidate, whose moaning cries became progressively weaker until he appeared lifeless, pale, and rigid when finally bedded in the cubicle.

Through the four days of the depatterning phase, the initiates are blindfolded. They are required to lie still, forbidden to talk or to move even in sleep, as they sweat under heavy covers on the fringes of which sit the so-called "babysitters." The initiates are starved, and their fluid intake is restricted; at the same time they are "teased" and "tested" with tasty salmon bits held close to their mouth. They are daily exposed to a reenactment of the "grabbing" procedure in order to make them "die" again. The novice's reentry into the desired altered state of consciousness is facilitated by the ceremonial workers' frequent "singing and drumming to the baby." These maneuvers aim at bringing forth the novice's "song." While lying in the "tent," the initiate perceives song, dance movements, and face painting in a state between sleep-dream and wakefulness.

The strict regime of what is called "sacrifice and torture" is continued until the initiate "gets the song straight," to be duly invested then with the traditional "uniform, hat and stick," outward signs of rebirth. The guardian spirit itself appears in a dream to the novice in the longhouse cubicle or in a visionary experience under conditions of physical exertion in the context of the training that follows the initiate's investiture. The phase of physical training is associated with intense indoctrination and is supposed to "make the newborn baby strong." It consists of daily "runs" around the longhouse hall or outside, often barefoot in snow; daily swimming (the new dancers are expected to jump into ice-cold waters and then rub their bodies with cedar boughs); and frequent rounds of dancing in the longhouse to the fast rhythms of many drums, driving the novices to exhaustion. Released from their incubation, the initiates feel their newly acquired power when the song bursts forth from them and the leaping steps of their first dance carry them through the longhouse, while they are spurred on by the rhythms of deerhide drums and the chanting and clapping of the crowd. To modern spirit dancers this blissful experience may appear comparable to that of altered states of consciousness induced by opiates:

> I was jumping three feet high, and I had such a thrill, a terrific feeling as if you were floating, as if you were in the air, you feel really high. I've only had such a feeling once before in my life, when I was on heroin mainlining, but then I went through hell afterwards, it was terrible; but with the spirit song's power you get this feeling without the terrible aftermath.[3]

Physical analysis of records of drumming revealed that rhythmic drumming encompasses a frequency range from 0.8 to 5.0 cycles per second with a mean frequency of 2.95 cps.[4] One-third of the recorded frequencies are above 3.0 cps, i.e. within or close to the frequency of the theta waves of the human electroencephalogram. Frequencies in this range are entirely predominant in drumming during initiation procedures. As a stimulus frequency in the theta range of the EEG (4 to 7 cps) is expected to be most effective in the production of trance states, Neher (1962) assumed drumming rhythms close to such frequencies to be preponderant in ceremonies associated with trance behavior. The analysis of our data confirms this hypothesis as far as contemporary Salish Indian spirit dancing is concerned.

Modern spirit dancers refer to the initiation as a salutary learning experience: "It teaches you physical, emotional, and mental well-being." While much of this is learning through nonverbal conditioning processes, theoretical indoctrination also plays an important role. It includes the direct teaching of the rules and sanctions of spirit power as well as the indirect reinforcement of collective suggestion through recounting of traditional lore presenting examples of the works of spirit, or "spiritual" power. It also includes what may be called culture propaganda, which is instrumental in helping the young Amerindian person to achieve a positive cultural identification.

The initiation process ends with the disrobing ceremony. The therapeutic implication of this ceremony is that it documents the candidate's successful cure from spirit illness through a duly performed initiation treatment. Together with the uniform, the initiate sheds the last vestiges of the old personality "as the snake sloughs off its old skin." The new dancer is presented to the public as yet another testifier to the healing and regenerating power of the guardian spirit.

Not only for those who have become active spirit dancers through initiation, and therefore continue to dance on frequent occasions each subsequent winter season, but also for their relatives and for many other Salish families who are involved in the ceremonial, the winter time now brings every year an immersion in seasonal spirit dance therapy, a complex therapeutic enterprise that in scope and duration is unparalleled in non-Indian society. The ceremonial combines the following therapeutic modes:

(1) *Occupational and activity therapy* by involving participants in a meaningful, goal-directed, and rewarding activity with healthy physical exercise during the vocational off-season.

(2) *Group therapy* by providing support, protection, acceptance, and stimulation, and, most relevantly, by turning the participant from egocentric preoccupation to group concerns and the pursuit of collective goals.

(3) *Cathartic abreaction* through the tension-releasing effect of "singing out one's song" in an affective discharge watched by a sympathetic audience.

(4) *Psychodrama* when at every dance the spirit dancer reenters an altered state of consciousness to feel and display the power of his guardian spirit by dramatized emotional expression in dance steps, tempo, miens, and gestures.

(5) *Direct ego support* resulting from the positive attention and encouragement that the ritualist leaders and the audience focus on the active dancer throughout the winter ceremonial (see also Ward, this volume).

Specific shamanic curing rites are also observed during the dances, for noninitiated patients requiring immediate therapeutic attention. Today the main area for traditional Amerindian therapy is that of conditions in which psychoreactive and psychophysiological mechanisms are prominent. In Amerindian clients the therapeutic effectiveness of indigenous treatment methods compares favorably with current Western therapies as far as such conditions are concerned, and with Western correctional management of behavior disorders associated with alcohol or drug abuse (Jilek, 1982).

PARADIGM II: SUN DANCE

The Sun Dance originated with the Plains Algonquians around 1700, diffused throughout the Plains tribes, and in the early 1800s became the most magnificent aboriginal ceremonial of this culture area, involving complex group rites associated with mythological themes revolving around war and the bison hunt. Sun Dances drew a large number of participants—dancers, singers, drummers, and spectators. Men danced for three to four days and nights, undergoing fasting, thirst, mutilation, and self-mortification in their quest for power and success in the hunt and in warfare. As Indian resistance to "Manifest Destiny" was finally overcome by the military might of dominant society in the United States and as there were no more bison to hunt, the traditional Sun Dance lost its function. By 1881 the Sioux Sun Dance was officially banned by the authorities on Pine Ridge Reservation, South Dakota. A desperate last effort to stem the white tide by resort to the supernatural means of the Ghost Dance religion ended with the bloody suppression of the Sioux outbreak of 1890. Around that time the shamans of the Wind River Shoshone of Wyoming shifted the concern of the Sun Dance from warfare and the hunt to the curing of illness and social misery. In doing this, they followed the lead of a Sun Dance chief who had been instructed by a dream vision to redirect the ceremonial.

In his historical analysis, Jorgensen (1972) concludes that the failure of the *transformative* movement (Aberle, 1966) of the Ghost Dance, which has aimed at a total change in the supraindividual system, led the ritualist leaders of the Shoshone to "retool" the old Sun Dance ceremonial. They changed the ceremonial into a therapeutic instrument dealing with health and community problems that, directly or indirectly, were the results of the white intrusion (see also Lambek and Stoller, this volume, for a discussion of the emergence of altered states of consciousness in relation to political and social factors). Under the vision-inspired guidance of the shamans, and in response to the deprivations of the early reservation period, the Sun Dance developed into a *redemptive* movement (Aberle, 1966) aimed at promoting a total change in individuals. As such a therapeutic movement, the Sun Dance continued on a small scale among the Shoshone and Ute of the central Rocky Mountains and Great Basin. It experienced a revitalization in the late 1950s and by the mid-1960s was flourishing as the major religious movement of Amerindian tribes in Wyoming, Idaho, Utah, and Colorado.

The focus of the Sun Dance religion is the asquisition of supernatural power. Power is sought for one's own health and for the community, to comfort the suffering and bereaved, or to dispel evil influences. We can define this as shamanic power and state that the Sun Dance has the characteristic features of shamanic initiation: calling and instruction by dream visions; guidance and teaching by a shaman; ordeal experience with fasting, thirst, pain, and privation; and finally questing for and receiving a personal vision in the last dance (see Krippner, this volume).

Since the Sioux Sun Dance was revived in the early 1960s (Nurge, 1966), several hundred participants and large crowds of spectators gather annually in August at Pine Ridge Reservation, South Dakota. The formerly outlawed self-mortification feature is now included in the revived ceremonies. Participants take sacred vows to dance with pierced flesh in consecutive annual ceremonies. After purification in the sweat lodge and the passing of the peace pipe, the dancers enter the arena in a procession led by a man carrying a buffalo skull and by the Sun Dance chief, the shaman-director who traditionally determines the course of the ritual procedures. Accompanied by rhythmic chanting and drumming, the dancers, blowing their eagle-bone whistles, dance four times in each cardinal direction, alternately charging toward and retreating from the center pole. Dancers who took the vow are tied to the center pole by a thong that the chief inserts in their chests. Holding on to a protective staff, they dance until "breaking the flesh." The contemporary Sun Dance is usually conducted throughout three days and three nights. In addition to the dancers, it involves teams of singer-drummers and many spectators who comfort and encourage the dancers. The great majority of Sun Dancers are male. Women play an important role in the Sun Dance teams but are in general not encouraged to dance themselves (Jorgensen, 1972). However, since the revival of the ceremonial, female dancers have been observed at Sioux Sun Dances on the Rosebud Reservation, South Dakota, and at Ute-Shoshone Sun Dances in Fort Hall, Utah. The shamanic Sun Dance chiefs not only plan and direct the ceremonies, but also guide the initiation process of new dancers. Among the Ute, shamans validate the candidate's calling by analyzing and interpreting dreams and offering counseling.

Sun Dance initiates among the Shoshone and Ute are instructed by their chief to dance at least twice in each of 12 ceremonials, to acquire supernatural power slowly over the years, to learn to control each dose of power before seeking more, and to exercise great caution in the use of supernatural power. Dancers must abstain from alcohol and from peyote. Other commandments oblige the Sun Dance participants to act in the interest of their people, to be generous and kind, to be respectful to their elders, and to be mindful of the integrity of traditional "Indian ways." During the ceremonials, shamans and leaders exhort dancers and audience to "maintain the beauty of Indian life." Railing against the materialism of the dominant white society, they belittle its forces in comparison with the supernatural "Indian power." Again, this is an exact analogy to what occurs at other contemporary Amerindian ceremonials, where the longhouses echo with the appeals of an emerging pan-Indian nationalism based on the assertion of an inherent superiority of Amerindian over white American culture, a nativistic culture propaganda based on opposition mythology (Jilek, 1977; see Stoller, this volume). There is identity and ego-strengthening significance in such teaching for many a culturally drifting young Amerindian person whose self-esteem has been undermined by experiences in the majority society.

In entering an altered state of consciousness, the vision-seeking Sun Dancer is helped by intensive rhythmic drumming in high frequencies close to the frequency range used in drumming during Salish Spirit Dance initiation. A stimulus frequency in the theta range of the human EEG is conducive to the production of altered states of consciousness via auditory driving in conjunction with other physiological features present in both ceremonials. At the Sun Dance, the dancer questing for a vision is encouraged by the other dancers, who blow their whistles while women in the audience beat willow wands in time and men yell war whoops. Dancing vigorously with quickening tempo for one hour or more, dancers finally receive a vision; seized by a jolt of power, they are lifted from their feet and thrown to the ground, where the "stone-cold," power-filled body lies motionless during the soul's archetypal shamanic journey.

Fellow dancers carry the visionaries to their stalls and position their heads toward the pole in the center of the "Thirst House" or Sun Dance corral. The central pole resembles a bare tree (cf. the classical *arbor vitae*) and is a source of power as well as the medium through which supernatural power is channeled. This power is symbolically equated with water but is derived from the sun's rays in daytime and from the light of the moon and the sacred fire at night. A "nest of water" in the form of a bundle of willows is placed in the crotch of the pole, and a bison head or stuffed eagle is attached below. Both are endowed with power and are also channels through which power flows. A dirt altar at the base of the pole represents the life-giving earth.

As in the Salish spirit dance ceremonial, specific shamanizing curing rites are also part of the Sun Dance. The people assist the shaman's curing through their "good hearts," uniting their minds in an effort at collective empathy. In the same manner, nondancing participants concentrate on the dancers and meditate about the power the dancers seek to win. The dancers feel supported by this well-meaning group spirit. At the end of the annual Sun Dance, a final blessing by respected shamans validates the power the dancers have obtained during the ceremonial. The ritual functions are then concluded as the dancers partake of the sacred water that has been blessed by the Water Chief.

The information I obtained in interviews with Sun Dance participants and the research data collected by Jorgensen (1972) provide evidence for the psychosociotherapeutic function of the Sun Dance, which can be defined in general terms as providing a means of achieving spiritual and emotional well-being, responsibility, and self-esteem when Amerindian people may find such feelings difficult to experience in North American society.

PARADIGM III: GOURD DANCE

Toward the end of the 1950s a revival of traditional Plains Indian medicine societies started among the Kiowa and extended to other tribes. The old pattern of medicine societies in the form of intertribal alliances such as the Black Leggings Society or the Flint and Dog Soldiers had been reestablished. From the 1960s both the revived traditional dance ceremonials and the syncretic religions have increasingly become foci of Amerindian identity with pan-Indian tendencies, and both serve psychosocial healing functions for individuals and for the community.

On the plains the Gourd Dance emerged as a successful cult dance movement. Ancestral to the modern Gourd Dance societies were the Warrior societies of the high plains and prairie tribes. These ceased to be functional in the reservation period following military "pacification" of the Amerindian tribes by federal and state forces. The last old-time Gourd Dance among the Kiowa was held in 1927. Descendants of Chief White Bear, the great orator of the plains, formed a Kiowa Gourd Dance "clan" in the 1950s and soon initiated members of other tribes into their "clan" as a mark of friendship and distinction. Small cadres of Gourd Dance singers developed into new intertribal Gourd Dance societies among the Kiowa, Comanche, Cheyenne, and Arapaho. During the 1960s and 1970s, enthusiastic adherents carried the Gourd Dance from its nuclear area in western Oklahoma to most plains tribes and to many prairie tribes in the United States and Canada. By the mid 1970s the ceremonial had spread south to the Navajo and north to the Blackfoot and Cree.

Modern gourd dancing has developed its own characteristic choreography. The dancers bob up and down in place, rattling their "gourds" and singing in time with a big war-dance-type drum placed in the center of the group. At the end of their song they often give a wolf howl, which is accompanied by a flurry of drumbeats and the vibration of rattles in unison. The "gourd" rattles are today usually made of cans or plastic containers filled with pebbles or shot. The rattle is shaken with the right hand while the left hand holds a fan of loose "peyote feathers," similar to the eagle-feather fan of Navajo peyote rituals (Aberle, 1966) and derived from the shaman's feathers of the Southern Plains and Southwest Indian tribes (Howard, 1976). The dancer's costume is of cowboy type with optional Amerindian jewelry, blanket, sash derived from the U.S. Cavalry uniform, or mescal bean necklaces that often are worn today as an expression of nativistic sentiment.

The classical Plains Indian style of the Gourd Dance, popularized by the media, appeals to the younger generation of Amerindians from diverse reservation backgrounds who strive to move beyond a tribal identity toward a pan-Indian identity. Among the growing numbers of urbanized Amerindians, recordings of Gourd Dance songs have become best-sellers. Participants see in the Gourd Dance a recognized means of expressing their Amerindian identity and a way to change their life to a more wholesome existence. The Gourd Dance has considerable ego-strengthening and rehabilitative potential, and the therapeutic effects of this dance ceremonial also account for its success as a popular movement among rural and urban Amerindian populations.

The Gourd Dance is credited with rehabilitating many participants who had become despondent alcoholics. Howard (1976, p. 255) quotes the leader of an urban Gourd Dance group: "I used to be an alcoholic, and not considered of much account . . . Since I have taken up gourd dancing my whole life has changed. I don't drink any more, and I have lots of friends. I tell my boy, who still drinks a lot, 'Try it, it may help you.'" Besides the aspects of ego strengthening, group support, and meaningful collective activity, Gourd Dance societies afford their members opportunities for socially sanctioned and approved abreactions. As a Gourd Dance session progresses, excitement builds during special "fast songs" played toward the end of the ceremony; drumming and rattling tempo increase to culminate in a trance-like state with psychodramatic discharges of aggressive feelings. "When everybody is in the mood and when they sing this fast song it's like an attacking, attacking the enemy and all of that, and it makes them want to go right on to the skirmishes" (Commentator on Kiowa Gourd Dance record, cited in Howard, 1976, p. 252).

The consciousness-altering effects of intensive sensory stimulation by rhythmic drumming and rattling appear to be operant in the Gourd Dance, as in other Amerindian ceremonials such as Salish spirit dancing and the Sun Dance. As in general with Amerindian dance ceremonials, the emotional responses of the participants in the Gourd Dance are guided by experienced ritualist leaders—the head singers and their assistants—who alternate the song sets in a way designed to influence the moods of dancers and spectators. Under the direction of skillful ritualist leaders, the revived

Amerindian cult dances hold considerable potential as organized group therapeutic ventures.

NEUROPHYSIOLOGY AND PSYCHOLOGY OF ALTERED STATES OF CONSCIOUSNESS

Altered states of consciousness are characterized by the following symptomatology, according to Ludwig (1966):

(1) Alterations in thinking, including predominance of archaic modes of thought, blurring of cause-effect distinctions, and cognitive ambivalence.

(2) Disturbed time sense.

(3) Loss of control and inhibition.

(4) Change in emotional expression toward affective extremes.

(5) Body-image changes and perceptual distortions.

(6) Change in meaning; attachment of increased or specific significance to subjective experience or external cues, leading to thrilling feelings of insight and revelation of "truth" that then carries an unshakable conviction.

(7) Sense of the ineffable; the essence of the personal experience is felt to be not directly communicable, and this is often explained by varying degrees of amnesia.

(8) Feelings of rejuvenation, of renewed hope or of rebirth.

(9) Hypersuggestibility.

Tart (1969, p. 2) offers a concise definition: "An altered state of consciousness for a given individual is one in which he clearly feels a *qualitative* shift in his pattern of mental functioning, that is, he feels not just a quantitative shift, but also that some quality or qualities of his mental processes are different."

Altered states of consciousness correspond to what Bleuler (1961) has defined as *Bewusstseinsverschiebung* (shifting of consciousness). In Western cultures, altered states of consciousness of a psychogenic type are mainly observed in (1) hypnosis, (2) religious revelation, and (3) "hysterical" dissociation. Anthropologists differentiate *possession trance*, an altered state of consciousness interpreted by subject and society as due to possession by a supernatural entity, from ordinary *trance*, an altered state of consciousness not so interpreted. In popular literature, the term "possession state" has been reserved for non-Western cultures and for states of diabolic provenance not approved of by Christian authorities—an arbitrary convention indicative of Eurocentric bias. It must be emphasized that the differences between all these states are cultural, not psychological or neurophysiological. Schlesinger (1962) has attempted a neuropsychological clarification of these hitherto vaguely defined experiences: "The neuropsychological basis of any trance or possession state is the dissociation of the self, which loses its experiential unity and is converted into a secondary dual system of relational experience, namely, the personal self and the para-personal self."

The capacity of attaining altered states of consciousness is a universal property of the human central nervous system, as evidenced by the ubiquitous occurrence of trance phenomena through time and space. However, the prevalence of these phenomena appears to be a function of sociocultural variables. Under the impact of rationalistic-positivistic ideologies, the normal faculty of manifesting psychogenic dissociation appears to have diminished among members of the Western urban middle class, who nowadays would not be expected to readily enter hysterical twilight reactions, demonic possessions, or religious frenzy, even though these states are by no means rare historically or in more tradition-oriented pockets of Western culture (see Kemp and Valla & Prince, this volume). They are also quite common in recently emerging "charismatic" Christian movements. Experimental studies of hypnotic trance have demonstrated beyond any doubt that the subject's motivation is essential for the induction of a hypnotic reaction; that the hypnotist is of importance only as a culturally approved sanctioning figure in whose influence the subject firmly believes, and as a focus for the projection of omnipotence fantasies; and that the hypnotic state serves the subject's wish fulfillment and the achievement of consciously or unconsciously desired goals (Barber, 1958; Schilder, 1953; Van der Walde, 1965, 1968). Above all, hypnotic trance is a "product of situational and cultural demands" (Van der Walde, 1968, p. 59). This is equally true of nonexperimental trance states (see Spanos, this volume, for a discussion of hypnosis and demonic possession). We may say that in trance the subject makes use of the capacity to enter a dissociative state in order to enact most efficiently a goal-directed role that his or her culture in certain situations permits or demands. While the induction of psychogenic dissociation unquestionably depends on the subject's motivation, it may be facilitated by the employment of techniques that result in changes of brain function with demonstrable electroencephalographic indicators.

Ludwig (1968) enumerated the factors operant in the production of altered states of consciousness:

1. Reduction of exteroceptive stimulation and/or motor activity.
2. Increase of exteroceptive stimulation and motor hyperactivity, emotional arousal leading to exertion and mental fatigue.
3. Focused and selective hyperalertness.
4. Decreased alertness; relaxation of critical faculties.
5. Somato-psychological factors.

The "somato-psychological factors" producing altered states of consciousness are hypoxyventilation and hyperventilation, which both can be carried on until loss of consciousness ensues, and which are associated with stage-specific EEG changes; further, hypoglycemia and dehydration due to fasting, sleep deprivation, and exposure to extreme temperatures. I would emphasize, however, the role of rhythmic sensory stimulation in the production of altered states of consciousness as deserving our special attention. While photic driving—i.e., the effects of stroboscopic photostimulation on electrical brain activity, perception, and consciousness—has been the main concern of neurophysiological research in this field ever since the pioneering work of Adrian and Matthews (1934), an analogous significance of acoustic stimulation has long been surmised by observers of rituals and ceremonies in which rhythmic sounds appeared to have a direct effect on the central nervous system. This was clearly expressed by Huxley (1961, p. 369):

> No man, however highly civilised, can listen for very long to African drumming, or Indian chanting, or Welsh hymn-singing, and retain intact his critical and self-conscious personality ... if exposed long enough to the tom-toms and the singing, every one of our philosophers would end by capering and howling with the savages.

In their now-classic treatise on rhythmic sensory stimulation, Walter and Grey Walter (1949) recorded the well-known physiological and psychological effects of photic flicker stimulation. With regard to acoustic stimulation, they concluded that

> rhythmic stimulation of the organ of hearing as a whole can be accomplished only by using a sound stimulus containing components of supra-liminal intensity over the whole gamut of audible

frequencies—in effect a steep fronted sound such as that produced by an untuned percussion instrument or an explosion. (p. 82)

This lead was not followed for some time. Instead of using rhythmic percussion, other researchers experimented with intermittent pure-tone sound stimulation. It was not until Neher's (1961, 1962) investigations that the neurophysiological effects of rhythmic drumming were demonstrated in controlled experiments. Neher (1961) exposed clinically and electroencephalographically normal subjects to a low-frequency, high-amplitude stimulus obtained from a snare drum without snares—an instrument quite similar to the Salish Indian deerskin drums employed in winter ceremonials. Auditory driving responses were demonstrated in the EEG of all subjects at the fundamental of each stimulus frequency (three, four, six, and eight beats per second), and also at second harmonics and second subharmonics of some stimulus frequencies. Subjective responses were similar to those obtained with photic driving by Walter and Grey Walter (1949) and included "fear, astonishment, amusement, back pulsing, muscle tightening, stiffness in chest, tone in background, humming, rattling, visual and auditory imagery." Due to the presence of theta rhythms (four to seven cycles per second) in the temporal auditory region of the cerebral cortex, sound stimulation by drumming in this frequency range appears to be most effective and would, therefore, be expected to predominate in ceremonies associated with trance behavior. As cited by Neher (1962), the response is heightened by accompanying rhythms reinforcing the main rhythm, and by concomitant rhythmic stimulation in other sensory modes, such as tactual and kinesthetic. Susceptibility to rhythmic stimulation is increased by stress in general, hyperventilation, hypoglycemia, and adrenaline secretion resulting from exertion and fatigue.

Neher (1962) reviewed some ethnographic reports on ceremonies involving rhythmic drumming from Siberia, Africa, Haiti, and Indonesia. A comparison of these data appeared to suggest that "unusual behavior observed in drum ceremonies is mainly the result of rhythmic drumming which affects the central nervous system" (p. 100). Prince (1968, p. 134) suggested that auditory driving is a "commonly used portal of entry into the dissociative state." His practical proposals for the study of possession states by telemetering the EEG of fully mobile "native" participants in ceremonies have not yet been taken up by field researchers. Sargant (1959) explains the induction of states of religious enthusiasm and spirit possession, as well as the so-called brainwashing and related therapeutic techniques, in terms of Pavlovian theory as transmarginal inhibition. He marshals evidence from historical and contemporary reports on methods of religious and ideological conversion and indoctrination and shows that the basic processes involved are analogous in all significant aspects, paralleling those Pavlov deduced from his experimental observations of dogs.

From the foregoing we conclude that both *trance* and *possession trance* are altered states of consciousness involving the universally human mechanism of mental dissociation. Their introduction is largely dependent on the subject's motivation and on the situational and sociocultural context but may be facilitated by certain conditions and techniques, some of which result in temporary changes of brain function. The pioneer of transcultural psychiatry, Professor Eric Wittkower, once remarked on the psychohygienic function of altered states of consciousness:

> There can be no doubt in anybody's mind that trance and possession states in the countries in which they play part of religious rituals have an important distress relieving, integrative, adaptive function. As far as mental illness is concerned, they may be of prophylactic value. An increase in mental illness may have to be expected when as a result of culture change they have ceased to exist. (Wittkower, 1970, p. 160)

In summarizing the ethnographic data on North American Indian dance ceremonials, we can clearly discern conditions that in conjunction with focused collective suggestion facilitate the production of altered states of consciousness. These are conditions of increased external stimulation and motor hyperactivity, alternating with conditions of reduced external stimulation and motor hypoactivity (see Katz, this volume). The ritual therapeutic modalities we have described involve some or all of the following *somatopsychological factors* conducive to the achievement of altered states of consciousness: (1) rhythmic acoustic stimulation; (2) kinetic stimulation; (3) forced hypermotility; (4) hyperventilation; (5) pain stimulation; (6) temperature stimulation; (7) dehydration and hypoglycemia; (8) sleep deprivation; (9) visual-sensory deprivation; (10) seclusion and restricted mobility.

As possible biochemical substrates of altered states of consciousness, the recently discovered endogenous opioid substances enkephalin and beta-endorphin, and probably also other neuroendocrine peptides, should be taken into consideration. In view of the neurophysiological research data summarized by Cleghorn (1977), Snyder (1980), Kline (1981), and Prince (1982a, 1982b), I suggest that in altered states of consciousness the neuroendocrine opioid system plays an important role because of: (1) its linkage with areas of the central nervous system (CNS) subserving the transmission, processing, and integration of signals in pain, auditory, visual, and kinetic perception; (2) its linkage with CNS areas involved in the emotional reaction to pain stimuli and in the control of affective states associated with food and fluid intake; (3) the finding that altered states of consciousness induced by suggestion or hypnosis, alone or in conjunction with other ASC-inducing techniques, can produce analgesia that is reversible by naloxone, the opiate-antagonist and opioid-blocker; (4) the finding that strong sensory stimulation inhibits the transmission of pain signals to brain areas where they are consciously perceived; (5) the transient antidysphoric, mood-elevating, anxiolytic, analgesic, and disinhibiting effects of beta-endorphin parenterally administered in clinical trials. I further suggest (1) that the body's neuroendocrine opioid system is activated under the same conditions that induce altered states of consciousness in the previously described ceremonials, notably rhythmic acoustic and kinetic stimulation in combination with physical exertion, hyperventilation, dehydration, hypoglycemia, and subliminal pain; (2) that *some* of the known therapeutic results observed in traditional ceremonials could be due to the antidysphoric, mood-elevating, and anxiolytic effects of endogenous opioids released in the course of these ritual procedures.

Finally, in reference to Levi-Strauss's (1963) ideas on the effectiveness of symbols, I propose that the therapeutic effects observed in the traditional healing rituals of many culture areas result from the skillful manipulation of culturally validated symbols. These symbols are patterned in accordance with neuropsychologically determined structural laws and thus find direct access to the unconscious through altered states of consciousness.

NOTES

1. The term *shock* is used here in analogy to the psychiatric treatment in which by electrical or chemical means a temporary *loss* of consciousness (coma) is induced that depatterns the morbid personality. In spirit dance initiation, the means are

psychophysiological and induce an *altered* state of consciousness that may have the appearance of coma.

2. Personal communication by Mr. R. P., at Chilliwack, B.C., December 19, 1971 (author's field notes).

3. Personal communication by Mr. A. J., at Agassiz, B. C., July 1, 1971 (author's field notes).

4. This physical analysis was conducted by Dr. Helmut Ormestad of the Fysisk Institutt Blindern of the University of Oslo.

REFERENCES

Aberle, D. F. (1966). *The peyote religion among the Navaho.* Chicago: Aldine.

Adrian, E. D., and Matthews, B. H. (1934). The Berger rhythm, potential changes from the occipital lobes in man. *Brain, 57,* 355-385.

Barber, T. X. (1958). The concept of "hypnosis." *Journal of Psychology, 45,* 115-131.

Bleuler, M. (1961). Bewusstseinsstoerungen in der Psychiatrie [Disturbances of consciousness in psychiatry]. In H. Staub & H. Thölen (Eds.), *Bewusstseinsstoerungen.* Stuttgart: Thieme.

Cleghorn, R. A. (1977). Morphine-like peptides of brain and their relation to hormonal neurotransmitters. *Psychiatric Journal of the University of Ottawa, 2,* 133-137.

Howard, J. H. (1976). The plains gourd dance as a revitalization movement. *American Ethnologist, 3,* 243-259.

Huxley, A. (1961). *The devils of Loudon.* London: Chatto & Windus.

Jilek, W. G. (1971). From crazy witch doctor to auxiliary psychotherapist: The changing image of the medicine man. *Psychiatria Clinica, 4,* 200-220.

Jilek, W. G. (1977). A quest for identity: Therapeutic aspects of the Salish Indian guardian spirit ceremonial. *Journal of Operational Psychiatry, 8,* 46-51.

Jilek, W. G. (1982). *Indian healing: Shamanic ceremonialism in the Pacific Northwest today.* Surrey, BC: Hancock House.

Jorgensen, J. G. (1972). *The Sun Dance Religion.* Chicago: University of Chicago Press.

Kline, N. S. (1981). The endorphins revisited. *Psychiatric Annals, 11,* 137-142.

Levi-Strauss, C. (1963). *Structural anthropology.* New York: Basic Books.

Ludwig, A. M. (1966). Altered states of consciousness. *Archives of General Psychiatry, 15,* 225-234.

Ludwig, A. M. (1968). Altered states of consciousness. In R. Prince (Ed.), *Trance and possession states* (pp. 69-95). Montreal: R. M. Bucke Memorial Society.

Neher, A. (1961). Auditory driving observed with scalp electrodes in normal subjects. *EEG and Clinical Neurophysiology, 13,* 449-451.

Neher, A. (1962). A physiological explanation of unusual behavior in ceremonies involving drums. *Human Biology, 34,* 151-160.

Nurge, E. (1966). The Sioux Sun Dance in 1962. *Actas, XXXVI Congreso Internacional de Americanistas, 3,* 105-114.

Prince, R. (1968). Can the EEG be used in the study of possession states? In R. Prince (Ed.), *Trance and possession states* (pp. 121-137). Montreal: R. M. Bucke Memorial Society.

Prince, R. (1982a). The endorphins. *Ethos, 10,* 303-316.

Prince, R. (1982b). Shamans and endorphins. *Ethos, 10,* 409-423.

Sargant, W. (1959). *Battle for the mind.* London: Pan Books.

Schilder, P. (1953). *Medical psychology.* New York: International University Press.

Schlesinger, B. (1962). *Higher cerebral functions and their clinical disorders: The organic basis of psychology and psychiatry.* New York: Grune & Stratton.

Snyder, S. H. (1980). Peptide neurotransmitters with possible involvements in pain perception. In J. J. Bonica (Ed.), *Pain* (pp. 233-243). New York: Raven Press.

Tart, C. T. (1969). Introduction. In C. Tart (Ed.), *Altered states of consciousness* (pp. 1-6). New York: John Wiley.

Van der Walde, P. H. (1965). Interpretation of hypnosis in terms of ego psychology. *Archives of General Psychiatry, 12,* 438-447.

Van der Walde, P. H. (1968). Trance states and ego psychology. In R. Prince (Ed.), *Trance and possession states* (pp. 57-68). Montreal: R. M. Bucke Memorial Society.

Walter, V. J., & Grey Walter, W. (1949). The central effects of rhythmic sensory stimulation. *EEG and Clinical Neurophysiology, 1,* 57-86.

Wittkower, E. D. (1970). Trance and possession states. *International Journal of Social Psychiatry, 16,* 153-160.

9

A CALL TO HEAL
Entry Patterns in Brazilian Mediumship
STANLEY KRIPPNER

HISTORICAL BACKGROUND AND ETHNOGRAPHY

African slaves were first brought to Brazil in about 1550 to work on plantations in the northeastern part of the Portuguese colony. It has been estimated that the total number of slaves who eventually arrived in Brazil exceeded four million, many of them appropriated, often with the complicity of avaricious people from their own tribes, from the West African coast. Permeating the belief systems of these tribes (e.g., Yoruba, Dahomey) were stories about the spiritual deities, or *orixás*. Powerful and terrifying, but so human that they could be talked to, pleaded with, and cajoled through special offerings, the *orixás* were part of the culture the slaves brought to Brazil.

Upon their arrival, however, the slaves were baptized as Christians and forced to attend Roman Catholic church services. They were allowed to hold their own religious meetings so long as they were Christian in nature. Devotion to the faith was demonstrated by the presence of pictures of Jesus, Mary, and the saints upon the slaves' altars. In this manner, the slaves cleverly adopted the Christian spirits, giving them "white masks" and combining them with the *orixás* (Bastide, 1960). Olorun, god of creation, became God the Father, or Jehova. In the Yoruba culture, Olorun (like the "High God" of the other West African cultures) was believed to be benevolent but uninterested in human affairs. It was Olorun's children who interceded in people's daily lives, and who, for the slaves, corresponded to Jesus and the Catholic saints. Obatalá, the god of heavens and of purity, became Jesus Christ. Obatalá's daughter, Iemanjá, became the Virgin Mary, and her children Ogum, Oxóssi, and Oxum became St. George (Jorge), St. Sebastian (Sebastião), St. Catherine (Catherina), and so on. There was no direct counterpart for Satan in Yoruba mythology. The closest resemblance was the Exús, the mes-

AUTHOR'S NOTE: Some of the field trips described in this paper were facilitated by private gifts from Dr. Lonnie Barbach and Ms. Zelda Suplee.

sengers of the gods, and the Ifás, the guardians of the temples. The Exús and the Ifás were quite mischievous, sometimes mixing up people's prayers and granting them someone else's request (Verger, 1985). The Exús were regarded as extremely clever and needed to be appeased, usually at the beginning or the end of a ceremony.

In some areas of Brazil, the "pure" form was altered and a few additional spirits entered the panoply. The Wise Old Black Slaves (*os pretos velhos*) were archetypal parent images, while the Indians of the Pathways (*os caboclos*) embodied the best traits of the native South American Indians and their part-Caucasian descendants. Both categories were considered very important in healing ceremonies, during which the spirits were said to work through the mediums who "incorporated" them. Other spirits credited with healing powers were as *crianças*, the babies who died in infancy, and practitioners' ancestors, any number of whom could surface during a healing session. Also, the *orixás'* Christian names varied regionally.

In early African cultures, as in many traditional cultures today, an individual was seen as being intimately connected to nature and the social group (see Katz, this volume). Each individual was thought to be part of a web of kinship relations, existing only in relationship to the larger family and community networks. Strained or broken social relations were the major cause of disease; anger, jealousy, and envy could lead to serious illness. A harmonious relationship with one's community was necessary for health; the relationships one's ancestors had with the community were also important (see Jilek, this volume). At the same time, an ordered relationship with the forces of nature, as personified by the *orixás*, was essential for maintaining the well-being of the individual and the community. Africans knew that illness had natural causes but believed that these factors were exacerbated on by discordant relations between people and their social and natural environment. Long before Western medicine recognized the fact, Africa's traditional healers had taken the position that ecology and interpersonal relations affected people's health (Raboteau, 1986).

African religious practitioners gained access to supernatural power in three ways: by making offerings to the *orixás*; by "divining," or foretelling the future with the help of an *orixá*; and by incorporating an *orixá* or an ancestor, who then warned the community about possible calamities, diagnosed illness, and prescribed cures. The medium, or person through whom the spirits spoke and moved, performed this task voluntarily, claiming not to remember the experience once it ended. The "trance" or altered state of consciousness required for incorporation (the purported voluntary surrender of the medium's mind and body to the discarnate entity) was brought about by dancing, singing, and drumming. Preventive medicine consisted of using charms and rituals, as well as of living within the social constraints of one's culture. Treatment for afflicted people included herbal preparations, prayers, and sacrifices. It frequently included spirit incorporation which had survived the transition to Brazil; it required no special equipment, only the dedication of a social group that could provide the music and emotional support to facilitate the experience.

Brazil declared its independence in 1822, and the slaves were freed in 1888. Between 1550 and 1888 some 15 generations of Brazilians had heard the stories of the *orixás*, of death by the evil eye, of illnesses cured by spirit counsel, and of marriages saved by spirit intervention. With a few exceptions (e.g., the Shango cult in Trinidad), the African religions did not survive among the slaves who were brought to the British colonies; however, the practices of the black "shouting churches" that grew out of the Protestant revival movement resembled some aspects of the West African rituals. But rather than "incorporating" *orixás*, slaves were "filled by the Holy Spirit" during their ecstatic experiences, which were triggered by the church service's emotionally arousing sermons, songs, and prayers (Raboteau, 1986).

Of the Brazilian spiritistic movements, Candomblé is the one most closely resembling the "pure" Yoruba religion of Africa, retaining the original beliefs and rituals. The name Candomblé seems to have derived from *candombé*, a community dance held by the slaves who worked on coffee plantations. In 1830 three black freedwomen bought an abandoned millhouse to set up Brazil's first permanent Candomblé temple. The three former slaves became *iyalorixás* (or *as mães de santos*, "the mothers of the saints") and their apprentices became *iaos as filhas de santos,* "the daughters of the saints."

In Africa males played a major role in sacred rituals. In Brazil, however, because male slaves were preoccupied with manual labor, these rituals often fell to the women. A number of slave women gained extra power upon becoming the concubines of their Portuguese masters, claiming that the practice of African rituals was necessary to maintain their sexual prowess. The three freedwomen who founded the first Candomblé temple excluded men from major responsibilities, although they were permitted to serve as assistants and to play the drums during the services.

Today the "daughters" still learn how to sing, beat the drums, and dance in order to alter their consciousness and incorporate their various spirit guides. They also learn about the herbs and special teas and potions often needed by the indisposed members of their congregation (McGregor, 1962). There are three main branches of Candomblé and some 700 Candomblé temples in the city of Salvador and other parts of the state of Bahia. The practice of Candomblé varies from region to region, and in some of these temples male mediums ("fathers" and "brothers of the saints") participate in the ceremonies.

In 1818, another spiritistic movement began and was organized around the principles of homeopathy, which claims that the most effective medicines are those that produce symptoms similar to those they are supposed to cure. By 1840 homeopathy was being practiced in Rio de Janeiro, and its philosophy was expanded to include prayer and the laying on of hands (St. Clair, 1971). In 1858, this spiritistic group was galvanized by the arrival of *The Spirits' Book* by Allan Kardec. Kardec's book was translated from the original French into Portuguese and created a sensation upon its publication. It described a faith more sophisticated than Candomblé that circumvented drum beating, rum drinking, and homage to the African *orixás*. Yet this faith upheld the doctrine of reincarnation and the importance of incorporating spirit guides in its healing services and religious ceremonies. Kardecist mediums alter their consciousness in a less dramatic way than Candomblé practitioners, usually by "turning inward" (often aided by soft music and the presence of a supportive social group) and providing an "opening" for the incorporation of their guide (Krippner & Villoldo, 1976).

Kardecismo, as this spiritistic movement became known, held that the human soul is enveloped in a semi-material body of its own called the "perispirit." During one's lifetime, the perispirit takes on the form of the material body; after death, the soul moves on to another body to continue its spiritual development. The laying on of hands is directed at the perispirit rather than at the physical body. Contemporary Kardecists continue to refer clients to homeopathic practitioners.

Umbanda, a third spiritistic movement, congealed in 1941. Its founder had claimed to be in contact with an American Indian guide who taught him how to "purify" the African rites. The name seems to have come from the Sanskrit term *Aum-bandha*, the "divine principle." Alterations of consciousness in the "low" Umbanda sects may be facilitated by drumming, chanting, smoking cigars, drinking rum, making sacrifices of fowl and small animals, and drawing cabalistic signs on the floor with chalk. Manifestations of altered states include not only spirit incorporation but walking barefoot on broken glass and handling snakes. The "high" Umbanda sects do not engage in these practices, but use trance-induction methods reminiscent of Kardecismo. Both groups emphasize the importance of spirit incorporation, and all Umbandistas venerate Jesus Christ. In addition, Christian names rather than African names are used for the saints (Herskovits, 1937).

There are other Brazilian spiritistic groups (e.g., Batuque, Caboclo, Quimbanda, Macumba, Xangô), but Candomblé, Kardecismo, and Umbanda are the three major groups. In some scholarly writings, Kardecismo is referred to as "Spiritism," while Umbanda, Candomblé, and other movements are called "Afro-Brazilian sects." Although the ceremonies and rituals of the three major groups vary, they share three beliefs: Humans have a physical body and a spiritual body; discarnate spirits are in constant contact with the physical world; humans can learn how to incorporate spirits for the purpose of healing.

METHODS OF CALLING

In the Yoruba culture and among the other West African societies from which the slaves originated, religion and medicine were interrelated and were articulated in myths and rituals that explained the nature of the world, of health, and of disease. Life was portrayed as positive; it was the way of nature for human beings to achieve health, fertility, prosperity, and success. However, the world contained several forces that might frustrate people's search for fulfillment. A major function of religion and medicine was to prevent misfortune and to ensure success (Raboteau, 1986). This worldview still permeates the sects. Many Brazilians become spiritistic practitioners in order to facilitate health and good fortune for themselves and others.

During six field trips to Brazil between 1973 and 1987, I met over 100 spiritistic healers and attended about 30 sessions in which they would enter altered states of consciousness, incorporate spirits, and attempt some type of healing. I interviewed two Candomblé, 15 Umbanda, and 14 Kardecismo healing practitioners, asking the medium how he or she had become adept at incorporating spirits and engaging in healing. I also interviewed eight practitioners who were eclectic, combining more than one spirit tradition, sometimes in combination with Western medicine, psychotherapy, or Eastern philosophy. Various methods of socialization appeared to operate for each individual, who eventually became comfortable with altered states of consciousness (or "trance"), the notion of incorporating spirits, and the commitment to dedicate part or all of one's life to the service of other people. Five methods of receiving the "call" emerged from these interviews, as described below.

(1) Some practitioners had dreams, "visions," or meditative imagery about past lives, spirit guides, or deceased relatives. These events had the function of stimulating an interest in spirits and, eventually, motivated the individual to begin a training program to become a healer and medium. Indeed, some of these individuals claimed to have incorporated spirits spontaneously, without expectation or effort, either during a formal ceremony or a ritual.

(2) Some practitioners came from families that had a history of mediumship. At an early age, these practitioners observed spirit incorporation by their parents, siblings, or other relatives. Later they were given the opportunity to develop their own abilities, thus carrying on the family tradition.

(3) Some practitioners began attending ceremonies out of curiosity, then volunteered their services for the charitable work of the spiritistic centers, spending time with the aged, the infirm, the sick, the handicapped, or the orphaned. Gradually, these individuals became assimilated into the movement and were given instructions in incorporation and healing.

(4) Some practitioners were identified as potential mediums when they came to the centers to request help or when a spiritistic healer came to their assistance when they were ill. As part of their treatment, they were advised to attend classes; spirit incorporation was seen as a necessary part of their therapy.

(5) Some practitioners were attracted to the sects by attending lectures or reading books on the topic, especially those describing the spiritist worldview with its emphasis on altruistic service, reincarnation, and the importance of spirit communication. The explanatory power of spiritistic philosophy attracted them, especially in regard to death, suffering, and the meaning of life.

Sometimes, the initial responses to my interview questions were vague, but when I asked for autobiographical accounts, one or more of these five methods of calling would emerge in our conversation. Sometimes an interview was casual, conducted over coffee. At other times it was formal, conducted in an office. Most interviews were one-on-one, but some were conducted with two or three people at a time. Some lasted for less than half an hour, while others took up to three hours. It was unusual for a medium to speak English, but a knowledgeable translator was always available to supplement my facility in conversational Portuguese. I took notes during the interview or, when this was not appropriate, immediately after. The mediums discussed a variety of topics, but for the purposes of this study I focused on how they had received the "call." A number of case studies will be presented to illustrate the three key spiritistic sects as well as the interplay of the five methods of entry into mediumship.

Candomblé

In 1983, I visited the Casa Branca (White Temple), one of the oldest Candomblé centers in Brazil. Its history goes back to the original millhouse that served as the first Candomblé center in 1830. The original "mothers of the saints" were succeeded by a woman named Marcelina, who reigned happily until her death. But the succession became difficult when two different "daughters of the saints" claimed priority. One of them left the millhouse with half the congregation and bought another building from a Frenchman named Gantois. Her successor, Pulqueria, became one of the most famous mediums in Salvador and was succeeded by her own niece, Maria Escolastica da Conceição Nazare, better known as Mãe Menininha de Gantois (Little Girl Mother of Gantois).

Mãe Menininha, who lived with her family at the Casa Branca, had celebrated her 83rd birthday the week before our arrival. She was pleased to reminisce about her past, telling me that her grandfather was a slave from Dahomey and her grandmother, Maria Julia Nazaré, was the priestess who had left the original millhouse. Mãe Menininha recalled, "Grandmother Nazaré could look at people and give their whole life story. I cannot do this because I am only the grandaughter."

Mãe Menininha's grandfather was not enthusiastic about his wife's devotion to the orixás. He asked why he had been permitted to become a slave if the orixás were as powerful as his wife claimed. Nor was Mãe Menininha's father pleased when she was "called" in her dreams and daytime "visions" to enter the Casa Branca. Indeed, Mãe Menininha told us that her father's objection to her initiation was probably the reason why he died handicapped. The low status of men in Mãe Menininha's branch of Candomblé, brought about in part by continued resentment that men had not prevented the tribe's enslavement, might have been one reason why her grandfather and father lacked enthusiasm for the sect.

According to Mãe Menininha, "Once the *orixá* calls, there is no other path to take." If you spurn the "call," you may become physically or mentally ill. The only remedy for this illness is to discover your spirit guide and follow the sacred path. If your *orixá* has not revealed itself in your dreams, you may discover its identity by having a medium enter an altered state of consciousness, "throw the *búzios*" (i.e., cowrie shells), and observe the resulting pattern. It is believed that the Ifas, who protect the temples, guide the falling cowrie shells in the proper way for the client's *orixá* to be revealed.

Before leaving the temple, I met Mãe Menininha's daughter, Cleosa Millet. She was extremely articulate as she expressed her dedication to the Candomblé tradition. She also described her mother's birthday party. A variety of celebrities had attended the festivities, among them Jorge Amado, Brazil's best known contemporary novelist, who often had assisted in local Candomblé rituals and whose work reflects this knowledge. In 1986, news reached me of Mãe Menininha's death; I felt fortunate that I had been able to interview her three years earlier. In her case, it was clear that the family tradition was a strong predisposing factor that had been activated by the "calls" she claimed to have received in the dreams and "visions" provided by the *orixás*.

Umbanda

I attended my first Umbanda healing ceremony in São Paulo in 1973. Following the evening session, I spoke to several of the *babalaôs* (male leaders) and *iyalorixás* (female leaders). (The terms "fathers of the saints" and "mothers of the saints" are also used in some Umbanda ceremonies.) They stated that they had been "invited" to mediumship in several ways. Two middle-aged women told me that they had been "called" to mediumship when they spontaneously incorporated spirits during some of their first candle and drum ceremonies. A young man told me that he had attended an Umbanda service when he was ill and was told by a medium that the illness was an "invitation" to enter training.

Three members of the group (two women, one man) had grown up in a household where family members were *babalaôs* or *iyalovishas*. One of them actually spurned the idea of mediumship in her youth, only to appreciate it later following a "call" in a dream. Four members of the group (all of them women) were assimilated into the movement through friendships with Umbandistas or by participating in some of the charitable projects sponsored by the sect.

Umbanda sessions are marked by drumming sessions that help evoke the incorporation of Indian or Negro guides as well as spirits of deceased relatives or *as crianças*, infants who died early in life. In some areas of Brazil, Oriental spirits also make their appearance. However, the major *orixás*, such as Ogum and Oxossi, are not generally incorporated because it is feared that the medium would explode from the "energy" involved in such a transaction.

During my 1973 visit, my colleague and I arrived late but received a warm welcome nevertheless. White-robed mediums were already dancing to the beat of a drum. There was an elaborate altar covered with pictures, photographs, and statues of Yoruba *orixás*, Christian saints, and deceased relatives. After half an hour of dancing, the mediums' movements became more frenzied, their eyes glazed over or rolled back, and they appeared to have entered altered states of consciousness. Their dancing displayed more energetic activity, and they sweated profusely as their colored bead necklaces swayed back and forth. A *babalaô* walked through the congregation with an incense holder to purify us for the forthcoming healing session.

As it was the second week of the month, the mediums were incorporating the Wise Old Black Slaves. During the first week, the Indians of the Seven Pathways had been featured. *As crianças* were to be venerated the third week of the month, followed by the ancestors during the final week. One by one, most of the mediums trembled with ecstatic jerks, shrieks, and spasms as *os prêtos velhos* possessed their bodies.

Having incorporated the spirits, the mediums were ready to heal those in need. Both my colleague and I went into the healing circle and received warm embraces; the hands of the *iyalorixás* massaged the ailing parts of our bodies intensely, then paused before moving on to the next client. After the healing session, homage was paid to the Exús so that these "trickster" deities would not undo the benefits of the healings. The mediums then filed out of the room. When we saw them again, once refreshments were served, they were dressed in street clothes and claimed to recall little of their experience once the incorporation had taken place.

In Rio de Janeiro, the center of Umbanda practice, I was a member of a small group that visited the Central Spiritist Union in 1983. The mediums in charge of the session were Terezinha Chaves, Alicia Soares, and Mario Soares. Senhora Chaves came from a family of Umbandistas and had begun incorporating spirits as an adolescent. Senhor Soares credits Umbanda mediums for restoring his health when he was critically ill with pneumonia; subsequently, he took an active role in Umbanda sessions and began to train as a medium. Senhora Soares supported her husband's interests, eventually becoming a medium herself.

About 50 people were present, sitting on wooden benches and facing the *iyalorixás*, who worked with their clients at the front of the temple's largest room. Each member of our group received a laying on of hands from one of the mediums, who used fire, water, and swords in their rituals. Each laying on of hands was unique, but all included prayers and concluded with a warm embrace. The mediums spent more time with the local clients than with us, as many of them had specific problems in need of attention. A dialogue preceded the actual attempt at healing, in which the clients discussed their ailments while the mediums suggested spiritual approaches (prayers, good works) that would assist the healing process. None of the mediums was in an obvious altered state, although several told me that they had meditated before the service. One *iyalorixás* remarked that Jesus comes to her as a "white light" during meditation; indeed, it was Jesus who had "called" her to enter mediumship training when she was an adolescent. She appeared to be one of the "conscious mediums" who maintains her awareness during trance and recalls the experience afterward.

That same evening, we visited the headquarters of the Followers of Truth. The building serves not only as a location for evening services, but also as an orphanage for 170 children, who stay there until they reach adulthood. Umbanda services alternate with Kardecismo services, and the rooms are decorated in a way that is suitable for members of both movements.

Upon arriving in the downstairs auditorium, we were greeted by musicians playing bombastic music and over 200 people sitting in wooden pews or lining up in front of a *babalaô* or an *iyalorixá*. The mediums were situated on a large stage facing the pews, and the musicians were sitting directly behind the mediums. There was a single drummer (as compared to the trio of drummers usually seen in Candomblé ceremonies); a few accompanying musicians shook *maracás* (gourd rattles) and *ganzás* (metal rattles).

Some members of our group were eager to experience another

laying on of hands. They were screened by a group of mediums to determine which ones needed an exorcism. For example, I was told that a "low spirit" of the river had entered my "energy field" when I came to Brazil and was sapping my strength. During the exorcisms I had witnessed a few minutes earlier, the mediums gently pushed their clients backward so that they would fall on the floor. As I complied with this aspect of the ritual, I began to feel extremely light-headed and disoriented. I was told that this was a common side effect of exorcisms and was encouraged to sit in a pew until I regained my composure.

After about 20 minutes, I felt more centered and proceeded to the next step of the ritual, which was to receive a laying on of hands by one of the *iyalorixâs* on the stage. She was smoking a cigar and blew its strong tobacco smoke into my face before laying on hands. The effect was highly stimulating and lasted for the rest of the evening. The *iyalorixâs* wore the headdress of an American Indian, because all the mediums were incorporating *os caboclos* that evening. One *babalaô*, Roberto Rojas—a "son of Oxossi"—told me that the Indians of the Pathways were directing the mediums' hands to the ailing portion of one's body, or to the segment of the client's "energy field" that needed to be cleansed and purified.

The following morning, we observed *despachos*—offerings of food, drink and tobacco—left by the Umbandistas on the beaches, street intersections, and crossroads as gifts to their *orixás*. We were told that even non-Umbandistas are reluctant to disturb these offerings for fear of incurring the wrath of the Umbandista deities.

Kardecismo

The spirit guides incorporated by the followers of Allan Kardec vary from place to place but can include *os caboclos, os pretos velhos*, Oriental teachers, deceased relatives, and spiritual masters from various world religions. Kardec's (e.g., 1857/1972) writings describe several types of mediumship, not all of which are primarily involved with diagnosis, counseling, and healing. For example, during a 1983 visit to São Paulo, our group spent an evening with João Pio de Almeida Prado, who was originally contacted by spirits during daytime visions. He now claims to incorporate the spirits of such artists as Manet, Picasso, Renoir, and Portinari as he paints and sketches in their style. He entered trance very dramatically—sighing, moaning, and contorting his body—then gave us a demonstration, producing ten credible pastel drawings in less than an hour.

In 1985 I spent time with another São Paulo medium, Luis Gasparetto, who was raised in a family of mediums and began incorporating spirits at the age of 12. A psychotherapist who runs his own clinic, Gasparetto said that he had incorporated the spirits of over 50 celebrated artists by the age of 20. He claims that their purpose in returning is to "create a revolution in the way humans think about life and death" (Villoldo & Krippner, 1987, p. 7). Gasparetto believes that the living must learn how to die in such a way that they can consciously enter into the spirit world and continue their spiritual development so that reincarnation is no longer needed.

At the São Paulo Spiritist Federation, which I visited in 1973 and again in 1983, diagnostic and prognostic work is carried out in a private room by half a dozen mediums seated around a table. Following a period of silence in which one's spirit guide is contacted, each medium receives a folded sheet of paper on which the name of a client has been written. A statement is made, supposedly dictated by the spirits, and recorded for later use by a secretary, for example:

> Reform. Pray. Persevere. See a physician for your ailment. Use homeopathic remedies. Return after seeing your physician.
> Cultivate security. Work toward unity in your family. Produce good vibrations in your home.

For especially critical cases, several mediums report on the same client and take a "majority vote" on the diagnosis and treatment.

In the treatment room, various "cleansing passes" are attempted by mediums who have incorporated spirit guides. Typically, the medium's hands move into the air, purportedly making connections with their guides. Then their hands shift into position around the "energy field" of the client at the part of the body where treatment is needed. The mediums stated that their hands are guided by the Spirits to the proper location. There is no physical contact with the client, as the "cleansing" is focused on the perispirit, which, in turn, is said to affect the physical body (Andrade, 1972).

Domingo Laudito, the director of the Federation, told me in 1983 that between 14,000 and 15,000 people are seen there each week; they are treated by some 3,000 mediums who volunteer their services. Treatment is free of charge at the various centers, although donations are permitted. The Federation sponsors a wide array of charitable programs, including homes for the elderly, the handicapped, and destitute children.

It was at the Spiritist Federation that I met dona Marta Gallego, who had worked for three dozen years as a medium and healer. Her original "call," in dreams and "visions," was to Umbanda, but she preferred the greater amount of control encouraged by the Kardecists. Dona (a term of respect) Marta claimed that as an Umbandista she sometimes would incorporate "immature spirits," sharing the feelings that they had experienced at the end of their lives. In Kardecismo she professes to incorporate "highly evolved spirits" who bring "delicious feelings" and "beautiful colors" into her awareness.

Dona Marta invited me to visit her circle of healers at the Noel Center, named after her favorite spirit guide. I noticed that mediums gave clients advice on diet, spiritual exercises, life style, and how frequently they should return to the Center. Homeopathic remedies were often advised, as were homeopathic physicians. I had observed similar sessions at the Evangelical Alliance in São Paulo, where I interviewed a medium who said that he had been told, in a dream, that it was necessary for him to work with poor people because he had victimized them in a previous life.

My original contact in São Paulo was Hernani Andrade, who converted from Roman Catholicism at the age of 17 after reading one of Kardec's books. Andrade commented, "I had been a Spiritist all along without knowing it." In 1963 he established the Brazilian Institute for Psychobiological Research. The author of several books, Andrade has recorded many instances of purported past life recall from his clients.

One of his clients, Carmen Marinho, told me that for several years she had been able to incorporate spirit guides, having been originally "called" in dreams. In one instance, however, the entity claimed to be her own past life as a gypsy. This entity is now Senhora Marinho's preferred guide and directs most of her mediumistic work with clients.

Her husband, Jarbas Marinho, a prominent São Paulo engineer, has developed a three-year training program for mediums at the Spiritist Federation, basing his typology of mediumship on Kardec's (1861/1971) work, primarily *The Medium's Book*, the volume that evoked Senhor Marinho's original interest in Spiritism. According to Kardec, some mediums specialize in one type of mediumship, while others combine several abilities:

(1) Intuitive mediums receive information and inspiration through hunches and internal feelings.

(2) Clairaudient mediums "hear" information as if it were being whispered to them.

(3) Clairvoyant mediums obtain information by "seeing" spirits and "looking into" the spirit world.

(4) Incorporation mediums allow discarnate spirits to communicate using the mediums' bodies and voices.

(5) Healing mediums act as receptors for various types of "energy," using it to heal by means of "magnetic passes" that "cleanse" a client's "energy field."

(6) Transportation mediums have the capacity for "out-of-body" experiences that transport them to the spirit world.

(7) Psychographic mediums allow the spirits to write with pen and ink by directing the mediums' hands.

(8) Precognitive mediums allow the spirits to look into the future.

During Senhor Marinho's training program, students purify their *chakras,* or "energy centers," and establish contact with their spirit guides. They are taught how to differentiate between spirit messages and those projected by their own personal needs. They learn the difference between "obsession" (in which a "low spirit" influences a person's behavior, producing repetitive thoughts, phobias, compulsive behavior, or psychosomatic illness) and "possession" (in which a "low spirit" takes control of an individual for short or long periods of time) (see Kemp, this volume). Students also learn that many of their clients' problems do not require intervention from the spirit world to be resolved.

Although São Paulo is the center of Kardecismo, I also met representatives of three affiliates in Rio de Janeiro. The Fiat Lux Fraternity claimed to have developed healing techniques for "cleansing" their clients' physical, mental, and spiritual "energy fields." For example, zinc and copper plates are placed in salt water, an electric charge is added, and, once imbibed, the "magnetized" water becomes a useful tonic.

The Spiritual Society of Ramatis combines religion, philosophy, and science. Ramatis, a purported Oriental spirit guide, has taught them how to assist clients for whom medicine has been unsuccessful. Over 3,000 clients are seen each week, many of whom experience "exorcisms" in which "high spirits" are enlisted to persuade "low spirits" to leave the body of an afflicted client. The "low spirits" are told that they need to grow spiritually so that they will be able to demonstrate what they have learned in their next incarnation.

A third group has organized the College of Bio-Psychic Science in an attempt to add a spiritual dimension to education. The curriculum of their college follows Kardec's teachings closely, applying them to an interdisciplinary study of the individual, society, and nature.

In 1985, I interviewed and observed Dr. Edson Calvacanti de Queiroz, a physician from Recife. He claims that some years earlier he had spontaneously incorporated the spirit of a deceased German physician who lived during the first part of this century. Twice a week, Queiroz operates on poor people free of charge, utilizing the purported spirit entity to work quickly, apparently without anesthesia or antiseptics (Rauscher, 1985). However, his procedures have been the object of criticism from both the Brazilian Medical Association and a Kardec-oriented medical group (Directorate, 1985).

Eclectic Practitioners

In 1986 and 1987, I spent several days at the Fraternity of the Rose and the Cross in Brasilia. Inspired by the Oriental spirit Ramatis, the Fraternity sponsors an active program of encounter groups for parents who engage in child abuse, counseling services for pregnant women, and educational programs for illiterate children. I spoke with two of the female volunteers who had worked in Fraternity projects for several years, discovering that their original interest had been in the social projects but that later they had joined study groups, eventually becoming mediums themselves.

The Fraternity's director, Dr. América Marques, has combined Kardec's teachings with Raja Yoga and humanistic psychology in formulating the guiding philosophy of the group. In 1969 Dr. Marques began to read psychology books; this reading stimulated her interest in body/mind connections, and she started to practice Raja Yoga. While reading the work of the American psychologist Carl Rogers, she was impressed by his comment that effective psychotherapists demonstrate "unconditional positive regard" toward their clients. Dr. Marques began to experience past-life recall, "out-of-body" travel, automatic writing, and spirit incorporation. Upon reading Kardec's books, she decided that the Kardecist framework provided the most useful explanation of these phenomena.

Dr. Marques has initiated a day-care center for children at her center, as well as an active educational program. Her group holds classes for pregnant women, for business executives, and for professional people interested in studying "abyssal psychology," the name that she gives her eclectic point of view. Abyssal psychology recognizes the "abyssal" or unfathomable nature of the human psyche and the importance of a holistic approach in dealing with the physical, emotional, intellectual, and spiritual issues in a person's life.

I interviewed Dr. Carlos Alberto Jacob in 1987. An anesthesiologist who has taught classes at the Federal Medical School of Triangulo Mineiro in Uberaba, Dr. Jacob found the writings of Allan Kardec helpful in explaining the past-life experiences reported by many of his patients. Eventually, he began incorporating spirits himself; he claims that this ability is useful in both diagnosis and therapy. In 1985 and 1987 I interviewed Dr. Eliezer Cerqueira Mendes, a physician who also became interested in spiritism through Kardec's books. He specializes in group therapy for epileptics, schizophrenics, and cases of multiple personality disorder (Krippner, 1987). Dr. Mendes believes that many of his patients can be treated through exorcism or through mediumship training.

In 1987, I met with Eliane Ignacio, a psychotherapist in Belo Horizonte who comes from a family of mediums and who has adapted Candomblé techniques to facilitate guided imagery sessions in her workshops. In Belo Horizonte I also interviewed Dalva Ferreira Nunes, a renowned spiritistic practitioner whose specialty is throwing the *búzios*, a skill she learned during the years in which she studied Candomblé. She also has studied Umbanda and has read the Kardec literature. When Senhora Nunes threw the cowrie shells for me, I observed her turn her attention inward, holding the 16 shells quietly before throwing them and observing the pattern in which they fell.

In 1986, I visited Mário Sassi, a healer who lives in the "Valley of the Dawn" outside of Brasilia. I attended an outdoor group meditation and indoor group healing session, and spoke to several members of this spiritual community. Senhor Sassi claimed that dreams, visions, and contacts with extraterrestrials motivated him to embark on his spiritual quest.

In total, I interviewed a total of 40 spiritistic practitioners, all of whom purported to incorporate spirits in their work. Of this number, 22 were women and 18 were men. In reviewing the most important factors in their "call," and assigning proportional values when more than one factor was mentioned, I found that an almost equal number of healers came from spiritistic families (11.5) as were "called" in dreams or "visions" (12.0). Eight entered mediumship through an assimilative process, and five through reading spiritist literature; a smaller number (3.5) developed mediumship abilities as a part of their own spiritist-directed therapeutic program.

Because my sample was neither random nor representative, I cannot claim that these proportions would necessarily generalize to all Brazilian mediums. Nor can I say with certainty that the responses were completely factual; distortion may enter into any interview study of this type. Nevertheless, the categories may prove to be useful to investigators instigating future studies.

DISCUSSION

Spiritistic groups are a major social force. Their social service projects are at least as extensive as those supported by the Roman Catholic church or the Brazilian government (St. Clair, 1971). The sects provide an important adjunct to medicine and psychotherapy, especially for those individuals who cannot afford to see a private practitioner or go to a clinic. It is a resource for those suffering from existential problems, psychosomatic illnesses, and ailments for which medication and traditional therapy have been ineffective (Torrey, 1986). Addressing the tension between their sects and Western medicine, a Brazilian governmental agency has issued a statement that physicians have something to learn from folk healers.

Spirit mediumship is exercised under the motto "Give freely what you have received freely" (Matthew 10:8). There are no entrance fees, charges for healing, or financial requests, but donations are always welcomed. Free homeopathic services are available at 1,700 Brazilian social assistance establishments. Indeed, Brazil's first spiritistic homeopaths reputedly have "returned" to the planet as spirit guides and dictate homeopathic prescriptions through mediums. In addition, a variety of prayers, rituals, good luck charms, laying on of hands (in Candomblé and Umbanda), and "magnetic passes" (in Kardecismo) are employed for healing purposes. Suggestions are also given regarding diet, family interactions, and changes in lifestyle. There are several spiritistic hospitals in Brazil; for example, the Psychiatric Hospital of Good Solitude in Curitiba specializes in treating cases of alcoholism and substance addiction.

Brazilian mediums are "called" to healing in several ways: through family background, through the spiritistic treatment of an illness, through the writings of celebrated healers, through contacts with practitioners in a charitable agency or other institution, and/or through dreams, "visions," or spontaneous incorporation of a spirit. As a result of these socialization processes, such behaviors as spirit incorporation, past-life recall, automatic writing, and "out-of-body" travel begin to lose their bizarre quality and seem to occur quite naturally.

The many mediums who report childhood experiences with spirits or who are "called" during altered states of consciousness resemble the "fantasy-prone" individuals identified by Wilson and Barber (1981), whose findings were confirmed and extended by other investigators (e.g., Lynn & Rhue, 1988; Wickramasekera, 1986; Zusne, this volume). Although no more or less emotionally stable than other people, Wilson and Barber's subjects were more prone to see "visions," hear voices, and touch imaginary companions. Possibly combining genetic inheritance and early experiences, fantasy-prone individuals, as children, lived in a world of make-believe much of the time. They pretended or believed that their dolls and toy animals were alive, they had imaginary playmates, and often they imagined they were a character in a book they were reading.

As adults, fantasy-prone individuals often "smell" or "see" what is being described in a conversation, find a special time or place to engage in imaginative activities, and have sexual fantasies so vivid they can lead to orgasm. Nine out of 10 report anomalous experiences such as automatic writing, "out-of-body" travel, "clairvoyance," "telepathy," or "precognition." More than two-thirds claim that they are able to heal sick people; three out of four claim to have encountered apparitions, ghosts, or spirits.

Wilson and Barber's subjects typically reported that they learned how to keep these activities secret as children and, as adults, discussed them with few—if any—other people. Wilson and Barber estimated that about 4% of the American population would be classified as fantasy-prone but stated that this percentage might be larger in cultures where these experiences were condoned or encouraged. Among the mediums I interviewed, it was apparent that their conversations with other practitioners provided a rational basis for these phenomena, had reinforced the behaviors, and had encouraged using the ensuing worldview to answer questions that arose about life's daily problems. It appears that for many Brazilians, the spiritist philosophy provided greater rewards than does that of secular society or orthodox religion.

The "mothers and fathers of the saints" in Candomblé and the di-

verse mediums I observed in both Umbanda and Kardecismo appeared to fall into this fantasy-prone category, as did the eclectic mediums who were most adept in entering trance. The "daughters and
sons of the saints" and the bulk of the other mediums were probably
not fantasy-prone but were able to enter altered states of consciousness as a result of their training, the social expectancy that exists
during the group sessions, and the cues (e.g., songs, charts, music)
that facilitate spirit incorporation (Bourguignon, 1976). Indeed, I
observed few instances of bizarre behavior during trance; the comportment that is most admired in mediums resembles ordinary social interaction. The training programs teach control, appropriate
role-taking, and support for one's fellow practitioners. For example,
if a spirit seems to be taking control too quickly, the other mediums
may sing a song that will slow down the process of incorporation
(Rouget, 1985).

    The altered state can be terminated abruptly (with head jerks,
rolling eyes, and body spasms) or gracefully (with farewells, bows,
and songs). Even if the medium claims not to recall the experiences,
there are other people who will recite the advice given to the client,
and who will tell the medium which spirit had been present on that
occasion. Sometimes the medium will claim amnesia except for the
chills, change in breathing, and/or dizziness that often signify the
onset of trance.

    Granted that these episodes are dissociative, are they pathologi-
cal? Leacock and Leacock (1972) observed that the mediums in
their study usually behaved in ways that were "basically rational,"
communicating effectively with other people; these are hardly
symptoms of psychosis or hysteria (p. 212). I would agree with their
assessments and would note that the role-taking behavior of the mediums reflects a higher degree of adaptation and imagination than is
characteristic of dysfunctional behavior. It is possible that some of
the mediums who are not fantasy-prone may "pretend" to be entranced at times, but the hard work and long training periods demanded of those who are called to this work make it highly unlikely
that pretense is frequently operative (Leacock & Leacock, 1972).
For those who are fantasy-prone, incorporation can occur spontaneously at any time of the day—and is not limited to a formal session.
After all, some spirits may have important news or advice that needs
to be shared immediately.

    The lure of becoming a spiritistic healer is especially strong for
those individuals who place great value on assisting other people. If
incorporation is positively experienced, the pattern of reinforce-

ment becomes so strong that the "call" to heal will be pursued. As long as spiritistic practice fulfills personal needs for status, for self-development, and for service, that "call" will be maintained.

REFERENCES

Andrade, H. G. (1972). *The psi matter.* Matão, Brazil: Clarim.
Bastide, R. (1960). *Les religions africaines au Bresil.* Paris: Universitaires de France.
Bourguignon, E. (1976). *Possession.* San Francisco: Chandler and Sharp.
Directorate of the Medical-Spiritist Association of São Paulo. (1985). A Associação Médico-Espírita de São Paulo contra o charlatanismo e a mistificação. *Boletim Médico-Espírita, 2*(3), x-xii.
Herskovits, M. J. (1937). African guides and Catholic saints in New World religious beliefs. *American Anthropologist, 39,* 635-643.
Kardec, A. (1971). *The mediums' book.* London: Psychic Press. (Original publication in 1861.)
Kardec, A. (1972). *The spirits' book.* São Paulo, Brazil: Lake. (Original publication in 1857.)
Krippner, S. (1987). Cross-cultural approaches to multiple personality disorder: Practices in Brazilian spiritism. *Ethos, 15,* 273-295.
Krippner, S., & Villoldo, A. (1976). *The realms of healing.* Millbrae, CA: Celestial Arts Press.
Leacock, S., & Leacock, R. (1972). *Spirits of the deep: Drums, mediums and trance in a Brazilian city.* Garden City, NY: Doubleday.
Lynn, S. J., & Rhue, J. W. (1988). Fantasy proneness: Hypnosis, developmental antecedents, and psychopathology. *American Psychologist, 43,* 35-44.
McGregor, P. (1962). *The moon and two mountains.* London: Souvenir Press.
Neher, A. (1962). A physiological explanation of unusual behavior in ceremonies involving drums. *Human Biology, 4,* 151-160.
Raboteau, A. J. (1986). The Afro-American traditions. In R. L. Numbers & D. W. Amundsen (Eds.), *Caring and curing: Health and medicine in the Western religious traditions* (pp. 539-562). New York: Macmillan.
Rauscher, E. A. (1985). Observations of a well known Brazilian psychic surgeon. *Psi Research, 4*(1), 57-65.
Rouget, G. (1985). *Music and trance: A theory of the relations between music and possession.* Chicago: University of Chicago Press.
St. Clair, D. (1971). *Drum and candle.* Garden City, NY: Doubleday.
Torrey, E. F. (1986). *Witchdoctors and psychiatrists: The common roots of psychotherapy and its future.* New York: Harper & Row.
Verger, P. F. (1985). *Lendas Africanas dos orixás.* Salvador, Brazil: Corrupio.
Villoldo, A., & Krippner, S. (1987). *Healing states.* New York: Fireside/Simon and Schuster.
Wickramasekera, I. (1986). A model of people at high risk to develop chronic stress-related somatic symptoms: Some predictions. *Professional Psychology: Research and Practice, 17,* 437-447.
Wilson, S., & Barber, T. X. (1981). Vivid fantasy and hallucinatory abilities in the life

histories of excellent hypnotic subjects ("somnambules"): Preliminary report with female subjects. In E. Klinger (Ed.), *Imagery: Concepts, results, and applications* (pp. 133-149). New York: Plenum Press.

10

HEALING AND TRANSFORMATION
Perspectives from !Kung Hunter-Gatherers

RICHARD KATZ

I. INTRODUCTION

Among the !Kung hunter-gatherers of the Kalahari Desert, healing is a central community ritual with significance far beyond affecting a cure.[1] In this article, I present field data on healing among the !Kung that support a definition of healing as "a process of transitioning toward meaning, balance, connectedness and wholeness" (Katz, 1982a). The data also suggest that the study of psychological healing provides special insights into processes of psychological development, education, and community, offering a transformational model.[2]

An enhanced state of consciousness, experienced most intensely by the healer, but also shared by the community, is at the core of !Kung healing. That enhanced state brings on a sense of connectedness between a spiritual healing power, the healers, and their community. Continual transitioning is the developmental pattern, as the relationship to power is in dynamic flux. The enhanced consciousness establishes the possibility of healing but does not remove healers from the context of daily life. Access to this healing power becomes significant only with its application within the daily life of the community. The healer serves as a vehicle to channel healing to the community, without accumulating power for personal use. The transformational model involves the experience of both accessing the enhanced state of consciousness and applying it within the community.

Individuals and communities that seek healing are often in the

AUTHOR'S NOTE: I wish to acknowledge the kind permission of the Government of Botswana to do the research reported in this chapter. The research was possible only because of the caring and wise support of the !Kung with whom I lived and worked, and who gave me so much. I hope this paper begins to reflect that understanding. I also want to thank Michael Murphy, Linda Levine, Susan Pollak, Becka Reichmann, and Merry White for their helpful comments, generously offered. Portions of this chapter are based on Katz (1986).

midst of crises, confusion, or a search for fulfillment (Katz, 1982a). In their vulnerability and openness to change, they reveal their fears and hopes. These fears and hopes are the context for the healing transition; their resolution or fulfillment, the aim of that transition.[3] Healing is not only a source of insight about human nature; it is also a vehicle for actualizing human potential (Bourguignon, 1979; Durkheim, 1968; Katz, 1982a; LeVine, 1982; Levi-Strauss, 1963; Van Gennep, 1960). Focusing as it does on vulnerability, healing deals with a critical link in the actualization of that potential, and thus with paradigmatic issues in community and individual development.

Healing also involves central tasks of psychological development, such as defining reality and making meaning; it is not merely confined to curing sick people. Focusing as it does upon the more intense disruptions and integrations in that reality definition and meaning making, healing can thus be studied as a paradigmatic developmental process. Among the !Kung, the process of becoming a healer exemplifies the process of healing itself; the key to both is an experience of transformation that benefits the community. As healers intersect with situations of crisis and opportunity in their efforts to construct reality and work on the dynamics of cultural balance, their education and development become inseparable processes. Thus, healing can also offer a paradigm for education.

The !Kung provide further support for considering healing in this paradigmatic fashion. The !Kung data offer a special evolutionary perspective. When I did fieldwork with the !Kung, they were living primarily as hunter-gatherers, a mode of adaptation rare today, though representative of what was the universal pattern of human existence for 99% of cultural history (Lee & DeVore, 1968). During that huge span of history, it is believed, basic patterns of human adaptation evolved (Lee & DeVore, 1968). Lee (1979) goes as far as to say that "basic human social forms, language and human nature itself were forged" during that span (p. 1). A study of !Kung healing may suggest principles fundamental to human healing and development, shedding light on their origins and evolution.[4]

The concept of healing explored in this paper suggests a tranformational model that can be applied to understanding processes of education, development, and community. The model is directly relevant to the healing enterprise, while offering an implicit generic perspective. For example, "education as transformation" describes a model of healer education, while offering a generic perspective on education. The transformational model emphasizes psychological and social transitioning and the sharing of valued resources, in striking contrast to comparable models that predominate in contemporary Euro-American culture, with their emphasis on linear, stage-wise progressions and the individual competition for, and accumulation of, valued resources.

While the cross-cultural relevance of this transformational model must be established with extreme care, the model presents an alternative to Euro-Western approaches that seems worth consideration (Katz, 1981; Katz & Craig, 1987, 1988; Katz & Kilner, 1987; Katz & Seth, 1986; Katz & St. Denis, 1988). The healing transition is an important key to a society's dominant issues in human potential; the transformational model suggests ways a society can encourage the communal generation and utilization of valued resources, a task Rappaport (1978) posits as critical for the survival of the human species.

We owe thanks to the !Kung because they have preserved this knowledge of healing at the cost of great suffering and nourished it in the context of oppression. Indigenous people have always offered their knowledge of healing as a gift to be shared with others for the benefit of the sick. We would be respecting that gift if we listened to their advice on using that knowledge. And as we realize the value of such advice, we can turn back to these indigenous people, returning their gift with our support of their present struggles for dignified self-determination in the various nation-states of the world in which they live.

II. ETHNOGRAPHIC DATA

In Botswana, Namibia, and southern Angola, there are about 50,000 San people, of whom some 5,000 live primarily as hunter-gatherers. My fieldwork, upon which this paper is based, occurred among a group of nearly 500 !Kung-speaking San, living as hunter-gatherers in the northwestern Kalahari Desert, Botswana.[5]

The economic system of the !Kung is based on sharing collected food resources (Lee, 1979, 1984; Lee & DeVore, 1976; Marshall, 1976). Local groups do not maintain exclusive rights to resources or defend territories; a reciprocal access prevails. Frequent visiting among different groups mitigates the effect of localized shortages. Allied groups cooperate, coming together in a given area, living apart when sources of food and water are widely scattered.

Resources of all kinds circulate among members of a camp and between camps, so that any one person draws upon resources far beyond his or her capacity. Little investment in a capital sector of the economy is necessary; elements of the material culture are easily made, with ample leisure time to make them. Since individuals must move around to get food, personal property is minimal, usually less than 25 pounds per adult (Lee, 1979). The environment itself acts as a storehouse. There is a marked absence of disparities in wealth and possessions among the !Kung. Egalitarianism is the rule (Lee, 1979).

The primary ritual among the !Kung, the all-night healing dance, epitomizes these characteristics of sharing and egalitarianism (Katz, 1981, 1982a, 1982b; Lee, 1968; Marshall, 1969). In the crucible of intense emotions and the search for protection that are the healing dance, sharing and egalitarianism are put to the test and relied upon as vehicles for survival. The healing power, or *n/um*, is the most valued resource at the dance, and one of the most valued resources in all community life (Katz, 1982a). It is released by the community and, through its healing effects, helps to recreate and renew that community. Though "strongest" at the dance, *n/um* has a primary significance throughout the !Kung universe of experience. Its existence and functioning harmonize with and help maintain !Kung life. !Kung healing involves health and growth on physical, psychological, social, and spiritual levels; it affects the individual, the group, the surrounding environment, and the cosmos. Healing is an integrating and enhancing force, far more fundamental than simple curing or the application of medicine.

As often as four times in a month, the women sit around the fire, singing and rhythmically clapping as night falls, signaling the start of a healing dance. The entire camp participates. The men, sometimes joined by the women, dance around the singers. As the dance intensifies, *n/um* ("energy") is activated in those who are healers, most of whom are among the dancing men. As *n/um* intensifies in the healers, they experience *!kia* ("a form of enhanced consciousness"), during which they heal everyone at the dance. The dance usually extends far into the night, often ending as the sun rises the next morning. Those at the dance confront the uncertainties of their experience and reaffirm the spiritual dimension of their daily lives. "Being at a dance makes our hearts happy," the !Kung say.

Kinachau, an experienced healer, talks about the *!kia* experience: "You dance, dance, dance, dance. Then *n/um* lifts you in your belly and lifts you in your back . . . *N/um* makes you tremble, it's hot . . .

When you get into *!kia*, you're looking around because you see everything, because you see what's troubling everybody . . ." (Katz, 1982a, p. 42).

Held in awe, *n/um* is considered very powerful and mysterious. As healers learn to control their boiling *n/um*, they can apply it to healing. They learn to heal, to "see the sickness and pull it out." The *n/um* in the healer must be activated for it to become a healing energy. The !Kung say that *n/um* must *gam,* or "rise up." The singing of the *n/um* songs helps "awaken" the *n/um* and "awaken" the healer's heart. The !Kung feel that their hearts must awaken before they can attempt to heal.

The *n/um* becomes stronger as it becomes hotter. The singing and the physical exertion of the dancing helps to heat up the healers' *n/um*. So do the various ways healers bring themselves into contact with the fire. When the *n/um* is hot from boiling up, *!kia* can result. One experienced healer says: "When we fall in *!kia*, our *n/um* is very hot, our *n/um* is as hot as it goes." Boiling *n/um* is painful. When *n/um* boils too rapidly, when it becomes too hot, the pain becomes so intense that fear overwhelms the healer. Then the clear perception necessary to see the sickness and heal is impossible. *!Kia* does not result in *!kia*-healing.

"Seeing properly" allows the healer to locate and diagnose the sickness in a person. /Wi, an old and experienced healer, speaks of ≠Dau, who is still comparatively "young in *!kia*":

> What tells me that ≠Dau isn't fully learned is the way he behaves. You see him staggering and running around. His eyes are rolling all over the place. If your eyes are rolling, you can't stare at sickness. You have to be absolutely steady to see sickness, steady-eyes, no shivering and shaking, absolutely steady . . . with a steady-gaze . . . you need direct looking. (Katz, 1982a, p. 106)

In seeing properly, one's "eye-insides are steady." One not only sees where and what the sickness is, but also, with that "absolutely steady" stare, one starts to treat the sickness.

This "proper seeing" allows the healer to see into and beyond many material manifestations. "Invisible" elements of the dance become "visible." /Wi talks further:

> [In *!kia*] you see the *n/um* rising in other healers. You see the singing and the *n/um*, and you pick it up . . . As a healer in *!kia*, you see everybody. You see that the insides of well people are fine. You see the in-

sides of the one the spirits are trying to kill and you go there. Then you
see the spirits and drive them away. (Katz, 1982a, p. 106)

In addition to describing the location and shape of a sickness inside
someone's body, healers may see at a distance—for example, warning persons of lions lurking out of sight or describing the activities in
a faraway camp. "Seeing properly" is an enhanced perception and
knowing, indicative of the healers' powers.

Sickness is pulled out as healers bring their vibrating hands close
to or in contact with a person. The healers are putting their *n/um*
into the other person and at the same time pulling the sickness out of
the other and into their own bodies. This is difficult, painful work.
The sickness is then expelled from the healer.

The laying on of hands is quite physical, direct, and penetrating:
"When I lay hands on a person, I take sickness into my hands. Then
I shiver from the sickness and then I throw it away." As /Wi speaks
these words, he makes a strong holding gesture, forming a cup with
both hands as he says, "I take sickness into my hands." The !Kung
word ≠*twe* refers to both the process of pulling out sickness and
the physical actions, such as the laying on of hands, that accomplish this process.

Beneath these healing behaviors a continuous, nonlinear process is occurring. The putting in of *n/um* and the pulling out of sickness are not different acts, nor even clearly delineated stages in the
same actions. This is particularly clear when healers in *!kia* heal
other healers not yet in *!kia*. In the very act of putting *n/um* into
the others, the healers who are already in *!kia* are not only pulling
out the others' sickness but also stimulating them into *!kia*. And, as
the other healers go into *!kia*, their own newly boiling *n/um* contacts the first healers, reintensifying their *!kia*. In this case, the
n/um is put in another to draw out the sickness and to activate
more *n/um*, which, among other things helps draw out the sickness.
The healing process is an even more dramatic unity when more experienced healers heal themselves. Their *n/um* and their sickness
exchange within themselves. Healing is an organic process
whereby a substance called sickness is transmuted by a substance
called *n/um*. It is not a mechanical process in which one substance
is replaced or erased by another.

≠Toma Zho, a powerful healer, spoke of the feeling *!kia* gives,
that of becoming more essential, more one's self: "I want to have a
dance soon so that I can really become myself again." A transcendent state of consciousness, *!kia* alters a !Kung's sense of self, time,

and space. *!Kia* makes healers feel they are "opening up" or "bursting open, like a ripe pod."

K"au ≠ Dau, a blind man who is one of the most powerful healers, describes his own transformation:

> God keeps my eyeballs in a little cloth bag. When he first collected them, he got a little cloth bag and plucked my eyeballs out and put them into the bag and then he tied the eyeballs to his belt and went up to heaven. And now when I dance, on the nights when I dance and the singing rises up, he comes down from heaven swinging the bag with the eyeballs above my head and then he lowers the eyeballs to my eye level, and as the singing gets strong, he puts the eyeballs into my sockets and they stay there and I cure. And then when the women stop singing and separate out, he removes the eyeballs, puts them back in the cloth bag and takes them up to heaven. (Katz, 1982a, p. 216)

During the *!kia* state he becomes more than himself because he can now see, and he means that both figuratively and literally.

Through *!kia*, the !Kung transcend ordinary life and can contact the realm of the gods and the spirits of dead ancestors. Sickness is a process in which the spirits try to carry a person off into their realm. In *!kia*, the healer expresses the wishes of the living to keep the sick person with them and goes directly into the struggle with the spirits. The healer is the community's emissary in this confrontation. When a person is seriously ill, the struggle intensifies. If a healer's *n/um* is strong, the spirits will retreat, and the sick one will live. This struggle is at the heart of the healer's art, skill, and power. In their search for contact with transcendent realms and in their struggle with illness, misfortune, and death, the healing dance and *n/um* are the !Kung's most important allies.

Fiercely egalitarian, the !Kung do not allow *n/um* to be controlled by a few religious specialists, but wish it to be spread widely among the group. All young boys and most young girls seek to become healers. By the time they reach adulthood, more than half the men and 10% of the women have become healers. Still, there is no stigma attached to those who do not become healers.[6] An unlimited energy, *n/um* expands as it boils. It cannot be hoarded by any one person.

The !Kung do not seek *!kia* for its own sake, but for its healing protection. At the healing dance, *n/um* is shared by everyone; all are given healing. As one person experiences *!kia* at the dance, others likely will follow. Though *!kia* may be experienced most intensely in the healers, they are channels to aid in the distribution of *n/um* to those at the dance.

The dance provides healing in the most generic sense: It may cure an ill body or mind, as the healer pulls out sickness with a laying on of hands; mend the social fabric, as the dance promotes social cohesion and a manageable release of hostility; protect the camp from misfortune, as the healer pleads with the Gods for relief from the Kalahari's harshness; and provide opportunities for growth and fulfillment, as all can experience a sense of well-being and some, a spiritual development.

These integrated functions of the dance reinforce one another, providing a continuous source of curing, counsel, protection, and enhancement. The healing dance is woven into !Kung hunting-gathering life without undermining the execution of everyday responsibilities. Healers are first and foremost hunters and gatherers, their primary obligation being to help in subsistence activities. A public, routine cultural event to which all have access, the dance establishes community, and it is the community, in its activation of *n/um*, that heals and is healed.

To heal depends upon developing a desire to "drink *n/um*," not on learning a set of specific techniques. Teaching focuses upon helping students overcome their fear, helping them to regulate the boiling *n/um* and resultant *!kia* so that healing can occur. Accepting boiling energy for oneself is a difficult process, because *n/um*, painful and mysterious, is greatly feared. The healer's education stresses not the structure of the dancing, but the importance of dancing so one's "heart is open to boiling *n/um*"; it emphasizes not the composition of the healing songs, but singing so that one's "voice reaches up to the heavens."

As they dance ever more seriously into the night, the potential healers' *n/um* may begin to boil, and *!kia* becomes imminent. As they feel *!kia* coming on, the potential healers try to regulate their condition, and they may resist the transition to an altered state. Others help to overcome this resistance. They try to help students to strike a balance between the oncoming intensity of *!kia* and their fear of it. It remains a dynamic balance. Experienced healers go as deeply into *!kia* as they can but must maintain control over the *n/um* to use it for healing. If the *!kia* is coming on so fast that fear escalates and prevents the experience of *!kia*, students may stop dancing for a while or drink some water to "cool down" the too rapidly boiling *n/um*. The *n/um* must be hot enough to evoke *!kia* but not so hot that it provokes debilitating fear. Throughout this work at the dance, extensive physical contact between the potential healers and experienced healers helps the students regulate the *n/um*.

The experience of *!kia* brings profound pain and fear, along with feelings of release and liberation. *N/um* feels "hot, like a fire that is inside." A respected healer described another dimension of this fear: "As we !Kung enter *!kia*, we fear death. We fear we may die and not come back!" When potential healers can face the fact of death and willingly die, they can overcome fear of *n/um*, and there can be a breakthrough to *!kia*. /Wi, an older healer, talks about this death and rebirth:

> [In *!kia*] your heart stops. You're dead. Your thoughts are nothing. You breathe with difficulty. You see things, *n/um* things; you see spirits killing people. You smell burning, rotten flesh. Then you heal, you pull sickness out. You heal, heal, heal. Then you live. Your eyeballs clear and you see people clearly. (Katz, 1982a, p. 45)

The process that teaches the !Kung to become healers also supports their continual efforts at healing. It is a process of education that engages the community.

The experience of healing among the !Kung involves the healers' acceptance of boiling *n/um* and an application of that *n/um* to healing. The fear and pain of boiling *n/um* must be felt; the fear and pain of dying during *!kia* must be faced. Embarking upon the search for *n/um* entails a risk—psychologically and physically—and the community offers its protective support for that journey. The fire that strengthens *n/um* can also burn. *!Kia*, an enhanced state of consciousness, represents a known mystery, experientially frightening though conceptually clear. The pain persists during the actual healing, though entering *!kia* brings transcendent feelings of release, and the unwinding or unfolding process of *//hxabe* brings pleasure. The painful transition into *!kia*, and then into *!kia*-healing, comes through the regulation of boiling *n/um*. The healers experience *!kia* as deeply as possible, provided they can control that *n/um* so as to direct it toward healing.

This transformation of consciousness, linking the spiritual power of *n/um* to the community through the healers, is expressed in a synthesis of phenomenological, behavioral, and environmental elements. When *n/um* is boiling, when it is potent for healing, it is seen as "hot," "heavy," "a lot." When it is weak, it is seen as "cold," "light," and "little." For example, as *n/um* boils, it is said to "heat up" or "rise up"; if it boils too rapidly, one must "cool" or "calm" or "bring down" the *n/um*. For the !Kung, the inner heat felt from boiling *n/um*, the heat of body temperature, and the heat of the fire are experienced as a connected—indeed, continuous—phenomena; likewise with their opposites.

The emphasis in this transformation of consciousness is on the process of transition rather than the nature of the barriers crossed or stages reached. Healers move continuously between their fear of the boiling *n/um* and their desire to heal others, their search for increased healing power and the increased difficulty of working with strong *n/um*. The regulation of *n/um* focuses upon transitions, balancing rising *n/um* with fear, pain, and the desire to heal. This balance is never a permanent one, so that within any one dance as well as over the career of a healer, the healer moves toward and away from boiling *n/um*, sometimes defeated by an unusually strong *n/um*, sometimes catapulted by that *n/um* into exceptionally strong healing. This intense experiential dialectic ensures that the balance is dynamic.

The career of healers can be seen as determined by the recurrent resolution—or lack of resolution—of one developmental task: to die to oneself in order to accept boiling *n/um*. Facing that task at increasing levels of difficulty is one sign of healers' increasing power. Powerful healers can accept especially hot and therefore painful *n/um* so that more potent healing becomes available. They can go deeper into *!kia* while maintaining finer control or turning *!kia* regularly toward the healing of serious illnesses. But it is rare that someone is considered "completely learned." Even the few most powerful healers, who represent the standard of what it means to be "completely learned," can experience an unexpectedly strong *n/um* at a dance and find themselves once again approaching and retreating from this boiling *n/um*.

III. TOWARD A TRANSFORMATIONAL MODEL

From the data on healing among the !Kung, we can extrapolate models of psychological development, education, and community, at whose crux are transformational experiences. For the !Kung, these experiences are epitomized in the process of "accepting boiling energy."[7] One expression of this transformation is a dramatically enhanced state of consciousness, such as *!kia*, but the transformational experience can also unfold during more subtle shifts in consciousness within the context of ordinary life events. Whether in its dramatic or ordinary context, transformation brings on an experience of reality in which the boundaries of self and social organization become more permeable to contact with a transpersonal realm. Accessing the enhanced state of consciousness and applying its effects within the community combine to constitute the transformational experience.

These transformational experiences can be said to unfold within and into a transformational model of psychological development (Katz, 1982b; Katz & Kilner, 1987); to be guided by a transformational model of education—"education as transformation" (Katz, 1981, 1982c); and to be structured by a transformational model of community—"synergistic community" (Katz, 1983/4; Katz & Seth, 1986). In fact, there is one transformational model, which, as it is applied to the areas of development, education, and community, interrelates those areas: Education and development merge, and community is a stimulant for, as well as an expression of, both. The model is offered as generic, originally derived from, but not necessarily limited to, healer or spiritual development and education, or healing communities. Though in contemporary Euro-American culture the spiritual is considered a separate or separable dimension, and healing a separate or separable role, the !Kung data describe a situation in which the spiritual is inseparable from other aspects of life, as is healing. The model reflects this integrated conception and offers an integrated perspective for understanding development, education, and community in the West.

The transformational model as applied to psychological development is clarified when compared with the Piagetian model, probably the most commonly accepted theory of developmental psychology in the West.[8] For example, the spiritual dimension plays a central role in the transformational model, in contrast to the focus on psychological, and especially cognitive, dimensions in the Piagetian approach.[9] That spiritual dimension is extraordinary only in its depth and intensity, not in its separation from ordinary life. It includes, in an integrative manner, the psychological and cognitive dimensions, as well as other dimensions such as the emotional and physical. The validity of the transition into an enhanced state, and of the state itself, is dependent on its application within daily life.

The transformational model emphasizes transitioning rather than stages achieved, process and experience rather than structures. A continual process of transitioning over the life course is viewed as the crux of development, rather than the Piagetian focus upon a linear (or spiral) progression through fixed stages that culminates in an equilibrated end-state, or stage, in adulthood. Life history in the transformation model becomes the continuous dialectic of meeting and being overwhelmed by one recurring developmental challenge: transcending the self to channel transpersonal resources to the community. This contrasts with the idea of different developmental challenges at different stages in the Piagetian model. Though healers have careers, and can be said to move through stages in their work, these are surface categories that do not organize the transitioning experiences.

Unlike the developmental process in the Piagetian model, the process of transitioning is neither unidirectional nor the basis of permanent structural gains. Transitioning occurs toward and away from meaning, balance, connectedness, and wholeness; and each movement is considered important in and of itself—regardless of direction—because it deals with the basic developmental challenge of transitioning. Once a particular meaning, for example, has been achieved in a certain setting, it is not thereby permanent. Meaning is undone as meaninglessness inevitably appears and old and new meaning are established. In their continual struggle to regulate their access to and control of the healing power, healers exemplify this fluidity in the developmental process. With each opportunity for transition, knowledge of how to transit must in the existential sense be relearned; at times it is unavailable, even to the experienced healers. The process of transitioning is also accompanied by a fundamental experience of vulnerability, both more frightening and more liberating than the feelings of perplexity, confusion, surprise, and insight that are spoken of as accompanying the developmental transitions in the Piagetian framework.

Finally, the merging of individual and social development in the transformational model contrasts with the more individualistic, even personal emphasis in Piagetian models. In the transformational model, development is a shared enterprise, a joining of self and community, with unexpected benefits to both. It is a way of giving support for the difficulties of transition as well as a way of distributing the benefits released by that transitioning.

By understanding the healer as a "moral explorer," we can see evidence for this merging of individual and sociocultural development. Healers are faced with the task of defining reality in their interactions with cultural mysteries. Defining reality, they impart meaning. Imparting meaning, they make judgments about mortality. None of these activities is predetermined. The community sends healers on a journey to new territories of experience, to formulate new questions of reality, meaning, and morality; and then it looks to them for guidance in these areas. In dynamic interaction with changing times, they can provide guidance for the direction of change.

The transformational model as applied to education—"education as transformation"—stresses character development rather than cognitive development as the critical context for knowledge (Hahn & Katz, 1985; Katz, 1981, 1982c). It is qualities of heart—courage, commitment, belief, and intuitive understanding—that open the healers to the healing potential, facilitate the learning of healing knowledge, and keep them in the healing work. Healing technologies become available to those with the necessary character. Technologies serve the healing aim, but they do not justify or measure the healing work. Character is the necessary foundation and result of developmental processes.

Education as transformation stresses process more than outcome, focusing on healing as a dynamic balancing rather than the achievement of specific cures. Such education respects both aspects of a dialectic that seem necessary to individual and community health (J. Rappaport, 1981; Turner, 1969). It connects experiences ordered by the structures of daily life as well as those that occur in transition between and beyond those structures. Education as transformation gives added weight to the experience of transition itself, emphasizing the intrinsic value of the psychological movement that animates that transition. The experience of the transpersonal is intensified during these transitions but not restricted to them. In a process we can call "envisioning," the experience of enhanced consciousness is continually reenacted and reaffirmed in the healers' daily lives. Transformation initiates the intensive phase of becoming a healer and also characterizes the healer's subsequent development.

Education as transformation is based upon a service orientation. The healer's commitment is to serve as a vehicle that channels healing to the community rather than to accumulate power for personal use. Education aims to connect the teaching-learning process to its community contexts. The cure of a particular patient assumes importance in the larger context of the general sense of dynamic balance in the community. Healers become a community's focal point of intensity, embodying a dedication to the healing work and reaffirming the community's self-healing capacities.

The transformation model as applied to community—"synergistic community"—is epitomized, for example, in the !Kung healing community. In a synergistic community, valued resources are renewable, expanding, and accessible (Katz, 1983/84; Katz & Seth, 1986). As these resources are shared equitably with all members of the community, the whole becomes greater than the sum of the parts, and what is good for one member becomes good for all. As a result, benefits to the community grow exponentially.

Synergy and scarcity represent paradigmatic alternatives, two ends of a continuum that in actual situations exist in some combination (Katz, 1983/84). What might be called a "scarcity paradigm" dominates Western thinking about the existence and distribution of a wide variety of resources. The paradigm assumes that valued resources are scarce; their presumed scarcity in fact largely determines their value. It further assumes that individuals or communities must compete with each other to gain access to these resources, struggling to accumulate their own supply, resisting pressures to share.[10]

An alternative paradigm is based on synergy. The term *synergy* describes a pattern of relationships among phenomena, including how people relate to one another and to other phenomena (Fuller, 1963; Katz, 1982a: Maslow, 1971; Maslow & Honigmann, 1970). A synergistic pattern exists when phenomena are interrelating, so that an often unexpected, new, and greater whole is created from disparate, seemingly conflicting parts. In that pattern, phenomena exist in harmony with one another, maximizing one anothers' potential. Within the synergy paradigm, a resource such as healing becomes renewable and expansively accessible, yet it can remain valuable (Katz, 1981).[11] Individuals and communities activate resources. They function as guardians, not possessors, of resources, and while guided by the motivation of service to others, they allow resources to be shared by all members of the community. Greater amounts of the resource become increasingly available to all, so that collaboration rather than competition is encouraged. Paradoxically, the more the resource is utilized, the more there is to be utilized.

Synergistic community is a perspective for understanding the functioning of synergy within a community as well as a guideline for increasing that synergy (Katz, 1983/4).[12] If, for example, healing is a valued resource for a community, the existence of a synergistic community would mean that that resource would expand and become renewable. The community would heal and become healed.

Synergistic community is initiated when members experience an enhancement of consciousness. As the boundaries of self become more permeable to the spiritual dimension, a transpersonal bonding between people can occur so that individuals realize and activate communal commitments. As persons "die to" or go beyond their individual needs, sharing of resources becomes possible, even predictable. Realizing their deep connectedness, persons realize they do not have to compete for resources, which have become shared and thereby expanding.[13] Synergistic community is established by the full transformational experience.

The transformational experience is based on access to and working with a resource that is highly valued in the culture and is also renewable and expanding when activated—for example, *n/um* for the !Kung. Transformation itself activates that resource. Given its sociocultural context, transformation releases that resource—now in the form of healing—to the community, making it accessible to all. A reciprocating web of valued resources becomes renewable and shared; for example, *n/um* is released in the process of healing, which stimulates and expresses developmental processes so that access to *n/um* is further facilitated.

The recurring developmental challenge is on behalf of one's community and the benefits channeled to that community, whether or not the challenge is met. In either case the community shares in the process of transitioning, supporting the healer's movement back and forth as it itself so moves. As one healer makes the transition, it becomes more likely that another will; it is not a zero-sum game, but a situation of renewable and expanding resources. The !Kung healing dance exemplifies this: healers, by their own *!kia*, stimulate *!kia* in others. In synergistic fashion, effects are produced that are far beyond what is possible from separate actions.[14]

The transformational model we have just presented has been deduced from the field data on !Kung community healing systems. But to what extent is this model culture-dependent, embedded in specific demographic, economic, technological, and other sociocultural conditions? The general validity of the model awaits further empirical work in other cultures. How valid is transformation as a paradigm for the processes of psychological healing, and in particular to healer development and education and healing communities? How valid is healing as a paradigm for generic processes of development, education, and community? A first step in this empirical effort demonstrates that "education as transformation" characterizes healer education among hunter-gatherers generally (Hahn & Katz, 1985), among traditional Fijian healers (Katz, 1981; Katz & Kilner, 1987), and among certain highly valued contemporary Western community psychiatrists (Cheever, 1988).

Despite the provisional nature of the proposed transformational model, its striking contrast with Euro-American models deserves comment. Transformational experiences are relatively absent in Euro-American models. These transformational experiences, epitomized in the healing transitioning, take individuals beyond the self and take communities beyond the usual boundaries of social organization. The result is a network of interconnections between individuals and within communities that makes sharing of resources a simple fact of living. The absence of such transformational experiences makes such sharing difficult, in spite of human motivation and intention.

Compelling arguments document the necessity of sharing, as well as other characteristics of the transformational model, for the survival of the human community (see e.g., Caplan & Killilea, 1976; Eliade, 1965; Freire, 1970, 1985; James, 1958; Jung, 1952; Lee, 1979; Light, 1980; Maslow, 1971; J. Rappaport, 1981; R. Rappaport, 1978; Sarason, 1977). There is, for example, the need to appreciate the nonlinear oscillation about a recurring central developmental issue rather than the relative Euro-American preoccupation with linear, "progressive" models of development; the need to focus on character and community service in education rather than the relative Euro-American emphasis on technical training in isolation from character and on the personal accumulation of skill and power; and the need to view resources as renewable and expanding rather than the relative Euro-American orientation that valued resources are scarce, requiring competition to access them.

From the perspective of most contemporary Euro-American communities, establishing a synergistic community would require a radical paradigm shift—a major shift in the way persons experience meaning and interpret data (Kuhn, 1970). Accepting—even cultivating—a sense of vulnerability would create the possibility for such a shift (Katz, 1987). Experiencing the self-embedded-in-community as a desirable state, along with the sense of the separate and separating self, would be one result. In a synergistic community, self and community work toward the common good while seeking to fulfill their own perceived needs. As healing is given, more rather than less becomes available. These apparently "illogical" events can be accepted or even encouraged when the synergy paradigm prevails. If change is to occur and persist, sociopolitical structures that initiate and express these new ways of making sense of experience must be established.

R. Rappaport (1978) suggests that rituals in which we experience a transpersonal bonding are essential for the survival for the species. He claims that only through participating in such rituals can we overcome our separateness as individuals and, by knowing the reality of the transpersonal, become able to accomplish the communal tasks so essential to the survival of the human community. The present individualism and consequent fragmentation of these communal efforts in industrialized society are well documented (Berger, Berger, & Kellner, 1973). The transformational model offers an alternative to this fragmentation, stressing a transpersonal, bonding within a supportive sociocultural context.

NOTES

1. The ethnographic data on the !Kung presented in this paper come largely from groups living primarily as hunter-gatherers in the 1950s and 1960s. The !Kung are also popularly known by the derogatory term "Bushmen."

2. The terms "transformation" and "transformational" have wide usage in the social sciences (see, e.g., "Education as transformation," 1981; Gould, 1978; Jung, 1952). But rather than working within a strictly comparative framework, I wish to devote this paper to generating a particular meaning constellation for the terms, and for the purposes of the paper, restrict the terms to those developed meanings.

Among the !Kung and in most traditional non-Western cultures, there are no significant differentiations between "physical" and "psychological" healing. But I have chosen the term "psychological healing" when dealing with the transformational model proposed, because the main application of that model in this paper will be to contemporary Euro-American thinking and practice, where such differentiations remain crucial. Assuming the validity of those distinctions, the model proposed would be more relevant to the psychological and sociocultural context of health and illness than the specific issues of tissue damage and repair. Yet this conservative stance may soon be unnecessary, as evidence is increasing within Western social science and medicine for the confluence of the psychological and physical elements of healing (see, e.g., Sobel, 1979).

3. Healing systems are among those parts of a culture most sensitive to change. Dealing as they do with points of crisis, confusion, and opportunity—transitions that are the essence of cultural change—healing systems often function as the barometers of, as well as the responses to, such change. Therefore, the study of healing could be focusing upon patterns of adaptation to change, perhaps even upon aspects of the culture that are most changed.

4. Contemporary hunter-gatherers or foragers are different from ancient foragers, changed as they are by their own history, which includes contact with other types of societies. Also, there are differences among contemporary foragers, such as the !Kung, the Inuit, and the Australian aboriginal (Lee, 1979). Yet the !Kung remain one of the few living groups whose lifestyle may be similar to that ancient foraging way: "The modern foragers do offer clues to the nature of the [foraging] way of life, and by

understanding the adaptations of the past we can better understand the present and the basic material that produced them both" (Lee, 1979, p. 433).

5. This fieldwork is reported primarily in Katz (1982a) and was conducted as part of the larger Harvard Kalahari Research Project (Lee & DeVore, 1976).

6. Healers are similar to non-healers in a broad range of social, economic, and political variables. While healers are not a privileged group, they do differ psychologically from non-healers in ways that both prepare them for the healing work and result from that work (Katz, 1982a). It is a distinction they are meant to carry within. "We (!Kung) are not meant to boast of our healing. It is . . . something we do to help others."

7. !Kung egalitarian social structure, with its emphasis on sharing, ensures that *n/um* is applied as healing that is distributed throughout the community. Therefore there is a relative emphasis in the !Kung data on accessing the enhanced state of consciousness. In Fiji, for example, the social structure cannot so clearly ensure that mana is applied to healing and distributed throughout the community. Therefore, there is a relative emphasis in the Fijian data on applying the enhanced state toward healing in the community (Katz, 1981).

8. Piaget's focus is on intellectual development and the development of moral reasoning, and thus has limitations as a general theory of development for the whole person. But other theorists have extended the Piagetian framework to such areas as social development (Selman, 1980), faith development (Fowler, 1982), and community development (Higgins, Power, & Kohlberg, 1984). Our discussion of the Piagetian model is based upon this broader conception of the Piagetian framework. The transformational model can be particularly confusing at this point, because some of those working within the Piagetian framework use the term "transformation" to refer to processes that are different from those described in this paper.

9. Fowler's (1981) work considers the influence of spiritual factors throughout development. But it is not until the final stage in his theory, "Universalizing Faith," that he deals with a spiritual influence as direct and pervasive as that which occurs in the transformational model of development. Even then Fowler's Universalizers are rare and often exist at odds with their culture, in contrast to the spiritual dimension of the transformation model, which is consonant with the cultural context.

10. The relation of actual scarcity of particular resources to cooperation or competition remains an empirical question. The relationship may differ according to the resource in question as well as the social structure governing access to and control of that resource. Water is a scarce and valued resource for the !Kung people of the Kalahari Desert, while building materials for their shelters are a plentiful and valued resource. Both resources are shared among the !Kung (Lee, 1979).

11. It can be argued that resources created at least in part by human activity and intention, such as healing, are intrinsically expanding and renewable. Yet the scarcity paradigm can dominate the generation and distribution of these human resources. In most Western psychotherapy techniques, healing is seen as existing in scarce supply. Value, expressed in varying fee schedules, becomes entrained to scarcity. People are forced to compete with one another for their share of healing. Here the scarcity paradigm seems to function more as an ideology than an empirically derived framework.

12. Synergy, it seems, is an inevitable aspect or phase of community. It exists in a dialectical relationship with its opposite. Most Euro-American communities function primarily within the scarcity paradigm, but they require moments of synergy in order to remain intact. "Synergistic community" refers both to the phase of synergy that is intrinsic to community and to those particular communities in which there is

relatively more synergy. But community cannot always function synergistically. In Turner's (1969) framework, anti-structure cannot exist without structure.

13. Synergistic community can exist even though its members are not altruistic, i.e., intentionally wishing to share or to help others. Sometimes the structure of synergistic communities is the dominant feature, overriding individual motivations. Members can act out of what they perceive as their own best, even individual, interests, but the structure makes what is good for one, good for all.

14. An important source for concepts of community in contemporary Western culture, as well as for strategies of introducing community change, is the discipline of "community psychology" (J. Rappaport, 1981; Sarason, 1977). Community psychology operates primarily within scarcity-paradigm thinking; its view of community is in sharp contrast to that of synergistic community. For example, community psychology assumes there is an inherent conflict between the individual and the community, because resources are insufficient to satisfy both; often, one is satisfied at the expense of the other. The inability of community psychology to fulfill its mandate to encourage individual and community change may be due in part to its commitment to the scarcity paradigm.

REFERENCES

Berger, P., Berger, B., & Kellner, H. (1973). *The homeless mind: Modernization and consciousness.* New York: Vintage Books.

Bourguignon, E. (1979). *Psychological anthropology.* New York: Holt, Rinehart & Winston.

Caplan, G., & Killilea, M. (Eds.). (1976). *Support systems and mutual help.* New York: Grune & Stratton.

Cheever, O. (1988). *The training of community psychiatrists: A test of the model of "Education as Transformation."* Doctoral dissertation, Harvard Graduate School of Education.

Durkheim, E. (1968). *The elementary forms of religious life.* New York: Free Press.

Education as transformation. 1981. [Special issue]. *Harvard Educational Review, 51*(1).

Eliade, M. (1965). *Rites and symbols of initiation.* New York: Harper & Row.

Fowler, J. (1981). *Stages of faith: Psychology of human development and the quest for meaning.* New York: Harper & Row.

Freire, P. (1970). Cultural action for freedom. *Harvard Educational Review,* Monograph Series No. 1.

Freire, P. (1985). *The politics of education: Culture, power and liberation.* South Hadley, MA: Bergin & Garvey.

Fuller, B. (1963). *Ideas and integrities.* New York: Simon & Schuster.

Gould, R. (1978). *Transformations.* New York: Simon & Schuster.

Hahn, H., & Katz, R. (1985). *Education as transformation: A test of the model.* Unpublished manuscript, Harvard University.

Higgins, A., Power, C., & Kohlberg, L. (1984). The relationship of moral atmosphere to judgments of responsibility. In W. Kurtines & J. Gerwirtz (Eds.), *Morality, moral behavior, and moral development.* New York: John Wiley.

James, W. (1958). *The varieties of religious experience.* New York: Mentor Books.

Jung, C. (1952). *Transformation.* Princeton: Princeton University Press.

Katz, R. (1981). Education as transformation: Becoming a healer among the !Kung and Fijians. *Harvard Educational Review, 51*(1), 57-78.

Katz, R. (1982a). *Boiling energy: Community healing among the Kalahari !Kung.* Cambridge, MA: Harvard University Press.

Katz, R. (1982b). Accepting "boiling energy": Transformation and healing. *Ethos, 10*(4), 344-368.

Katz, R. (1982c). Commentary on "Education as Transformation." *Harvard Educational Review, 52*(1), 63-66.

Katz, R. (1983/4). Empowerment and synergy: Expanding the community's healing resources. *Prevention in Human Services, 3*(2/3).

Katz, R. (1986). Healing and transformation. In M. White & S. Pollak (Eds.), *The cultural transition: Social transformation in the Third World of Japan.* New York: Routledge & Kegan Paul.

Katz, R. (1987). The role of vulnerability in field-work. In A. Schenk & H. Kalweit (Eds.), *The healing forces of knowledge* (German Language Edition). Munich: Wilhelm Goldman Verlag.

Katz, R., & Craig, R. (1987). Community healing: The rich resource of tradition. *The Exchange, 8*(2).

Katz, R., & Craig, R. (1988). Health is more than not being sick. *The Exchange, 9*(2).

Katz, R., & Kilner, L. (1987). The straight path: A Fijian perspective on development. In C. Super (Ed.), *The role of culture in developmental disorder.* New York: Academic Press.

Katz, R., & Seth, N. (1986). Synergy and healing: A perspective on western health care. *Prevention in Human Services, 5*(1).

Katz, R., & St. Denis, V. (1988). Teacher as healer: A renewing tradition. In R. Barnhardt (Ed.), *Cross-cultural issues in Alaskan education* (Vol. 3). Fairbanks: University of Alaska (Center for Cross-Cultural Studies).

Kuhn, T. S. (1970). *The structure of scientific revolutions* (2nd ed., enlarged). Chicago: University of Chicago Press.

Lee, R. B. (1968). The sociology of !Kung Bushman trance performances. In R. Prince (Ed.), *Trance and possession states.* Montreal: Bucke Memorial Society.

Lee, R. B. (1979). *The !Kung San: Men, women and work in a foraging society.* Cambridge: Cambridge University Press.

Lee, R. B. (1984). *The Dobe !Kung.* New York: Holt, Rinehart & Winston.

Lee, R. B., & DeVore, I. (Eds.) (1968). *Man the hunter.* Chicago: Aldine.

Lee, R. B., & DeVore, I. (1976). *Kalahari hunter-gatherers: Studies of the !Kung San and their neighbors.* Cambridge, MA: Harvard University Press.

LeVine, R. (1982). *Culture, behavior and personality* (2nd ed.). Chicago: Aldine.

Levi-Strauss, C. (1963). *Structural anthropology.* New York: Basic Books.

Light, D. (1980). *Becoming psychiatrists: The professional transformation of the self.* New York: Norton.

Marshall, L. (1969). The medicine dance of the !Kung Bushmen, *Africa, 39,* 347-381.

Marshall, L. (1976). *The !Kung of Nyae Nyae.* Cambridge, MA: Harvard University Press.

Maslow, A. (1971). *The farther reaches of human nature.* New York: Viking.

Maslow, A., & Honigmann, J. (1970). Ruth Benedict's notes on synergy. *American Anthropologist, 72,* 320-333.

Rappaport, J. (1981). In praise of paradox: A social policy of empowerment over prevention. *American Journal of Community Psychology, 9*(1), 1-25.

Rappaport, R. (1978). Adaptation and the structure of ritual. In N. Blurton-Jones &

V. Reynolds (Eds.), *Human behavior and adaptation* (Vol. 18). New York: Halsted Press.

Sarason, S. (1977). *The psychological sense of community: Prospects for a community psychology.* San Francisco: Jossey-Bass.

Selman, R. (1980). *The growth of interpersonal understanding: Developmental and clinical understanding.* New York: Academic Press.

Sobel, D. (Ed.). (1979). *Ways of health.* New York: Harcourt Brace Jovanovich.

Turner, V. (1969). *The ritual process.* Chicago: Aldine.

Van Gennep, A. (1960). *The rites of passage.* Chicago: University of Chicago Press.

PART IV

Alternative Perspectives on Altered States of Consciousness

> Possession [and other forms of altered states of consciousness], in fact, is not a solitary act or an isolated phenomenon. It represents just one aspect of a particular world view . . . It is intrinsically linked to social structures, religious philosophy, political institutions and indigenous theories of mental health and illness. (Ward, 1980, p. 150)

While the primary focus of this volume has been upon the relationship between altered states of consciousness and mental health, the authors in this section suggest alternative avenues for the analysis of altered states of awareness. A diversity of theoretical perspectives, methodological approaches, and content areas are presented in the cross-cultural study of ASC's. Theoretical contributions are made from perceptual-cognitive psychology, sociology, and political anthropology, including examples of signal detection theory, dramaturgical analyses, social-psychological and sociopolitical theories of power, and macro-analysis of social change. Investigative approaches include ethnographic studies and naturalistic observations as well as archival research reliant on early-twentieth-century writings and ancient pottery and art works. A diversity of altered states of consciousness is also described and discussed: vivid imagining, hallucinogenic states, trance, and possession.

Zusne opens the section with a critical review of Ludwig Staudenmaier's autobiographical account and analysis of magic as an experimental natural science. Staudenmaier, an early-twentieth-century chemist, utilized introspection to "report objectively on self-induced altered states of consciousness" and attempted to subject to scientific scrutiny and experimentation such diverse phenomena as automatic writing, possession, hallucinations, and psychokinetics. Zusne, however, dismisses Staudenmaier's "scientific" theorizing on ASC's as magical thinking camouflaged by scientific language and then provides an insightful alternative analysis of Staudenmaier's psychic experiences. While Zusne argues that Staudenmaier possessed an exceptional ability as an imager and that he was unlikely to be psychologically disturbed despite the frequent onset of ASC's, he acknowledges that many of the states could be described as near-psychotic. Preferring to consider Staudenmaier as a fantasy-prone individual, Zusne discusses the ASC experiences in terms of signal detection theory with reference to eidetics and hallucinations and the distinction between controlled and autonomous imagery. The chapter presents an impressive piece of archival research and a clever extension of mainstream perceptual-cognitive theory to explain altered states of awareness in this unusual context.

Lee diverges from subjective psychological accounts of altered states of awareness and takes a more critical sociological perspective on such phenomena. The author voices vigorous objections to the tendency for researchers to rely somewhat uncritically on reference to private feelings and notes that these are verifiable only by participating individuals. He argues that private feelings are shaped by larger social contexts and that researchers can assess the social rules governing the display of ritual ASC's. Lee, therefore, applies a dramaturgical analysis to altered states of awareness in Malaysian healing practices, with the objective of diminishing the overemphasis on internal processes. In this context three areas of the ritual activities are examined and discussed: the medium's behavior, the audience's response, and the rules of trance performance. Lee concludes that ASC's in healing practices are "not only physiological and psychological events, but also a function of the social relationship between mediums and clients."

While Stoller contemplates the relationship between ASC's and mental health in his study of Songhay possession, his analysis occurs on the societal rather than the individual level, and emphasis is placed upon the relationship between ceremonial altered states of awareness and rapid social change. Stoller convincingly argues that Africans have historically employed a range of satiric symbolic devices as a means of cultural resistance to disruptive social influences. Hauka trance and possession in the Songhay, for example, are described as emerging as a parody of the French colonial imposition of the early twentieth century. Sasale possession activities, by contrast, are rude and sexually explicit and have recently evolved to mock the moral premises of Islam in contemporary Niger. Both forms of ceremonial trance and possession function as societal means of protecting cultural identity. Stoller argues that they constitute a "psychologically stabilizing response to social change and cultural dissolution brought on by stressing social change." While this position has been hinted at throughout this volume, Stoller makes the argument more explicit with his macro-analysis and provides a fitting complement to the earlier focus on the individual.

Finally, Dobkin de Rios assumes a novel approach to the study of ASC's both in her selection of hallucinogenic states as depicted in pre-Columbian art and her analysis of these phenomena in relation to psychological and anthropological theories of power. Hallucinogenic plant use by the ancient Moche is documented by early art works, as are shamanic activities and powers—healing, neutralizing misfortunes, and initiating military victories, as well as the ability to transform into *naguals* (animal familiars). Although acknowledging the potential significance of power for the individual healer, Dobkin de Rios concentrates on a macro political analysis, postulating that as societies become more complex, access to ASC's is regulated by an elite. In the case of the Moche it is argued that shamans utilize psychoactive plants in order to enable them to focus in accordance with the power needs of their culture. Dobkin de Rios, then, offers an insightful political analysis of the utilization of nonordinary states of consciousness for religious and healing purposes, complementing the psychological and psychiatric interpretations that have predominated in this volume. All in all, the chapters in this section extend the cross-cultural perspectives on altered states of consciousness.

REFERENCE

Ward, C. (1980). Spirit possession and mental health: A psychoanthropological perspective. *Human Relations, 33*(3), 149-163.

11

ALTERED STATES OF CONSCIOUSNESS, MAGICAL THINKING, AND PSYCHOPATHOLOGY
The Case of Ludwig Staudenmaier

LEONARD ZUSNE

In 1912 there appeared a book with the curious title *Magic as an Experimental Natural Science*, written by a chemist, Ludwig Staudenmaier.[1] Staudenmaier's ambition was to establish a new discipline by subjecting to scientific scrutiny and experimentation phenomena that traditionally had been considered under the rubric of magic and by introducing systematic training for its practitioners. Of much greater interest to the psychologist, however, are the altered states of consciousness, dissociation of personality, and paranormal phenomena that Staudenmaier writes about in connection with his work on magic. Most case histories of hallucinators, eidetikers, stigmatists, or alternate personalities are second-hand reports by observers, investigators, or therapists. *Magic as an Experimental Natural Science* is significant because it is a first-person account of unusual imagery by an individual who combines an educational background in both theology and chemistry with an exceptional ability as an imager. Another reason that prompts me to examine the case of Ludwig Staudenmaier is his ability to report objectively on self-induced altered states of consciousness and the associated abnormal and paranormal behaviors and experiences even when in a state that ordinarily would be considered to be at least near-psychotic.

LUDWIG STAUDENMAIER'S LIFE

Staudenmaier was born in Krumbach, Bavaria, on February 14, 1865. After graduating from high school at the age of 19, he took a year of philosophy and three years of theology at a Catholic *Lyzeum* in Bavaria, a university-level school specializing in philosophy and theology. After a year's practical experience in ecclesiastic service, Staudenmaier enrolled at the University of Munich to study zoology and chemistry. He does not say what the reason for the switch was. He passed his doctoral examination in chemistry, stayed on as assistant at a natural sciences laboratory for 18 months, then, in 1896, was appointed professor of experimental chemistry at the Royal *Lyzeum* in Freising, near Munich. He still held that position in 1922. Staudenmaier died in Rome on August 20, 1933.

Staudenmaier seems to have been unmarried and to have lived alone. He mentions his mother once briefly as a witness who heard the same mysterious (and presumably paranormal) noise that he had heard, but not his father, and he tells us nothing about his childhood or youth. He gives a few tantalizing details concerning his physical appearance and health when this becomes necessary in connection with his description of his experiences. He must have been a very slight individual (64½ inches tall, weighing 110 pounds, dropping to an all-time low of 83 pounds in 1915), a condition that must have been related to his lifelong gastrointestinal problems. His low weight, combined with a very flexible body, inclined him to gymnastics, and he describes with considerable pride his performance, remarkable for a person of his age, as a member of a Bavarian *Turnverein*. His somatotype and his chronically "nervous" stomach tie in with his self-description as a very intense person.

Staudenmaier apparently published more than one paper on chemistry in professional journals. His book indicates that he must have done a considerable amount of reading outside the field of chemistry. Apart from authors of spiritualist and occult literature, he mentions the names of Alzheimer, Exner, Kraepelin, Nissl, and Rank in connection with their views on the organicity of mental disorders and briefly alludes to the case of a patient of Joseph Breuer's and the founding of psychoanalysis. Freud is mentioned once in passing, although it appears that Staudenmaier read his *Five Lectures on Psychoanalysis*. Various other psychologists, psychiatrists, and physiologists are mentioned, mainly for two reasons: either their names are associated with psychical research (Dessoir, Flournoy, Haeckel, Huxley, Münsterberg, Pfungst, Richet, Stumpf, Zöllner) or they had made statements concerning the localization of mental functions or the psyche (Ebbinghaus, Flechsig, Jung), two subject matters of considerable concern to Staudenmaier. Theodor Lipps is quoted approvingly concerning the importance of the unconscious to psychology, while Wundt is cited in order to disagree with him concerning the possibility of doing experimental self-observation.

Staudenmaier began his imagery experiments in 1901. He reported them first in a 38-page article that appeared in 1910 in *Annalen der Naturphilosophie*, a journal published in Leipzig by Wilhelm Ostwald, the Nobel-prize-winning chemist. Ostwald personally endorsed the publication of Staudenmaier's paper. Expanded to book form, Staudenmaier's work was first published in 1912, was reprinted in 1918 and 1920, saw an enlarged edition in 1922, and was reprinted once again in 1968. The publication history of the book shows that it enjoyed a measure of success. It was received enthusiastically in some quarters and severely criticized in others. Staudenmaier, who never responded to individual published critiques of his work, cites the most important ones in the last chapter of the second edition of his book, a chapter in which he responds to all critics at once.

THE EXPERIMENTS

At first Staudenmaier did not have any plans to conduct experiments. The instructions for imaging that he gives were formulated after he had lived through some disturbing experiences. The instructions and the theorizing that Staudenmaier offers may therefore be seen as either a rationalization of what to most would appear a psychosis or a genuine and partly successful attempt to place mental disorders, imagery, altered states of consciousness, and paranormal phenomena within the same explanatory framework. Even though some rationalization is evident in Staudenmaier's book, I think the latter possibility is more in accord with what he has to say.

Staudenmaier began his excursions into the realm of altered states of consciousness and imagery when, upon the suggestion of an acquaintance, he tried automatic writing.[2] He soon found that he was rather good at it, and various entities began to report themselves through the writing, entities which Staudenmaier knew from the outset were the products of his own mind because they bore the names of discarnate spirits that he had just finished reading about in the spiritualist literature. He also realized that the spirits did not convey any new information but simply re-presented that which he already knew. (When Staudenmaier first mentions "spirits," he places the term in quotation marks. The understanding throughout is that he never considered the spirits to be anything but the product of his own mind.)

As Staudenmaier became increasingly adept at automatic writing, it was only necessary for him to move his hand in an approximation of writing in order to begin to hear the corresponding message. Eventually he became an "auditory medium," asking questions of the "spirits" mentally and receiving audible replies. Again, Staudenmaier uses the term "auditory medium" in quotes and indicates that he is merely borrowing the term from the spiritualists as a descriptive and not an explanatory term. Gradually, the voices became more distinct and individualized and, in time, associated with corresponding visual images. The images, internal at first, later became externalized. In accord with modern usage of the term, Staudenmaier called these images hallucinations. His explanation of them, however, as will be seen later, was quite at variance with scientific knowledge. Through association, some of the hallucinations, especially those of human or human-like figures, which Staudenmaier called "personifications," combined visual, auditory, and olfactory dimensions, behaving in a very realistic manner. Some of the personifications acquired considerable autonomy, affecting his motor and physiological functioning.

Much of what Staudenmaier has to report has to do with his attempts to cope with the wishes and demands of a large number of personifications, many of which were selfish, lying, and mischievous at best and downright evil at worst. At times, a whole host of them seem to have taken turns in controlling Staudenmaier's behavior, making him confess that "in naive medieval terms I was possessed" (see Kemp, this volume). Some of the personifications were indeed those of the devil and similar figures ("Cloven Foot," "Horse Foot") that appeared bent on influencing Staudenmaier along the classical lines of sex and evildoing. Other personifications included "Highness," represented by a variety of noble, princely, and powerful personages (Napoleon, the German Kaiser, Field Marshall von Moltke), "Child," "Worker," "Wise Old Man," "Roundhead" (a jester figure), and others. While the personifications just mentioned were clearly archetypal and recurred many times over a period of years, others were more mundane and ephemeral:

Once a beautiful young lady visited me over a period of several days. She made a definite impression on me which, however, quickly vanished once she was gone. A couple of days later I was lying in my bed on my left side, occasionally conversing with my inner voices. As I turned on the other side, I was greatly surprised to see to the right of me the head of this woman, as if she was lying right next to me. The image was magically clear, of enchanting beauty, ethereally transparent, and shone with a soft light in the almost complete darkness of the room for there was only an arc light shining in the street some distance away. For an instant I was completely bewildered, then in the next it became quite clear to me what it was all about, especially since at the same time a rough, uncanny voice began whispering to me in a mocking tone of voice. Indignant and uttering a hearty cussword I therefore turned back on my left side without worrying about the phantom any further. Later a friendly voice told me, "The girl is now gone." I looked and, since there was nothing to be seen, went to sleep. (p. 26)

For the most part Staudenmaier's contacts with the personifications took the form of inner conversation, but the personifications would also appear as projected visual images, and, on occasion, affect his behavior. For instance, his facial expression, posture, eating habits, and the like would change toward nobler features, military bearing, and finer food under the control of the Highness personification; Horse Foot would make him paw the ground while walking, or painfully hit the ankle of one foot with the shoe of the other. Staudenmaier would feel compelled to visit toy shops and experienced increased interest in childlike things when under the influence of the Child, make faces under the influence of Roundhead, and so on (see Spanos, this volume).

Were Staudenmaier's personifications alternate personalities? Was he suffering from a psychotic delusion of possession? He assesses the situation himself, answering both questions with a no, and we must concur with him: The personifications fail to show the usual personality dynamics involved in alternate personalities; for instance, they are all aware of each other, and Staudenmaier is aware of all of them. They are heard and seen more than they are acted out. Neither is Staudenmaier under the delusion that he is really the Kaiser, von Moltke, and so on. Some aspects of his condition do look like possession, but he is too well-informed ever to accept the idea literally. Eager to achieve results quickly, he had pushed too hard, and now the various entities, particularly the evil ones, began to dominate his life:

Sometimes it seemed as if all hell had broken loose . . . Convinced that there were fundamental discoveries to be made here, I had conducted my experiments with all my energy, making sacrifices and enduring great stress. The progress that I had made in the course of only three months was astounding. It appeared that I should soon become an excellent medium who would find it easy to convince the world of the reality of magic phenomena . . . I had welcomed almost every reporting entity with too much openness and trust and had paid too little attention to warnings, because deep in my heart I had never believed that there were actual spirits, let alone evil spirits, involved in my experiments. In addition, I had often been driven as if by an evil genius, pushing myself in an excess of eagerness to the outer limits of pain and staying up nights. My health was therefore seriously affected, and my friends thought I would soon die. I therefore decided to change my whole lifestyle and tactics, try to establish, on the basis of my experiences, the laws that govern the phenomena, and to conduct planned, independent experiments, whereas before I had often allowed the reporting entities to lead and to mislead me . . . With a change in lifestyle my mediumship declined, never to return to the previous high level. (pp. 27-29, passim)

Staudenmaier's condition would be characterized by many as psychotic, at least during the first few years of his experiments. He himself admits that he was often on the brink of insanity. Being on the brink of insanity rather than being insane is a crucial difference here, because Staudenmaier was able to remain an objective observer of his condition throughout. His account shows none of the telltale language that often marks the schizophrenic. Nor is he in any way defensive about his excursion into what must have appeared as bizarre experiences and behaviors to his contemporaries. On the contrary, his language is lucid and matter-of-fact, and he freely discusses the possibility that he may have had alternate personalities or been a schizophrenic. This could also mean, of course, that he wrote his book some time after what could have been real psychotic episodes and with the benefit of hindsight and current rationality, aided by rationalizations developed to explain these experiences in a manner that would make their account sound scientifically objective. I rather think that the internal evidence is such as to speak against this interpretation.

Staudenmaier's explanations of his experiences are naturalistic, although the specific mechanisms he invokes are bad science. He refuses to admit the existence of supernatural or paranormal forces or entities. His explanations, both correct and incorrect, are couched in the language of psychophysical relationships. Staudenmaier theorizes that the personifications, being the creation of his own unconscious, are associated with the activity of nerve centers not under his voluntary control, such as the ganglia of the autonomic nervous system. He was in fact told by some of his friendly entities that the centers corresponding to the personifications of Highness, Cloven Foot, and Horse Foot were located in his small intestine, the transverse colon, and the rectum, respectively. Staudenmaier's lifelong problems with digestion and elimination clearly dictated this particular choice of bodily sites. Furthermore, Staudenmaier developed the hypothesis that blood congestion in any part of the body facilitates the activity of the corresponding personifications by stimulating the associated brain centers and, accordingly, tried to combat the evil personifications by using purgatives to reduce the swelling of his intestines caused by constipation, constricting his waist very tightly, and placing a balled-up towel under the 10th and 11th thoracic vertebrae at night. By contrast, in order to experiment with the personifications, he would deliberately create blood congestion in his legs through binding and in his head by choking himself and by rhythmically beating on his head with his fists (see Jilek, this volume). Outside the context of Staudenmaier's experimentation on himself to identify the best means for the controlled observation of imagery, his behavior must have appeared disturbed indeed.

Staudenmaier's congestion or erection theory (he likened the swelling of any organ because of blood congestion to tissue erection in sexual excitement) in itself is not as farfetched as it seems. For instance, there may be some basis to his speculation that "the so-called magical or ecstatic look as well as the look of some psychotic hallucinators, etc., is based on an intentional or unintentional erection of the eyes" (p. 62). Marks and McKellar (1982) state that "the deliberate induction of eidetic imagery in the visual modality may be accompanied by a feeling of ocular pressure or 'eyestrain' which may persist after the eidetic image has finished" (p. 4), and Ahsen (1977) comments on accommodation tension in eidetic imagery and other associated somatic changes, such as an increase in blood pressure.

THE THEORY AND PRACTICE OF MAGIC

Staudenmaier's view of magic and magic creation has two aspects, one dealing with the nature of magic, the other with its two branches, magic of the conscious self and magic of the unconscious self. Magic, according to Staudenmaier, is all those things that traditionally have been called magic and have existed at all times and in all human societies. They are the "extraordinary and wonderful phenomena that cannot be produced by means of known natural forces or known human abilities" (p. 8). Staudenmaier feels that there is nothing unnatural or supernatural about any of these phenomena, however. The human body is an instrument for recreating whatever exists in the external world. Only vivid imagination and strong motivation are required. Given these, the eyes and the ears will project to the outside whatever the magician has vividly conjured before the mind's eyes and strongly wishes to become real. If the external world can produce a subjective image in us by casting an optical image on the retina and causing the latter to produce a pattern of nervous excitation, then, by reversing the process, a vivid image may set up a reverse flow of nerve impulses toward the retina, where it is transduced to light and in this form may be projected outward as an objective image, visible to others. In the same manner, voices heard inwardly will, by reverse action, stimulate the eardrums, producing sound audible to others.

Staudenmaier apparently thought that if an organ was capable of responding to light or sound, it was also capable of generating light or sound energy. Rather than inquiring whether this was in fact the case, Staudenmaier simply cites instances of light-producing animals (fireflies, marine fish) to support his contention. Here he not only uses analogy as a substitute for establishing cause-effect relationships but also reifies the subjective by turning a purely psychological process, the outward projection of sensory experiences, into an objective event external to the perceiver. Thus, ironically, instead of putting magic on a scientific footing, in his attempt to do so Staudenmaier overdoes it and himself succumbs to magical thinking. The seeming reality of inner visions and hallucinations is so overwhelming that one refuses to believe that the thing seen is not "out there." Paradoxically, this is especially so when one realizes that the image is indeed the creation of one's own mind.

The other aspect of Staudenmaier's view of magic has to do with the locus of origination of the magical phenomena within the human psyche. Although the processes are identical, Staudenmaier holds that the origins of imagery are twofold, conscious and unconscious. He deplores having started in magic by experiencing hallucinations that originated in his unconscious self, because he could not exercise any control over them at first. The specific instructions that he gives for doing magic of the conscious self are quite simple:

Look at an object that has been set up at a convenient viewing distance as attentively as possible, close the eyes, and now, without turning the head or changing bodily posture, try to see it as vividly as if it were real and at the same distance, using only the power of imagination. As the clear picture of the object gradually dissipates, open the eyes for a while and look again at the object carefully. This is a purely hallucinatory copying of a visual display. With time it will become possible to see quite clearly a hallucination of the object with one's cycs closed. The main thing here is to practice the stimulation of the visual apparatus in the unaccustomed, opposite direction and to learn to really see the image, i.e., develop it into a hallucination. (p. 53)

Staudenmaier warns that most people, and especially people whose occupations do not call for the use of visual imagery, will require much time and patience, that there are individual differences in the ability to visualize, and that various conditions affect the goodness of the visualization. Staudenmaier adds instructions for photographing the hallucinations thus produced, but, in another place, he tellingly confesses that he has never taken such photographs himself. For auditory hallucinations the recommended procedure is analogous: strain to hear the sound of a ticking watch that is being moved away, for instance, until the sound heard is that of a watch next to the ear, although the watch itself has been removed. Hallucinations in other sensory modalities arise almost automatically through association: Once a vivid hallucinatory image of a rose is achieved, for instance, its smell will also be perceived.

EIDETICS OR HALLUCINATIONS, DISSOCIATION OR PSYCHOSIS?

Some of Staudenmaier's ideas concerning the nature of his experiences are not inadequate even in the light of contemporary knowledge of imagery and abnormality. As already mentioned, Staudenmaier distinguished between hallucinations brought about by magic of the conscious self and those brought about by magic of the unconscious self. It is clearly the same distinction as that between controlled imagery and autonomous imagery (McKellar, 1977), although the idea goes back to Erich Jaensch (1930). It is also clear from the directions given by Staudenmaier for producing the first kind of hallucinations that the images he obtained were not hallucinations but eidetics in the broader, current sense of the term

(Ahsen, 1977; Marks & McKellar, 1982). His directions are practical instructions for improving the quality of imagery. This aspect of Staudenmaier's experiences bears no mark of psychopathology and conforms exactly to Ahsen's (1977) definition of the eidetic as a

> normal subjective visual image which is experienced with pronounced vividness: Although not necessarily evoked at the time of the experience by an actual external object, and not necessarily dependent on a previous experience of an actual situation, it is "seen" inside of the mind or outside in the literal sense of the word, and this "seeing" is accompanied by certain somatic events as well as a feeling of meaning; the total experience in all its dimensions excludes the possibility that it is pathological. (p. 6)

All of the characteristics of the imagery experiences, both autonomous and controlled, that are described by Staudenmaier are part of the list of such charcteristics presented by Ahsen (1977), including such relatively esoteric aspects as the aura or lighting of the visual field that precedes an eidetic.

Hallucinations of the unconscious (autonomous imagery) are somewhat more complicated. Here, instead of attempting to "copy," in imagination, a sensible object, Staudenmaier suggests that one should lay oneself open to whatever images may come around unbidden, just as one does in the course of ordinary perception. His examples of automatic writing, drawing, and painting suggest that the effect and purpose of the exercise is to achieve some degree of dissociation and to allow unconscious contents to manifest themselves, as in dreams or free association. The archetypal nature of the personifications—the Child, Highness, Wise Old Man, Cloven Foot, Jester—indicates that Staudenmaier's technique worked. Not knowing any better, he started with automatic writing. It developed into bizarre auditory and visual imagery, with accompanying behavior disturbances. Without a guide to what was happening, Staudenmaier did not have much control over his imagery, but he attempted to gain it by various physical means, as the mentally disturbed will sometimes do. But was Staudenmaier mentally disturbed?

Using Marks's (1983) signal detection theory approach to imagery, it may be seen that the difference between eidetics and hallucinations consists solely in the position of the reality-testing criterion with respect to that region of imagery designated as eidetic (Figure 11.1)—that is, how much of the realm of eidetic images

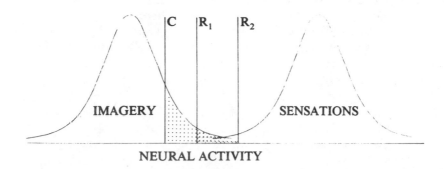

Figure 11.1. Hallucinations and Imagery as a Function of the Position of the Reality-Testing Criterion (R) with Respect to Imagery, Sensations, and the Criterion of Consciousness (Awareness) (C).

At R_1 only that portion under the imagery curve that is to the left (the dotted area) is perceived as eidetic images (not objective reality); the crosshatched portion under the imagery curve is perceived as real, although it is not (hallucinations). At R_2, all imagery experiences (entire dotted area between C and R_2) are perceived for what they are, imagery.

one decides to call real and, therefore, whether one will present oneself to others as hallucinating and, consequently, as disturbed. On the other hand, the degree of reality of an eidetic/hallucination is inversely correlated with the degree of control that one has over it. In fact, a remission of hallucinations may be achieved by teaching the individual how to control them, as was the case with Morton Schatzman's (1980) patient, Ruth, who was tormented by apparitions of her still-living father. Staudenmaier's struggle with the personifications of his unconscious, therefore, may be seen as attempts to gain control over them, or, in signal detection terms, to move the reality-testing criterion for imagery as far to the right as possible.

It appears that there is a need to introduce another criterion in Mark's model, a reality-testing criterion for sensory experience. Without this additional criterion, it is difficult to depict experiences such as those of Staudenmaier. Figure 11.2 represents his condition using the additional criterion of reality testing for sensory experience. According to Staudenmaier's account, he never thought of the images produced by his unconscious or those produced deliberately as real in any way. Spontaneous or voluntary, they were vivid enough to be called eidetics. To explain the phenomena he called illusions, it is necessary to make the distributions of imagery and sensation overlap partially, which differs from the case of the "normal" individual in the waking state (Figure 11.1). The "illusions" then fall in the area that is under both curves. By the imagery-reality criterion, the imagery part of the "illusion" is judged to be unreal, and by the sensation-reality criterion that portion of the total image that is stimulus-bound is judged to be real. Incidentally, if everything remains the same but the positions of the two reality criteria are switched, we have an individual suffering from hallucinations that are thought to be real (portion of the imagery distribution to the right of the R_i criterion) and experiencing the Perky effect frequently (portion under the sensation curve to the left of the R_s criterion), as well as a combination of the two (the overlapping portion of the two distributions).

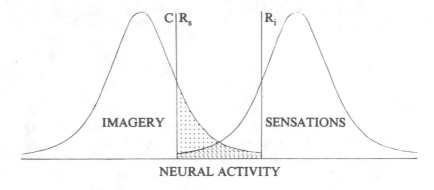

NEURAL ACTIVITY

Figure 11.2. Hypothesized Waking State of Ludwig Staudenmaier.

Separate reality criteria are applied to images (R_i) and sensations (R_s). By the R_s criterion all sensations are judged real, and by the R_i criterion all images are judged not real (eidetics—dotted area). The area where both distributions overlap (crosshatched) is the area of Staudenmaier's "illusions," or eidetic images superimposed upon suitable sensory perceptions.

In reading Staudenmaier's book one cannot help but empathize with him and see his behavior as a necessary aspect of his experiments and of his initial lack of understanding of what he was getting into. Staudenmaier never attributes external causation to his personifications, never blames anybody for his problems but himself, and at every step relates his experiences to physiological, psychological, and psychiatric concepts known to him. For instance, he discusses at length the different types and characteristics of schizophrenia, concluding in a very nondefensive manner that he did not suffer from it. Staudenmaier speaks like an objective scientist relating his experiences to the public. Although the experiences may have been traumatic at the time, they are now presented as data for examination. This is an important point. Had the same experience occurred to someone to whom the language of science was unavailable, he or she would quite likely have described them in the language that was available to the individual, namely the everyday language of the common person that pivots on the idea of a body-mind duality, reifies subjective experience, and accepts supernatural and paranormal causation. Because those who make psychiatric diagnoses are themselves users of scientific language, it is obvious who will be diagnosed as suffering from mental impairment and who will not (see Lambek, this volume). "What separates the normal individual from the hallucinatory schizophrenic, then, are the expectancies, biases, life experiences, and judgment skills brought to the task of distinguishing perceptions from mental images" (Starker, 1982, p. 44). And, I may add, language.

It seems to me that Staudenmaier's case may be best described as one of a fantasy-prone individual in the sense recently used by Wilson and Barber (1983). Of the 14 characteristics[3] that describe the 26 women who in the Wilson and Barber study "responded profoundly to and passed all or virtually all of the items" on an imagination scale and a suggestibility scale and all or virtually all of the suggestions given during hypnosis, 7 may be found in Staudenmaier's self-description. (1) His fantasies were both extensive and vivid; they lasted over a period of many years, occurred daily or almost daily, and were vivid enough to be confounded with reality. (2) The fantasies were hallucinatory, as vivid as reality, and experienced in at least the visual, auditory, and olfactory sense modalities, if not in all of them. (3) Staudenmaier's experiences of the "personifications" taking over or influencing his behavior are the equivalent of Wilson and Barber's subjects pretending to be someone else and becoming totally absorbed in the character. (4) Physical effects associated with vivid fantasies are reported by Staudenmaier throughout his book. His imaginal processes were powerful enough not only to affect his motor behavior and produce psychosomatic intestinal changes but to show up in somatic manifestations isomorphic to certain features of his personifications. In other words, he could have easily become a stigmatist:

> As soon as Horse Foot comes on stronger, which is accompanied by an increasing tendency to develop my (middle) foot [*sic!*] into a horse foot, the skin of the heels shows many wildly crisscrossing tracks that quickly deepen and finally begin to hurt and bleed unless I apply a remedy. (p. 134)

(5) Most of the 26 women experienced phenomena of extrasensory perception. Although Staudenmaier says that he did not experience any ESP phenomena, he does describe his experiments with psychokinesis and other, poltergeist-like phenomena: a chemical substance that was not known to do so suddenly disintegrated before his eyes (and those of a witness); unaccountably, unripe apples were knocked down from a tree as he was standing by it; and

> Occasionally there would be knocks on the window, the floor, or the wall, as well as cracks and crashes. Once there was a rapid succession of about a dozen strong knocks against some books in my bedroom. Another time, I was quite taken aback when half a bread roll that was lying on the table in front of me was flung powerfully to the floor. (p. 31)

(6) The fantasy-prone personality is also prone to have out-of-body experiences. Staudenmaier reports having experienced an autoscopic hallucination once, actually an eidetic image of himself:

> When walking up and down the garden at night I imagined as vividly as possible that besides me there were present three additional, similar figures. Gradually the corresponding sensory hallucinations developed. It appeared to me that there were three other "Staudenmaiers" walking in front of me, all dressed like me and walking at the same pace. They stopped when I stopped, stretched out their hands when I did, and so on. (p. 106)

(7) Automatisms were reported by 50% of Wilson and Barber's subjects. Staudenmaier began his experiments with automatic writing. His proficiency at it led him to abandon it and switch to auditory imagery.

Except for a brief mention of the personification of the Wise Old Man and the suggestion that images like this and that of Cloven Foot may be useful in comparative studies of religion, Staudenmaier does not report any religious imagery. This may have had something to do with his switching from the study of theology and philosophy to the study of chemistry and the subsequent adherence to explanations of phenomena that meticulously avoid anything supernatural. Having adopted this stance precluded him from labeling any of his imagery as ghosts or apparitions, an experience reported by 73 of Wilson and Barber's subjects. To Staudenmaier, these fell in the same category as all other hallucinations: they were outward projections of subjective images.

THE PARANORMAL

Paranormal visual and auditory phenomena of the kind that presumably occur in mediumistic seances are explained by Staudenmaier in terms of his projection theory: apparitions, voices, knocks, and so on, are nothing but the outward projections of light and sound energies by the medium and originate in his or her vivid imagination. While energy can be externalized by the reversal of nervous processes, Staudenmaier states that such a reversal would not enable the nose to produce odorous substances. He apparently drew a line between externalizing informational and energetic processes and the materialization of substance.

With regard to psychokinetic phenomena, Staudenmaier's explanation was that, for instance, a vivid image of the hand moving the object, not accompanied by actual movements of the hand, could lead to the actual movement of objects at a distance as if they had been displaced by a hand. He describes his experiments with a chemical balance and being able to tip the scales by producing an image of movement—but not in a very reliable manner, because he could not predict which scale would go up. Following such a failure, a derisive face with a long nose would appear where the pointer was, grinning at him mockingly. It apparently never occurred to Staudenmaier that he himself had provided an entirely adequate explanation of psychokinesis in his definition of an "illusion" as a modification of the image of a perceived object by a superimposed "hallucination" (eidetic image), an explanation that does not require the assumption of impossible physical processes. Somehow, to Staudenmaier the tipping of the scales was real but the mocking face that was part of the balance was not.

In general, Staudenmaier had become quite familiar with occultism and spiritualism, especially the latter, and he dedicates a whole chapter of his book to explanations of the various spiritualist phenomena, such as telepathy, precognition, materialization, spirit rappings and voices, apparitions, and the like, in terms of his theory of the reversibility of nervous excitation. Wilson and Barber (1983) report that 92% of their group of fantasy-prone women saw themselves as psychic or sensitive and reported numerous ESP experiences, whereas only 16% in a control group reported any such experiences. It is easy to see how the ability to produce imagery of objects moving of their own accord—the tipping of the scales, in Staudenmaier's case—could be mistaken for an actual ability to move objects at a distance by mind alone. One of the characteristics of individuals absorbed in an LSD hallucination, an intense daydream, or an eidetic fantasy is the unwillingness to check the empirical content of their experiences. Thus Staudenmaier never did obtain any consensual validation that the scales he willed to tip were actually tipping; nor did he obtain any photographs of the light images that presumably were emanating from his eyes, even though the nature of his entire previous experience with imagery should have alerted him to the possibility of confounding imagery and reality. Somehow the vividness of a projected image, "more real than real," appears to the imager to be self-evident proof of its ontological status, requiring no further validation.

The reification of the subjective, the confusion of the self with the non-self, and the attribution of causation to phenomena linked only by similarity and contiguity lie at the root of magical thinking. Reasoning by analogy, that is, invoking contiguity and similarity as causal principles, affects an easy shift from that which is physically possible to that which is not. For instance, if I can communicate with another person and affect that person's behavior via speech, why shouldn't I be able to do likewise via thought? After all, speech only expresses thought. In Staudenmaier's thinking, reification of the subjective and reasoning by analogy are inextricably linked, but in his book they wear the camouflage of scientific language. This kind of thinking leads not only to his acceptance of the reality of paranormal phenomena but also to the particular kind of explanation that he seeks for them.

CONCLUSION

The case of Ludwig Staudenmaier has been examined as an illustration of the relationship between imagery, psychopathology, altered states of consciousness, and paranormality. His book is a remarkable first-person account of a prolonged excursion into the realm of various types of imagery, altered states of consciousness, and the paranormal, combined with an attempt to present an objective report of his experiences and experiments and a scientific explanation of what is ordinarily thought of as belonging in the realm of magic. Staudenmaier's magic was indeed naturalistic, but his worldview was not naturalistic enough for him to avoid the pitfalls of reasoning by analogy and magical thinking. He was right in his view that magic is part of the natural order. He was mistaken as to which part it is. There is only one kind of true magic, and that is magic of the self or self-transformations—all those informational processes that, originated by a source, affect energetic changes in a target, source and target being the same system, the individual: self-control, therapeutic imagery (including supplicatory prayer), biofeedback, and other self-healing situations. They constitute the link between the subjective and the objective *within* the individual. To think of magic as anything else is to think magically.

NOTES

1. Portions of the second, enlarged edition of the book (Staudenmaier, 1922) that are relevant to the present discussion have been translated and published (Zusne, 1983). Page numbers for quotations are from the German original.

2. Automatic writing is one of the automatisms observed in states of divided consciousness (cf. Hilgard, 1977) that also include glossolalia and ideomotor movements (such as those observed in water witching, radiesthesia, and table-tilting phenomena) (cf. Zusne & Jones, 1982). When automatic writing occurs in the use of the popular Ouija board, the hand rests on an easily movable planchette and approaches the letters of the alphabet, one at a time, to spell words. Otherwise the arm may be suspended from a sling, with only the writing implement touching the paper. In practiced subjects any such devices may be dispensed with. For genuine automatic writing to occur, a state of at least partial dissociation must be achieved. Even with training, only about 10% of the general population may produce automatic writing. Its content often reveals the workings of the unconscious, the handwriting will often differ from the person's normal handwriting, and the author of the writing may be perceived as an alien, intruding entity.

3. Extensive and vivid fantasy; hallucinatory intensities of fantasies; pretending to be someone else; vivid sensory experiences since childhood; vivid personal memo-

ries; physical effects associated with vivid fantasies and memories; telepathy, precognition, and other psychic experiences; out-of-body experiences; automatic writing; religious visions; healing; experiences with apparitions; hypnagogic imagery; social awareness and secret fantasy life.

REFERENCES

Ahsen, A. (1977). Eidetics: An overview. *Journal of Mental Imagery, 1*(1), 5-38.

Hilgard, E. R. (1977). *Divided consciousness: Multiple controls in human thought and action.* New York: John Wiley.

Jaensch, E. (1930). *Eidetic imagery and typological methods of investigation.* London: Kegan Paul, Trench, Trubner.

Marks, D. (1983). Signal detection theory applied to imagery and states of consciousness. *International Imagery Bulletin, 1*(1), 39-51.

Marks, D., & McKellar, P. (1982). The nature and function of mental imagery. *Journal of Mental Imagery, 6*(1), 1-124.

McKellar, P. (1977). Autonomy, imagery, and dissociation. *Journal of Mental Imagery, 1*(1), 93-108.

Schatzman, M. (1980). Evocations of unreality. *New Scientist, 87,* 935-937.

Starker, S. (1982). *Fantastic thought.* Englewood Cliffs, NJ: Prentice-Hall.

Staudenmaier, L. (1922). *Die Magie als experimentelle Naturwissenschaft* [Magic as an experimental natural science] (2nd ed.). Leipzig: Akademische Verlagsgesellschaft.

Wilson, S. C., & Barber, T. X. (1983). The fantasy-prone personality: Implications for understanding imagery, hypnosis, and parapsychological phenomena. In A. A. Sheikh (Ed.), *Imagery* (pp. 340-387). New York: John Wiley.

Zusne, L. (1983). Translation of portions of Ludwig Staudenmaier's *Magic as an experimental natural science. Psychological Documents, 14,* 9 (Ms. No. 2617).

Zusne, L., & Jones, W. H. (1982). *Anomalistic psychology.* Hillsdale, NJ: Erlbaum.

12

SELF-PRESENTATION IN MALAYSIAN SPIRIT SEANCES
A Dramaturgical Perspective on Altered States
of Consciousness in Healing Ceremonies

RAYMOND L. M. LEE

Ever since altered states of consciousness (ASC's) became an accepted phrase of discourse, it has been used as an analytical tool for
exploring the therapeutic aspects of spirit possession (e.g. Jilek, this
volume; Ludwig, 1966; Ward, 1979). Researchers in this area tend
to assume that the ASC's in spirit possession provides a cathartic
discharge for the entranced individual. To speak of ASC-related
emotional release in spirit possession implies a reference to the private feelings that are verifiable only by the participating individual.
Such analyses depend on the ability of the subjects to articulate their
experiences. The important distinction between public and private
events in spirit possession is underemphasized in these analyses.

Other researchers, however, have noted the significance of the
private-public dimension in the analysis of trance and possession
(Bourguignon, 1970; Lewis, 1971; Schwartz, 1976), but it is worth
bringing up this point again for two reasons. First, our present methods of cross-cultural observation cannot determine the actual state
of the possessed or entranced person. Observation of such behaviors
is not the same as personally experiencing them. Even if it were possible for the observer to participate in such behaviors, she or he may
be able only to identify, not claim verisimilitude with, the subject's
possession experiences, since each person's experiences are unique.
Second, private feelings are to a certain extent shaped by the larger
social context. People are socialized to attribute particular meanings
to their private experiences (see Chandra shekar, Kemp, Ward, this
volume). In other words, there are common arenas, such as language
and symbols, for articulating such experiences even though they
may remain the closed property of each individual. Thus, the study
of ASC's and spirit possession must first and foremost assume that
the behaviors observed are externally determined in the form of a

relationship between the performer and the audience. Private feelings are of secondary importance in the sense that they are merely based on personal statements, the authenticity of which is not easy to verify.

Given these assumptions, we may now proceed to discuss the structure of expectations in possession rituals. By "structure of expectations," I refer to the social rules that govern the relationship between the possessed and nonpossessed. Within the context of ritualized possession, these rules become vital in demarcating the behaviors of the possessed from those of the nonpossessed. These social boundaries are important to the extent that they define roles for, or elicit role expectations from, the participating individuals. An analysis of these role requirements entails an examination of how possession performances are staged and received. To paraphrase Goffman (1959), the relationship between the performer and the audience is essentially a presentation of appearances and manners that signal the former's status at a particular moment and what is expected from him or her.[1]

Goffman (1959) argues further that the self "is a *product* of a scene that comes off, and is not a *cause* of it" (p. 252). When applied to the case of spirit possession, this principle implies that the possessed self in spirit mediumship is a performed character that is imputed through the interpretive activity of the audience. In other words, the spirit medium does not operate *in vacuo* but through the interpretations of the audience, so that a complementary set of expectations develops between them that maintains the reality of possession. For this reality to work, these expectations must rest upon wider cultural assumptions concerning supernaturalism (see Kemp, Spanos, this volume), and more immediately upon what Goffman has termed "the back and front regions of self-production." The front regions are concerned mainly with behavioral manipulations by the performer to achieve certain desired effects with the audience, while the back regions conceal various forms of activity that may be discrepant with the performed character but nevertheless are necessary for its fabrication.[2] Thus, the drama of ritualized possession rests upon a role-specific relationship between the spirit medium and the audience that comes to fruition in a staged performance within an idiom of accepted supernatural beliefs.

The purpose of this chapter is to explore the structure of expectations in several Malaysian possession performances by examining the different styles of spirit mediumship and the responses of the audience. My data are based on observations of several spirit seances and festivals in urban Malaysia made between 1977 and 1981. Before proceeding to a description and analysis of these seances, it is necessary to divert briefly to discuss the nature of spirit mediumship in Malaysia.

MALAYSIAN SPIRIT MEDIUMSHIP

Malaysia is an ethnically plural society comprising approximately 52% Malays, 35% Chinese, 11% Indians, and 2% others (Eurasians, Europeans, aborigines, etc.).[3] Although the three major ethnic groups are culturally divergent, they share common beliefs in spirit possession and mediumship. Convergence in supernaturalism among ethnic groups living side by side implies that the exchange of practices and paraphernalia of spirit mediumship among the ethnic groups concerned is almost inevitable (see Krippner, this volume, for a Brazilian parallel). This is evident in the Malaysian case, where there is a constant exchange in styles between Malay, Chinese, and Indian mediums. The clientele also moves from one ethnic medium to another in search of solutions to daily problems, fortunes, cures for illnesses, and various favors. Thus, it is not surprising to witness a Chinese client consulting a Malay spirit medium on one occasion and an Indian medium on another occasion. While this type of syncretism exists in Malaysian spirit mediumship, there are practicing mediums who prefer their own traditional styles because they consider them superior or because they are unaware of other styles.[4]

This pluralism cannot be understood further without some preliminary knowledge of the different types of spirit mediums that exist in Malaysian society. The Malay spirit medium, alternately known as the *bomoh*, is treated not only as a mediator between spirits and humans but is sometimes also a specialist in herbal cures, an advisor of mundane matters, or a practitioner of Malay martial arts *(silat)*.[5] However, most *bomohs* usually gain their reputations as specialists in particular areas, such as exorcism, drug rehabilitation, and so on, even though they may have acquired varieties of esoteric knowledge *(ilmu)*. A *bomoh* gains *ilmu* either through inheritance or through apprenticeship, although there are cases in which a person may seek *ilmu* from both family members and unrelated *bomohs*.[6] A *bomoh* with inherited knowledge (through the family, dreams, or various supernatural encounters) is generally held in higher esteem than one who *menuntut* (learns from others) because of the former's status as a selected individual (Winstedt, 1961). However, in the practicalities of day-to-day living, many people are more concerned with the power of a *bomoh*, as reflected in the number of "successful" treatments, than in the origins of *ilmu*.

In contemporary Malaysia, public seances that were once popular in the Malay royal courts and among the commoners are now rarely seen, except in the northeastern state of Kelantan, where a public seance that has developed into an unique art form called *main puteri* (literally, play of the princess) is still observed and performed (Firth, 1967; Wright, 1980). The rare occurrence of public seances in Malay society, however, does not mean the gradual demise of such phenomena. Rather, many seances continue to be conducted, but within the confines of the *bomoh*'s or the patient's house. I was privileged to witness such a seance for two successive nights in August 1980 in Kuching, Sarawak. The performance (described in the following section) was conducted by a Malay female *bomoh* named Sarimah (a pseudonym), a housewife in her early forties married to a Malay, a former army captain, from West Malaysia. Sarimah is a *bomoh* by descent. She is the only one among her siblings who had continuously experienced trances and mystical dreams, experiences she had undergone since the age of 17 (see Krippner, this volume, for a discussion of entry into healing practices). She claimed that she had reluctantly agreed to be tutored in the magical arts by her father because the spirits would not leave her alone. As a full-time *bomoh*, Sarimah conducts seances regularly except on Fridays and during the Muslim month of Ramadan, when her spirit helpers are believed to be fasting and praying.

The Chinese spirit medium, known popularly as *dang ki*, also performs roughly the same functions as the *bomoh*.[7] However, unlike the *bomoh*, Chinese spirit mediums fall into two general categories: those who operate mainly in temples and those who consult with their clients in private homes. In the former case, many such mediums either use an established temple as a base of operation or turn their homes into temples, with living quarters occupying only a small section of the temple and the rest of the floor space used for ritual purposes. The other mediums either practice their trade at home without turning their houses into elaborate temples or travel to a client's home for special consultations. These mediums usually have a smaller clientele than the temple practitioners. Unlike the Malay *bomoh*, who hardly participates in public ritual festivals, the Chinese spirit medium is usually obligated to lead these annual events to appease the spirits. These festivals and the practice of Chinese mediumship have been described in depth by Elliott (1955) and Lee (1986).

The Chinese believe that spirit mediums are gifted people who have chosen their profession as a result of family tradition or because of a special calling. Spirit mediums are believed to possess a trait called *sin kuat* (Cantonese meaning "spiritual bone") that gives them the ability to communicate with deities and other spiritual beings. The two Chinese mediums described in this chapter did not acquire their skills from their families but from temple mediums, although both are regarded as individuals with unique talents. In the first case, Lim (a pseudonym), a former Catholic in his thirties, claimed that he had accidentally discovered his ability to enter into trance during a temple seance. However, he was unable to control his trance experiences until he came under the tutelage of a temple medium who instructed him in various techniques of "disciplined trance." Since then he has abandoned his career as a pop musician, and for the last ten years he has been a full-time medium in a small temple (cum family residence) in Petaling Jaya, the satellite town of Kuala Lumpur. The second case concerns Tan (a pseudonym), a former salesman who had also accidentally discovered his trance abilities while meditating in a temple.[8] Unlike Lim, he does not practice mediumship in a temple but serves a small group of clients either at his home in Petaling Jaya or at their homes. Tan is now quite inactive as a medium, having become a partner with an ex-client, a Malay, in operating a pub in Petaling Jaya. Lim and Tan live close to each other and were once associates. They are now not on speaking terms and pursue separate careers.

The majority of Indians in Malaysia are Tamil-speaking Hindus, who define a spirit medium as *samiyati* (god dancer) or *arul vantu sollupavan* (one who speaks through divine grace).[9] Two types of mediumship are said to be characteristic of popular Hinduism in Malaysia. The first type is often observed at temple festivals, such as Thaipusam, when certain Hindu deities are asked to descend upon a devotee, who enters into a trance and is occasionally treated as a vehicle for divination and blessings. The second type of medium goes into a trance to seek direct supernatural help for clients. This type of medium is either a part-time practitioner or a temple priest of the nonorthodox (or non-agamic) tradition. Hindu mediums acquire their abilities by apprenticing themselves to an experienced medium and taking over the business upon the latter's retirement or death. Alternatively, they become mediums in response to a divine command or some other supernatural encounter.

While most Hindu mediums are of working- or lower-class backgrounds, the one I met in November 1977 comes from a middleclass background. Govinda (a pseudonym), who is in his thirties, works as an assistant manager in a large hotel in Kuala Lumpur. He lives with his family in a two-story house in Petaling Jaya. He maintains a Shakti shrine in the backyard of his house and a Shiva shrine in one of the rooms. Govinda goes into trance and is possessed by the mother goddess, Shakti, several evenings a week, and he is usually consulted by a small clientele of mostly Indian women. Govinda claims that he became a medium as a result of Shakti's calling, and he has been a medium for more than 17 years.

It is obvious from this brief description that there is no dearth of opportunities for the cross-fertilization of ideas and styles of mediumship, given the many parallels between Malay, Chinese, and Indian mediumship. Innovative syncretism is the outcome of active experimentation by individuals who have been exposed to a variety of beliefs and styles in mediumship. Thus, Tan is often possessed by seven legendary Malay warrior spirits during seances. When possessed by these spirits, he dons a Malay costume and headgear and speaks only in Malay to his clients. Sometimes he is possessed by Siamese deities, an obvious influence of his mediumship experiences in Penang, which has a small Thai community. Similarly, Lim is also a vehicle for Malay warrior spirits at some seances. Like Tan, he dresses Malay style and converses only in Malay under those circumstances. Elliott (1955) has also reported on a Sino-Malay medium cult that he observed in Singapore. From these accounts, it would appear that Chinese mediums tend to be more syncretic in their practices than Malay or Indian mediums, although this is not to say that Malay and Indian attempts at syncretic mediumship are totally absent. These questions on comparative mediumship in Malaysia are still open to further exploration (see Lee, 1983).

There is no lack of demand for spirit mediums in contemporary Malaysia. A medium's clientele typically includes not only lower- or working-class individuals but also middle class, Westernized professionals. From a functional perspective, these mediums play an important role in delivering thaumaturgical services to a Malaysian public that has not yet readily accepted the practices of Western psychiatry.[10] Modernization in Malaysia has not obscured the practice of spirit mediumship. Instead, mediumship has blended unobtrusively into the urbanized and industrialized environment of contemporary Malaysia. A reason for this persistence is that the supernatural ethos is not perceived by many Malaysians as contradictory to the "scientific" outlook ushered in by modern technology. Spirit mediums will continue to thrive because medical science provides only an alternative healing method, not a radical substitute to supernatural healing services in Malaysia.

FRONTAL PERFORMANCES

In discussing the relationship between the spirit medium and the audience, it is necessary to focus on the outward forms of display that the medium puts on to increase credibility and to sustain audience attention. The most obvious outward form that projects an image as medium is the ceremonial costume worn for the seance. Although most clients attending the seance know beforehand who the medium is, the main purpose of the special costume is to identify and differentiate the medium's unique status. The costume is in fact a badge of distinction that confers prestige upon the medium and elicits deference during the seance.

Sarimah wears a multicolored robe and loose red slacks during her seances. Each of the seven colors (bright red, crimson, pink, turquoise, yellow, white, black) on her robe represents one of seven royal Malay spirits that possess her during the seance. Sarimah announces the arrival of a particular spirit by covering herself briefly with a colored cloth, the hue of which is allegedly favored by that spirit. These pieces of cloth are folded and placed within easy reach of the medium. Tan also wears a colored Malay costume, but only at a spirit festival. At one of the festivals I attended in October 1980, Tan was observed wearing a green Malay costume and headgear. The color green symbolizes *Datuk Hijau*, the Malay spirit that regularly possesses Tan.[11] When he is possessed by other spirits, Tan removes his green headgear and replaces it with one of another color that represents a different spirit. He does not change his costume, however. At seances, Tan merely wears a pair of shorts but wraps his forehead with a colored cloth to signal the presence of a particular spirit. Lim, on the other hand, wears only a loose pair of yellow pajama bottoms at seances. He hardly changes into other costumes, since he is regularly possessed by a Hokkien deity, *Kong Teik Choon Ong*. However, at a spirit festival I observed in March 1981, Lim wore a special costume that was lined with rhinestones and elaborate patterns and that resembled a Vietnamese *ao dai*. Like Lim, Govinda communicates mainly with one spirit, and during seances he wears only a short brown *lungi* (a wraparound loin cloth of South Indian origin).

The significance of the medium's attire at these seances is that it underscores a select individuality not shared with the clients. But dress alone does not sanctify a medium. The medium's behavior before, during, and after the seance is also crucial in the presentation of self. All the four mediums described here mingle freely with their clients prior to a seance. This lowering of boundary strictures as a prelude to the medium's metamorphosis is necessary in maintaining certain conceptions of self. First, by emphasizing mortal human qualities in those interactions, the medium reassures clients of the earthly self, a role the medium adopts when not entranced. Second, the transformation from natural to supernatural self provides dramatic effect, thus enhancing the reality of the oracular self in trance. The casual nature of these pre-seance interactions is terminated with the medium's timed display of certain behaviors that suggest the successful descent of spirits into his or her body.

At Sarimah's ritual seance, she sat in the center of her living room, chanting quietly with eyes closed, breathing in *kemunyan* (benzoic) fumes, and throwing *beras bertih* (yellow rice) behind her back for protection. Then she covered her head with a black cloth. A slight quiver was observed, and when the cloth was removed, her facial expression had changed. Her eyes were wide and staring, delivering a fierce look. It was whispered among the audience that *Datuk Bono* (a warrior spirit) had arrived. The entrance and exit of each spirit were signaled by changes in Sarimah's demeanor upon removal of various colored cloths from her head at regular intervals. At the medium's festival at Tan's house, he was seen sitting cross-legged in full regalia in front of a large altar, inhaling *kemunyan* smoke with eyes closed, and violently regurgitating a piece of charm paper swallowed earlier. Suddenly, he spoke in Malay demanding his *bendera*, a small flag, to signal the arrival of *Datuk Hijau*. Throughout the trance he kept his eyes closed. When Tan performs at a seance, he also inhales *kemunyan* smoke with closed eyes in front of the same altar to induce trance. But in contrast to the performance at the festival, the arrival of the spirit is indicated by a violent shaking of his head from left to right. Only when he has ceased this action does he tie a cloth around his forehead. Violent head swinging is also practiced by Lim at festivals and regular seances. In addition, Lim trembles all over while in trance, and the timbre of his voice changes as he speaks in Mandarin to his clients. Tan, on the other hand, trembles only slightly, and no noticeable changes in his voice are observed. Govinda also induces trance by inhaling deeply, but without benzoic fumes, while sitting and facing the Shakti shrine. At the seance I had attended, he knocked his head against the shrine door and rang bells hung on that door to announce the arrival of Shakti. Then he scratched his head and ran his hands through his hair as though the mother goddess was letting her hair down. He whispered in a hoarse voice to clients who approached him.

During a seance, each of the four mediums acts out the character of the possessing deity. In the case of a medium who is possessed in turn by several spirits, such as Sarimah and Tan, the characteristics and idiosyncracies of the various spirits are enacted in succession through changes in the medium's mood, expression, and style, all of which are recognizable by the audience. Thus, Sarimah adopts the gait of a warrior when possessed by *Datuk Bono*. She stalks around the living room with a stern look, holding a large spear in one hand and mumbling incomprehensible incantations. When she is possessed by *Putera Bongsu*, she becomes unrestrained in speaking her mind. She jokes and exchanges gossip with her clients, smokes a cigar, and chews betel leaves. The entrance of *Jin Jambol* (the protector spirit of the house) is characterized by a serious expression on Sarimah's face. She moves around the room with a dagger in one hand, beats her chest several times, and mutters *bagus, bagus* (good, good). Tan becomes irritable, vituperative, and ill-tempered when possessed by *Datuk Hijau* but changes to a pleasant mood when *Datuk Merah* (red *datuk*) takes over. The arrival of *Datuk Hitam* (black *datuk*) is usually accompanied by demonstrations of feats of strength. At the festival, while under the influence of *Datuk Hitam* Tan stabbed himself in the abdomen with several *kris* (curved Malay daggers) but without injuring himself; instead he bent all the *kris*. However, the deities that possess Lim and Govinda are less colorful characters. Since each of them is identified only with one deity, there is very little variation in their performance styles. They speak either in monotones or in low whispers, without any observable changes in temperament. Even though Lim demonstrated various feats at the spirit festival— such as drinking boiling oil and walking barefoot over hot coals and a bridge of knives—his mood remained constant. At the end of a seance, a medium is drenched in sweat and totally exhausted. Sarimah usually gets a rubdown from her husband or some members of the audience. The others normally retire to a back room to rest or talk with family members and friends.

These repertoires of behaviors are, in effect, the props by which the supernatural self is distinguished from the natural self in spirit mediumship. Although mediums are for the most part treated by others as ordinary people, it is the ephemeral nature of the non-routine behaviors in trance that is associated with spirit possession. In other words, the performed self of the medium in seances is respected, feared, and perhaps tolerated because it is not identified as a continuous aspect of the normal, waking self. Both supernatural and natural selves occupy the same body, but the former is only deliberately invoked as a limited, prearranged affair. However, the emergence of the supernatural self in seances must be responded to as such, since spirit possession is by earlier definition an imputed event (see Lambek, this volume).

AUDIENCE RESPONSES

The clients of these mediums come from assorted backgrounds. Most of Sarimah's patients are poor, working-class Malays, although clients of different ethnicities and class backgrounds also approach her for help. In contrast, Govinda's clientele comprises largely middle-class Indians, although there is a Chinese professional who attends his seances regularly. The people who consult Tan and Lim are mostly Chinese, both middle- and working-class, although there are occasional Malay and Indian patients. All these individuals believe in the efficacy of divine intervention in healing, changing fortunes, and other mundane matters. Their involvement with these spirit mediums presupposes an adherence to a broad set of supernatural beliefs that facilitates receptivity to trance performances.

Sarimah's audience responds to her varyingly, according to her characterization of the various possessing deities. The appearance of *Datuk Bong*, *Jin Jambol*, and other reputedly fierce spirits is usually greeted by sharp silence. No one in the audience moves; the only person who seems to do anything is Sarimah's husband, who hurriedly records in a notebook the spirit's requests for various sacrificial and healing items. The atmosphere becomes more tense as each of the warrior spirits prances around the room, armed with a variety of weapons. Tension turns to gambol with the arrival of *Putera*

Bongsu. The audience exchange greetings with *Bongsu* in Arabic and throw coins amounting to three, seven, or nine cents into a bowl as offerings. Howls of laughter from the audience reverberate through the room as *Bongsu* delivers risqué jokes while performing divinations and healings. The more seasoned members of the audience would instruct the newly arrived patients on how and where to sit as the possessed Sarimah strokes their bodies with leaves as if driving out the illnesses from them. When Sarimah is possessed by a water spirit, she shivers and speaks in a shrill voice, complaining that she is cold. The members of the audience immediately cover her with the colored cloths to keep her warm.

The exchange between Govinda and his clients is relatively more restrained. The arrival of Shakti is greeted by devotees clasping their hands above their heads in supplication. Some devotees cry out softly "Mother has come" to inform naive observers that the seance has begun and to ready themselves for worship and consultation. They sit at a fair distance from the medium, waiting for his signal to begin private consultations. Govinda whispers advice to his clients, unlike Sarimah, who voices her opinion loud enough for all to hear. Because Govinda is possessed only by Shakti and no other deities, there is little variation in audience response. The somewhat subdued response of Govinda's clients suggests their respect and reverence for the goddess.

Audience response in the case of Lim's seances is also subdued. His clients wait patiently outside the temple, queue number in hand, for their turn to consult with Lim, who speaks to them in private in high-pitched Mandarin but is assisted by his wife. The same type of interaction between medium and patients is observed at Tan's seances. Patients who are waiting their turns sit around in the living room but at a fair distance from the main altar, where consultation is conducted. At these seances, Lim and Tan are each possessed by only one deity for the specific purpose of advising and healing their clients. The businesslike atmosphere of these seances seems to dampen the enthusiasm of the clients, who are mainly concerned with receiving advice, medicine, and charms, and leaving quickly.

At the festivals, however, the audience respond excitedly to the various spectacles that unfold before them, while the medium's assistants rush around to prepare food, offerings, and ritual paraphernalia. Unlike the seances, spirit festivals are more open affairs that are not restricted to clients seeking cures. Members of the public are usually invited to attend elaborate festivals that feature trance, Chinese opera, and other sideshows performed over a few consecutive evenings. At these festivals, Lim and Tan are assisted by several mediums, each of whom in turn is possessed by one or few deities. Audience reactions are likely to vary widely, depending on the character of the descending deities. Thus, at the festival that Tan put on in 1980, the audience moved hurriedly away from an assistant medium who, possessed by the tiger spirit, was crawling around on all fours. But some joined in the dancing led by another medium possessed by a jovial spirit.

These descriptions of audience responses suggest that the context of possession is the main determinant of audience behavior. Clients tend to become familiar with the routines of these occasions and develop certain expectations of trance performances. Some regular clients are even able to tell in advance the medium's next move. But all these expectations are predicated on their belief that the medium's soul has departed from the body, turning it into a temporary receptacle for the gods. This is evident in their acts of submission and deference to the medium during a seance, in contrast to the somewhat open and casual interactions before possession occurs. In deferring to the entranced medium, the patient is in fact treating possession as a necessary condition for physical and mental healing. The patient is more likely to accept the advice of a medium in trance than one in a "normal" frame of mind.

The degree of receptivity to trance performance is an important measure of the medium's reputation. Mediums who are known to be powerful and efficacious in healing tend to attract larger clienteles. Individuals who attend seances are usually eager to obtain charms and various power objects for protection and good fortune. Sarimah attracts many clients who are aware of her alleged abilities to materialize gemstones through the intervention of her spirit helpers. Many stories have circulated concerning the power of these gemstones in effecting cures and fulfilling various needs. Similarly, Lim, Tan, and Govinda distribute charms that are expected by their clients to possess supernatural qualities. Clients also evaluate the moral standing of the mediums through their actions in trance and non-trance states. Lim and Tan are believed to be morally pure because they feel no pain and bleed little when they mutilate themselves in trance performances. On the other hand, Govinda and Sarimah do not engage in practices of self-mortification but are known for their honesty and discipline. Many of Govinda's clients are aware of his strict regimen of meditation and devotional prayers. They also claim that Govinda makes no profits as a medium. This allegation also applies to Sarimah, who performs out of obligation to the spirits rather than for personal profit.

THE RULES OF TRANCE PERFORMANCE

The acceptance of ASC's in spirit seances can be understood as an interaction event based on three rules of role performance: mood changes, status distance, and power display. Mood changes in spirit mediums signal their entries into a different state of consciousness. These changes are observed by clients at a seance or festival as a set of recognizable behaviors, such as changes in pitch of voice, continuous head shaking, trembling, violent coughing, or a sudden collapse. These behaviors must be performed within the context of a seance or spirit festival for an ASC interpretation to be legitimate; otherwise, such behaviors may be attributed to other conditions, such as madness, illness, or a form of malingering. Clients usually do not critically question the authenticity of a medium's mood changes, especially a medium with an untarnished reputation. In fact, in some cases the medium's reputation alone is a legitimate guarantee of the transformation in a seance. The clients of the four mediums mentioned above have expressed no doubts about their mood changes; on the contrary, they ask "How can he or she heal if there is no trance?" Thus, the clients' interpretation of mood changes as an ASC-related phenomenon is contingent upon the context of observation and expectation.

Mood change in a medium is followed by status elevation. As a medium sheds the earthly self in a seance, he or she becomes the embodiment of divine power and expects treatment commensurate with the changed status. Mediums routinely expect deference by virtue of their mood changes, but more importantly they maintain status distance from clients by the intermediation of one or more assistants. Even though the clients are in visual contact with the medium, they communicate indirectly through a third person. The presence of the assistant reinforces the notion of sacred boundaries implied in the higher psychic state of the medium. The assistant does not usually become entranced but performs the role as interpreter in a normal state of consciousness. A medium's assistant is therefore a special individual who bridges the status gap without necessarily invoking mood changes. To meet this requirement, an assistant must be thoroughly familiar with the unique demands of mediumship. Spouses, close friends, and colleagues of mediums make up a special pool of people from which individuals are selected to fulfill the assistant's role. Thus, Lim's wife, Tan's neighbor, Govinda's colleague (a Hindu priest), and Sarimah's husband provide their resources in regulating the unequal relationship between the medium and clients. However, not all mediums have assistants, especially those with limited reputation and small clienteles. Status distance, in this instance, is assumed in the medium's transformation but not accentuated by the presence of an assistant.

Since a medium in trance is, by definition, an individual imbued with supernatural powers, he or she must demonstrate the ability to meet the clients' expectations (see Dobkin de Rios, this volume, for a discussion of shamanic power). Physical mutilations and oracular accuracy are the major means of power display. Lim and Tan specialize in the former method, inflicting cuts on various parts of their bodies without grimacing or showing any outward signs of pain to emphasize the physical invulnerability induced by trance. Sarimah and Govinda, on the other hand, avoid the techniques of bloodletting and rely more on their oracular skills to underscore their abilities in trance. Acts of physical mutilations are meant largely to awe the audience, especially at festivals, but their performance in conjunction with the production of charms amounts to a special technique of power display; for example, Tan very often cuts his tongue and daubs the blood on paper charms for his clients. Specific substances emitted from a medium's body during trance are considered by clients to be efficacious healing agents. Thus, even though Sarimah does not cut herself in a seance, she uses her saliva as a liniment for healing. Compared with displays of self-mortification, oracular accuracy is more difficult to achieve because the medium is required to demonstrate consistency in predictive abilities. Most clients are highly sensitive to the precision of a medium's advice, especially in matters relating to lotteries, business, jobs, marriage, and other earthly predicaments. They are always prepared to seek out other mediums should their regular medium provide ineffective advice. Most mediums are therefore hard-pressed to produce an impressive oracular record in order to remain in business. Lim, Tan, Govinda, and Sarimah apparently hold untainted records as effective soothsayers, since the clients I interviewed all spoke highly of them in terms of the beneficial advice they had received.

CONCLUSION

These rules of trance performance suggest that ASC's in healing ceremonies are not only physiological and psychological events but also a function of the social relationship between medium and clients. The interpretation of the physiological and psychological changes in an entranced medium is contingent upon the clients' knowledge and understanding of these rules, which in turn are grounded in the larger cultural milieu. The dramaturgical approach to mediumship provides an important corrective to the overemphasis on internal processes in healing rituals. This approach focuses on the role behaviors and expectations in trance performances but does not cover the question of how these roles are learned. In many ways, this is an important research question, because it opens the area of ASC's to further inquiry; i.e., to what extent are ASC's learned or naturally acquired? Some moves have already been made in this direction (e.g., Bateson, 1976). The data in this chapter are silent on this question but stress the need to understand further the social components of ASC's in ritual healing.

NOTES

1. Unlike Goffman, I am not interested in discussing whether the performer believes in his or her own act or is cynical about it. Rather, I am more concerned with how the act is presented and perceived.

2. In this chapter, I focus on the front regions of ritualized possession for two reasons: (1) I aim to compare the different styles of several selected Malaysian spirit mediums and to relate these styles to various rules of trance performances; (2) my data on the back regions are very meager, since they are guarded closely by the spirit mediums, whose livelihoods and reputations depend on the outward appearances they successfully forge.

3. Malaysia consists of a peninsula (known as West Malaysia) with 11 states, together with 2 states, Sabah and Sarawak, in Borneo (collectively known as East Malaysia). The statistics presented here are relevant only to West Malaysia.

4. Even these traditional styles of mediumship are not entirely "pure." Many of these styles have incorporated other cultural elements over long periods of time but are deemed traditional in the sense that they are relatively stable and have been practiced for a long time by many generations of mediums.

5. In some parts of Malaysia, the term *pawang* is used. Sometimes, a *pawang* is considered more powerful than a *bomoh*, although this is not necessarily so all the time.

6. In one case I studied, the *bomoh* revealed that he had studied with his father and seven other *bomohs* before setting up his own practice.

7. *Dang ki* is a Hokkien term meaning "divining youth." The Cantonese term is *kong t'ung*. A local term that is used is *jinjang*.

8. It is unclear whether Tan had undergone rigorous training with mediums, although he hinted of his close association with temple mediums in Penang, the island state in northern Malaysia.

9. Very little research has been done on spirit mediumship among the Hindus in Malaysia. Most of the description of Hindu mediums in this section is based on data provided by Rajoo (1975).

10. A short survey conducted by Teoh, Kinzie, and Tan (1973) found that in a sample of 175 patients who had sought psychiatric help at the University of Malaya medical center in Kuala Lumpur, 54, or 31%, had consulted spirit mediums prior to admission at the center.

11. *Datuk* is a Malay term of respect for an older person. It can also mean grandfather. *Hijau* is Malay for green.

REFERENCES

Bateson, G. (1976). Some components of socialization for trance. In T. Schwartz (Ed.), *Socialization as cultural communication* (pp. 51-63). Berkeley: University of California Press.

Bourguignon, E. (1970). Hallucination and trance: An anthropologist's perspective. In W. Keup (Ed.), *Origin and mechanisms of hallucinations* (pp. 183-190). New York: Plenum.

Elliott, A. J. A. (1955). *Chinese spirit-medium cults in Singapore*. London: Athlone Press.

Firth, R. (1967). Ritual and drama in Malay spirit mediumship. *Comparative Studies in Society and History, 9*, 190-207.

Goffman, E. (1959). *The presentation of self in everyday life*. New York: Anchor Books.

Lee, R. L. M. (1983). Dancing with the gods: A spirit medium festival in urban Malaysia. *Anthropos, 78*, 355-368.

Lee, R. L. M. (1986). Continuity and change in Chinese spirit mediumship in urban Malaysia. *Bijdragen Tot de Taal-, Land- en Volkenkunde, 142*, 198-214.

Lewis, I. M. (1971). *Ecstatic religion*. Harmondsworth: Penguin.

Ludwig, A. M. (1966). Altered states of consciousness. *Archives of General Psychiatry, 15*, 225-234.

Rajoo, R. (1975). *Patterns of Hindu religious beliefs and practices among the people of Tamil origin in West Malaysia*. Unpublished master's thesis, University of Malaya, Kuala Lumpur.

Schwartz, T. (1976). The cargo cult: A Melanesian type-response to change. In George A. DeVos (Ed.), *Responses to change* (pp. 157-206). New York: Van Nostrand.

Teoh, J. I., Kinzie, J. D., & Tan, E. S. (1973). Referrals to a psychiatric clinic in West Malaysia. *International Journal of Social Psychiatry, 18*, 301-307.

Ward, C. (1979). Therapeutic aspects of ritual trance: The Shango cult in Trinidad. *Journal of Altered States of Consciousness, 5*, 19-29.

Winstedt, R. O. (1961). *The Malay magician*. London: Routledge & Kegan Paul.

Wright, B. S. (1980). Dance is the cure: The arts as metaphor for healing in Kelantanese Malay spirit exorcisms. *Dance Research Journal, 12*, 3-10.

13

STRESSING SOCIAL CHANGE AND SONGHAY POSSESSION

PAUL STOLLER

The whole history of humanity has been one of cultural struggles, migrations and fusions. (Bastide, 1978, p. 12)

Roger Bastide's view of cultural life is one that is marked by ongoing cultural contact. Peoples of different languages and cultures come in contact with one another, and cultural struggles ensue, followed by some kind of resolution, a cultural fusion. And when this fusion occurs, the social structure of both groups is in some way transformed. This transformation, in turn, precipitates social change.

Scholars generally agree that rapid social change creates cases of severe social stress (Hughes, 1969; Jilek, this volume; Kiev, 1972; Lambo, 1964). Having undergone rapid social and technological change, the peoples of Africa are no exception. How have African peoples adapted to irrevocable social change and the stress that it has produced? Like other peoples throughout the world, Africans have used a variety of cultural resources to protect themselves from the devastating psychological ramifications of rapid social change (see Cole, 1981; Ranger, 1975). More specifically, Africans faced with social and cultural dissolution have employed a number of generally satiric symbolic devices as a means of "cultural resistance . . . an endeavor not to let vital values inherited from ancestors . . . perish, but to reestablish them through symbolic or military means" (Bastide, 1978, p. 156).

People in African societies have a long history of using satiric ex-

AUTHOR'S NOTE: The research upon which the present chapter is based was made possible through funds provided by a Fulbright-Hays Doctoral Disseration Fellowship (G00-76-03569), a grant from the Wenner-Gren Foundation for Anthropological Research (#3175), a NATO Postdoctoral Fellowship in Science for the academic year of 1979-80, two grants from the American Philosophical Society (1981, 1982), and a series of Faculty Research Grants from West Chester University (1981, 1982, 1983). I thank these institutions for their generous support. For their comments and advice I thank Cheryl Olkes, Ivan Karp, and Jean-Pierre Olivier de Sardin.

pressive forms to resist the disruptive influences of powerful strangers. In some Dogon masks, for example, the exaggerated portrayal of the Peul woman serves to critique the ways of the stranger as it buttresses the traditions of the Dogon (DeMott, 1982). The masks of the Yorouba *Gelede* society appear to ridicule those strangers who have precipitated unwanted social change. "In preserving the traditions by ridiculing the unacceptable changes and praising acceptable actions, the imagery entertains, placates and honors the gods of society" (Drewal, 1974, p. 10).

This paper focuses upon possession as a form of cultural resistance among the Songhay people of the Republic of Niger. In Songhay society, I shall argue, the creation of the possession movement has been

> connected to great social upheavals, to wars and massacres. This connection stems from a general hypothesis on the emergence of possession cults. Following it, they [possession cults] appear in particularly troubled periods when human beings desire the intimate presence of the gods. Due to the need of greater security, they call to the gods to descend upon them. (Gibbal, 1982, p. 163)

When confronted with powerful and influential others, the Songhay have resisted those "realities" that have threatened to vitiate their cultural identity by incorporating them into the symbolic framework of their possession rituals. Taking the bodies of mediums, most Songhay spirits invariably violate expectations of social appropriateness through exaggerated, satiric behavior. Evidence from studies of the two most recent groups of Songhay deities—the *Hauka*, spirits that burlesque French colonial society in Niger, and the *Sasale*, spirits that mock the moral premises of neoconservative Islam in Niger—powerfully reinforces my premise: that Songhay possession is a psychologically stabilizing cultural response to social and cultural dissolution brought on by stressing social change.

POSSESSION IN SONGHAY SOCIETY

The Songhay live today primarily in the republics of Mali and Niger, though a considerable population of Songhay speakers lives in northern Benin. The Songhay trace their origins to the latter part of the seventh century when Aliaman Dia, reputedly a Berber from

Libya, traveled west and eventually conquered the peoples living along the banks of the Niger River south of the present-day region of Gao (Republic of Mali). Aliaman Dia settled along the Niger River and established the *Dia* (or *Za*) dynasty of Songhay. Despite the rise and fall of Ghana and Mali, the *Dia* dynasty remained intact until the latter part of the thirteenth century, when Ali Kolen temporarily freed the Songhay from the rule of Mali. Ali Kolen and his descendants took the title *Si* rather than *Dia* and considered themselves a new Songhay dynasty. Mali soon reestablished its hegemony over the Songhay, however, and it was only with the ascendance of the 18th and last *Si*, Sonni Ali Ber (1464–1491), that Songhay at last gained total independence from Mali. Sonni Ali Ber expanded considerably the power and influence of Songhay. The empire reached the height of its power, however, during the reign of Sonni's successor, Mohammed Touré (1493–1528), who established the Askiad (1493–1591), the third and last dynasty of Songhay (see Hama, 1968; Hunwick, 1966, 1972; Konare Ba, 1977; Olivier de Sardin, 1982, 1984; Rouch, 1953).

Songhay cosmology expanded with historical experience. Prior to the Askiad, the Songhay developed the central theme of their belief system: human beings are powerless actors in a universe filled with powerful forces that can at any moment destroy society. Individuals attempted to control the powerful unseen forces through ritual offerings to their lineage altars (*tooru*). The historical patterns suggest, moreover, that prior to the Askiad, Songhay religion consisted of a series of localized and private rites in which sacrifices were made to the land, to the mountains, to the sky, and to the Niger River. Other offerings were no doubt made to the ancestors of a person's lineage (see Boulnois & Hama, 1953; Hama, 1968; Olivier de Sardin, 1982; Rouch, 1960).

With the onset of the Askiad and the planned Islamization of the Songhay Empire, Songhay religious practices appear to have become more public: Private offerings to the spirits of the *tooru* (altar) of a lineage became public offerings to the *Tooru* spirits that now manifested themselves in the bodies of mediums. Like the old altar spirits, the *Tooru* controlled the most powerful forces of nature: the sky (wind, lightning, clouds, rain) and the Niger River. What precipitated this transformation? The policies of the Askiad promoted Islamization, the dispersion of entire populations, and the dissolution of the lineage as a decision-making body. In this climate of irrevocable change, the possession ritual (*holi hori*) became a stage of resistance from which the Songhay dodged the influences of the Askiad (Olivier de Sardin, 1982).

The same pattern of resistance and incorporation emerged during the other periods of Songhay historical contact and crisis. From contact with the non-negroid and Islamized Tuaregs came the *Genji Kwarey*, or white spirits. In the spirit world, the *Genji Kwarey* are Islamic clerics that settle disputes. From nineteenth-century contact with Hausa-speaking peoples, the Hausa spirits became part of the Songhay pantheon. On the eve of the colonial period (1898–1960), there existed five distinct "families" of spirits in the Songhay pantheon:

1. *The Tooru*: the nobles of the spirit world, which control such natural forces as the wind, the clouds, the Niger River, fire, lightning, and thunder.
2. *The Genji Kwarey*: the "white spirits," which are the Islamic clerics and dispute arbitrators of the spirit world.
3. *The Genji Bi*: the "black spirits," which control forces governing soil fertility and pestilence.
4. *The Hargay*: the spirits of the cold, which govern many illnesses, especially those associated with the reproductive cycle.
5. *The Hausa Genji*: the Hausa spirits, which precipitate madness and various kinds of paralysis.

From the Askiad to the eve of the colonial period, then, Songhay possession had been a continually evolving aesthetic form. From its humble beginnings at the dawn of Songhay civilization it grew in importance and complexity to become, along with Islam, a major religious force of the precolonial social order.[1]

The Songhay theory of possession devolves from their view of the human body. The body consists of flesh (*ga*), the life force (*hundi*), and the double (*bia*). Flesh is the material essence of the human being. The life force resides in the human heart; it is the energy of life. When a person is born, he or she receives the life force. When Songhay die, the life force immediately leaves the body and rises to the heavens. *Bia* is the human double. Adamu Jenitongo, the possession priest of Tillaberi, Niger, says that people can see their own double when they look into a placid pool of water. The same might be said when a person sees his or her shadow on the sand. When a person sleeps, the double leaves the body and travels about the village seeking adventure. Songhay believe that dreams are the representation of the double's nocturnal travels. The double is the essence of a human being's personality.

Possession among the Songhay results from the temporary displacement of a person's double. When dancers are taken by their spirits, the deity displaces the dancer's double with its own. It is for this reason that the possessed dancer's body shakes in uncontrolled fashion. When the double of the deity is firmly established in the body of the dancer, the deity screams and dances wildly. The medium's body has become the deity. (Similar manifestations of possession are cited by Krippner and Lee, this volume.)

There is widespread disagreement about where the medium's double is displaced. Adamu Jenitongo says that the dancer's double leaves the body and deposits itself in a *lolo*, a tall iron staff that specialists use to repel witches. Other ritual priests suggest that the dancer's double finds temporary residence in the sanctified wooden poles of the ritual canopy under which possession musicians play their sacred instruments.

When mediums are possessed, they enter an altered state of consciousness in which they drink blood, perform acrobatics, and read minds. In this state the medium's comportment and voice change. Possessed mediums are impervious to fire, boiling water, and poison (see Chandra shekar, this volume). Adamu Jenitongo says that the mediums derive great strength from their spirits. "If we mediums make offerings to our spirits, they will protect us from our enemies. That is why we walk our paths with great confidence. If we mediums neglect our spirits, they make us sick. Sometimes, they kill us."[2]

Possession rituals have always been staged in the same manner. The *zima*, or priest of the possession cult, organizes a dance that features the music of the monochord violin (*godji*) and the calabash drum (*gasi*). When the music of these instruments is combined with the sacred verse of spirit praise-poetry and the movement of dancer-adepts, the spirits are lured from their domain in the heavens and take the bodies of their mediums on earth. When the spirits arrive in the social world, members of the cult give them food and drink and dress them in their respective costumes. Attendants also give them objects associated with their respective roles in the spirit world.

THE HAUKA, SATIRE, AND THE COLONIAL PERIOD

There has been no greater time of precipitous social change in Songhay history than the colonial period. The coming of the French in 1899 marked a significant turning point in Songhay experience. Before the colonial era, the traditions of the Songhay had never been threatened significantly by military or cultural invasion. During the incessant wars of the nineteenth century, for example, the victors would take their slave-prisoners or their tribute and return to their own lands. The combatants in these precolonial wars were unconcerned about such European notions as cultural evolution. With the onset of French colonialism, however, the Songhay confronted the way of the European, a path of progress culminating in "civilization." To rescue Africans from their uncivilized ways, the French introduced a policy of "cultural renaissance." The colonial administrators designed this policy to train a small educated elite and to instill in the masses a deep shame over their ancient ways. In Songhay country and elsewhere in French West Africa, people

> had their old life broken by the shock of European contact; the old order of tribal society, with its cohesion based on unquestioned rule of custom, has been forced into the background; and the native, deracialized by the shattering of everything which has previously guided him, drifts disillusioned and despairing now knowing no hope, and now with the insane joy of the iconoclast aiding the outside forces in rending his life from top to bottom. (Roberts, 1963, pp. 312–313)

Cultural renaissance succeeded in radically transforming the social and political foundations of the precolonial social order. Out of this decay, however, there emerged a revolutionary cultural phenomenon, the *Hauka*, a new "family" of Songhay spirits. Through their outrageous mockery of such colonial identities as *King Zuzi* (the colonial chief justice) and *Gomno Malia* (the governor of the Red Sea), the *Hauka* burlesqued European ways.

As the French began to consolidate their power in Niger, the *Hauka* movement emerged. During the course of a dance of young adults, the first *Hauka* took a medium. Jean Rouch's informant, *El Hadj* Mohammadou of Filingue, said:

> It all began during a dance of girls and boys. During the dance a Soudye woman, Zibo, who was married to a Timbucktu *sherif*, began to be possessed by a spirit. They asked who it was. It said: "I am *Gomno Malia* (Governor of the Red Sea)." The people said that they did not know this spirit. Then others came and took bodies of some of the young boys. They too spoke their names, and the people did not know them. The spirits said: "We are the *Hauka*, the guests of *Dongo*." This occurred at Chikal, very close to Filingue. A few days

later all the boys and girls of Filingue had been possessed by the *Hauka*. (Rouch, 1960, p. 73)

The *Hauka* movement spread rapidly. By February 1927 the French administration noted that there were *Hauka* mediums in all the villages of Filingue district. Indeed, the French considered the *Hauka* "rivals of the established order, represented by the chieftaincy, the backbone of the administrative system created by the French" (Fugelstad, 1975, p. 204).

As time passed by, the *Hauka* family and the mythology that reinforced the place of the *Hauka* in Songhay cosmology took form. In all cases the deities and identities associated with the *Hauka* aped French colonial society. Continuing to assert that they were from the Red Sea and the guests of *Dongo* in Songhay country, the following characters emerged as the most important of the early *Hauka* deities:

1. *Istanbula*, who lives in Istanbul and who is both a pious Muslim and the chief of all the *Hauka*.
2. *Gomno*, the colonial governor (of the Red Sea).
3. *Zeneral Malia*, the general of the Red Sea.
4. *King Zuzi*, the king of judges, or colonial chief justice.
5. *Mayaki*, the warrior or great soldier.
6. *Korsasi*, the wicked major who sometimes kills his mediums.
7. *Sekter*, the secretary or clerk.
8. *Kapral Gardi*, the corporal of the guard who is the assistant to Korsasi, and who knows how to break iron with his bare hands.
9. *Rabule*, the blacksmith.
10. *Falimata Malia*, the wife of *Zeneral Malia* who had her son, *Cehmoko*, with *Kapral Gardi*.
11. *Cemoko*, the young boy who knows how to pull silver out of the ground. (Rouch, 1960, pp. 74-75)

The *Hauka* boldly expressed their refusal of colonialism through satire. In the bodies of their mediums, the *Hauka* deities routinely handled fire, consumed poison plants, and knocked down mudbrick walls with their bare hands. They made verbal statements in a mixture of Pidgin French, Pidgin English, and Songhay. Having the "Colonial Governor" or the "General of the Red Sea" speak to an audience in Pidgin, still a stigmatized linguistic form in West Africa, constituted a negative message about the colonial authorities. Imagine a French colonial official being aped by possessed Songhay. The mediums' bodies are contorted. Their eyes are bulging, and like all *Hauka* they froth at the mouth. And to add insult to injury, the "official" speaks a mixture of Pidgin and Songhay. The result of this complex of symbolic messages is a combination of fright, for the *Hauka* is a terrifying sight, and burlesque, for the *Hauka* mocks the identity he or she represents. So shocking was this mockery that the ritual priests completely disassociated themselves from the *Hauka*. The *Hauka* were outlaws in both the spirit and social worlds. Given their popularity, however, the possession priests eventually created a *Hauka* mythology that justified their incorporation into the Songhay pantheon (Stoller, 1984).[3]

The *Hauka* were popular during the colonial period because their exaggerated antics diminished some of the stress associated with social change precipitated by French colonialism. At the same time, the *Hauka* expressed a pride in the cultural traditions of the Songhay. Indeed the satiric action of the *Hauka* was the only weapon—a cultural weapon—that the Songhay could use to protect their cultural identity from the disruptive influences of colonialism.

THE SASALE, SATIRE, AND THE CONTEMPORARY PERIOD IN NIGER

Just as the *Hauka* spirits emerged in response to the cultural disruption of French colonialism, so the *Sasale* spirits have emerged today partly in response to the increasing influence of neo-conservative Islam in the Republic of Niger. French colonial policy undermined the political autonomy and symbolic importance of chiefs, introduced money into the Songhay economy, and promoted French language and culture to the detriment of Songhay culture. The *Hauka* brutally satirized the symbols of French supremacy in order to reaffirm and to protect the traditions of Songhay culture. (Spanos, this volume, also discusses possession and propaganda.)

The policies of the Government of Niger (GON) today emphasize values associated with scripturalist Islam—individual industriousness, sexual vigilance, and interethnic harmony in a nation of believers in which all people are considered equals. These recent social policies are designed to solve the monumental set of problems facing the Republic of Niger; many of them seek to dismantle old eth-

nic hierarchies. From the GON perspective, outmoded social con-
figurations like those of the Songhay precipitate both recalcitrance
to change and ethnic divisiveness, both of which prevent the emergence of a national consciousness. In this tense climate of change,
the *Sasale* have emerged. Having first appeared in 1965, the *Sasale*
spirits flaunt sexual excess and social perversion (drinking alcohol;
foul language; gambling); in so doing they have become opponents
of the increasingly popular neoconservative Islam that has recently
undermined many of the themes central to Songhay cultural
identity.

Songhay Society in the Republic of Niger

The Songhay constitute roughly 40% of the population of the Republic of Niger. Like other ethnic groups in Niger (Hausa, Peul,
Tuareg, Kanuri), Songhay has remained a distinct social grouping.
Consciousness of one's Songhay identity very often supersedes consciousness of national identity. Indeed, the persistence of what some
call "tribalism" is a major problem facing the GON, which desires
to forge a nation-state from ethnic elements that have long histories
of mutual enmity (Stoller, 1980, 1981).

There are other socioeconomic problems facing the Songhay in
the Republic of Niger. These include chronic agricultural underproduction, continuous migration, and uncontrolled urbanization.
The problems are compounded by their interrelatedness. The need
for money forces young men to leave the countryside for the city,
where they exchange labor for wages; consequently, since many of
these young men never return to the countryside, the rural labor
force has been depleted. As cities such as Niamey have grown exponentially, the amount of millet produced in the countryside has
dwindled. Shortages of millet, in turn, increase the price of this
Sahelian staple, bolstering the resolve of young men to leave their
villages to seek waged labor. Songhay in remote rural areas would
not be able to remain in their villages if not for the money sent
home by their departed sons (see World Bank, 1981). Add to this
cycle of economic horrors the chronic pattern of drought in the
Sahelian climate, and one can envisage the socioeconomic situation faced by rural Songhay as well as the policy perspective of the
GON, which would like to heal the wounds of ethnic enmity and
better incorporate the groups into the nation-state (Franke &
Chasin, 1980; Sidikou, 1974).

Just as the policies of the Askiad displaced the lineage as an important social institution, so the cycle of socioeconomic problems—underproduction, migration, urbanization—has diminished the importance of village life among the Songhay of the Republic of Niger. This decline of village life is a stressing social situation not dissimilar to those critical events in Songhay history when social dissolution sparked the emergence of new deities into the pantheon of spirits.

Islam in the Republic of Niger

The GON has attempted to solve the problems of underproduction, migration, urbanization, and ethnic enmity. Indeed the government of Seyni Kountché, which took power in 1974, recognized that if Niger is to become a viable nation-state, there must emerge a radically new social order. To achieve these social goals, the GON has promoted a set of social policies based upon the tenets of scripturalist Islam. The reassertion of the basic message of the Koran in the face of the overgrown garden of magic in late medieval Islam

> has had a profoundly modernizing consequence. Awakening membership in the universal community of Islam has often been the first mode of consciousness to break through stagnant localisms ... Anticolonialist and nationalist impulses as well as all kinds of social reform efforts have originated at this source. There can be no clearer tribute to the universalistic, progressive and indeed, revolutionary potential of Quaranic religion. (Bellah, 1970, p. 160)

Following this prescription the GON has begun to appeal to the population not as Songhay, Hausa, or Peul, but as citizen-believers in the Islamic community of *Umma*. In a speech made in February 1981, President Kountché said that *Umma* "gives us the wherewithal to follow the straight road ... All Muslims, despite their variation in color and language, are one community. They follow the same path and are of one culture" (Government of Niger, 1980, p. 4). GON policy planners have also argued that if there is moral purity in a Niger united through Islam, the citizen-believers will be mobilized to meet the goals of agricultural and industrial self-sufficiency in a climate of national harmony. The Songhay today are confronted not only with the continuing erosion of their social autonomy but also with the planned desires of the GON to make them model citizens of an Islamically vigilant nation-state. Although almost all Songhay are Muslims, many of them continue to resist those elements of Islam that threaten themes central to Songhay identity and consciousness.

The *Sasale* Movement

The term *sasale* originally denoted a group of slaves who were notorious for their dancing. When they danced for chiefs,

> they took off their clothing, sang sexual songs and danced sexual dances. And the spectators paid them to stop. You see the idea: It's a kind of strip-tease, only you pay them not to go on! Well, when the *Sasale* possess boys and girls they do the same thing, they start to take off their clothes and start to make love when they are possessed. It was considered shameful, it was forbidden by the Niger police, and they were put in jail ... (Rouch, 1978, p. 1010)

Unlike other Songhay spirits, the *Sasale* flaunt the immorality that the GON abhors: permissive sexuality, foul language, womanizing, gambling, laziness, and prostitution. The first *Sasale* appeared in the mid-1960s, and the movement continues to grow in the wake of more than 15 years of the GON's socioeconomic policies.

The *Sasale* Deities

The deities are the reincarnations of famous womanizers, prostitutes, singers, and gamblers who have died in the recent past. The first *Sasale* to appear was *Alibiyo* ("black Ali"). *Alibiyo* was

> a young and very handsome man who had been a propagandist for the RDA, the *Rassemblement Democratique Africain*, a political party in the fight for independence. In '61 the minstrels, guitar players, fiddle players—the griot—composed a very famous song about him called "*Alibiya*." The Niger army was looking for some traditional tunes to play and chose "Alibiya." When *Alibiya* appeared three years later he said, "You are calling me all the time, even the army is calling me. Well, here I am, I'm *Alibiyo*, the playboy," and that was the beginning. (Rouch, 1978, p. 1010)

Of *Alibiyo* is it said that he is a treacherous playboy. He will betray the best of his friends. And he will grab and have intercourse with any woman who pleases him.

Many of the *Sasale* deities, however, are women, the reincarnations of prostitutes and other free spirits who are, from the vantage of Koranic Islam, social deviates. Some of the female *Sasale* are

1. *Ramu Kong'izo*, or Ramu, the daughter of a female slave, who was a famous prostitute.
2. *Bell'izo*, or the daughter of a Bella, a former slave of the Tuareg. She is the chief of the *Sasale* who is especially foul-mouthed.
3. *Kadidja Cendag'izo*, or Kadidja, a daughter of the town of Cendaggi. Kadidja approaches men, strangers in a possession audience, and attempts to thrust her hands into their trousers and grab their penises.
4. *Fadimata Idrissa*, or Fadimata, the daughter of Idrissa, who attempts to grab the testicles of men in a possession audience.

Sasale and Possession Dance

Ritual priests use the same means to bring the *Sasale* to the social world—music, dance, and the recitation of sacred texts—as they do for other spirit "families" in the Songhay pantheon. However, the *Sasale* possession songs, chanted by the ritual musicians, are far more scatological and sexual than the songs sung for the other spirits. Generally speaking, *Sasale* songs are sung at dusk, when the regular audience of a possession ritual goes home. When calling for the *Sasale*, musicians sing the following verses:

1. Nya ngoko
   "Fuck your mother."
2. Nya dufe
   "Your mother's cunt."
3. Duf'izey kule bene
   "All clitori are above [with God]."
4. Fulan benda, a ga wey ngoko
   "A Peul's penis fucks women."
5. Benda, benda a si ngoko weybora kala gina, gina, nga hari kogo
   "The penis, penis, it will only fuck women again and again [but] its water [sperm] is dried up."
6. Duf'izey kosu, a ga labduru ga dang tonka
   "Into the clitori and cunt, he/she will pour porridge with hot pepper."

These insults, of course, are designed to compel the *Sasale* to take the bodies of their mediums, and when they do, they begin their own barrage of insults. They insult the musicians, the praise-singers, and members of the audience. At one possession dance in June 1981, *Ramu Kong'izo* picked me out in the crowd. She announced to the more than 100 people assembled that "this European had brains of dried semen." She repeated this statement five times and then asked me for money.[4]

Just as older possession participants disassociated themselves from the *Hauka* in 1925, so older ritual priests, like Adamu Jenitongo of Tillaberi, Niger, disassociate themselves today from the *Sasale*. When *Sasale* songs are played today, the audience consists mostly of teenagers and young adults—the population category that seems to be most entertained by the sexual and scatological antics of the *Sasale* deities. When the singers, for example, chant "Fulan benda a ga wey ngoko," ("A Peul's penis fucks women"), a woman dancer will take a long piece of cloth and twist it into a phallic shape. Then she places the cloth between her legs and twirls it in a circle as she dances. This kind of behavior is a far cry from that which the GON endorses for its Islamically inspired national society.

The Sociocultural Messages of *Sasale*

The *Sasale* movement celebrates people in Songhay society who have violated the moral code of Islam in one way or another. Opposition to the moral preeminence of Islam is expressed through ritually framed sexual perversion. Rouch (1978) has called the *Sasale* movement a new religion:

> This new religion is . . . absolutely underground because the government is against sex. I began a film about it, but they [the GON] asked me not to show it because, of course, the people were, well, they were not making love in front of the camera, but all the dances, all the songs were about sex: "Look at my clitoris," "Oh, your testicles are wonderful," and so on . . . These religions are a kind of *inconscient collectif.* The people can't explain what they're doing, they can only show what they're thinking of, and it means that during these years from the 20's to Independence they were thinking of power, military, administrative and bureaucratic power, and now they are thinking of sex . . . (p. 1010)

It is too simple to say that the *Sasale* represent the "antistructure" of Songhay social life in independent Niger (see Turner, 1969, 1974). Why are many Songhay thinking about sex today? Perhaps the answer can be found by looking at the problem historically. Initially, possession in Songhay emerged in reaction to the Askiad, imperial Islam, and the dissolution of the lineage. As an aesthetic form, possession stretched with Songhay experience. Eventually, the *Hauka* movement emerged at a time when French colonialism undermined the precolonial social order. In both the imperial and colonial cases possession emerged in response to profoundly stressing social change, and reflected—often with mockery—the influential other. By contrast, the *Sasale* movement is a parody of the Songhay themselves. Despite GON Islamic propaganda, sexual promiscuity is commonplace, at least in the villages where I have lived. Women in their late teens and early twenties who are recently divorced fend for themselves by renting their bodies to eager customers. These may be young men who have not yet amassed the necessary amount of money to pay a bride price, men who have been recently divorced, or married men seeking sexual gratification. But sex in Songhay social life is generally a private affair; it never reaches the public excess of the *Sasale*. Public discussion of sex is absolutely shameful.

But the *Sasale* have burlesqued these long-standing sexual practices. Why? By flaunting sexual excess in the wake of prudish GON policy, the *Sasale* register a public social protest. More profoundly, neoconservative Islam is perhaps a more disquieting challenge to Songhay cultural identity than threats of the past, for it threatens to break the links of past and present; it threatens to undermine the Songhay concept of self. The importance of village life has diminished. Islamic practices are more valued than possession, a religious practice of the ancestors. Perhaps the *Sasale's* shameful public display of sex is a way of saying to the GON: "Look what you are doing to us. This is what you have forced us to become." On yet a deeper level the *Sasale* may represent a warning to their Songhay audiences: "We will disintegrate into sexual deviants unless we reaffirm our links to the past." In the past other deities have reaffirmed collective themes central to Songhay society; the *Sasale* seem to assert personal themes central to the psychological stability of individual Songhay, themes of individual freedom in a climate in which the individual has lost his or her sociocultural autonomy.

SUMMARY AND CONCLUSIONS

In this article I have argued that the Songhay have responded to stressing sociocultural change in the present in much the same way they responded to the devastating military and cultural contacts of their past. When confronted with powerful Others the Songhay have resisted those "realities" that have threatened to vitiate their cultural identity. Since the time of the Askiad the pattern has been to neutralize powerful foreign influences by incorporating them symbolically into Songhay possession rituals. The first Songhay deities seemingly emerged in response to the Askiad, the policies of which promoted Islamization, the dispersion of entire populations, and the dissolution of the lineage. In the colonial period, when European contact undermined much of the foundation of Songhay social life, there emerged the *Hauka* deities, who brutally satirized European colonial society. With the *Sasale* movement, the Songhay use the imagery of sexual perversion to satirize themselves—a plea for individual freedom in a situation of increasing personal loss.

Underlying all of the varied sociocultural dynamics of possession in Songhay society is the fact that it is a stage from which the unspeakable is expressed through ethnic, religious, or sexual imagery; possession becomes, then, an index of the Songhay *inconscient collectif*. Possession among the Songhay is one outlet for the stress associated with collective and individual loss of autonomy. By viewing possession as a stage of cultural resistance, moreover, I affirm that Songhay, like all people, are intentional subjects, who, despite the sociocultural and psychological devastation of irrevocable change, have maintained a strong sense of their cultural identity. The *Sasale* deities represent the unarticulated concerns of rural Songhay. In the coming years there will doubtless emerge unimagined Songhay deities that through satire, will ease the psychological burdens of the sociocultural challenges of the future.

NOTES

1. From oral accounts we have some idea when the various families of Songhay spirits were incorporated into the Songhay pantheon. Clearly, the *Tooru* spirits are the most ancient; they appear to date to the Askiad. The *Genjio Kwaarey* may well have been incorporated into the Songhay pantheon prior to the nineteenth century (Olivier de Sardin, 1982). Some specialists think that the *Genji Bi*, the spirits of the

land, represent the first non-Songhay inhabitants of the land. They are, therefore, considered to have long been part of the Songhay pantheon. Olivier de Sardin disagrees with this premise. We do know that the *Hargey, Hausa Genji,* and *Hauka* appeared in the late nineteenth or early twentieth century. According to Adamu Jenitongo, the *Hausa Genji* emerged just after the great drought of 1911–14.

2. This statement is from an interview with Adamu Jenitongo, zima of Tillaberi, conducted in Tillaberi on December 20, 1982.

3. To illustrate the combination of horror and humor in *Hauka* possession dances, I shall describe one case from my field notes. The ritual occurred in the town of Tillaberi in June 1981 during a *yenaandi,* the rain dance during which Songhay make offerings to the spirits that control the heavens. The Songhay believe that if they make offerings to these spirits, the spirits will bring enough rain during the planting season (June through September). A good rainy season usually ensures a good millet harvest in October. The *yenaandi* is primarily a *Tooru* dance, for the *Tooru* are a family of spirits that control the winds, the clouds, lightning, and thunder—forces associated with rain. When the *Tooru,* the nobles of the Songhay spirit world, come to the social world, they travel with an entourage of lesser spirits. When there are visiting *Tooru,* those *Hauka* who personify French soldiers swoop down to earth, take the bodies of their mediums, and serve as sentries to the *Tooru.*

The following slice of interaction took place when the *Tooru* held court during this rain dance (see Stoller, 1984). The *Tooru* were seated on overturned mortars and received the people of Tillaberi. Before approaching the *Tooru* to receive advice, however, the townspeople had to endure the horrific comedy of the *Hauka,* whose role it was to bring the people to the masters of the heavens. *Commandamant Bashirou*(CB) and *Lieutenant Marseille*(LM) were the two *Hauka* who provided this service.

CB: (Goose-steps from the center of dance ground to audience. Stops in front of young woman [YW]. Slaps his legs together and salutes YW.) You are a fool, young woman. (Sprays saliva in her face.)

YW: (Recoils.)

CB: (Grabs her hand and yanks her away from audience.)

YW: (Falls to ground, and says as she is dragged:) I don't want to go. I don't want to go.

CB: (Stops. Stands on one foot and looks at audience.) You are all stupid Songhay. How can you resist? (Looks at YW and smiles.) Come, you daughter of a donkey. (He laughs, audience laughs, and he pulls YW to a standing position and takes her to the *Tooru.*)

(Minutes later)

LM: (Starts toward the crowd and stands on one foot gazing at the audience for a few moments. Then he struts toward a young man [YM] and salutes him.) In the name of the army, in the name of God, in the name of the spirits, in the name of the *Tooru* . . .

YM: . . . In the name of idiocy? (General laughter.)

LM: (Extends his hand to YM.) You . . . you, the one with the limp penis. Come and seek a solution. (More laughter.)

YM: (Pointing at LM and laughing.) And you with the empty head?

LM: (Grabs arm of YM and shoves him toward the *Tooru.*)

4. The following description from my field notes of January 1980 describes graphically the symbolic context and satiric antics of *Sasale* possession.

It is almost dusk. The dull edges of the mudbrick houses to the west are silhouetted against the darkening sky. The Songhay possession dance in the compound of Adamu Jenitongo, a ritual priest, is almost over. Adamu Jenitongo had attempted to bring the *Hausa* spirits to Tillaberi because one of his clients had been suffering from a partial paralysis of the left arm. The spirit had come and suggested that the partially paralyzed man present the old ritual priest with a jar of honey, which the latter would place in the spirit house. The old ritual priest, Adamu Jenitongo, considers the dance a success and leaves the crowd to seek the privacy of his hut. But only part of the crowd had dispersed. Most of the people have remained to listen and dance to possession music. Suddenly, there is movement in the crowd just to the left of the musician's canopy. People move away from the dance grounds to make way for the coming of a spirit. A young woman, a medium, is wailing, "wo, wo, wo, woo," as she places the palms of her hands to either side of her head. She struts around the dance ground in this manner, wailing, as though she had lost her way. But soon the spirit settles more comfortably in the body of her medium. *Ramu Kon'izo* (RK), the *Sasale* prostitute, has come to visit the people of Tillaberi. Keeping the palms of her hands to either side of her head, she approaches the crowd.

RK: Wo, wo, wo, woo. Yes, I am greeting you. (She undulates her hips as she presses her body against one of the men.) How much will you give?
Man: (Backs away from the spirit.) Uh, uh, I don't want . . .
RK: (Following the man into the crowd, waving her finger in his direction.) You do not want? You are a worthless Moslem. You have no penis.
Man: (Leaves the dance area.)

REFERENCES

Bastide, R. (1978). *The African religions of Brazil.* Baltimore: Johns Hopkins University Press.

Bellah, R. (1970). *Beyond belief: Essays on religion in a post-traditional world.* New York: Harper & Row.

Boulnois, J., & Hama, B. (1953). *L'Empire de Gao: Histoire, cotumes, et magie des Songhay.* Paris: Maisonneuve.

Cole, H. (1981). *Mbari: Art and life among the Owerri Igbo.* Bloomington: Indiana University Press.

DeMott, B. (1982). *Dogon masks: A structural study of form and meaning.* Ann Arbor: University of Michigan Press.

Drewal, J. H. (1974). Gelede masquerade: Imagery and motif. *African Arts, 7,* 8-20, 62-63.

Franke, R. W., & Chasin, B. H. (1980). *Seeds of famine: Ecological destruction and the development dilemma in the West African Sahel.* Totowa, NJ: Allanhead, Osman.

Fugelstad, F. (1975). Les Hauka: Une interpretation historique. *Cahiers d'Etudes Africaines, 58,* 203-216.

Gibbal, J-M. (1982). *Tambours d'eau: Journal et enquete sur un culte de possession au Mali occidental.* Paris: Le Sycomore.

Government of Niger. (1980). *Le voix du Sahel: Journal quotidien du Niger,* p. 4.

Hama, B. (1968). *Historie des Songhay.* Paris: Presence Africaine.

Hughes, Charles C. (1969). Psychocultural dimensions of social change. In J. P. Finney (Ed.), *Culture, change, mental health and poverty.* Lexington: University of Kentucky Press.

Hunwick, J. O. (1966). Religion and state in the Songhay empire. In I. M. Lewis (Ed.), *Islam in tropical Africa* (pp. 296-316). London: Oxford University Press.

Hunwick, J. O. (1972). Songhay, Bornu and Hausaland in the 16th century. In J. Ajayi & M. Crowder (Eds.), *The history of West Africa* (Vol. 1, pp. 202-240). New York: Columbia University Press.

Kiev, A. (1972). *Transcultural psychiatry.* New York: Free Press.

Konare Ba, Adam. (1977). *Sonni Ali Ber* (Etudes Nigeriennes No. 40). Niamey: Université de Niamey.

Lambo, T. A. (1964). Malignant anxiety: A syndrome associated with criminal conduct in Africans. *Journal of Mental Science, 108,* 256-264.

Olivier de Sardin, J-P. (1982). *Concepts et conceptions Songhay-Zarma.* Paris: Nubia.

Olivier de Sardin, J-P. (1984). *Les sociétés Songhay-Zarma.* Paris: Karthala.

Ranger, T. O. (1975). *Dance and society in East Africa.* Berkeley: University of California Press.

Roberts, S. (1963). *The history of French colonial policy, 1870-1925.* London: Archon.

Rouch, J. (1953). *Les Songhay.* Paris: P.U.F.

Rouch, J. (1960). *La religion et la magie Songhay.* Paris: P.U.F.

Rouch, J. (1978). Jean Rouch talks about his films to John Marshall and John W. Adams. *American Anthropologist, 80,* 1005-1022.

Sidikou, A. H. (1974). *Sedentarité et mobilite entré Niger et Zagret* (Études Nigeriennes No. 34). Niamey: Université de Niamey.

Stoller, P. A. (1980). The negotiation of Songhay space: Phenomenology in the heart of darkness. *American Ethnologist, 7,* 419-431.

Stoller, P. A. (1981). Social interaction and the management of Songhay sociopolitical change. *Africa, 51,* 765-780.

Stoller, P. A. (1984). Horrific comedy: Cultural resistance and the Hauka movement in Niger. *Ethos, 12,* 165-188.

Turner, V. (1969). *The ritual process: Structure and anti-structure.* Ithaca, NY: Cornell University Press

Turner, V. (1974). *Dramas, fields and metaphors.* Ithaca, NY: Cornell University Press.

The World Bank. (1981). *Accelerated development in sub-Saharan Africa.* Washington, DC: International Development Bank.

14

POWER AND HALLUCINOGENIC STATES OF CONSCIOUSNESS AMONG THE MOCHE
An Ancient Peruvian Society

MARLENE DOBKIN DE RIOS

Studies of shamanism, both contemporary and historical, often allude to its political function and to the shamans' control over their peers in stateless societies. Few studies, however, have focused particularly on the variable of political power, control, and domination (see, however, Langdon, 1983). In particular, in those societies of the world where, prior to European contact, plant hallucinogens have been utilized to achieve nonordinary states of consciousness for religious and healing purposes, cross-cultural data suggests that political variables played an extremely important role in motivating such drug use (Dobkin de Rios, 1976, 1977; Dobkin de Rios & Cardenas, 1980). In an earlier paper (Dobkin de Rios & Smith, 1977), my colleague and I examined social stratification and access to drug-induced altered states of consciousness. We argued that as societies became more complex and segmentation occurred, access to altered states induced by drugs was controlled and regulated by elite groups. When such societies underwent social change and conquest, drug rituals and esoteric knowledge were often lost to posterity, although clues to these beliefs and rituals remained coded in art.

In 1973, I received a contract from the Second National Commission on Marihuana and Drug Abuse to survey the non-Western use of plant hallucinogens. As a result of that study (Dobkin de Rios, 1973, 1976, 1984a), a series of cross-cultural themes connected to the use of plant hallucinogens appeared that provide a series of working hypotheses to test in other societies of the world. This paper examines the role of plant hallucinogens and political variables of control and domination by shamans in one pre-Colombian society of ancient Peru—that of the Moche—in which access to altered states of conciousness induced by drugs provided mechanisms of social control. In the process, the function of the shaman as healer was enhanced, as the shaman created exceptional emotional states in his or her clients, due to the degrees of power and dominion the shaman was acknowledged to possess, as well as the animal familiars the shaman could call upon to do his or her bidding.

As an anthropologist who has specialized in the study of plant hallucinogens and culture, I have conducted field research on the north coast of Peru and in the Amazon, among urban and rural populations of peasants who utilize plant drugs in the treatment of illness. As the result of several periods of field research in 1968-9, 1977, and 1979 (Dobkin de Rios, 1969, 1971, 1972, 1973), I extended my analysis from populations currently using plant hallucinogens to prehistoric ones of the same region, based on an analysis of their archaeological remains. In this paper, I examine what I believe to be pivotal in traditional Moche life—namely, the use by ancient peoples of various plant hallucinogens to achieve contact with supernatural realms and to permit the magical manipulation of supernatural forces by religious hierophants to serve social goals. Moche art can best be interpreted as an interplay of complex shamanistic notions of good and evil, power and its manipulation and expression, and the magical control over nature by religious hierophants in serving their clients and community. To explore these themes in more detail, the paper first summarizes features of contemporary plant hallucinogenic use on the Peruvian north coast and documents the hallucinogenic plants available. Hallucinogenic-linked themes, documented for other New World prehistoric populations, will then be discussed as they occur in Moche art. While this paper focuses on the variables of power and authority in one pre-Colombian society of ancient Peru, the implication for healing effectiveness in traditional societies in general must not be overlooked.

A MODEL FOR THE STUDY OF POWER IN SOCIETY

In 1975, David McClelland, long interested in the psychology of motivation and needs achievement, published the book *Power: the Inner Experience*, in which he examined the human fascination with power. He drew upon earlier works of Freud and Erikson, who classified power based on whether the source of power is believed to be outside or inside the "self" and whether the object of power is the "self" or someone or something outside the "self." This book is important to any discussion of drug-adjuncted shamanic healing. My medical-anthropological research among peasants in cities and rural areas of Peru and other analyses of illness etiology among traditional peoples of the world generally bring forth the conclusion (e.g., Seguin, 1979) that the source of power to bewitch and cause illness or misfortune to an individual is believed to be outside the self (see Kemp, Ward, Chandra shekar, this volume).

McClelland classified the variable of power according to four modalities, in terms of whether it strengthens the individual, whether the individual strengthens himself or herself, whether power has an impact on others, and whether power moves an individual to do his or her duty. McClelland presents a typology of power, including its pathological manifestations, in four stages, viewed as invariant and irrespective of culture; indeed, from an anthropological perspective, the typology is quite ethnocentric. In particular, McClelland views Stage IV of power acquisition as more mature, from a Freudian perspective, than others. Thus, in this stage of power, where individuals are motivated by duty and see themselves as instruments of a higher authority, their actions have a morality and ethic apart from personal power needs. Westerners may acknowledge this as the only, or at least the most appropriate, way to seek and contain power, where the well-being of the collectivity rather than that of the individual and his or her immediate circle is involved.

McClelland's four stages are as follows.

Stage I: In this stage, power strengthens the individual. Here pathology exists when forces outside the individual govern what a person does to such an extent that the individual is not in control. According to McClelland, this gives rise to dependent people, because they can feel strong only when they are near a source of strength. Although he never explicitly describes it as such, McClelland implies that this condition is pathological.

Stage II: The individual strengthens himself or herself. In this stage, obsessive-compulsive pathology exists when the person tries to control every thought and action. One might collect prestigious possessions or discipline oneself to feel strong.

Stage III: In this stage, the individual has an impact on others by controlling them. He or she can persuade, bargain, and maneuver. Anthropologically speaking, I would argue that the mutual exchange of gifts could be seen as used by societies in an attempt to minimize power relationships. A pathology in this stage would be to overwhelm the individual with giving.

Stage IV: The individual in this stage is moved to his or her duty. A person is viewed as an instrument of a higher authority that causes the individual to try to influence others or to serve them. Personal goals are subordinated to a higher authority, and a psychological approach exists, recommended by many great world religions, involving service toward the collective well-being. Again, while the point is not explicitly stated, this stage is thought by McClelland not only to lack pathology but to represent an ideal state of personal development to be sought after by one and all.[1]

From a cross-cultural perspective, McClelland has examined Eastern traditions compared to those of the West, where there is a need for power primarily to feel strong and, secondarily, to act powerfully. In contrast, Eastern societies do not prefer to exercise power but rather to accumulate it, by concentrating the power and preserving it. To my knowledge, McClelland's model has not been tested against the evidence concerning shamanic power and its accumulation and exercise in traditional societies of the world.

Before doing this, however, it might be useful to compare an anthropological approach to power and authority with McClelland's psychological one. Fried, in his book *The Evolution of Political Society* (1974), takes an approach to the question of power and authority that is quite different from that which one might expect from a social psychologist. Fried examines power and authority from a sociocultural, not individual, perspective and delineates four major types of societies: egalitarian, ranked, stratified, and state societies. In egalitarian societies, authority can be evoked without the use of power or applications of sanctions, while power is the ability to channel the behavior of others by threat or use of sanctions. In egalitarian societies, many people can wield power by means of personal strength, influence, and authority, and there are no orders of dominance or paramountcy. Fried points out that in simple egalitarian societies, it is difficult to find cases in which one individual tells others to do a certain thing. It is the authority of the individual that is in question, not his or her power. The example I enjoy using to distinguish between authority and power is that I can lecture my students not to use the word "ain't" and point to the authority of a major dictionary to show them that "ain't" is not the correct form of the verb. However, should I wish to exercise sanctions in this case, I might have to hit one or two over the head to change the offensive behavior.

Leaders in ranked societies, too, have few sanctions to compel compliance from their followers except by setting examples for their peers. Nonetheless, authority is regular and repetitive. As societies become more stratified, there is a change in the number of persons who are capable of exerting power. The state-type of social organization is one of the few in which warfare and killing can become monopolies of the state and carried out "only at times, in places and under the specific conditions set by the state" (Fried, 1974). In this regard, only the state maintains an actual physical force such as an army, militia, or police force in its task of preserving social order and defending the central order of stratification.

Fried makes it very clear that we need to distinguish between reinforcements and sanctions. "Reinforcements, coextensive with learning, comprise the broadest grouping of directives of behavior. Including sanctions, they comprise all events that favor the adoption or extinction of modes of conduct, whereas "sanctions are distinctly social and usually cultural as well and must be consciously applied" (Fried, 1974, p. 10). Needless to say, breaches of correct behavior occur in all societies; when these are too large to go unnoticed, they are referred to as deviations, wrongful acts, or crimes. In some types of political organizations, these breaches are corrected by means of sanctions that are the *only* major mechanisms for correcting breaches. What makes egalitarian and ranked societies so interesting anthropologically is that apart from uttering the advice, no action may be taken to ensure that the course of behavior that will be followed is the one recommended. Thus, authority may be all that a society can fall back upon to enforce preferred codes of behavior.

In pre-Colombian societies like that of the Moche, religious and ritual authority are coded in the plastic arts of the society as a means of signaling to everyone the extent of the power and control (however ritualistic) of the religious/political leaders. In this paper, I will try to integrate both the political and psychological variables connected to shamanic/priestly power among the Moche. As Wallace (1974) points out, one of the most important aspects of shamanism is the control and domination of the psychopomp—the spiritual guardian of the community—over forces that may be much more powerful than the individual or society can control. In this process, the individual and the group can achieve ontological security. In this sense, one can argue that particular ways of accumulating and exercising power in traditional societies of the world are adaptive, given the low level of technological control that individuals possess over resources. This is so despite McClelland's presentation of shamanic-like power accumulation and exercise. He compares this stage to that of the infant, following some early Freudian notions of the primitive as neurotic, childlike, etc., and looks to the oral stage, since the infant's mouth is initially the chief organ through which the baby gathers strength. Some of the characteristics of subjects studied by McClelland at this Stage I of power orientation included being psychic-minded, very involved with personal fantasies and dreams, and quick to see natural objects as possessing human qualities.

THE MOCHE

The Peruvian coast, a dry, arid desert occasionally watered by rivers flowing from east to west, is dotted by agricultural villages, such as Salas in the north, that are famous because of the prevalence of specialized healers who use a psychoactive cactus, *San Pedro,* in their rituals. Called *maestros,* they treat disease through the use of a variety of plant hallucinogens such as *San Pedro (Trichocereus pachanoi),* which contains 1.29 g of mescaline in a given kilo sample of fresh material. The cactus is cut into small pieces and boiled several hours, with additives such as *misha (Datura arborea), condorillo (Lycopodium* sp.), and *hornamo* (unidentified) added to the brew. In addition, tobacco mixed with water is used as a snuff and drawn into the healer's lungs to enhance the drug's effect. Wilbert (1987) has argued convincingly that *Nicotiana rustica,* used by many South American peoples, including Mestizos, by itself produces many powerful and long-lasting effects without the aid of hallucinogens. Effects of drug additives, as Shultes (1972) pointed out, have still to be studied.

Since the sixteenth-century Spanish conquest, many Roman Catholic beliefs have been syncretized with traditional use of the *San Pedro* plant. Its major use at present is to treat illness believed to be caused by witchcraft. Like other hallucinogenic plants, *San Pedro* is used as a revelatory agent to make known the source of bewitchment deemed responsible for illness and misfortune (Dobkin de Rios, 1972). Healing sessions take place at night in *tambos,* shelters without walls that are found in fields some distance from houses. Healers (almost always males), an assistant, and several patients assemble around a cloth laid on the ground, called a *mesa.* A large number of ritual items, including polished shields and staffs, are set up as defenses against the evil machinations of witches, with other magical elements placed on the *mesa.* In interviews with healers in 1967, I elicited statements that polished stones are believed to assume the form of persons and animals who attack enemies. During the session, the *maestro* sings and whistles to facilitate the recognition of disease etiology and to elicit spirit forces he wishes to evoke in healing. The healers claim that visions from the cactus enable them to learn which magical illness afflicts their patients.

A Re-Creation of Moche Religion

The pre-Incaic civilization of the Moche flourished in the north coastal area of Peru from 100 B.C.–A.D. 700. The Moche were a state society with subsistence based on intensive agriculture and the use of irrigation, enabling large populations to exploit both maritime and farming areas. As G. Willey (personal communication, 1975) has expressed it, "The Mochica built castle-like fortifications over a hundred feet high, out of thousands or millions of adobe bricks. They ran stone and adobe defensive walls for miles across the desert and built great aqueducts of equal length." Moche society was probably theocratically organized. There was a complex division of labor, with specialization of occupations and crafts. From the pottery, often interpreted as realistic in nature, we find data on the regional foods, costumes, and animal species known. Lanning (1967) has written that the Moche potters portrayed at least 35 different species of birds, 16 mammals, and 16 fish, as well as other animals. Fishing was a major activity conducted in one-person canoes made of totora rushes. Throughout the ceramic representations, we see the Mochica warrior, weaver, beggar, and shaman/priest. Moche society was highly stratified, a pattern reflected in dress, ornament, and temple form. Professions were symbolized by details of dress and ornament, and variations in architecture indicate cult centers.

Some ceramics are devoted to surgical and medical practices, while shamanistic sessions, very much like those described by myself and others in present-day regional healing (Dobkin de Rios, 1968), are found in the pottery. Bennett and Bird (1946) have described shamans performing cures by massaging patients and sucking the affected part of the body to remove a foreign substance, a procedure reminiscent of present-day practices. Stylized decorative motifs on Moche pottery described by the ethnobotanist Friedberg (1960), as interpreted to her by the late Dr. Larco of the Larco Herrera Museum in Lima, depict what seem to be Moche sorcerers carrying stumps of cacti in their hands. Friedberg suggests that one such representation showed a remarkable likeness to *San Pedro,* which is easily recognized by its lack of thorns. She has also described Moche pottery showing individuals transformed into animals in association with a thornless cactus. This is a commonplace theme. Supernatural forces of a magical nature are also represented in the art, including various animals that probably correspond to the *nagual,* or animal familiar, as well as what Lavallee (1970) has called animal, vegetable, and object demons.

Moche Plant Use

Before discussing Moche religion, it is important to reiterate the evidence for Moche hallucinogenic plant use. As mentioned earlier, various uprooted cacti are represented in the art, including *San Pedro.* Towle (1961) has written that cereus cacti are found frequently among the art of this region. Shultes (1967, 1972) has referred to an ancient drink called *cimora* on the Peruvian north coast, which includes the cactus *Neoraimondia macrostibas.* Coca *(Erythroxylon coca),* a plant stimulant, played an important economic role in Moche civilization. It is quite possible that coca may have been used by the Moche, as attested to in numerous ceramics. Disselhoff (1967) has reproduced a ceramic of a man drinking *chica,* a fermented corn drink, with his hand in his coca pouch. Multiple drug use, moreover, was not infrequent, and coca may have been ingested along with other hallucinogenic plants. The effects of mixing hallucinogenic plants remain an uncharted area (Schultes, 1972).

Themes in Moche Art

In this section I argue that Moche art eminently represented a combative shamanistic ethos, which was reflected in the expansionist militaristic activities of these people. Combative elements in shamanistic/priestly beliefs have been reported by me for two distinctive contemporary Peruvian drug-using regions (Dobkin de Rios, 1968, 1984a) and by Furst (1965) for West Mexico. Despite themes of peace and love reflected in the drug use of runaway American youth in the 1960s, we must not be ethnocentric in our analysis and extend the ethos of one subculture to that of another people far removed in time and space. Much of nuclear American hallucinogenic plant use, in fact, occurs in societies with overriding martial activity, to wit, the Aztec and the Inca. Certainly, a commonly expressed belief over the last 50 years, reiterated by La Barre (1970), is that shamanistic beliefs, particularly direct revelation of the supernatural, are a dominant motif of many New World Indian populations.

In his classic study of shamanism, the historian of religions Eliade (1958) has discussed the vital role of shamans as psychopomps who are obliged to confront and combat their group's adversaries. A major part of this activity includes healing disease and neutralizing misfortunes caused by enemies that have occurred to members of the community. In Moche life, shaman/priests probably had an important role as protectors of seafaring activities as well. This was witnessed by a student of *San Pedro* use who observed a healer in Trujillo, Peru, called upon to bless a forthcoming fishing expedition with the cactus drink (D. Sharon, personal communication, 1970). Shamans are famous for their abilities to transform themselves into powerful animal figures—familiars or *naguals*—whom they send to do their bidding, to rectify evil or redress harm caused to their clients. Amazonian shamanic healers often boasted to me of their apprenticeship period, during which they obtained magical powers over their allies—a long, arduous, and often lethal task. The shaman often descends to nether worlds to consult with ancestral spirits, found in Moche ceramics, or travels to celestial realms whence he returns with special chants and auguries of future happenings. In addition, when the shaman emerges triumphant, he indeed is believed to be possessed of impressive power. (I use the male gender almost consistently because in my 1967 study of a north coast Peruvian community, Salas, 90% of practicing shamans were male, with only one female actively practicing drug healing, and then only after menopause. Additionally, in the Peruvian Amazon, where I worked with more than a dozen drug healers, no woman healer practiced in the community, although several women were said to be witches who caused harm to their clients' enemies.)

The Shaman and Metamorphosis into Animal Familiars

The metamorphosis of human beings into animals, or, less frequently, into plants, is a common drug-linked motif and a pan-American theme in general. These resultant metamorphoses are known as spirit familiars. In Moche art, they never appear in battle scenes, but only are associated with individual human beings. A study by Pitt-Rivers (1970) on spiritual power in Central America can be generalized to interpret beliefs linked to hallucinogenic plant use. The author speaks of the term *nagual* (animal familiar) as a prototype, illustrating a type of relationship between an individual person and an animal species. The *nagual* in Chiapas and parts of Mexico has been shown by Pitt-Rivers to be linked to the spiritual power of an individual. Just as there are differences among *naguals* in strength, activity, and power in the world of nature, so, too, do the *naguals* represent a spiritual hierarchy of individual human beings. For example, Pitt-Rivers points out that the jaguar or tiger is more powerful than the dog, who is more cunning than the raccoon. The animal familiar has an analogous function in making explicit the relative spiritual power of the shaman. In many Moche pots, animal familiars are represented in great number and include snakes, numerous felines, foxes, and so on.

The hummingbird, a frequent motif, may represent, once again in an analogous sense, the aerial voyage linked to hallucinogenic drug use and shamanistic activity when the shaman's animal familiar travels through time and space to effect the master's bidding (Dobkin de Rios,1974). Sharon and Donan (1974) have also suggested that the sucking of the hummingbird may metaphorically relate to the animal familiar of a shaman, who throughout all of Indian America commonly treats illness by sucking at afflicted parts of a patient's body. As predators, the jaguar and eagle, when shown in their *nagual* function, may signal malevolent intentions on the part of their owners, while vegetarian animals might not. The *nagual* could also indicate the way in which an individual uses power. Certainly, the parallel between the shamanistic animal familiar and the shaman's warrior nature is not surprising. Pitt-Rivers points out that dangerous animals and high-flying birds in Central America are usually reserved for mature individuals, in particular, curers. In many parts of the New World, there is a belief that disease and misfortune are the outcome of a combat between shamanistic *naguals*. In curing, shamans must combat the opponent's *nagual* at the same time that they are working on the corporeal presence of patients by sucking, blowing tobacco smoke, and other techniques.

Shamans or witches can transform themselves into the shape of a given animal to perform evil. Lavallee (1970) cites the widespread myth in South America that shamans can metamorphose into jaguars. Several Moche pots photographed by Benson (1972) show the process of metamorphosis or transformation. Benson's study of a feline motif in Moche art discusses instances of the portrayal of trancelike states. The head of the feline is often prominent in the Moche trophy head, and the paws and head of the feline are always somewhere near the human figure's head. She suggests among other alternatives a shaman's state of exhilaration or intoxication while hallucinating the feline or undergoing initiatory wounding. Various drug plants could be candidates for shamanic transformation following their use. It is interesting to note that in Moche art beans are the only vegetable appearing truly anthropomorphized, with a head, arms, and legs. Benson has suggested that this plant was a representation of a warrior or messenger, but the beans are not rendered in a naturalistic fashion; in fact, they float in the air in various ritual scenes.

When an individual is transformed into a *nagual,* he or she demonstrates possession of a particularly powerful spiritual nature represented by the animal (Pitt-Rivers, 1970). The *nagual,* then, is part of an analogy system in which the specific animal species defines the social personality of the individual vis-à-vis other members of the community. The plant hallucinogens, in this case, serve always as a vehicle of transformation and control.

CONCLUSION

This paper has argued that the Moche used plant hallucinogens in their religious rituals. Certainly, plant hallucinogens were present in northern Peru and available for use by the Moche. Ceramic motifs and the shamanic belief system connected to it parallel those of other drug-using New World cultures where we have independent verification of plant hallucinogenic drug use from ethnohistorical sources.

This article on the use of plant hallucinogens among one ancient Peruvian peoples suggests that shamanic/priestly leaders, within the framework of a desire for power over fellow tribespeople and nature, may have ingested such psychoactive plants to enable them to function in accordance with the power needs of their culture. To better understand the concept of power in general, we must return to McClelland's typology and his four stages that delineate types of power and how they are exercised in human societies.

We see the comparison between the role of supplication in major world religions and shamanic beliefs concerning the value placed on individual power, control, and domination that appear to have lingered in stage-level societies such as the Moche. The first three stages of power that McClelland delineates are applicable in ranked/

stratified societies like that of the Moche. Power clearly strengthens the individual potentate/shaman in those societies, so that all powerful animal familiars are viewed as controllable by the shaman via ingestion of plant hallucinogens, although there are difficulties in estimating just how many adult male shamans existed and the specificity of the control they claimed to render over the animal familiars who did their bidding.

Nonetheless, encyclopedias of animal life, written for young children, can be consulted to explain the metaphoric significance of animal familiars that might be important to shape-shifting shamans. Thus, the sucking of hummingbirds, metaphorically compared to the sucking action of the shaman in a healing ceremony in New World societies, may be the crucial element in understanding the significance of that animal familiar. The characteristic of flight among avians may be important, too, particularly in the awe and respect that traditional peoples must have felt for the unusual visual properties they possess. This is likened metaphorically to a diviner or seer, who as a shamanic leader can prophesy the future and concern himself or herself with the well-being of the community (Dobkin de Rios, 1984b). Stage II of McClelland's typology, in which individuals strengthen themselves by power acquisition, again may be related to shamanic animal familiars. In the case of the Moche and other New World societies, a powerful individual attaches to his or her personage (represented in the plastic arts) numerous animal familiars, as well as the trophy heads of vanquished foes, which are indicative of power and dominion. In Stage III, the powerful regional political/religious figure, with appended animal familiars, is able to advertise widely by means of the society's plastic arts concerning the power sources to which he or she affiliates.

In Western society in recent times, scholars have expressed a real ambivalence concerning the romanticization of the role of the shaman in traditional societies. On the one hand, one can easily pay money for weekend training to have an out-of-body experience evoked or else learn a series of dances and techniques for acquiring power from a personal animal familiar. The anthropologist interested in this phenomenon may argue that the hiatus in true control that human beings exercise over their physical environment in traditional societies could give rise to attempts by individuals to dominate their milieu, however tenuously they may succeed. Psychological control and domination of their personal and physical environment through the ingesting of plant hallucinogens is an important technology, especially in light of global beliefs that plant drugs are vehicles of personal transformation. In this manner, shamans can transform themselves into power animals and/or plant familiar(s) who have powers of control over life and death that is awe-inspiring.

From the perspective of political anthropology, however, it may be that structural characteristics of traditional societies, particularly in non-state-level societies, make options available to their members to enhance personal authority so that they can better exercise power. The particular power and reputation of an individual shamanic political/religious leader might depend upon iconic representation of animal and plant familiars—much like a shield and coat of arms—as portrayed in the visual arts. In the shaman's healing function, he or she established omnipotence in terms of the authority accompanying him or her, heightening the ability to treat a patient's disorder or misfortune. These cultural manifestations of power, however much they lack esteem in typologies such as those of McClelland (with its decided Western bias), give us insight into political behavior in general. Insofar as the omnipotence of healers evokes exceptional emotional states in their clients that contribute to the efficacy of healing (Prince, 1982), the way of the shamans in all their dominion and their posturing to exercise power in traditional societies may be the key to understanding the successful psychological treatment of a client's illnesses. Freud may give us little solace here, in that political and psychological variables get all mixed up. In Moche society, well-developed mechanisms may not have existed to allow individuals to exercise social control over their peers. Full authority and power may have been possible only by means of a certain type of religious/ritual posturing, given the dangers and despairs to be expected in hostile environments. The boldness of the visual arts in representing the shaman's personal power may have been the mechanism that allowed authority to be utilized for the benefit of the commonweal, while at the same time serving the individual's need for control.

Thus, from the perspective of the psychological consequences of the use of hallucinogens for mental health, it would appear that in societies like that of the Moche, the power that individuals believed to reside in the hallucinogenic plants and their use by powerful, omnipotent individuals enabled cures to take place, enemies to be routed, and ontological security to be provided. From a historical point of view, we cannot really talk about the perception of power by the individual, but merely speculate and certainly argue that schemes like that of McClelland have little or no place in understanding drug use in traditional societies of the past.

NOTE

1. In *Beyond Freedom and Dignity,* B. F. Skinner (1971) reiterates this point by arguing that human beings do not have the freedom to choose that they think they have and that their behavior is controlled by forces in the environment outside of themselves. Because of this, it is essential that they acknowledge the superior strength and power of the contingencies that control their behavior.

REFERENCES

Bennett, W. C., & Bird, J. B. (1946). The archaeology of the Central Andes. In Julian Steward (Ed.), *Handbook of South American Indians* (Vol. 2, pp. 307-351). Washington, DC: Smithsonian Institution.

Benson, E. P. (1972). *The Mochica.* New York: Praeger.

Disselhoff, H. D. (1967). *Daily life in ancient Peru* (A. Jaffa, Trans.). New York: McGraw-Hill.

Dobkin de Rios, M. (1968). *Trichocereus pachanoi*—a mescaline cactus used in folk healing in Peru. *Economic Botany, 22*(2), 191-194.

Dobkin de Rios, M. (1969). Curanderísmo psícodelico en el Perú: Continuidad y cambio [Psychedelic curing in Peru: Continuity and change]. In *Mesa Redonda de Ciencias Prehistoricas y Antropológicas.* Lima: Catholic University of Peru.

Dobkin de Rios, M. (1971). Peruvian hallucinogenic healing: An overview. *Proceedings, 5th World Congress of Psychiatry.* Mexico: Excerpta Medica.

Dobkin de Rios, M. (1972). *Visionary vine: Hallucinogenic healing in the Peruvian Amazon.* San Francisco: Chandler Press.

Dobkin de Rios, M. (1973). The non-western use of hallucinatory agents. *Second report of the National Commission on Marihuana and Drug Abuse* (Vol. 2, Appendix). Washington, DC: U.S. Government Printing Office.

Dobkin de Rios, M. (1974). The influence of psychotropic flora and fauna on Maya religion. *Current Anthropology, 15*(2), 147-164.

Dobkin de Rios, M. (1976). *Wilderness of mind.* Beverly Hills, CA: Sage.

Dobkin de Rios, M. (1977). Plant hallucinogens and the religion of the Mochica—an ancient Peruvian people. *Economic Botany, 31*(2), 189-203.

Dobkin de Rios, M. (1984a). *Hallucinogens: Cross-cultural perspective.* Albuquerque: University of New Mexico Press.

Dobkin de Rios, M. (1984b). The vidente phenomenon in third world traditional healing: An Amazonian example. *Medical Anthropology, 8*(1), 60-70.

Dobkin de Rios, M., & Cardenas, M. (1980). Plant hallucinogens, shamanism and Nazca ceramics. *Journal of Ethnopharmacology, 2*, 233-246.

Dobkin de Rios, M., & Smith, D. E. (1977). Drug use and abuse in cross-cultural perspective. *Human Organization, 36*(1), 14-21.

Eliade, M. (1958). *Shamanism: Archaic techniques of ecstasy* (W. Trask, Trans.). New York: Pantheon.

Fried, M. (1974). *The evolution of political society.* New York: Random House.

Friedberg, C. (1960). Utilisation d'un cactus a mescaline au nord du Perou (*Trichocereus pachanoi*) [The use of mescaline in northern Peru]. *Proceedings, 6th International Congress of Anthropological and Ethnological Sciences, 2,* 21-26.

Furst, P. J. (1965). West Mexican tomb sculpture as evidence for shamanism in prehistoric Mesoamerica. *Antropológica, 15,* 29-34.

La Barre, W. (1970). Old and new world narcotics: A statistical question and an ethnological reply. *Economic Botany, 24,* 73-75.

Langdon, E. J. (1983, August). Dau: Power of the shaman in Siona religion and medicine. Paper presented at 11th International Congress of Anthropological and Ethnological Sciences, Vancouver.

Lanning, E. (1967). *Peru before the Incas.* Englewood Cliffs, NJ: Prentice-Hall.

Lavallee, D. (1970). Les representations animales dans la ceramique Mochica [Animal representations in Moche ceremonies]. *Memoires de l'Institut d'Ethnologie* (Vol. 4). Paris: Musée de l'Homme.

McClelland, D. (1975). *Power: The inner experience.* New York: Irvington.

Pitt-Rivers, J. (1970). Spiritual power in Central America: The *naguals* of Chiapas. In Mary Douglas (Ed.), *Witchcraft confessions and accusations* (pp. 186-206). New York: Tavistock.

Prince, R. (1982). The endorphins: A review for psychological anthropologists. *Ethos, 7*(4), 303-316.

Schultes, R. E. (1967). The place of ethnobotany in the ethnopharmacological search for psychotomimetic drugs. In D. Efron (Ed.), *Ethnopharmacological Search for Psychoactive Drugs* (Publication No. 1645, pp. 35-58). Washington, DC: Public Health Service.

Schultes, R. E. (1972). The ethnotoxicological significance of additives to New World hallucinogens. *Plant Science Bulletin, 18,* 34-40.

Seguin, C. A. (1979). *Psiquiatria folklórica.* [Psychiatric folklore]. Lima: Erdmar.

Sharon, D., & Donan, C. (1974). Shamanism in Moche iconography. In *Ethno-Archaeology,* published by Institute of Archaeology. Los Angeles: University of California.

Skinner, B. F. (1971). *Beyond freedom and dignity.* New York: Knopf.

Towle, M. (1961). The ethnobotany of pre-Colombian Peru. *Viking Fund Publications in Anthropology* (No. 30). New York: Wenner Gren Foundation.

Wallace, A. F. C. (1974). *Religion: An anthropological view.* New York: Random House.

Wilbert, J. (1987). *Tobacco and shamanism in South America.* New Haven: Yale University Press.

AUTHOR INDEX

SUBJECT INDEX

ABOUT THE AUTHORS

C. R. Chandra shekar currently works in the Department of Psychiatry, National Institute of Mental Health and Neuro Sciences (NIMHANS), Bangalore, India. His main interest is in the field of community and social psychiatry. Along with his colleagues, he is developing cost-effective models to extend mental health care into the community through the existing health and welfare infrastructure. Dr Chandra shekar is involved in many community-based studies, including epidemiological studies, home care of patients, follow-up and evaluation of intervention programs, and studies of belief and attitudes. He is a popular science writer and has published more than 300 articles as well as 42 books on mental health in Kannada (state language of Karnataka, South India) and English. He is a Fellow of the Indian Psychiatric Society and served for two years as secretary of the society's Karnataka Branch.

Marlene Dobkin de Rios is Professor of Anthropology at California State University, Fullerton, and holds a consulting clinical appointment at the University of California Irvine Medical Center's Burn Center. She is former Health Science Administrator at the National Institute of Mental Health and the author of two books and more than 100 articles and book chapters in medical anthropology, particularly ethnobotany/ethnopharmacology and transcultural psychiatry.

Wolfgang G. Jilek is Clinical Professor, Department of Psychiatry, University of British Columbia, and Affiliate Professor of Psychiatry, University of Washington; currently he is also UNHCR Refugee Mental Health Coordinator in Thailand. He served as mental health consultant with WHO and is active in the World Psychiatric Association as Secretary, Transcultural Psychiatry Section. Trained in Austria, Switzerland, the United States, and Canada, he holds degrees in medicine, social psychiatry, and anthropology. His primary research interest is comparative cultural psychiatry and ethnomedicine, in which fields he has conducted investigations in Tanzania, Haiti, Ecuador, Paraguay, Thailand, Papua New Guinea, Tonga, and among North American indigenous and ethnic populations. Dr. Jilek has published three books and over 60 journal articles and chapters.

Richard Katz received his Ph.D. in Clinical Psychology from Harvard University, where he taught for nearly 20 years. His research focuses on indigenous community healing systems and their critique of, and contributions to, Western approaches to help. He has completed fieldwork in the Kalahari Desert, the Fiji Islands, India, and Alaska. After three years of work in Alaska, he is now teaching at the Saskatchewan Indian Federated College in Saskatoon, Saskatchewan. Katz's work emphasizes community healing systems as vehicles of cultural revitalization and political liberation. He is the author of *Boiling Energy: Community Healing among the Kalahari !Kung* (Harvard University Press).

Simon Kemp is Senior Lecturer in Psychology at the University of Canterbury, Christchurch, New Zealand. He received his Ph.D. from the University of Auckland and has been a Humboldt Fellow and held research posts in West Germany. His research interests include perception, memory, and psychology in the Middle Ages.

Stanley Krippner is Professor of Psychology at Saybrook Institute Graduate School, San Francisco. He formerly directed the Child Study Center, Kent State University, Kent, Ohio, and the Dream Laboratory, Maimonides Medical Center, Brooklyn. Krippner is a former president of the Association for Humanistic Psychology and the Parapsychological Association. He is a Fellow of the American Psychological Association and the American Society of Clinical Hypnosis, and a Charter Member of the International Society for the Study of Multiple Personality and Dissociation. Krippner is co-author of *Dreamworking, Dream Telepathy, Healing States*, author of *Human Possibilities: Mind Exploration in the USSR and Eastern Europe*, and series editor of *Advances in Parapsychological Research.*

Michael Lambek is Associate Professor of Anthropology at the University of Toronto. Among his interests are the relationship between social structure and personhood in nonindustrial societies and interpretive approaches in the study of culture, religion, and ritual. He is the author of *Human Spirits: A Cultural Account of Trance in Mayotte* as well as several articles on spirit possession, ritual, kinship, women, and the life course among Malagasy speakers of Mayotte (Comoro Islands, Western Indian Ocean). Lambek has also carried out fieldwork in Botswana and is currently at work on a book on ethnomedical practice in Mayotte.

Raymond L. M. Lee is Associate Professor, Department of Anthropology and Sociology, University of Malaya, Kuala Lumpur, Malaysia. He received his Ph.D. from the University of Massachusetts, Amherst, in 1979. He has published several papers on religion and ethnic relations in Malaysia and is coauthor of *Heaven in Transition: Non-Muslim Religious Innovation and Ethnic Identity in Malaysia* (University of Hawaii Press, 1987).

Raymond H. Prince (M.D., M.Sc., University of Western Ontario) is Professor and Director of the Division of Social and Transcultural Psychiatry, Department of Psychiatry, McGill University. He is editor of *Transcultural Psychiatric Research Review* and was founder, in 1964, and subsequently President (1964–84) of the *R. M. Bucke Memorial Society for the Study of Religious Experience*. His field research has been in Nigeria, Jamaica, and Malaysia, and his interests are generally in distinguishing the universal from the culturally contingent in phenomena relevant to psychiatry and psychology.

Nicholas P. Spanos is Professor of Psychology and Director of the Laboratory for Experimental Hypnosis at Carleton University. He received his Ph.D. from Boston University in 1974 and from 1967 to 1975 was a clinical consultant and psychotherapist at the Medfield State Hospital and a research psychologist at the Medfield Foundation. He joined the Department of Psychology of Carleton University in 1975. He has conducted extensive research on hypnotic phenomena as well as on pain perception, mystical experience, glossolalia, multiple personality, and historical aspects of witchcraft and demonic possession. Recently he has begun research on expert testimony and its effects on jury deliberations. His research is published regularly in such journals as *Science, Psychological Bulletin, Journal of Abnormal Psychology, The Journal of Personality and Social Psychology,* and *Psychosomatic Medicine.*

Paul Stoller is Professor of Anthropology and Chair of the Department of Anthropology-Sociology at West Chester University in West Chester, Pennsylvania. His publications include *In Sorcery's Shadow: A Memoir of Apprenticeship among the Songhay of Niger* (1987) and *Fusion of the Worlds: An Ethnography of Possession among the Songhay of Niger* (forthcoming in 1989), as well as numerous articles in scholarly journals. His publications are based on research conducted during seven field missions to Niger between 1976 and 1987.

Jean-Pierre Valla (M.D., M.Sc.) is Associate Professor at the University of Montreal. He received his M.D. and psychiatric training in Paris, France, and his M.Sc. in the Department of Psychiatry, McGill University. He is the author of *L'experience Hallucinogene,* which will shortly be published in English. His major interests include altered states of consciousness, child psychiatry, and psychiatric epidemiology.

Colleen Ward (Ph.D., Dunelm) is currently in the Department of Psychology, University of Canterbury, Christchurch, New Zealand. She has formerly held an Organization of American States Postdoctoral Fellowship (religion, altered states of consciousness, and mental health) at the University of the West Indies, Trinidad, and lectureships at the Science University of Malaysia and the National University of Singapore. Her major research interests are in cross-cultural psychology and psychology of women. She serves on an editorial board of the *Journal of Cross-cultural Psychology* and *Counselling Psychology Quarterly* and is co-author of *Victims of Sexual Violence* (in press).

Leonard Zusne is Professor of Psychology at the University of Tulsa. He received his doctorate in general-experimental psychology from Purdue University. His primary areas of research and teaching have been perception and history of psychology. He is the author of six books and many articles in these areas. He has identified the area of anomalistic psychology, and he and Warren H. Jones are currently preparing a revised edition of their 1982 text under that title.

Series Editors: Walter J. Lonner *and* John W. Berry

Volumes in the

CROSS-CULTURAL RESEARCH AND METHODOLOGY SERIES

LIFE'S CAREER-AGING
Cultural Variations on Growing Old
edited by **BARBARA G. MYERHOFF** and **ANDREI SIMIC**
Volume 4 / ISBN 0-8039-0867-9 cloth / ISBN 0-8039-6000-X paper

CULTURE'S CONSEQUENCES
International Differences In Work-Related Values
by **GEERT HOFSTEDE**
Volume 5 / ISBN 0-8039-1444-X cloth (Unabridged Edition) /
  ISBN 0-8039-1306-0 paper (Abridged Edition)

MENTAL HEALTH SERVICES
The Cross-Cultural Context
edited by **PAUL B. PEDERSEN, NORMAN SARTORIUS** and
  ANTHONY J. MARSELLA
Volume 7 / ISBN 0-8039-2259-0 cloth

FIELD METHODS IN CROSS-CULTURAL RESEARCH
edited by **WALTER J. LONNER** and **JOHN W. BERRY**
Volume 8 / ISBN 0-8039-2549-2 cloth

INTERCULTURAL INTERACTIONS
A Practical Guide
by **RICHARD W. BRISLIN, KENNETH CUSHNER,**
  CRAIG CHERRIE and **MAHEALANI YONG**
Volume 9 / ISBN 0-8039-2558-1 cloth / ISBN 0-8039-3441-6 paper

HEALTH AND CROSS-CULTURAL PSYCHOLOGY
Toward Applications
edited by **P. R. DASEN, J. W. BERRY** and **N. SARTORIUS**
Volume 10 / ISBN 0-8039-3039-9 cloth

THE CROSS-CULTURAL CHALLENGE TO SOCIAL PSYCHOLOGY
edited by **MICHAEL HARRIS BOND**
Volume 11 / ISBN 0-8039-3042-9 cloth

ALTERED STATES OF CONSCIOUSNESS AND MENTAL HEALTH
A Cross-Cultural Perspective
edited by **COLLEEN A. WARD**
Volume 12 / ISBN 0-8039-3277-4 cloth

NOTES

NOTES

NOTES

ACN 9892